Adobe® Illustrator® CS4

The Professional Portfolio

AGAINST THE CLOCK
mastering graphic technology

Managing Editor: Ellenn Behoriam
Cover & Interior Design: Erika Kendra
Copy Editor: Laurel Nelson-Cucchiara
Proofreader: Angelina Kendra

10 9 8 7 6 5 4 3 2   978-0-9815216-7-1

AGAINST THE CLOCK
mastering graphic technology

4710 28th Street North, Saint Petersburg, FL 33714
800-256-4ATC • www.againsttheclock.com

Acknowledgements

ABOUT AGAINST THE CLOCK

Against The Clock has been publishing graphic communications educational materials for more than 17 years, starting out as a Tampa, Florida-based systems integration firm whose primary focus was on skills development in high-volume, demanding commercial environments. Among the company's clients were LL Bean, The New England Journal of Medicine, the Smithsonian, and many others. Over the years, Against The Clock has developed a solid and widely-respected approach to teaching people how to effectively utilize graphics applications while maintaining a disciplined approach to real-world problems.

Against The Clock has been recognized as one of the nation's leaders in courseware development. Having developed the *Against The Clock* and the *Essentials for Design* series with Prentice Hall/Pearson Education, the firm works closely with all major software developers to ensure timely release of educational products aimed at new version releases.

ABOUT THE AUTHORS

Erika Kendra holds a BA in History and a BA in English Literature from the University of Pittsburgh. She began her career in the graphic communications industry as an editor at Graphic Arts Technical Foundation before moving to Los Angeles in 2000. Erika is the author or co-author of more than fifteen books about graphic design software, including QuarkXPress, Adobe Photoshop, Adobe InDesign, and Adobe PageMaker. She has also written several books about graphic design concepts such as color reproduction and preflighting, and dozens of articles for online and print journals in the graphics industry. Working with Against The Clock for more than seven years, Erika was a key partner in developing the new Portfolio Series of software training books.

Gary Poyssick, co-owner of Against The Clock, is a well-known and often controversial speaker, writer, and industry consultant who has been involved in professional graphics and communications for more than twenty years. He wrote the highly popular *Workflow Reengineering* (Adobe Press), *Teams and the Graphic Arts Service Provider* (Prentice Hall), *Creative Techniques: Adobe Illustrator*, and *Creative Techniques: Adobe Photoshop* (Hayden Books), and was the author or co-author of many application-specific training books from Against The Clock.

CONTRIBUTING AUTHORS, ARTISTS, AND EDITORS

A big thank you to the people whose artwork, comments, and expertise contributed to the success of these books:

- **Ramon Llorens, Jr.,** International Academy of Design & Technology
- **Dana Huber,** Hunterdon County Polytech Career Academy
- **Pam Harris,** Missouri Southern State University
- **Debbie Davidson**, Sweet Dreams Design
- **Dean Bagley**, Against The Clock, Inc.
- **Robin McAllister**, Against The Clock, Inc.

Thanks also to **Laurel Nelson-Cucchiara**, editor, and **Angelina Kendra**, proofreader, for their help in making sure that we all said what we meant to say.

Walk Through

Project Goals

Each project begins with a clear description of the overall concepts that are explained in the project; these goals closely match the different "stages" of the project workflow.

The Project Meeting

Each project includes the client's initial comments, which provide valuable information about the job. The Project Art Director, a vital part of any design workflow, also provides fundamental advice and production requirements.

Project Objectives

Each Project Meeting includes a summary of the specific skills required to complete the project.

Real-World Workflow

Projects are broken into logical lessons or "stages" of the workflow. Brief introductions at the beginning of each stage provide vital foundational material required to complete the task.

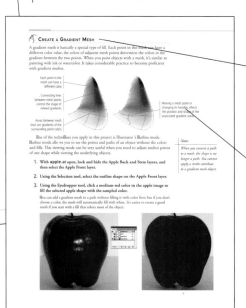

Step-By-Step Exercises

Every stage of the workflow is broken into multiple hands-on, step-by-step exercises.

Visual Explanations

Wherever possible, screen shots are annotated so students can quickly identify important information.

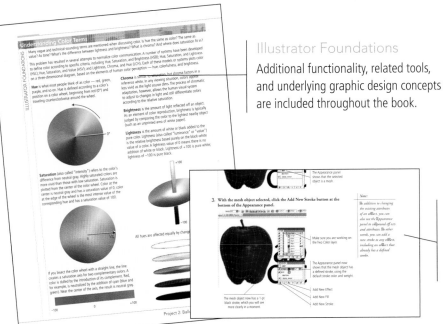

Illustrator Foundations

Additional functionality, related tools, and underlying graphic design concepts are included throughout the book.

Advice and Warnings

Where appropriate, sidebars provide shortcuts, warnings, or tips about the topic at hand.

Project Review

After completing each project, students can complete these fill-in-the-blank and short-answer questions to test their understanding of the concepts in the project.

Portfolio Builder Projects

Each step-by-step project is accompanied by a freeform project, allowing students to practice skills and creativity, resulting in an extensive and diverse portfolio of work.

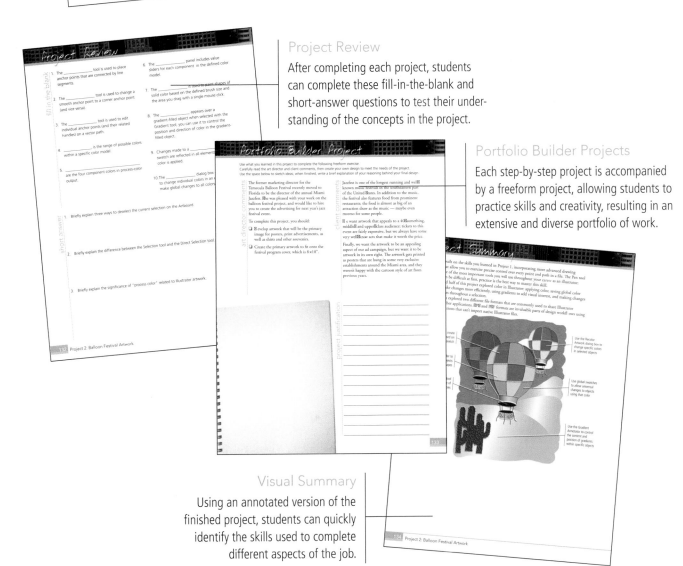

Visual Summary

Using an annotated version of the finished project, students can quickly identify the skills used to complete different aspects of the job.

Projects at a Glance

The Against The Clock *Portfolio Series* teaches graphic design software tools and techniques entirely within the framework of real-world projects; we introduce and explain skills where they would naturally fall into a real project workflow. For example, rather than including an entire chapter about printing (which most students find boring), we teach printing where you naturally need to do so — when you complete a print-based project.

The project-based approach in the *Portfolio Series* allows you to get in depth with the software beginning in Project 1 — you don't have to read several chapters of introductory material before you can start creating finished artwork.

The project-based approach of the *Portfolio Series* also prevents "topic tedium" — in other words, we don't require you to read pages and pages of information about text (for example); instead, we explain text tools and options as part of larger project (e.g., creating a logotype, building a folding brochure).

Clear, easy-to-read, step-by-step instructions walk you through every phase of each job, from creating a new file to saving the finished piece. Wherever logical, we also offer practical advice and tips about underlying concepts and graphic design practices that will benefit students as they enter the job market.

The projects in this book reflect a range of different types of Illustrator jobs, from creating a series of icons to designing a corporate identity to building a Web page. When you finish the eight projects in this book (and the accompanying Portfolio Builder exercises), you will have a substantial body of work that should impress any potential employer.

The eight Illustrator CS4 projects are described briefly here; more detail is provided in the full table of contents (beginning on Page viii).

project 1 — International Symbols

- ❏ Digital Drawing Basics
- ❏ Drawing Basics

project 2 — Balloon Festival Artwork

- ❏ Drawing Complex Artwork
- ❏ Coloring and Painting Artwork
- ❏ Exporting EPS and PDF Files

project 3 — Identity Package

- ❏ Working with Gradient Meshes
- ❏ Working with Type
- ❏ Working with Multiple Artboards
- ❏ Combining Text and Graphics

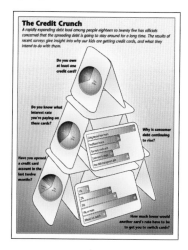

Some experts claim most people use only a small fraction — maybe 10% — of their software's capabilities; this is likely because many people don't know what is available. As you complete the projects in this book, our goal is to familiarize you with the entire tool set so you can be more productive and more marketable in your career as a graphic designer.

It is important to keep in mind that Illustrator is an extremely versatile and powerful application. The sheer volume of available tools, panels, and features can seem intimidating when you first look at the software interface. Most of these tools, however, are fairly simple to use with a bit of background information and a little practice.

Wherever necessary, we explain the underlying concepts and terms that are required for understanding the software. And we're confident that these projects provide the practice you need to be able to create sophisticated artwork by the end of the very first project.

Contents

Contents

CONTENTS

PREREQUISITES

The entire Portfolio Series is based on the assumption that you have a basic understanding of how to use your computer. You should know how to use your mouse to point, click, and drag items around the screen. You should be able to resize and arrange windows on your desktop to maximize your available space. You should know how to access drop-down menus, and understand how check boxes and radio buttons work. It also doesn't hurt to have a good understanding of how your operating system organizes files and folders, and how to navigate your way around them. If you're familiar with these fundamental skills, then you know all that's necessary to use the Portfolio Series.

RESOURCE FILES

All of the files that you need to complete the projects in this book are on the provided Resource CD in the **RF_Illustrator** folder. This folder contains nine subfolders, one for each project in the book (including the Interface); you will be directed to the appropriate folder whenever you need to access a specific file. Files required for the related Portfolio Builder exercises are in the **RF_Builders** folder.

The Resource CD also includes a **WIP** folder, which also contains (mostly empty) subfolders for each project in the book. This is where you will save your work as you complete the various projects. In some cases, the location of a file will be extremely important for later steps in a project to work properly; that's why we've provided a specific set of folders with known file names.

Before you begin working on the projects in this book, you should copy the entire WIP folder to your hard drive or some other recordable media such as a flash drive; when we tell you to save a file, you should save it to the appropriate folder on the drive where you put that WIP folder.

ATC FONTS

You must install the ATC fonts from the Resource CD to ensure that your exercises and projects will work as described in the book; these fonts are provided on the Resource CD in the **ATC Fonts** folder. Specific instructions for installing fonts are provided in the documentation that came with your computer. You should replace older (pre-2004) ATC fonts with the ones on your Resource CD.

SYSTEM REQUIREMENTS

As software technology continues to mature, the differences in functionality from one platform to another continue to diminish. The Portfolio Series was designed to work on both Macintosh or Windows computers; where differences exist from one platform to another, we include specific instructions relative to each platform.

One issue that remains different from Macintosh to Windows is the use of different modifier keys (Control, Shift, etc.) to accomplish the same task. When we present key commands, we always follow the same Macintosh/Windows format — Macintosh keys are listed first, then a slash, followed by the Windows key command.

Minimum System Requirements for Adobe Illustrator CS4:

Windows

- 2 GHz or faster processor
- Microsoft® Windows® XP with Service Pack 2 or Windows Vista® with Service Pack 1
- 512 MB of RAM (1 GB recommended)
- 2 GB of available hard-disk space for installation
- 1,024×768 display with 16-bit video card
- DVD-ROM drive

Macintosh

- PowerPC® G4 or G5 or Intel® processor
- Mac OS X v10.4.11–10.5.4
- 512 MB of RAM (1 GB recommended)
- 2 GB of available hard-disk space for installation
- 1,024×768 display with 16-bit video card
- DVD-ROM drive
- QuickTime 7.2 required for multimedia features

Illustration is a very broad career path, with potential applications in virtually any industry. In other words, mastering the tools and techniques of Adobe Illustrator can significantly improve your range of career options. Within the general category of illustration, many Illustrator experts specialize in certain types of work: logo design, technical drawing, and editorial illustration are only a few subcategories of artwork you can create with Illustrator.

Adobe Illustrator is the industry-standard application for creating digital drawings or **vector images** (graphics composed of mathematically defined lines instead of pixels). Our goal in this book is to teach you how to use the available tools to create different types of work that you might encounter in your professional career.

Some projects, such as Projects 1 through 4, focus specifically on creating graphics and illustrations — which is the true heart of the application. And although we do not advocate doing *all* page layout work in Illustrator, we do recognize that many people use the application to create complete designs; Project 5, for example, uses Illustrator to combine different elements into a finished product.

Although not intended as a page-layout application, you can use the tools in Illustrator to combine type, graphics, and images into a single cohesive design. Many people create flyers, posters, and other one-page projects entirely within Illustrator. With the multiple-artboard capability added to CS4 (explained in Projects 3 and 5) we will likely see more of this type of Illustrator work in the future.

The simple exercises in this introduction are designed to allow you to explore the Illustrator user interface. Whether you are new to the application or upgrading from a previous version, we highly recommend you follow these steps to click around and become familiar with the basic workspace. When you work on Project 1, you will be better prepared to jump right in and start creating digital artwork.

Note:

Some people argue that Adobe Illustrator should not be used for page layout and that Adobe InDesign is the preferred page-layout application. However, the tools needed for basic page design are built into Illustrator CS4, so many people use Illustrator for that type of job, rather than buying a second application.

Illustrator Menus

ILLUSTRATOR FOUNDATIONS

Like most applications, Illustrator has a menu bar across the top of the workspace. Nine menus provide access to virtually all of the available options. Macintosh users have two extra menus. The Apple menu provides access to system-specific commands. The Illustrator menu follows the Macintosh system-standard format for all applications; this menu controls basic application operations such as About, Hide, Preferences, and Quit. You will explore most of the specific menu options as you complete the projects in this book, but you should understand what different indicators mean within the application menus.

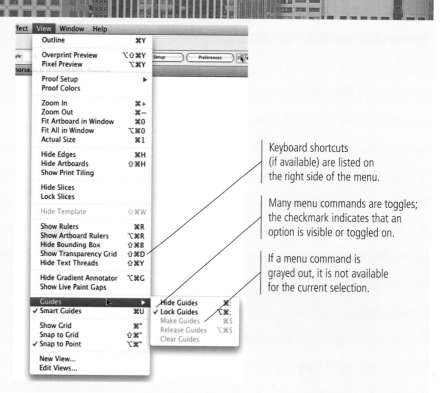

Keyboard shortcuts (if available) are listed on the right side of the menu.

Many menu commands are toggles; the checkmark indicates that an option is visible or toggled on.

If a menu command is grayed out, it is not available for the current selection.

EXPLORE THE ILLUSTRATOR INTERFACE

The user interface (UI) is what you see when you launch the Illustrator application. The specific elements you see — including which panels are open and where they appear on the screen — depend on what was done the last time the application was open. The first time you launch Illustrator, you'll see the default workspace settings defined by Adobe. When you relaunch the application after you or another user has quit, the workspace defaults to the last-used settings — including specific open panels and the position of those panels on your screen.

1. **Launch Illustrator. If you do not see the Welcome Screen, choose Help>Welcome Screen.**

    By default, the **Welcome Screen** appears when no files are open. This screen provides easy access to recently opened files, as well as one-click commands for creating a variety of new documents. At the bottom of the Welcome Screen, a number of options provide quick links to HTML pages on the Adobe Web site, where you can find resources about the Illustrator application. If you check the Don't Show Again box, the Welcome Screen does not appear when all files are closed.

2. **Macintosh users: Open the Window menu. If Application Frame is not checked (active), choose that command in the menu.**

Note:

Most screen shots in this book show floating panels so we can focus on the most important issue in a particular image. In our production workflow, however, we make heavy use of docked and iconized panels and take full advantage of saved custom workspaces.

Note:

If you or someone else checked the Don't Show Again box, you can display the Welcome Screen by choosing Help>Welcome Screen.

The Macintosh Application Frame

ILLUSTRATOR FOUNDATIONS

On Windows, each running application is contained within its own frame; all elements of the application — including the Menu bar, panels, tools, and open documents — are contained within that Application frame.

In CS4, Adobe introduced the Application frame concept to Macintosh users as an option for controlling the workspace. When you activate the Application frame, the entire workspace shifts into a self-contained area that can be moved around the screen; all elements of the

workspace (excluding the Menu bar) move when you move the Application frame. The Application frame is inactive by default; you can toggle it on or off in the Window menu.

Using the Application frame is purely a matter of personal preference. It can be particularly useful for Windows users who recently made the switch to Macintosh, because the Application frame more closely resembles what you are used to seeing on Windows. The screen shots throughout this book show the Application frame in use.

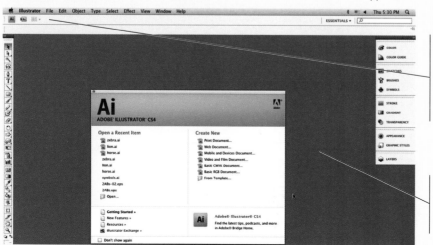

When the Application frame is not active, the Application bar appears immediately below the Menu bar; in this case, the Application bar can be moved or turned off.

When the Application frame is not active, the desktop is visible behind the workspace elements.

3. Choose Window>Workspace>Essentials.

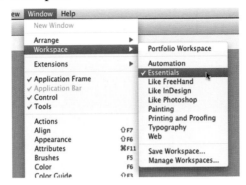

This step might or might not do anything, depending on what was done in Illustrator before you started this project. If you or someone else changed anything and then quit the application, those changes are remembered when Illustrator is relaunched. Because we can't be sure what your default settings show, by completing this step you are resetting the user interface to one of the built-in default workspaces so your screen shots will match ours.

Saved **workspaces** (accessed in the Window>Workspace menu, or in the Workspace switcher on the Application/Menu bar) provide one-click access to a defined group of tools that might take ten or more clicks to create each time you need the same toolset.

The Essentials workspace includes the Tools panel on the left of the screen, the Control panel at the top, and a set of **iconized** (collapsed) and docked panels on the right. (The area where the panels are stored is called the **panel dock**.)

On Macintosh systems, the Application bar includes a link to the Adobe Bridge application, a widget for tiling multiple open documents, a menu for accessing different saved workspaces, and a search option. On Windows systems, those options are available on the right side of the Menu bar.

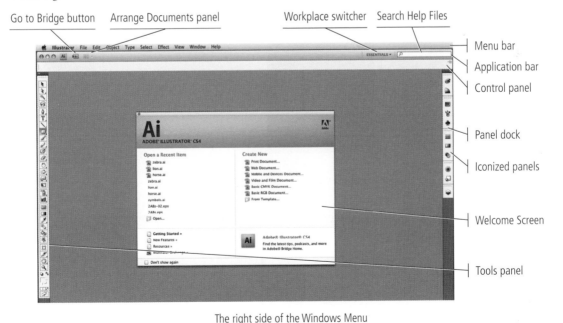

Go to Bridge button · Arrange Documents panel · Workplace switcher · Search Help Files · Menu bar · Application bar · Control panel · Panel dock · Iconized panels · Welcome Screen · Tools panel

The right side of the Windows Menu bar offers the same options that are in the Macintosh Application bar.

Menu bar · Control panel

4. Click the Welcome Screen close button to dismiss this window.

The Welcome Screen, which appears by default when no files are open, includes links to recently opened files (on the left) and links to create different types of new documents (on the right). The bottom section provides easy links to online resources from Adobe.

Click here to close the Welcome Screen.

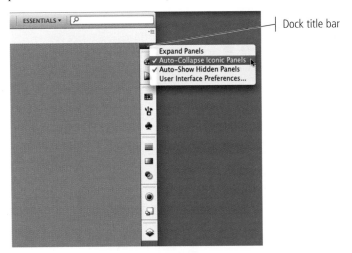

Note:

The Welcome Screen appears by default whenever no files are open. If you check the Don't Show Again option, it will not appear again unless you choose Help>Welcome Screen.

5. Control/right-click the title bar above the docked panel icons. If Auto-Collapse Iconic Panels is not checked, choose that item to toggle the option on.

Control/right-clicking a dock title bar opens the dock contextual menu, where you can change the default panel behavior. If the Auto-Collapse Iconic Panels option is not active, a panel remains open until you intentionally collapse it, or until you open a different panel in the dock.

Dock title bar

Note:

If you're using a Macintosh with a mouse that doesn't have right-click capability, we highly recommend that ou purchase one that does. They're inexpensive, can be purchased in most retail stores, and will save you significant amounts of time when accessing contextual options.

6. In the panel dock, click the third icon (Swatches) from the top.

Most Illustrator functionality is accessed in one of more than 30 panels. Virtually everything you do in Illustrator requires interacting with at least one panel; more often than not, you'll use multiple panels to complete any given project.

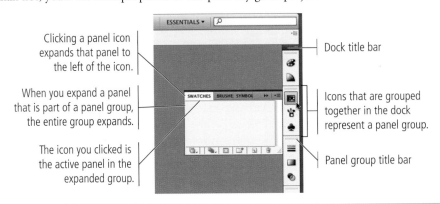

Clicking a panel icon expands that panel to the left of the icon.

When you expand a panel that is part of a panel group, the entire group expands.

The icon you clicked is the active panel in the expanded group.

Dock title bar

Icons that are grouped together in the dock represent a panel group.

Panel group title bar

Note:

The Auto-Collapse Iconic Panels option is also available in the User Interface pane of the Preferences dialog box, which you can open directly from the dock contextual menu.

7. **Click away from the expanded panel, anywhere in the application workspace.**

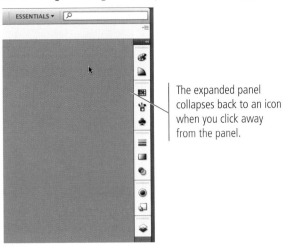

The expanded panel collapses back to an icon when you click away from the panel.

8. **Click the left edge of the docked panels (on the right side of the screen) and drag left.**

When panels are iconized, you can expand the icons to show the panel names as well as the panel icons. This can be particularly useful until you become more familiar with the application and the icons used to symbolize the various panels.

Click here...

...and drag left to show the panel names in addition to the icons.

Using Adobe Bridge

The Illustrator Application/Menu bar includes a Go to Bridge button, which is especially useful for managing files. Adobe Bridge is a stand-alone application designed to assist in the sharing of projects and project components between different Creative Suite applications, including Adobe Photoshop, Adobe Illustrator, and Adobe InDesign, to name a few. But Bridge doesn't stop there; it can help you manage virtually any digital and graphic file.

Bridge includes a Favorites area, where you can save quick links to specific locations on your system. The center displays thumbnail images of all the files in the location you choose. File-specific information (such as Preview, Metadata, and Keywords) appears in the panes on the left and right sides of the window. You can customize Bridge however you prefer. To find out more, visit the Adobe site and search for Bridge tutorials.

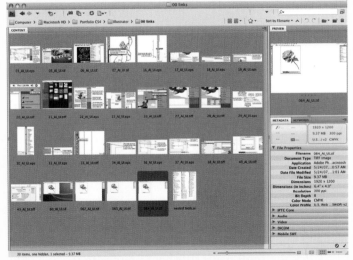

If you have other Creative Suite applications, Bridge can be accessed from and share data between all of them.

9. Click the dock title bar above the docked icons to expand the docked panels.

Clicking the dock title bar expands or collapses the entire dock column.

Note:

You can create multiple columns of panels in the dock. Each column, technically considered a separate dock, can be expanded or collapsed independently of other columns.

10. On the left side of the workspace, click the Tools panel title bar.

The Tools panel can't be expanded, but it can be displayed as either one or two columns; clicking the Tools panel title bar toggles between these two modes.

The one- or two-column format is a purely personal choice. The one-column layout takes up less horizontal space on the screen, which can be useful if you have a small monitor. The two-column format fits in a smaller vertical space, which can be especially useful if you have a laptop with a widescreen monitor.

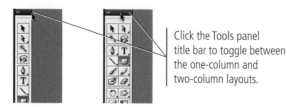

Click the Tools panel title bar to toggle between the one-column and two-column layouts.

Note:

The Tools panel can also be floated by clicking its title bar and dragging away from the edge of the screen. To re-dock the floating Tools panel, simply click the title bar and drag back to the left edge of the screen; when the blue line highlights the edge of the workspace, releasing the mouse button places the Tools panel back into the dock.

11. Click the Tools panel title bar to return to the one-column format.

Throughout this book, our screen shots show the Tools panel in the one-column format. Feel free to work with the panel in two columns if you prefer.

12. Continue to the next exercise.

Identifying and Accessing Tools in Illustrator

Like most industrial-strength programs — especially ones from Adobe — Illustrator has no shortage of tools. The Tools panel appears to contain 28 tools; however, many of the primary tools also have variations or similar tools nested under the primary tools.

Nested Tools and Keyboard Shortcuts

Tool icons that show a small black mark in the lower-right corner have **nested tools**. You can access nested tools by clicking the primary tool and holding down the mouse button until a pop-up menu shows the nested variations.

This arrow means the tool has other nested tools.

When you roll the mouse cursor over the tool, a tool tip shows the name of the tool.

If you drag the mouse cursor to the bar on the right of the nested-tool menu, the nested-tool options separate into their own floating toolboxes so you can more easily access the nested variations. (The primary tool is not removed from the main Tools panel.)

If you hover your mouse over a tool, a pop-up **tool tip** shows the name of the tool, as well as the associated keyboard shortcut for that tool if one exists. If a tool has a defined shortcut, pressing that key activates the associated tool. (If you don't see tool tips, check the Show Tool Tips option in the General pane of the Preferences dialog box.)

Hold down the mouse button to show the nested tools.

While holding down the mouse button, drag to here, then release the mouse button...

...to tear off a separate panel with all of the related tools.

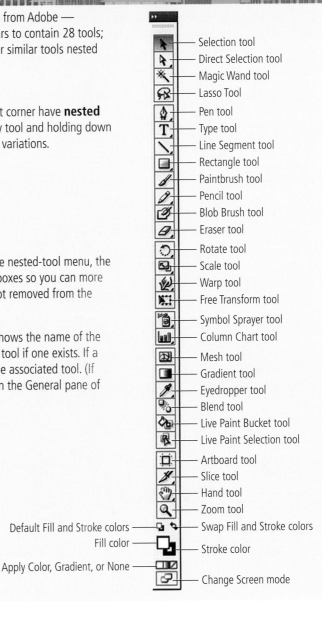

- Selection tool
- Direct Selection tool
- Magic Wand tool
- Lasso Tool
- Pen tool
- Type tool
- Line Segment tool
- Rectangle tool
- Paintbrush tool
- Pencil tool
- Blob Brush tool
- Eraser tool
- Rotate tool
- Scale tool
- Warp tool
- Free Transform tool
- Symbol Sprayer tool
- Column Chart tool
- Mesh tool
- Gradient tool
- Eyedropper tool
- Blend tool
- Live Paint Bucket tool
- Live Paint Selection tool
- Artboard tool
- Slice tool
- Hand tool
- Zoom tool

Default Fill and Stroke colors — Swap Fill and Stroke colors
Fill color — Stroke color
Apply Color, Gradient, or None — Change Screen mode

Nested Tools and Keyboard Shortcuts

The following chart offers a quick reference of nested tools, as well as the keyboard shortcut for each tool (if any).

- Selection tool (V)
  - *Direct Selection tool (A)*
  - *Group Selection tool*
- Magic Wand tool (Y)
- Lasso tool (L)
- Pen tool (P)
  - *Add Anchor Point tool (+)*
  - *Delete Anchor Point tool (-)*
  - *Convert Anchor Point tool (Shift-C)*
- Type tool (T)
  - *Area Type tool*
  - *Type on a Path tool*
  - *Vertical Type tool*
  - *Vertical Area Type tool*
  - *Vertical Type on a Path tool*
- Line Segment tool (\)
  - *Arc tool*
  - *Spiral tool*
  - *Rectangular Grid tool*
  - *Polar Grid tool*
- Rectangle tool (M)
  - *Rounded Rectangle tool*
  - *Ellipse tool (L)*
  - *Polygon tool*
  - *Star tool*
  - *Flare tool*
- Paintbrush tool (B)
- Pencil tool (N)
  - *Smooth tool*
  - *Path Erase tool*
- Blob Brush tool (Shift-B)
- Eraser tool (Shift-E)
  - *Scissors tool (C)*
  - *Knife tool*
- Rotate tool (R)
  - *Reflect tool (O)*
- Scale tool (S)
  - *Shear tool*
  - *Reshape tool*
- Warp tool (Shift-R)
  - *Twirl tool*
  - *Pucker tool*
  - *Bloat tool*
  - *Scallop tool*
  - *Crystallize tool*
  - *Wrinkle tool*
- Free Transform tool (E)
- Symbol Sprayer tool (Shift-S)
  - *Symbol Shifter tool*
  - *Symbol Scruncher tool*
  - *Symbol Sizer tool*
  - *Symbol Spinner tool*
  - *Symbol Stainer tool*
  - *Symbol Screener tool*
  - *Symbol Styler tool*
- Column Graph tool (J)
  - *Stacked Column Graph tool*
  - *Bar Graph tool*
  - *Stacked Bar Graph tool*
  - *Line Graph tool*
  - *Area Graph tool*
  - *Scatter Graph tool*
  - *Pie Graph tool*
  - *Radar Graph tool*
- Mesh tool (U)
- Gradient tool (G)
- Eyedropper tool (I)
  - *Measurement tool*
- Blend tool (W)
- Live Paint Bucket tool (K)
- Live Paint Selection tool (Shift-L)
- Artboard tool (Shift-O)
- Slice tool (Shift-K)
  - *Slice Select tool*
- Hand tool (H)
  - *Print Tiling tool*
- Zoom tool (Z)

EXPLORE THE ARRANGEMENT OF ILLUSTRATOR PANELS

As you gain experience and familiarity with Illustrator, you will develop personal artistic and working styles. You will also find that different types of Illustrator jobs often require specific sets of tools. Adobe recognizes this wide range of needs and preferences among users, so they designed Illustrator to include a number of options for arranging and managing the numerous panels. You can use these options to customize and personalize the workspace to suit your specific needs.

We designed the following exercise to allow you to explore different ways of controlling panels in the Illustrator user interface. Because workspace preferences are largely a matter of personal taste, the projects in this book direct you to use certain tools and panels, but where you place those elements within the interface is up to you.

1. **With Illustrator open, choose Window>Symbols.**

   All panels can be toggled on and off using the Window menu.

   - If you choose a panel that is already open but iconized, the panel expands to the left of its icon.

   - If you choose a panel already open in an expanded group, that panel moves to the front of the group.

   - If you choose a panel not currently open, it opens in the same position as when it was last closed.

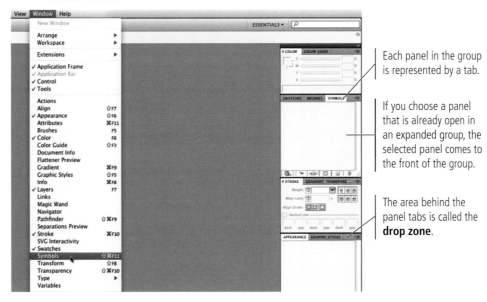

Each panel in the group is represented by a tab.

If you choose a panel that is already open in an expanded group, the selected panel comes to the front of the group.

The area behind the panel tabs is called the **drop zone**.

2. **Control/right-click the Symbols panel tab and choose Close from the contextual menu.**

   The panel's contextual menu is the only way to close a docked panel. You can also close an entire panel group by choosing Close Tab Group from the contextual menu.

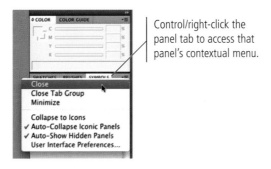

Control/right-click the panel tab to access that panel's contextual menu.

3. **Click the drop zone in the remaining panel group (the one with Swatches and Brushes) and drag away from the dock.**

Panels and panel groups can be **floated** away from the dock by clicking a panel tab or the panel group's drop zone and dragging away from the dock.

This is the panel group drop zone.

When a group is expanded, click the group's drop zone to move the entire panel group.

When you release the mouse button, the panel group floats freely in the workspace.

Panel group title bar

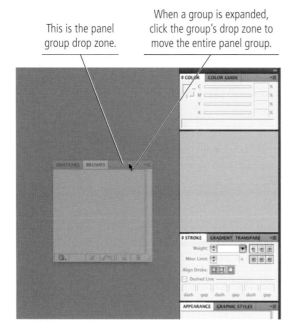

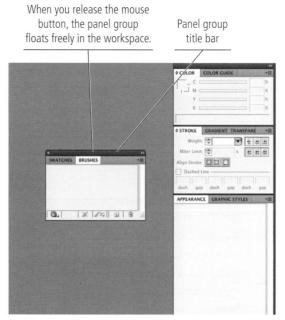

4. **Click the title bar of the floating panel group to iconize the group.**

Floating panels (and panel groups) can be iconized just like panels in the dock.

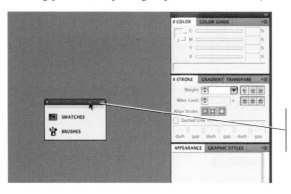

Click the title bar at the top of the floating group to collapse or expand it.

Note:

You can independently iconize or expand each floating panel (group) and each column of docked panels.

5. **Click the Swatches panel icon (in the floating panel group) and drag the panel into the dock, below the second panel group. Don't release the mouse button.**

Individual panels can be dragged to different locations (including into different groups) by dragging the panel's tab. The target location — where the panel will be located when you release the mouse button — is identified by the blue highlight.

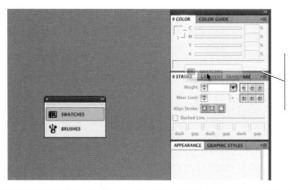

The blue highlight shows where the panel will be placed if you release the mouse button.

6. **Drag the Swatches panel onto the drop zone area of the top panel group in the dock, and then release the mouse button.**

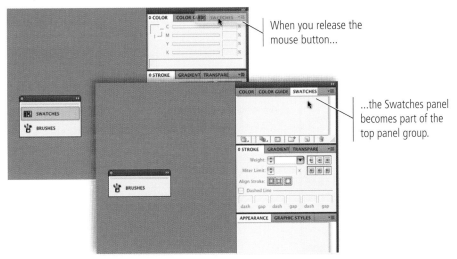

When you release the mouse button...

...the Swatches panel becomes part of the top panel group.

7. **Click the drop zone of the third panel group in the dock, and drag the group to the left until the blue highlight shows a second column added to the dock.**

As we mentioned previously, you can create multiple columns of panels in the dock. This can be very useful if you need easy access to a large number of panels, and you have a monitor with enough available screen space.

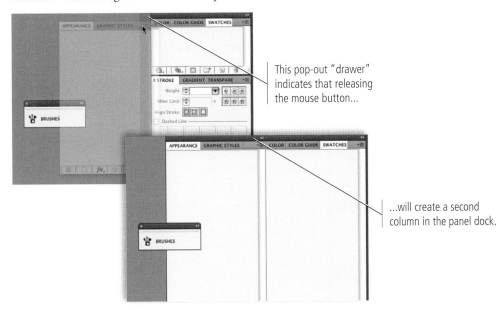

This pop-out "drawer" indicates that releasing the mouse button...

...will create a second column in the panel dock.

8. **Click the title bar above the left dock column to collapse the left column.**

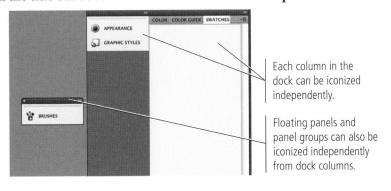

Each column in the dock can be iconized independently.

Floating panels and panel groups can also be iconized independently from dock columns.

Note:

When you have more than one column in the dock, each column can be expanded or iconized independently of the other column(s).

9. **Click the left edge of the right dock column and drag left.**

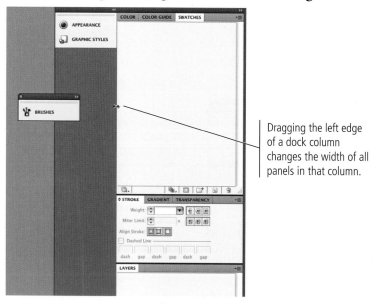

Dragging the left edge of a dock column changes the width of all panels in that column.

10. **Click the bottom edge of the first panel group in the right column of the dock and drag down.**

When you drag the bottom edge of a docked group, other variable panels in the same column expand or contract to fit the available space. By "variable panels", we mean any panel that has an undefined number of options. Some panels, such as the Strokes panel that is visible here, have a fixed number of options so they do not expand or contract. The Links panel, on the other hand, can list a variable number of items so it can be made larger or smaller.

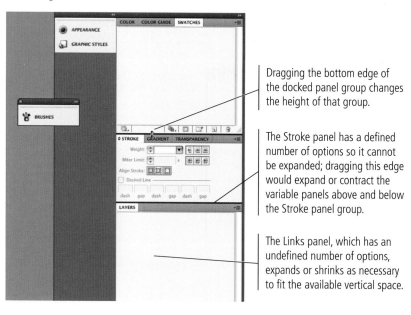

Dragging the bottom edge of the docked panel group changes the height of that group.

The Stroke panel has a defined number of options so it cannot be expanded; dragging this edge would expand or contract the variable panels above and below the Stroke panel group.

The Links panel, which has an undefined number of options, expands or shrinks as necessary to fit the available vertical space.

11. **Continue to the next exercise.**

CREATE A SAVED WORKSPACE

By now you should understand that you have virtually unlimited control over the appearance of your Illustrator workspace — what panels are visible, where and how they appear, and even the size of individual panels and panel groups.

Over time you will develop personal preferences based on your work habits and project needs. Rather than re-establishing every workspace element each time you return to Illustrator, you can save your custom workspace settings so you can recall them with a single click.

1. **Click the Workspace switcher in the Application/Menu bar and choose Save Workspace.**

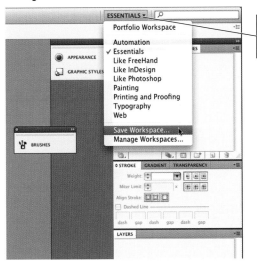

The Workspace switcher shows the name of the last-called workspace.

2. **In the Save Workspace dialog box, type Portfolio and click OK.**

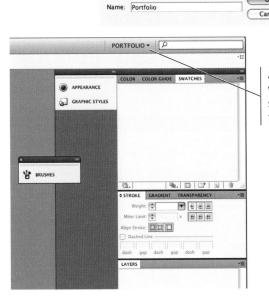

After saving the current workspace, the Workspace switcher shows the name of the new saved workspace.

3. **Click the Workspace switcher and choose Essentials from the list of available workspaces.**

   As we explained earlier, saved workspaces — whether part of the default set or ones you create — call specific sets of panels in specific places. This step restores the default set of panels, iconized without the panel names.

   Custom workspaces are listed at the top of the Workspace switcher.

4. **Continue to the next exercise.**

EXPLORE THE ILLUSTRATOR DOCUMENT WINDOW

There is much more to using Illustrator than simply arranging panels around the workspace. What you do with those panels — and which panels you need — depends on the type of work you are doing in a particular file. In this exercise, you open an Illustrator file and explore interface elements that will be important as you begin creating digital artwork.

1. **In Illustrator, choose File>Open.**

2. **Navigate to the RF_Illustrator>Interface folder on your Resource CD and select lion.ai in the list of available files.**

   The Open dialog box is a system-standard navigation dialog box. This is one area of significant difference between Macintosh and Windows users.

Note:

Press Command/Control-O to access the Open dialog box.

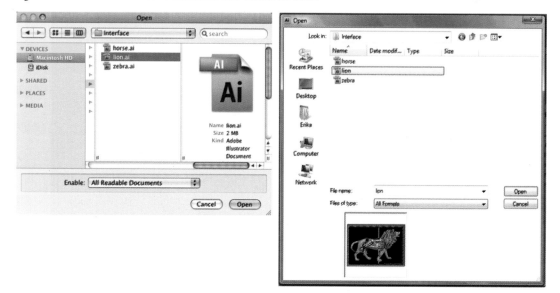

3. Click Open.

By default, documents appear in Preview mode, which shows the artwork in color.

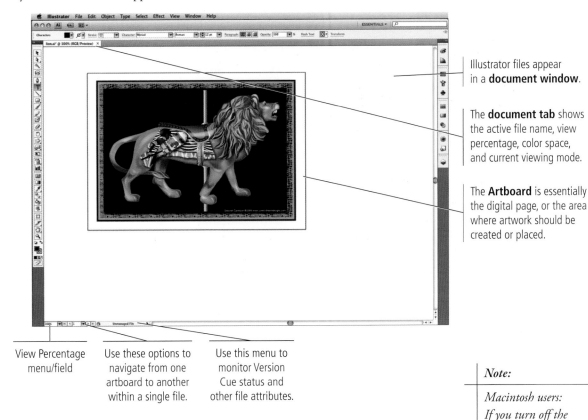

Illustrator files appear in a **document window**.

The **document tab** shows the active file name, view percentage, color space, and current viewing mode.

The **Artboard** is essentially the digital page, or the area where artwork should be created or placed.

View Percentage menu/field	Use these options to navigate from one artboard to another within a single file.	Use this menu to monitor Version Cue status and other file attributes.

Note:

Macintosh users: If you turn off the Application frame, the new document will have its own title bar.

4. Open the View Percentage menu in the bottom-left corner of the document window and choose 200%.

Different people prefer different view percentages, depending on a number of factors such as eyesight, monitor size, and so on. As you complete the projects in this book, you'll see our screen shots zoom in or out as necessary to show you the most relevant part of a particular file. In most cases we do not tell you what specific view percentage to use for a particular exercise, unless it is specifically required for the work being done.

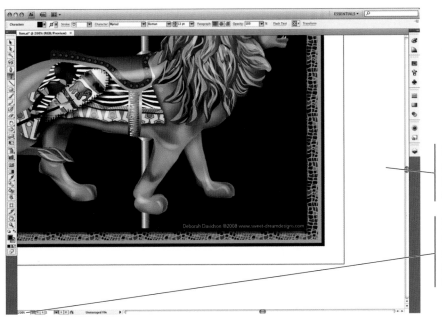

Changing the view percentage of the file does not affect the size of the document window.

Type a specific percentage in the field or choose one of the predefined percentages from the attached menu.

5. Choose View>Fit Artboard in Window.

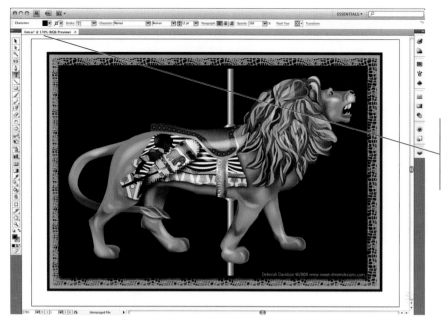

The Fit Artboard in Window command automatically calculates view percentage based on the size of the document window.

Note:

You can zoom an Illustrator document from 3.13% to 6400%.

6. Review the options in the Control panel.

We will not discuss all 30-something Illustrator panels here, but the Control panel deserves mention. This panel appears by default at the top of the workspace below the Menu bar (and the Application bar on Macintosh systems). It is context sensitive, which means it provides access to different options depending on which tool is active and what is selected in the document.

When nothing is selected in the file, the most important Control panel options open the Document Setup dialog box and the Preferences dialog box (more about these specific elements in the projects). Other options set the default stroke and fill attributes for the next object you create.

Note:

Many of the options available in the Control panel duplicate options in other panels or menu commands.

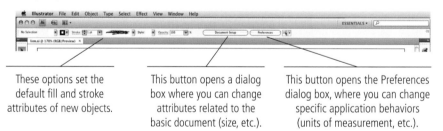

These options set the default fill and stroke attributes of new objects.

This button opens a dialog box where you can change attributes related to the basic document (size, etc.).

This button opens the Preferences dialog box, where you can change specific application behaviors (units of measurement, etc.).

7. Click the Selection tool at the top of the Tools panel to make sure that tool is active.

The Selection tool (the solid arrow) is used to select entire objects in the file.

8. Click the black area behind the lion to select that object in the file.

Note:

For now, don't worry about the specific options that are available. You only need to realize that the Control panel options change depending on what is selected in the file.

9. Review the options in the Control panel.

When an object is selected in the file, the Control panel shows the attributes of the selected object.

Selection tool

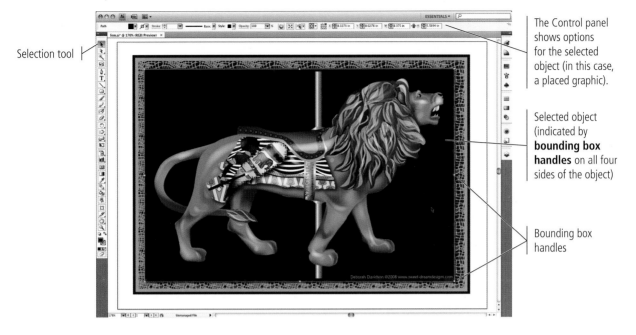

The Control panel shows options for the selected object (in this case, a placed graphic).

Selected object (indicated by **bounding box handles** on all four sides of the object)

Bounding box handles

10. Click the text near the bottom of the artwork to select the text object.

Again, the Control panel changes to show options related to text objects.

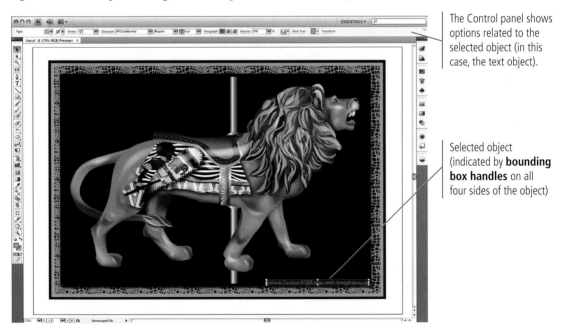

The Control panel shows options related to the selected object (in this case, the text object).

Selected object (indicated by **bounding box handles** on all four sides of the object)

11. Continue to the next exercise.

Most Illustrator projects require some amount of zooming in and out to various view percentages, as well as navigating around the document within its window. As we show you how to complete different stages of the workflow, we usually won't tell you when to change your view percentage because that's largely a matter of personal preference. But you should understand the different options for navigating around an Illustrator file so you can efficiently get to what you want.

To change the view percentage, you can type a specific percent in the **View Percentage field** of the document window or choose from the predefined options in the related menu.

You can also click with the **Zoom tool** to increase the view percentage in specific, predefined intervals (the same intervals you see in the View Percentage menu in the bottom-left corner of the document window). Pressing Option/Alt with the Zoom tool allows you to zoom out in the same defined percentages. If you drag a marquee with the Zoom tool, you can zoom into a specific location; the area surrounded by the marquee fills the available space in the document window.

The **View menu** also provides options for changing view percentage. (The Zoom In and Zoom Out options step through the same predefined view percentages as clicking with the Zoom tool.)

Zoom In	Command/Control-plus (+)
Zoom Out	Command/Control-minus (-)
Fit Artboard in Window	Command/Control-0 (zero)
Fit All in Window	Command-Option-0/ Control-Alt-0 (zero)
Actual Size (100%)	Command/Control-1

Whatever your view percentage, you can use the **Hand tool** to drag the file around in the document window. The Hand tool changes what is visible in the window; it has no effect on the actual pixels in the image.

The Navigator Panel

The **Navigator panel** (Window>Navigator) is another method of adjusting what you see, how close your viewpoint, and what part of the page you currently see (if you're zoomed in close enough that you can't see the whole page). The Navigator panel shows a thumbnail of the active file; a red rectangle represents exactly how much of the document shows in the document window.

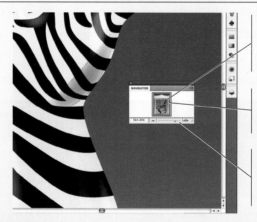

The red rectangle shows the area of the file that is visible in the document window.

Drag the red rectangle to change the visible portion of the file.

Use the slider and field at the bottom of the panel to change the view percentage.

Saved Views

Named views can be helpful if you repeatedly return to the same area and view percentage. By choosing View>New View, you can save the current view with a specific name.

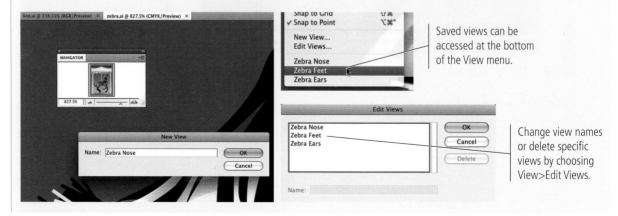

Saved views can be accessed at the bottom of the View menu.

Change view names or delete specific views by choosing View>Edit Views.

EXPLORE THE ARRANGEMENT OF MULTIPLE DOCUMENTS

More often than not, you will need to work with more than one Illustrator file at once. Illustrator CS4 incorporates a number of options for arranging multiple documents. We designed the following simple exercise to allow you to explore these options.

1. **With the lion.ai file open in Illustrator, choose File>Open.**

   The Open dialog box defaults to the last-used location, so you should not have to navigate back to the RF_Illustrator>Interface folder.

2. **Click horse.ai in the list to select that file.**

3. **Press Command/Control, and click zebra.ai to add it to the active selection.**

   You can open more than one file at a time, as long as those files are in the same folder. Pressing Shift allows you select multiple contiguous (consecutive) files; pressing Command/Control allows you to select non-contiguous files.

Customizing the Toolset

ILLUSTRATOR FOUNDATIONS

Keyboard Shortcuts

In addition to positioning specific panels in precise locations, you can also add to or modify the keyboard shortcuts used for different functions in the application. Choosing Edit>Keyboard Shortcuts opens a dialog box where you can modify the shortcuts for menu commands and tools. If you assign a shortcut that isn't part of the default set, you have to save a custom set of shortcuts (Illustrator won't let you modify the default set of keyboard shortcuts). When more than one set of shortcuts exists (i.e., if you or someone else has added to or changed the default settings), you can switch between the different sets using the menu at the top of the dialog box.

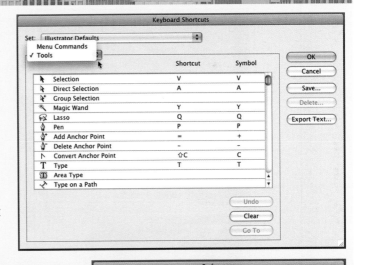

Illustrator Preferences

You can also customize the way many of the program's tools and options function. On Macintosh systems, the Preferences dialog box is accessed in the Illustrator menu. Windows users access the Preferences dialog box in the Edit menu.

The right side of the Preferences dialog box (Illustrator>Preferences on Macintosh or Edit>Preferences on Windows) allows you to move forward and backward through the twelve sets of Preferences available in Illustrator. As you work your way through the projects in this book, you learn not only what you can do with these collections of Preferences, but also *why* and *when* you might want to use them.

4. Click Open to open both selected files.

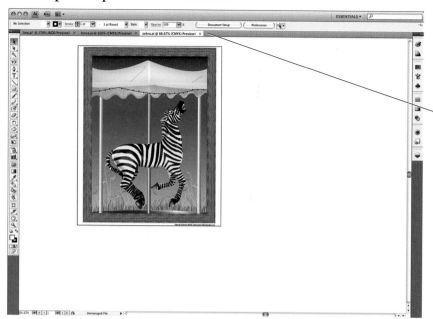

When multiple files are open, each file is represented by a tab at the top of the document window.

5. Click the horse.ai tab at the top of the document window.

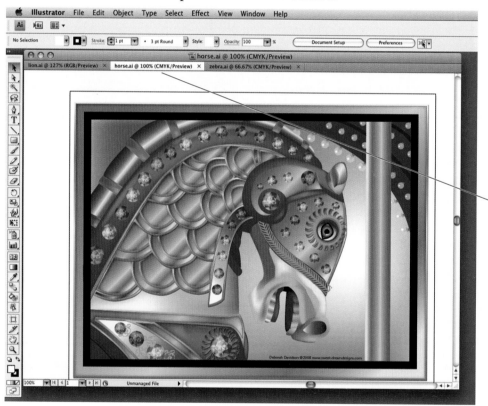

Clicking a specific tab makes that file active in the document window.

6. Choose Window>Arrange>Float in Window.

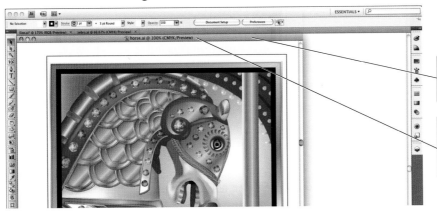

Floating a document separates the file into its own document window.

The title bar of the separate document window shows the same information that was in the document tab.

7. In the Application/Menu bar, click the Arrange Documents button to open the panel of defined arrangements.

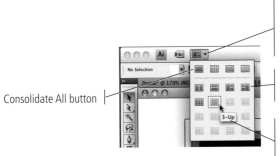

The Arrange Documents panel includes a number of tiling options for arranging multiple open files in the workspace.

The appearance of each icon suggests the result of each option.

Consolidate All button

Rolling your mouse cursor over an icon shows the arrangement name in a tool tip.

Note:

You can separate all open files by choosing Window>Arrange>Float All In Windows.

Note:

On Macintosh systems, the Application bar must be visible to access the Arrange Documents button.

8. Click the Consolidate All button (top-left) in the Arrange Documents panel.

The Consolidate All button consolidates all floating documents into a single tabbed document window (the same as you see in the default arrangement).

The remaining buttons in the top row separate all open files into individual document windows, and then arrange the different windows as indicated.

The lower options use a specific number of floating documents (2-Up, 3-Up, etc.); if more files are open than an option indicates, the extra files are consolidated as tabs in the first document window.

Note:

When multiple floating documents windows are open, two options in the Window>Arrange menu allow you to cascade or tile the different document windows.

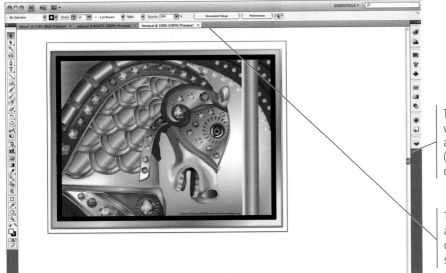

The consolidated document window snaps to fill the available monitor space (within the boundaries of docked panels).

The Consolidate All arrangement restores all open documents into a single document window.

9. **Click the button at the bottom of the Tools panel to show the screen mode options.**

Illustrator has three different **screen modes**, which change the way the document window displays on the screen. The default mode, which you saw when you opened these three files, is called Normal mode.

Note:

All open files are listed at the bottom of the Window menu. You can use these menu options to navigate from one file to another, which is particularly useful if you're working in Full Screen Mode with Menu Bar because the document tabs are not visible in this mode.

10. **Choose Full Screen Mode with Menu Bar from the Screen Mode menu.**

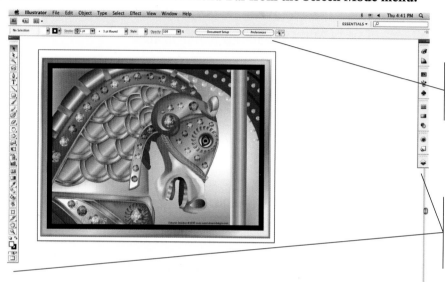

In Full Screen Mode with Menu Bar, the document tabs are hidden behind the Menu bar.

In Full Screen Mode with Menu Bar, the document window fills the entire workspace and extends behind the docked panels.

11. **Click the Screen Mode button at the bottom of the Tools panel and choose Full Screen Mode.**

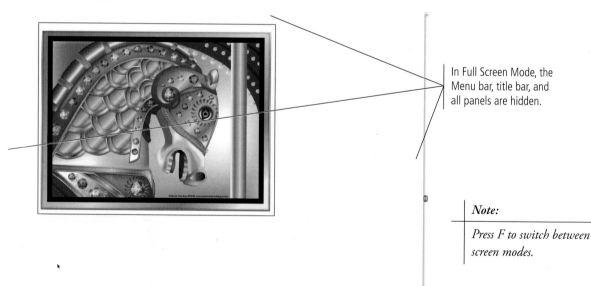

In Full Screen Mode, the Menu bar, title bar, and all panels are hidden.

Note:

Press F to switch between screen modes.

12. **Press the Escape key to exit Full Screen Mode and return to Normal Screen mode.**

13. **Click the X button on the horse.ai tab.**

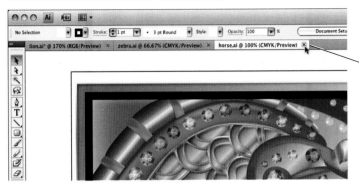

When multiple files are open, clicking the close button on a document tab closes only that file.

14. **Click the Close button in the zebra.ai and lion.ai document tabs. If asked to save changes, click Don't Save in the warning message.**

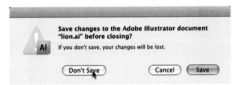

International Symbols

Biotech Services manages large-scale manufacturing facilities specializing in everything from digital photographic equipment to machines used to drill for oil. The company builds plants all over the world that in many cases handle dangerous chemicals and undertake dangerous tasks — which means they must prominently display danger warnings. Biotech Services hired you to create a digital collection of universal symbols they can use to create signs, print on the side of large machines, place as icons on their Web sites, and embroider onto employee uniforms.

This project incorporates the following skills:

❏ Placing raster images into an Illustrator file to use as drawing templates

❏ Creating and managing simple shapes and lines

❏ Using various tools and panels to transform objects' color, position, and shape

❏ Cloning objects to minimize repetitive tasks

❏ Using layers to organize and manage complex artwork

❏ Drawing complex shapes by combining simple shapes

Project Meeting

client comments

We have a set of universal warning symbols on our Web site, but we need to use those same icons in other places as well. Our printer told us that the symbols on our Web site are "low res," which can't be used for print projects. The printer also said he needs vector graphics that will scale larger and still look good. The printer suggested we hire a designer to create digital versions of the icons so we can use them for a wide variety of purposes, from large machinery signs to small plastic cards to anything else that might come up. We need you to help us figure out exactly what we need and then create the icons for us.

art director comments

Basically, we have the icons, but they're low-resolution raster images, so they only work for the Web, and they can't be enlarged. The good news is that you can use the existing icons as templates and more or less trace them to create the new icons.

The client needs files that can be printed cleanly and scaled from a couple of inches up to several feet. Illustrator vector files are perfect for this type of job. In fact, vector graphics get their resolution from the printer being used for a specific job, so you can scale them to any size you want without losing quality.

project objectives

To complete this project, you will:

- ❏ Create a grid that will eventually hold all fourteen icons in one document
- ❏ Control objects' stroke, fill, and transparency attributes
- ❏ Import and use the client's raster images as templates, which you can then trace
- ❏ Use layers to manage complex artwork
- ❏ Use the Line tool to create a complex object from a set of straight lines
- ❏ Lock, unlock, hide, and show objects to navigate the objects' stacking order
- ❏ Rotate and reflect objects to create complex artwork from simple shapes
- ❏ Use the Pathfinder to combine simple shapes into a single complex object

Stage 1 Digital Drawing Basics

There are two primary types of digital artwork: vector graphics and raster images. (**Line art**, sometimes categorized as a third type of image, is actually a type of raster image.)

Vector graphics are composed of mathematical descriptions of a series of lines and points. Vector graphics are **resolution independent**; they can be freely scaled and are automatically output at the resolution of the output device.

Raster images, on the other hand, are pixel-based, made up of a grid of individual **pixels** (**rasters** or **bits**) in rows and columns (called a **bitmap**). Raster files are **resolution dependent**; their resolution is determined when you scan, photograph, or create the file.

Why is it important for you to know the difference between rasters and vectors? Many of the files you build in Illustrator will be placed in various print projects, so you have to build the files with the appropriate settings for commercial printing. As a professional graphic designer, you should have a basic understanding of the following terms and concepts:

- **Pixels per inch (ppi)** is the number of pixels in one horizontal or vertical inch of a digital raster file.

- **Lines per inch (lpi)** is the number of halftone dots produced in a horizontal or vertical linear inch by a high-resolution imagesetter, which simulates the appearance of continuous-tone color.

- **Dots per inch (dpi)** or **spots per inch (spi)** is the number of dots produced by an output device in a single line of output. DPI is sometimes used interchangeably with ppi.

CREATE A NEW DOCUMENT

In this project, you work with the basics of creating vector graphics in Illustrator using a number of different drawing tools, adding color, and managing various aspects of your artwork. The first step is to create a new document for building your artwork.

1. **On any writable disk, create a folder named WIP. On your desktop, drag the Symbols folder from the WIP folder on your Resource CD to your WIP folder where you will save your work.**

   Use this folder to save all files in this project. When you work on a specific project, it can be helpful to use this type of "job folder" for all files so you don't have to hunt for the files you need at a given point in the project.

2. **In Illustrator, choose File>New.**

3. **In the resulting New Document dialog box, type icons in the Name field.**

   The New Document dialog box defaults to the last-used settings.

4. **Choose Print in the New Document Profile dialog box, and make sure the Number of Artboards field is set to 1.**

   Illustrator CS4 includes the ability to create multiple **Artboards** (basically, Illustrator's version of "pages"). You work with multiple Artboards in Project 3.

5. **Choose Letter in the Size menu, choose Points in the Units menu, and choose the Portrait Orientation option.**

   The **point** is a standard unit of measurement for graphic designers. There are 72 points in an inch. As you complete this project, you will work with other units of measurement; you'll convert the units later.

6. **Set all four bleed values to 0.**

   Bleed is the amount an object needs to extend past the edge of the Artboard or page to meet the mechanical requirements of commercial printing.

Note:

You learn more about bleeds in Project 3.

7. **If the Advanced options aren't visible, click the arrow button to the left of the word Advanced.**

8. **Make sure the Color Mode is set to CMYK and the Preview Mode is set to Default.**

   CMYK is the standard color mode for printing, and RGB is the standard color mode for digital distribution. You learn much more about color and color modes in Project 2.

   Don't worry about the Raster Effects setting because the artwork you create in this project doesn't use raster effects. You work with those effects in Project 6.

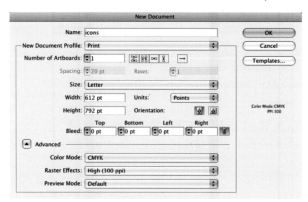

9. **Click OK to create the new file.**

   In the resulting document window, the letter-size "page" (or Artboard) is represented by a dark black line. The Artboard concept will be important in the final stage of this project, when you save the icon files for use in other applications.

   As we explained in the Interface chapter, the panels you see depend on what was done the last time you (or someone else) used the application. Because workspace arrangement is such a personal preference, we tell you what panels you need to use, but we don't tell you where to place them. (Remember: Panels can be accessed in the Window menu.)

   In our screen shots, we typically float panels over the relevant area of the document so we can focus the images on the most important part of the file at any particular point. As you complete the projects in this book, feel free to dock the panels, grouped or ungrouped, iconized or expanded, however you prefer.

Note:

Our screen shots show the Macintosh operating system using the Application frame. If you're on a Macintosh system and your screen doesn't look like our screen shots, choose Window>Application Frame to toggle on that option.

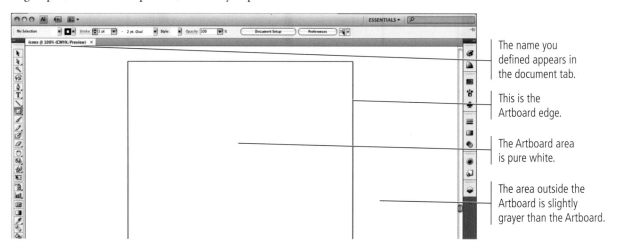

The name you defined appears in the document tab.

This is the Artboard edge.

The Artboard area is pure white.

The area outside the Artboard is slightly grayer than the Artboard.

10. Choose File>Save As and navigate to your WIP>Symbols folder.

If you assign a name in the New Document dialog box (as you did in Step 3), that name becomes the default file name in the Save As dialog box.

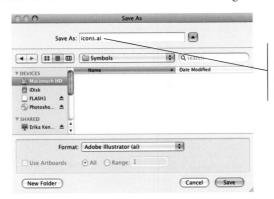

The file name defaults to the name you defined when you created the file, including the ".ai" extension.

Note:

Press Command/Control-S to save a document, or press Command/Control-Shift-S to open the Save As dialog box.

Note:

The Save As dialog box is a system-standard format.

11. Click Save in the Save As dialog box. Review the options in the resulting Illustrator Options dialog box, and then click OK.

These options determine what is stored in the file. The default options are adequate for most files.

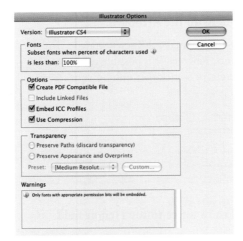

12. Continue to the next exercise.

DRAW BASIC SHAPES

Now that you have a place to draw (the Artboard), you're ready to start creating the icon artwork. The first step of this project requires a set of background shapes — simple rectangles with rounded corners — to contain each icon. Illustrator includes a number of shape tools that make it easy to create this kind of basic shape — rectangles (or squares), ellipses (or circles), and so on.

1. With icons.ai open, click the Rectangle tool in the Tools panel and hold down the mouse button until the nested tools appear. Choose the Rounded Rectangle tool from the list of nested tools.

2. Click the Default Fill and Stroke button at the bottom of the Tools panel.

In Illustrator, the default fill is white and the default stroke is 1-pt. black.

Rounded Rectangle tool

Rounded Rectangle
tool cursor

Default Fill and
Stroke button

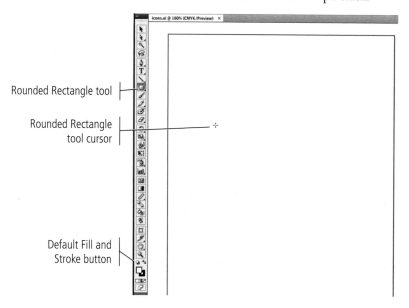

3. Click the Rounded Rectangle tool anywhere on the Artboard.

The resulting dialog box asks you how big you want to make the new rectangle. The default application measurement system is points; however, it is possible to change the default units, so you might see inches, millimeters, or some other unit on your screen (i.e., if someone changed the default settings).

Note:

A point is a unit of measurement that comes from the traditional typesetting industry; there are 72 points in an inch.

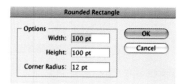

4. Type 1.5″ in the Width field and press Tab to move to the Height field.

Regardless of what unit you see in the dialog box, you can enter values in whatever system you prefer, as long as you remember to type the correct unit in the dialog box fields (use ″ for inches, mm for millimeters, and pt for points; there are a few others, but they are rarely used). Illustrator automatically translates one unit of measurement to another.

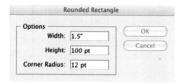

When you move to the next field, Illustrator calculates the conversion of 1.5 inches (the value you placed in the Width field) to 108 pt (the value that automatically appears in the Width field after you move to the Height field).

5. Type 1.5″ in the Height field. Set the Corner Radius field to 12 pt, and then click OK.

A shape appears on the Artboard with its top-left corner exactly where you clicked the Rounded Rectangle tool.

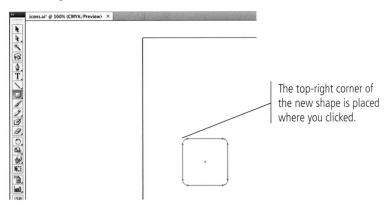

The top-right corner of the new shape is placed where you clicked.

Note:

If you Option/Alt-click with the Rectangle tool, the place where you click becomes the center of the new rectangle shape.

6. Click the Selection tool in the Tools panel and zoom in to 200%.

When the object is selected, the **bounding box** marks the outermost edges of the shape. **Bounding box handles** mark the corners and exact horizontal and vertical center of the shape. If you don't see the bounding box, choose View>Show Bounding Box.

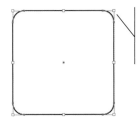

The bounding box handles show the actual corners, where the corner radius cut off the corners of the rectangle.

Note:

A rounded-corner rectangle is simply a rectangle with the corners cut at a specific distance from the end (the corner radius). The two sides are connected with one-fourth of a circle, which has a radius equal to the amount of the rounding.

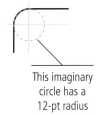

This imaginary circle has a 12-pt radius

7. Select the Rounded Rectangle tool in the Tools panel.

When you choose a nested tool, that variation becomes the default option in the Tools panel. You don't need to access the nested menu to select the Rounded Rectangle tool again.

8. Move the cursor to the right of the top edge of the existing shape.

Note:

As a rule, we don't tell you what view percentage to use unless we want to highlight a specific issue. As you work through the projects in this book, we encourage you to zoom in and out as necessary to meet your specific needs.

9. **When you see a green line connected to the top edge of the first shape, click, hold down the mouse button, and drag down and right to begin creating a second shape.**

Note:

If you don't see the cursor feedback or Smart Guides, choose View>Smart Guides and make sure the option is toggled on (checked).

The green line is a function of the Smart Guides feature, which provides instant feedback while you draw.

As you drag, notice the cursor feedback showing the size of the new shape. Also notice that as you drag near the bottom edge of the first shape, a Smart Guide appears to indicate your position.

Cursor feedback and Smart Guides provide precise control over what you're creating — as individual objects and in relation to other objects on the Artboard.

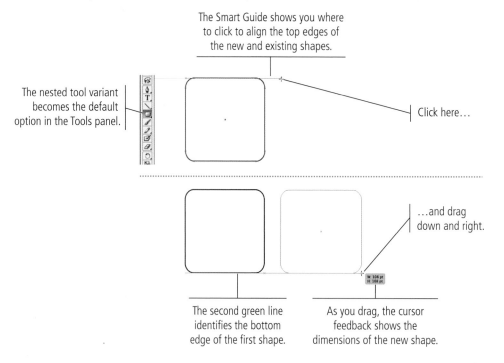

The Smart Guide shows you where to click to align the top edges of the new and existing shapes.

The nested tool variant becomes the default option in the Tools panel.

Click here…

…and drag down and right.

The second green line identifies the bottom edge of the first shape.

As you drag, the cursor feedback shows the dimensions of the new shape.

10. **While still holding down the mouse button, press the Shift key. When the cursor feedback shows both Width and Height values of 108 pt, release the mouse button to create the second shape.**

Note:

You can control the specific Smart Guides options in the Smart Guides pane of the Preferences dialog box.

Pressing Shift **constrains** the shape to equal height and width. Although you can accomplish the same result by carefully monitoring the cursor feedback, pressing the Shift key makes the process faster and easier.

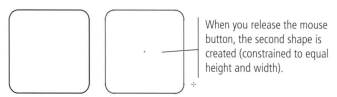

When you release the mouse button, the second shape is created (constrained to equal height and width).

Note:

Press Shift while dragging with a shape tool to create a shape with equal height and width. This is called constraining the shape.

11. **Move the cursor to the right of the second shape until a green line connects to the center of the shape. Click, press Option/Alt-Shift, and drag down and right.**

Pressing the Option/Alt key allows you to create a shape from the center out; in other words, the point where you click will be the exact center of the resulting shape.

Pressing Shift as well constrains the new shape to equal height and width, growing out from the center point where you first clicked.

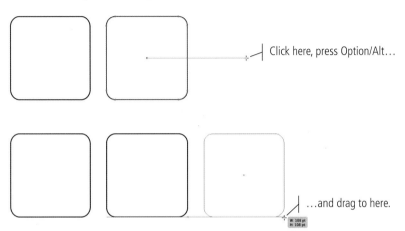

Click here, press Option/Alt…

…and drag to here.

W 108 pt
H 108 pt

Note:

If you do something wrong, or aren't happy with your results, press Command/Control-Z to undo the last action you took.

12. **When the cursor feedback shows both Width and Height values of 108 pt, release the mouse button.**

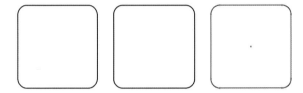

13. **Save the file and continue to the next exercise.**

 ## CONTROL FILL AND STROKE ATTRIBUTES

At the beginning of the previous exercise, you clicked the Default Fill and Stroke button in the Tools panel to apply a white fill and 1-pt black stroke to the objects you created. Obviously, most artwork requires more than these basic attributes. Illustrator gives you almost unlimited control over the fill and stroke attributes of objects on the Artboard.

As you complete the projects in this book, you learn about styles, patterns, gradients, effects, and other attributes that can take an illustration from flat to fabulous. In this exercise, you learn about a number of options for changing the basic fill, stroke, and color attributes for objects on the page.

1. **With icons.ai open, choose the Selection tool at the top of the Tools panel. Click the left rectangle on the Artboard to select it.**

The Selection tool is used to select entire objects.

2. **Open the Swatches panel.**

The Swatches panel includes a number of predefined and saved colors, which you can use to change the color of the fill and stroke of an object. You can also save custom swatches, which you learn about in Project 5.

Note:

Remember: Panels can always be accessed in the Window menu.

Most Illustrator objects (including shapes like rounded-corner rectangles) contain two basic building blocks: anchor points and paths. In fact, these building blocks are the heart of vector graphics. Fortunately, you don't really need to worry about the geometric specifics of vectors because Illustrator manages them for you. But you do need to understand the basic concept of how Illustrator works with anchor points and paths. You should also understand how to access those building blocks so you can do more than create basic shapes.

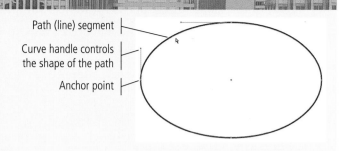

Path (line) segment

Curve handle controls the shape of the path

Anchor point

When you select an object with the **Selection tool** (the solid arrow), you can see the bounding box that identifies the outermost dimensions of the shape. Around the edges of the bounding box you see the bounding box handles, which you can use to resize the shape. (Press Command/Control-Shift-B to show or hide the bounding box of selected objects.)

When you select an object with the **Direct Selection tool** (the hollow arrow), you can see the anchor points and paths that make up the selected object rather than the object's bounding box. As you work with Illustrator, keep this distinction in mind: Use the Selection tool to select an entire object; use the Direct Selection tool to edit the points and paths of an object.

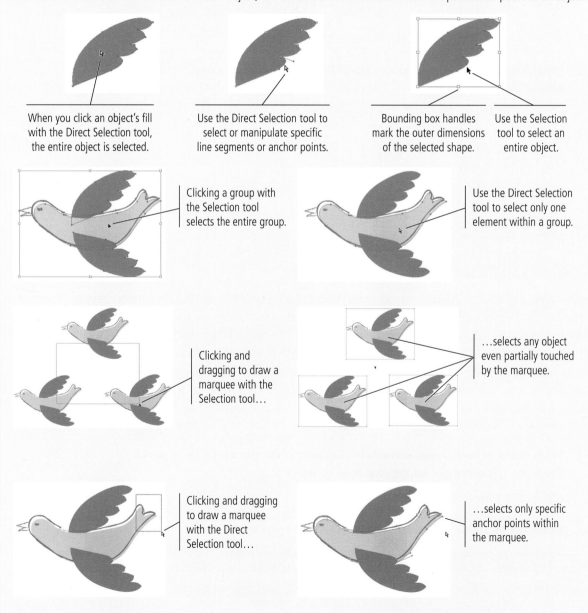

When you click an object's fill with the Direct Selection tool, the entire object is selected.

Use the Direct Selection tool to select or manipulate specific line segments or anchor points.

Bounding box handles mark the outer dimensions of the selected shape.

Use the Selection tool to select an entire object.

Clicking a group with the Selection tool selects the entire group.

Use the Direct Selection tool to select only one element within a group.

Clicking and dragging to draw a marquee with the Selection tool…

…selects any object even partially touched by the marquee.

Clicking and dragging to draw a marquee with the Direct Selection tool…

…selects only specific anchor points within the marquee.

3. Near the bottom of the Tools panel, click the Stroke icon to bring it to the front of the stack.

The Fill and Stroke icons in the Tools panel are used to change the color of the related attributes. Clicking one of these buttons brings it to the front of the stack (makes it active) so you can change the color of that attribute.

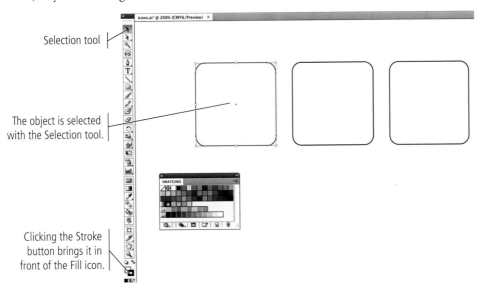

Selection tool

The object is selected with the Selection tool.

Clicking the Stroke button brings it in front of the Fill icon.

4. In the Swatches panel, click the gold swatch at the beginning of the second row.

Because the Stroke icon is active in the Tools panel, the color of the selected object's stroke (border) changes to gold.

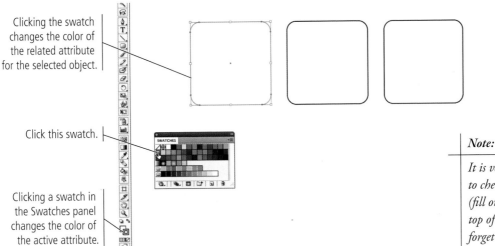

Clicking the swatch changes the color of the related attribute for the selected object.

Click this swatch.

Clicking a swatch in the Swatches panel changes the color of the active attribute.

5. In the Tools panel, click the Fill icon to bring it to the front of the stack.

Note:

It is very easy to forget to check which icon (fill or stroke) is on top of the stack. If you forget and accidentally change the color of the wrong attribute, simply undo the change (press Command/Control-Z) and bring the correct attribute to the front before changing colors.

6. In the Swatches panel, click the black swatch in the first row.

Because the Fill icon is active in the Tools panel, clicking the black color swatch changes the fill color of the selected object.

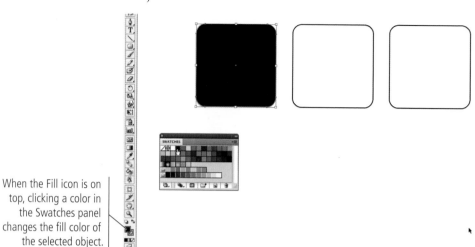

When the Fill icon is on top, clicking a color in the Swatches panel changes the fill color of the selected object.

Transforming Objects with the Bounding Box

Bounding box handles make it easier to transform an object on the Artboard without using the Transform dialog boxes. You can resize an object by dragging any handle, and even rotate an object by placing the cursor directly outside a corner handle. (If Smart Guides are active, cursor feedback helps if you want to make specific transformations, or you can work freestyle and drag handles until you're satisfied with the results.)

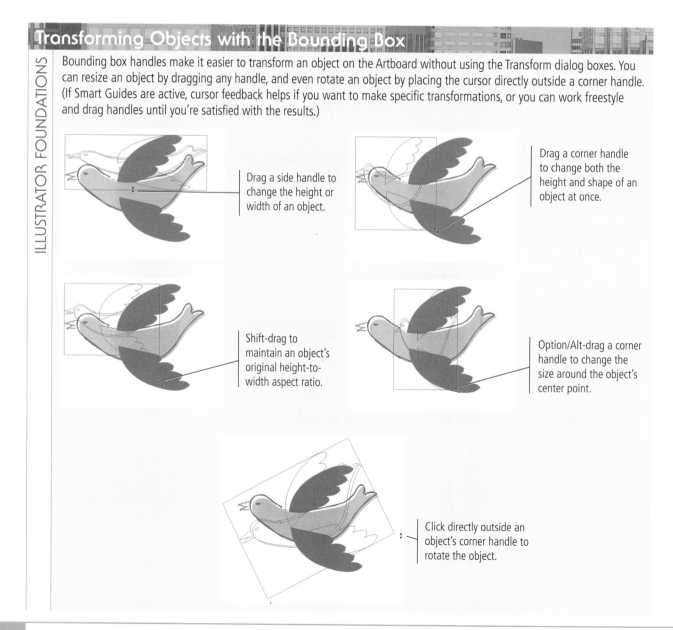

Drag a side handle to change the height or width of an object.

Drag a corner handle to change both the height and shape of an object at once.

Shift-drag to maintain an object's original height-to-width aspect ratio.

Option/Alt-drag a corner handle to change the size around the object's center point.

Click directly outside an object's corner handle to rotate the object.

7. **Open the Stroke panel. With the rounded rectangle still selected on the Artboard, change the Stroke Weight to 3 pt.**

   The Stroke icon in the Tools panel does not need to be active to change the stroke weight. The Tools panel icon relates to the stroke color only.

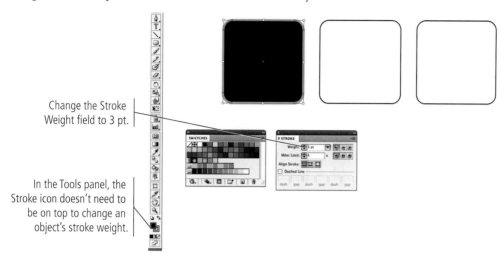

Change the Stroke Weight field to 3 pt.

In the Tools panel, the Stroke icon doesn't need to be on top to change an object's stroke weight.

8. **With the rectangle still selected, click the Swap Fill and Stroke button in the Tools panel.**

   This button makes it easy to reverse the fill and stroke colors of an object; the stroke weight remains unaffected when you swap the colors.

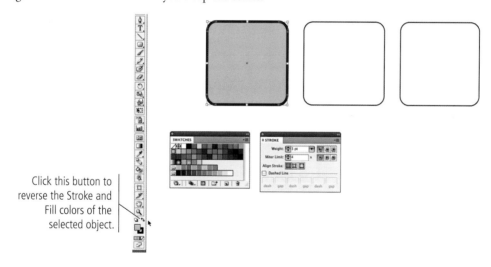

Click this button to reverse the Stroke and Fill colors of the selected object.

9. **Using the Selection tool, click the second rectangle on the Artboard.**

   The Fill and Stroke icons change to reflect the colors of the selected objects.

10. **Click the Fill color swatch in the Control panel. Choose the gold swatch in the second row to change the fill color for the selected object.**

When an object is selected with the Selection tool, the Control panel provides quick access to the stroke and fill attributes of the selected object.

Clicking the Fill color swatch opens an attached Swatches panel so you can change the fill for the selected object without opening the separate Swatches panel.

Note:

When you use the Control panel options, you don't need to worry about which icon is active in the Tools panel.

Click this color swatch to change the fill color of the selected object.

Click this color swatch to change the stroke color of the selected object.

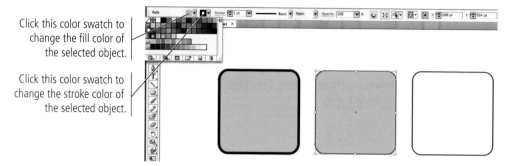

11. **In the Control panel, change the Stroke Weight value to 3 pt.**

Again, the Control panel options allow you to change the attribute value without opening the Stroke panel. The Control panel can be a significant time-saver for common operations such as changing stroke and fill attributes.

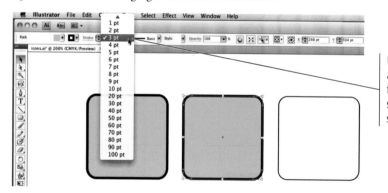

Use the menu or type a value in the attached field to change the stroke weight of the selected object.

12. **Using the Selection tool, click the third rectangle on the Artboard.**

Again, the Fill and Stroke icons in the Tools panel change to reflect the colors of the selected object.

13. **Select the Eyedropper tool in the Tools panel, and then click the first or second rectangle on the Artboard.**

The Eyedropper tool copies fill and stroke attributes from one object (the one you click) to another (the one you first selected).

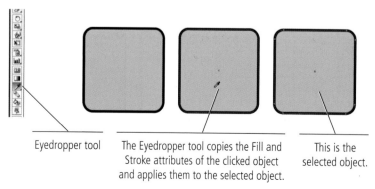

Eyedropper tool

The Eyedropper tool copies the Fill and Stroke attributes of the clicked object and applies them to the selected object.

This is the selected object.

14. **Press Command/Control and click anywhere on the Artboard away from the three rectangles.**

Pressing Command/Control temporarily switches to the Selection tool. By clicking on the empty Artboard area, you can quickly deselect the selected object(s). When you release the Command/Control key, the tool reverts to the one you last used.

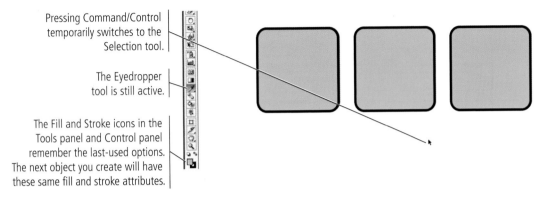

Pressing Command/Control temporarily switches to the Selection tool.

The Eyedropper tool is still active.

The Fill and Stroke icons in the Tools panel and Control panel remember the last-used options. The next object you create will have these same fill and stroke attributes.

15. **Choose the Rounded Rectangle tool in the Tools panel.**

16. **To the right of the third shape on the Artboard, use any method you learned in the previous exercise to draw a fourth rounded rectangle that is 108 pt square.**

The new rectangle has the same heavy black stroke and gold fill as the others.

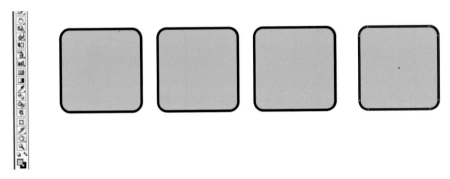

17. **Save the file (File>Save or Command/Control-S) and continue to the next exercise.**

 CONTROL OBJECT POSITIONING

The ability to move objects around on the Artboard is one of the advantages of digital drawing. On paper, you have to manually erase items and then redraw them in their new locations. Illustrator offers a number of tools that make it easy to move existing objects around the Artboard, either as isolated objects or in relation to other elements on the page. In this exercise, you learn several techniques for moving objects around on the Artboard.

1. **With icons.ai open, change your zoom percentage so you can see the entire top of the Artboard.**

2. **Choose the Selection tool from the top of the Tools panel. Click the left rectangle on the Artboard to select it.**

3. **Choose View>Show Rulers to show the rulers at the top and left edges of the document window.**

Because you created this file using points as the default unit of measurement, the rulers — and fields in dialog boxes and panels — show measurements in points.

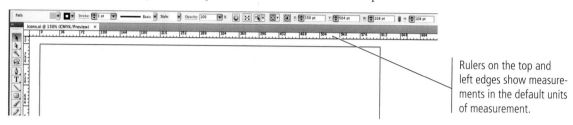

Rulers on the top and left edges show measurements in the default units of measurement.

4. **Control/right-click the top ruler and choose Inches from the contextual menu.**

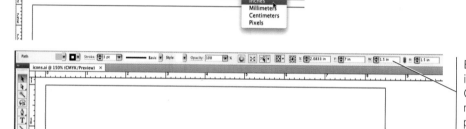

By changing the rulers to inches, measurements in the Control panel and other areas now appear in terms you are probably more familiar with.

If you don't see the X, Y, W, and H fields in the Control panel, you must click the Transform hot-text link to open the pop-up Transform panel, where you can make changes to the object's position or dimensions.

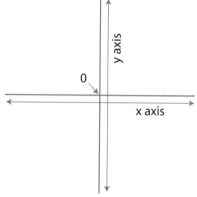

If you have a small monitor (or have reduced the Application frame width), the X, Y, W, and H options are replaced by a hot-text link that opens the Transform panel

In Illustrator, the **zero point** (the source of measurements) is the bottom-left corner of the Artboard; the X and Y positions of an object are measured relative to that location. This is an important distinction because most of the English-speaking world tends to think of "zero" as top-left — the same way we read, from left to right and top to bottom.

Mathematically, however, "zero" is the bottom-left; because vectors (what you are creating in Illustrator) are basically mathematical functions, the measurements default to the bottom-left corner of the Artboard. The X axis is the horizontal value and the Y axis is the vertical value.

Keep these ideas in mind when you move something in an Illustrator file:

- Moving something up requires adding to the Y value.
- Moving something down requires subtracting from the Y value.
- Moving something right requires adding to the X value.
- Moving something left requires subtracting from the X value.

You can change the zero point by clicking where the horizontal and vertical rulers meet and dragging to a new position.

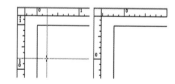

5. With the left rectangle selected, look at the right side of the Control panel.

The reference point corresponds to the bounding box handles of the selected object. The selected square in this icon identifies which point of the selected object is being measured.

6. Click the top-left reference point (if it's not already selected).

The X and Y fields now show the position of the top-left bounding box handle for the selected object.

7. Highlight the X field in the Control panel and type .5. Press Return/Enter to apply the change.

You don't need to type the measurement unit ("), or the preceding "0". Because the rulers are showing inches, Illustrator automatically applies inches as the unit to whatever value you type.

Note:

As with dialog boxes, you can enter values in a unit of measurement other than the default, as long as you remember to type the unit abbreviation.

The selected reference point determines which point on the selection is being measured.

Because the top-left reference point is selected in the Control panel, measurements correspond to this point of the selected shape.

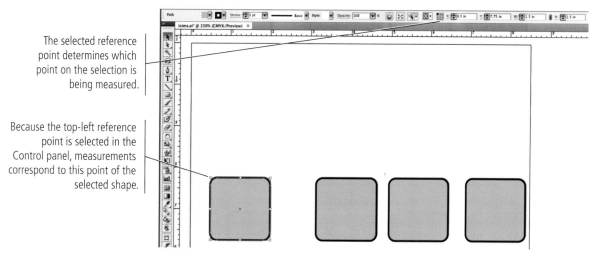

8. Highlight the Y field and type 10.5, then press Return/Enter to apply the change.

The top-left handle of the selected object is now 1/2″ from the top and left edges. The numbers you typed correspond to the measurements you see on the rulers.

The rulers show that the selected point of the object is at X: 0.5″, Y: 10.5″.

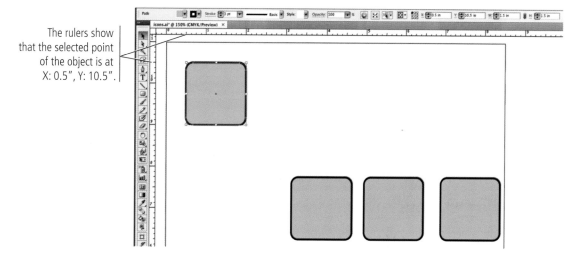

9. **Using the Selection tool, click the second rectangle on the Artboard and drag until a green line appears, connecting the center points of the first and second shapes.**

As you drag the cursor, feedback shows the relative position of the object. In other words, you can see the change (difference) in the object's position, both horizontally (X) and vertically (Y) — hence the "dX" and "dY" values.

In addition to cursor feedback, Smart Guides can be very useful for aligning objects on the Artboard. As you drag, Illustrator identifies and highlights relative alignment, and snaps objects to those alignment points as you drag.

Note:

Remember, moving left decreases the X value and moving down decreases the Y value. If the cursor feedback shows a negative value, you've moved left or down (or both).

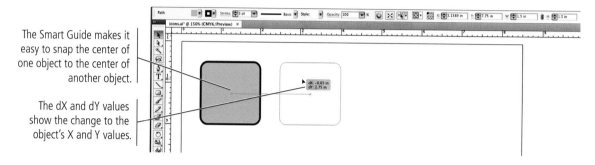

The Smart Guide makes it easy to snap the center of one object to the center of another object.

The dX and dY values show the change to the object's X and Y values.

10. **Release the mouse button while the center Smart Guide is visible.**

11. **Click the fourth shape on the page. In the Control panel, select the top-right reference point, type 8 in the X field, and type 10.5 in the Y field.**

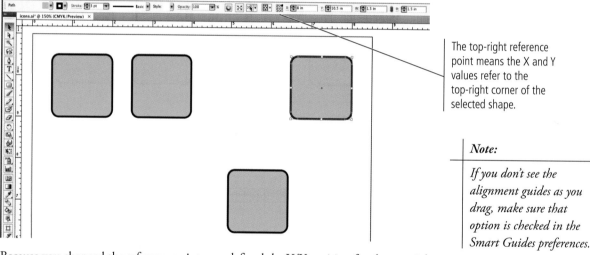

The top-right reference point means the X and Y values refer to the top-right corner of the selected shape.

Note:

If you don't see the alignment guides as you drag, make sure that option is checked in the Smart Guides preferences.

Because you changed the reference point, you defined the X/Y position for the top-right bounding box handle of the fourth rectangle.

12. **Save the file and continue to the next exercise.**

The Transform Panel

Using the Transform panel fields, you can change the position, size, angle, or skew of an object. If you use the panel to resize an object, you can constrain the object's height-to-width aspect ratio by clicking the chain icon. (The same options are available in the Control panel between the W and H fields.)

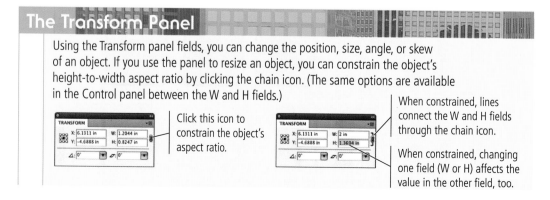

Click this icon to constrain the object's aspect ratio.

When constrained, lines connect the W and H fields through the chain icon.

When constrained, changing one field (W or H) affects the value in the other field, too.

ALIGN AND DISTRIBUTE OBJECTS

In addition to dragging objects around the Artboard, the Illustrator Align panel makes it very easy to align and distribute selected objects relative to one another, to a specific key object in the file, or to the overall Artboard. In this exercise, you learn how to use the Align panel to align shapes.

1. **With icons.ai open, use the Selection tool to drag a marquee that touches some part of all four objects on the page.**

   The Selection tool selects objects, so the selection marquee only needs to touch the objects you want to select. The marquee doesn't need to surround the objects entirely.

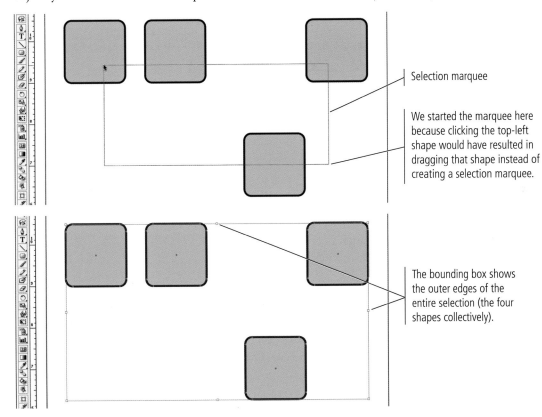

Selection marquee

We started the marquee here because clicking the top-left shape would have resulted in dragging that shape instead of creating a selection marquee.

The bounding box shows the outer edges of the entire selection (the four shapes collectively).

2. **Open the Align panel (Window>Align) and click the Vertical Align Top button.**

   By default, alignment and distribution functions occur relative to the selected objects. In other words, when you click the Vertical Align Top button, Illustrator determines the topmost edge of the selected objects, and then moves the top edges of all other selected objects to that point.

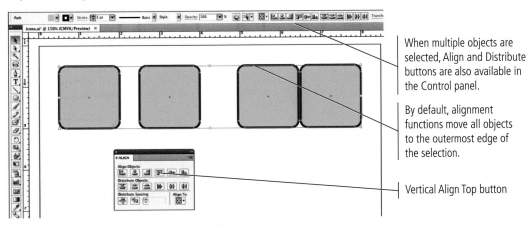

When multiple objects are selected, Align and Distribute buttons are also available in the Control panel.

By default, alignment functions move all objects to the outermost edge of the selection.

Vertical Align Top button

3. **With all four objects selected, click the Horizontal Distribute Center button.**

By default, the distribution functions create equal distance between the selected point of the selected objects.

In this case, Illustrator distributed the center points along the horizontal axis. Illustrator determined the center-point positions of the outermost selected objects, and then moved the middle two objects to create equal distance between the center points of all four selected objects; the positions of the two outer objects remained unchanged.

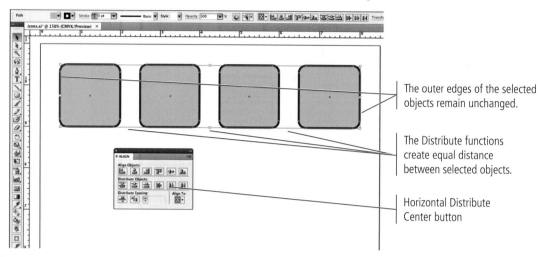

The outer edges of the selected objects remain unchanged.

The Distribute functions create equal distance between selected objects.

Horizontal Distribute Center button

4. **With all four objects selected, choose Object>Group.**

When you group multiple objects, the group is essentially treated as a single object. A single bounding box surrounds all objects within the group.

5. **Click inside any of the grouped objects, press the Option/Alt key, and drag down.**

6. **Use the Smart Guides and cursor feedback to drag exactly vertical (the dX value should be 0). When the dY value in the cursor feedback is –2 in, release the mouse button.**

Pressing Option/Alt while you drag makes a copy of the original selection. This technique, called **cloning**, can save significant amounts of time when you build illustrations that contain numerous repetitive elements.

Note:

Press Command/ Control-G to group selected objects. Press Command/Control-Shift-G to ungroup grouped objects.

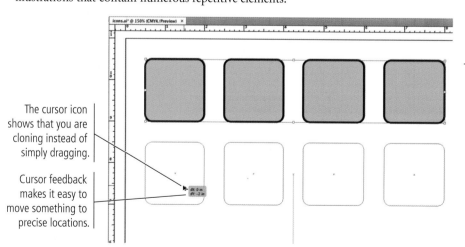

The cursor icon shows that you are cloning instead of simply dragging.

Cursor feedback makes it easy to move something to precise locations.

Note:

You can press Command/ Control-D to repeat the last-used transformation. In this case, the last transformation was the cloning movement, so Command/Control-D would create the third row of rectangles.

7. Repeat Steps 5–6 to create a third row of rectangles.

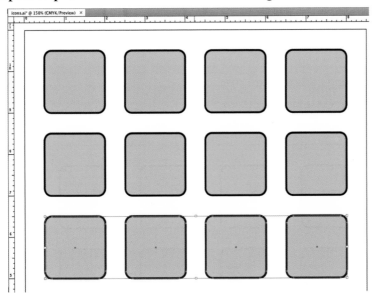

Note:

As you might have guessed by now, there is almost always more than one way to accomplish a specific task. The Align panel is useful for certain functions (especially distribution), but Smart Guides make object-to-object alignment very easy.

8. Click anywhere outside the rectangle shapes to deselect all objects and groups.

9. Save the file and continue to the next exercise.

 ## EDIT INDIVIDUAL GROUPED ELEMENTS

The client in this project requested only ten icons, so you don't need two of the rectangles in the third row. As you know, the Selection tool selects entire objects on the page. You also know that grouped objects are treated as a single object — which means you can't use the Selection tool to select part of a group. In this exercise, you use two techniques to work with component pieces of a group.

1. With icons.ai open, use the Selection tool to click the fourth rectangle in the third row.

Because the four objects are grouped, the Selection tool selects the entire group. You need to use a different method to select certain elements within the group.

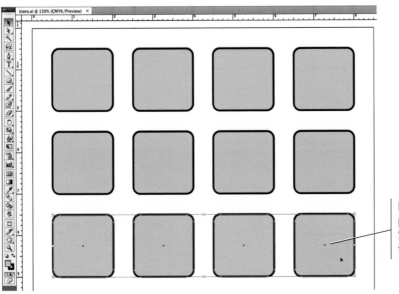

Because this object is part of a group, the Selection tool selects the entire group.

2. **Click anywhere outside the rectangle shapes to deselect the group, then choose the Direct Selection tool in the Tools panel.**

   The Direct Selection tool selects pieces of an object — specific paths, anchor points, or individual elements in a grouped object.

3. **Click the gold fill of the fourth rectangle in the third row.**

   Because you clicked the fill, you basically selected the entire object.

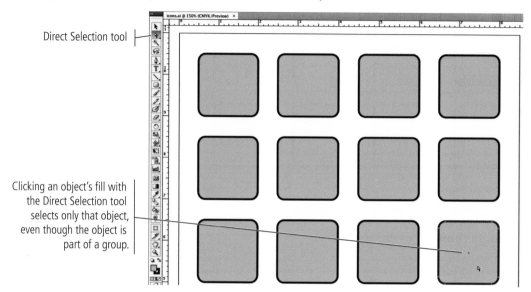

Direct Selection tool

Clicking an object's fill with the Direct Selection tool selects only that object, even though the object is part of a group.

4. **Press Delete to remove the selected object.**

   Easy enough, especially because this is a very simple group of objects that don't overlap. When you start working with complex files that have multiple levels of grouping, however, it can be challenging to manipulate objects within a group using only the Direct Selection tool.

5. **Choose the Selection tool in the Tools panel, and then double-click the third rectangle in the third row.**

   Double-clicking a group enters into Isolation mode, where only objects within the selected group are available. Basically, Isolation mode provides access to objects in the group without ungrouping the objects on the main Artboard.

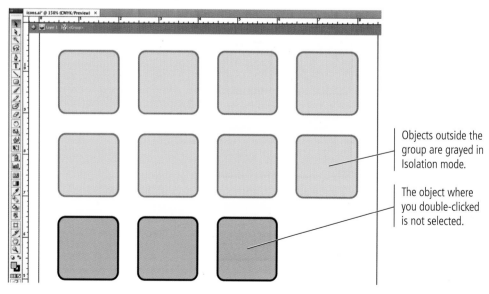

Objects outside the group are grayed in Isolation mode.

The object where you double-clicked is not selected.

6. **Using the Selection tool, click the third rectangle in the third row to select it, and then press Delete.**

   Because you created only a single level of grouping, you can now use the Selection tool to select individual objects.

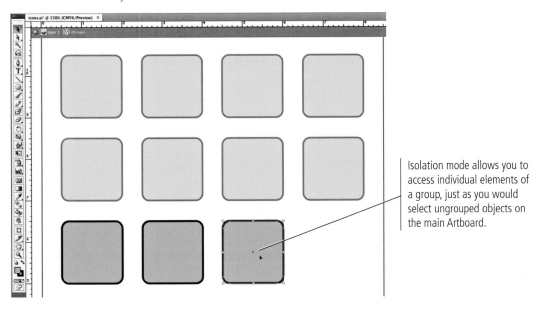

Isolation mode allows you to access individual elements of a group, just as you would select ungrouped objects on the main Artboard.

7. **At the top of the document window, click the Arrow button twice to return to the main Artboard.**

   The third row, now with two rectangles, is still a single group on the main Artboard.

Click this button to exit Isolation mode.

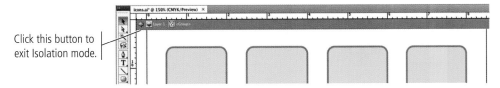

8. **Save the file and continue to the next exercise.**

 ## IMPORT TEMPLATE IMAGES

Many Illustrator projects require you to start with something that's already been captured — a sketch, photograph, or low-resolution image (which is the case in this project). Illustrator makes it easy to place existing digital files to use as templates for your new artwork. You will use this feature in this exercise.

1. **With icons.ai open, choose File>Place. Navigate to the RF_Illustrator> Symbols folder on your Resource CD and click cold.tif to select that file.**

2. **At the bottom of the Place dialog box, make sure the Link option is unchecked.**

   If the Link option is unchecked, the placed file is **embedded** — it becomes part of the file where it's placed. The original external file is not necessary for the artwork to output properly. We will explore the details of placed files in later projects.

   If you check the Link option, the placed file is not a part of the actual file where you're working. For the file to output properly, Illustrator must be able to locate the linked file in the same location (hard drive, CD, etc.) as when you placed it.

3. Check the Template option.

When you place an object as a template, it's added to the file on a separate, non-printing layer that is partially grayed, making it easier to work with (you'll see what we mean in the next exercise).

If this option is checked, the placed file is not stored (embedded) as a part of your Illustrator file.

4. Click Place.

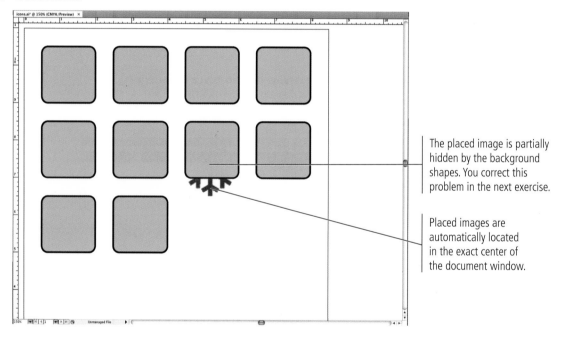

The placed image is partially hidden by the background shapes. You correct this problem in the next exercise.

Placed images are automatically located in the exact center of the document window.

5. **Choose File>Place again. Select** radiation.tif **in the list, check the Template option, and click Place.**

The Place dialog box remembers the last-used location, so you don't have to re-navigate to the Symbols folder. The Link option also remembers the last-used settings. The Template option, however, always defaults to off, so you have to manually check this box for each template object.

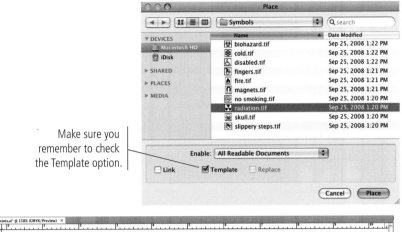

Make sure you remember to check the Template option.

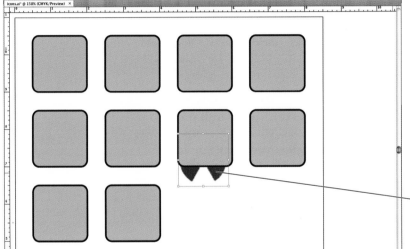

This image is also placed in the center of the document window, directly on top of the first placed image.

6. **Repeat Step 5 to place** fire.tif **into your file as a template image.**

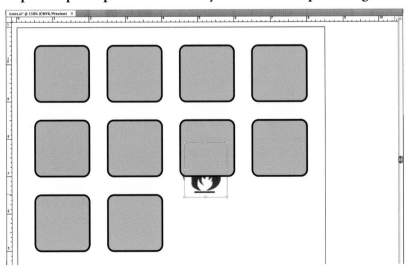

7. **Save the file and continue to the next exercise.**

MANAGE MULTIPLE LAYERS

When you create digital artwork in Illustrator, you almost always end up with more than one object on the Artboard. In many cases, a completed file has dozens or hundreds of objects, arranged in specific order on top of one another. As files become more and more complex, it can be difficult to find and work with exactly the pieces you need. Illustrator layers are one of the most powerful tools available for solving this organizational problem.

1. **In the open icons.ai file, open the Layers panel.**

   By default, all files have a single layer, named Layer 1. Your file has three additional layers — the template layers — below Layer 1. Template layers are locked by default, which means you can't select or modify objects on those layers.

   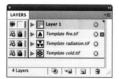

2. **In the Layers panel, click the Layer 1 name and drag it below all three template layers in the stack.**

   The top-to-bottom position of objects or layers is called **stacking order**. Objects and layers typically appear in the stack based on the order in which they are created — the first-created is at the bottom, the last-created is at the top, and so on in between.

   Placed template objects are the exception; these layers are placed *below* the currently selected layer (i.e., lower in the stacking order). In this case, the rectangle shapes have a fill color other than None. You can't see the template image behind the shapes because the template layer is below the layer containing the filled shapes. To see the template images, you need to move the template object layers above the layer containing the background shapes. Rather than moving three layers above Layer 1, you can save a few clicks by moving Layer 1 below the template layers.

   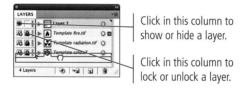

   Click in this column to show or hide a layer.

   Click in this column to lock or unlock a layer.

3. **Using the Selection tool, click the top-left rounded rectangle to select it.**

   Remember, this object is grouped with the other rectangles in the same row. You need to align the placed object to only the first rectangle, which means you need to be able to select only that object.

   As you saw in an earlier exercise, you can use Isolation mode to access a single element of a group. However, each rectangle shape is ultimately going to be a separate icon; you're simply creating them all in the same workspace. The best choice here is to simply ungroup the rectangles, returning them to individual objects.

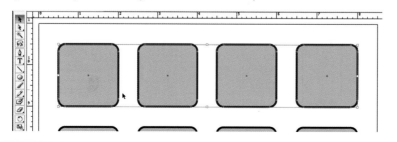

4. **With the top-row group selected, choose Object>Ungroup.**

5. **Click away from the selected objects to deselect them, and then click the top-left rectangle to select that object only.**

6. **In the Layers panel, click the Lock icon for the Template cold.tif layer.**

   Because you need to move the placed template object into the correct position, you need to first unlock the layer.

7. **With the Selection tool still active, press Shift and click anywhere inside the area where the template images are placed.**

   Pressing Shift allows you to add objects to the current selection. The first rectangle and the image should both be selected.

Note:

Press Command/Control-Shift-G to ungroup objects in a group.

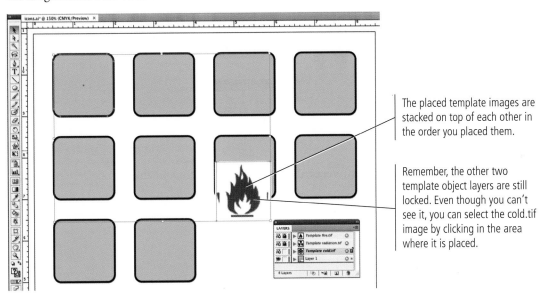

The placed template images are stacked on top of each other in the order you placed them.

Remember, the other two template object layers are still locked. Even though you can't see it, you can select the cold.tif image by clicking in the area where it is placed.

8. **With both objects selected, click the Align To button in the Control panel and choose Align to Key Object from the menu.**

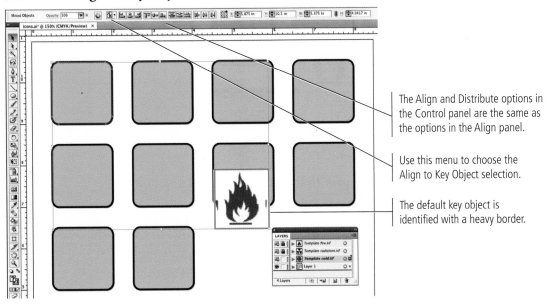

The Align and Distribute options in the Control panel are the same as the options in the Align panel.

Use this menu to choose the Align to Key Object selection.

The default key object is identified with a heavy border.

9. **Click the selected rounded rectangle on the Artboard.**

   Key Object alignment allows you to define where you want other objects to align. By selecting the key object, you're telling Illustrator which object to use as the basis for alignment.

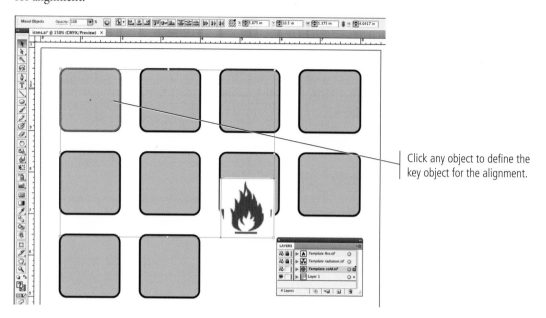

Click any object to define the key object for the alignment.

10. **Click the Horizontal Align Center and Vertical Align Center buttons in the Control panel.**

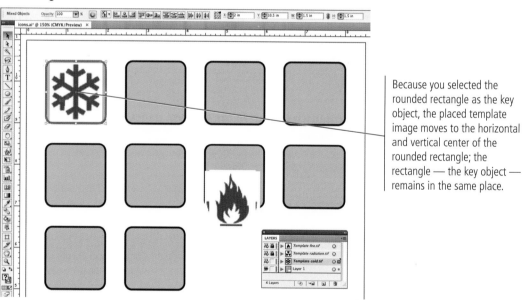

Because you selected the rounded rectangle as the key object, the placed template image moves to the horizontal and vertical center of the rounded rectangle; the rectangle — the key object — remains in the same place.

11. **In the Layers panel, click the empty space to the left of the Template cold.tif layer to lock the layer.**

   Now that the template object is in place, it's a good idea to lock it again so that you don't accidentally move the object.

12. **In the Layers panel, double-click the name of the Template cold.tif layer.**

   Double-clicking a layer name opens the Layer Options dialog box for that layer, where you can change a number of attributes for the selected layer.

13. Change the Dim Images To field to `30`, and then click OK to close the Layer Options dialog box.

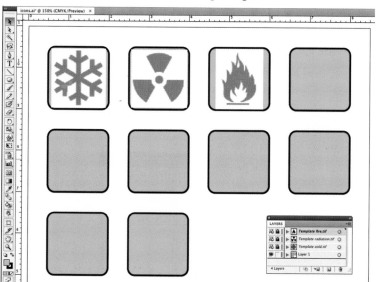

The dimmed template image makes it easier to see your artwork when you start drawing.

14. Repeat Steps 6–13 to position the other two template images in the first-row rectangles (as shown in the following image).

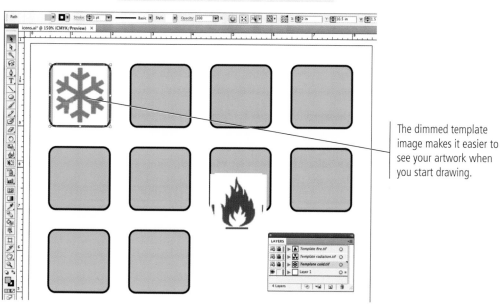

15. In the Layers panel, double-click the Layer 1 name to open the Layer Options dialog box. Change the Layer Name field to Background Shapes and click OK.

Whenever you have more than one working layer, it's a good idea to use names that tell you what is on each layer. Doing so avoids confusion later when you or someone else needs to change a particular item.

16. In the Layers panel, click the empty space immediately left of the Background Shapes layer.

This step — locking the Background Shapes layer — is simply a safeguard to avoid accidentally changing the background rectangles while you're drawing the icon artwork.

Lock the Background Shapes layer to protect the objects on that layer.

17. In the Layers panel, click the New Layer button at the bottom of the panel.

In the next exercise, you start tracing the object in the template. The completed icon will be a black icon on top of the rounded rectangle with the gold background color.

At this point, most of the gold color in the background shapes is obscured by the placed images, because the template layers are above the layer containing the rectangles. If you tried to draw the icon shapes on the existing non-template layer, you'd be drawing *behind* the template — in other words, you wouldn't be able to see what you were drawing. Instead, you need another layer above the template layers, where you can create the icon artwork.

New Layer button

18. In the Layers panel, drag Layer 5 to the top of the layer stack.

New layers are automatically placed immediately above the selected layer. You need this new layer to be above the template layers so you can see what you're drawing.

19. Double-click the Layer 5 name in the Layers panel. Change the layer name to Icon Art. Choose Dark Green from the Color menu and click OK.

The Color option determines the color of bounding box handles and other visual indicators for objects on a layer. (The default for Layer 5, Yellow, can be very difficult to see. We chose Dark Green because it shows better in our screen shots.)

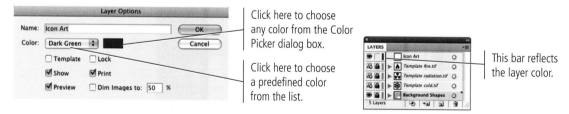

Click here to choose any color from the Color Picker dialog box.

Click here to choose a predefined color from the list.

This bar reflects the layer color.

20. Save the file and continue to the next stage of the project.

Stage 2 **Drawing Basics**

At this stage of the project, you've already developed many of the necessary skills for creating Illustrator drawings. The next step is to draw something more complex than simple rectangles. If you remember from the client meeting, the client's bitmap icons work fine on the Web, but they look terrible in print. After you redraw the icons in Illustrator, the client will be able to print the icons anywhere, with no loss in quality — which is the primary advantage of vector-based artwork vs. raster-based images.

A number of tools and utilities — either in addition to or in combination with the basic shape tools — can be used to create complex Illustrator artwork. Creating the three icons in this project gives you an opportunity to experiment with some of these tools and options. As you complete the other projects in this book, you delve deeper into complex drawing techniques.

CREATE ARTWORK WITH LINES

The snowflake icon is really nothing more than a series of straight lines — which makes it an ideal image to introduce the Illustrator Line tool. In this exercise, you create simple lines, and then use some basic modification techniques to create the final icon.

1. **With icons.ai open (from your WIP>Symbols folder), make sure the Icon Art layer is selected. Zoom in to the top-left rectangle (the one with the snowflake image).**

2. **In the Tools panel, select the Line tool, and then click the Default Fill and Stroke button.**

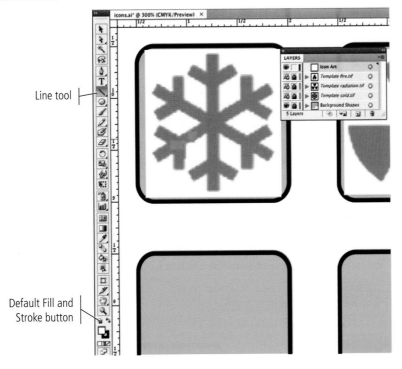

Line tool

Default Fill and Stroke button

3. **Click at the bottom of the vertical line in the snowflake image, and then drag up to the top of the snowflake image. Release the mouse button while the cursor feedback shows the line at 90°.**

   As you drag, the cursor feedback shows the length and — more importantly in this case — the angle of the line you're drawing. If you don't see the cursor feedback, choose View>Smart Guides to toggle on that option.

Note:

You can also press Shift to constrain a line to increments of 45°.

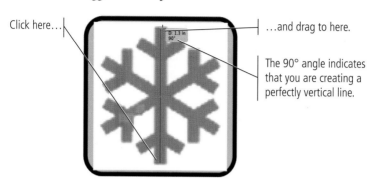

Click here...

...and drag to here.

The 90° angle indicates that you are creating a perfectly vertical line.

D: 1.3 in
90°

4. **With the Line tool still active, click the cursor on the top of the left flake branch in the template image.**

5. **Drag until you see the word "path" appear near the cursor, then release the mouse button.**

   The word "path" is another function of Illustrator's Smart Guides; when you drag near an existing path, Illustrator identifies the path so you can place a point exactly on top of the existing path.

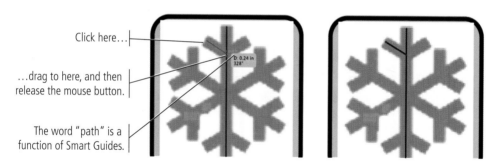

Click here...

...drag to here, and then release the mouse button.

The word "path" is a function of Smart Guides.

D: 0.24 in
328°

6. **Move the cursor to the top of the right flake branch until you see a green line connecting to the top of the left branch that you drew in Steps 4–5.**

7. **Click the mouse button, and then drag down and left until the word "anchor" appears next to the cursor, and then release the mouse button.**

   The "anchor" label indicates that you've dragged to the position of an existing anchor point (in this case, the endpoint of the left flake branch). As you can see, Illustrator makes it easy to create precise lines and shapes in relation to other objects on the page.

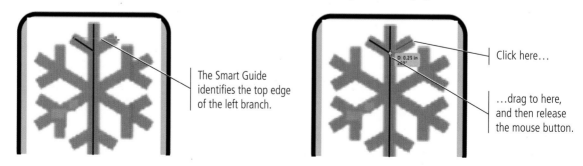

The Smart Guide identifies the top edge of the left branch.

Click here...

...drag to here, and then release the mouse button.

D: 0.25 in
268°

8. **Choose the Selection tool from the Tools panel, and then click the vertical line you drew in Step 3. Choose Object>Lock>Selection.**

When an object is locked, you can't select or change it — just as locking a template layer protects the template object from being moved. In the next few steps, you select and join the endpoints of the two angled lines, which is much easier if the vertical line can't be selected (you want the vertical line to remain unchanged).

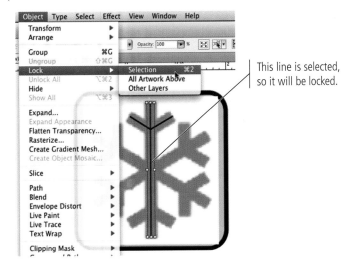

This line is selected, so it will be locked.

9. **Using the Direct Selection tool, drag a marquee around the bottom points of both angled lines.**

You want to join the lines' endpoints, so you need to select only those specific points (instead of the entire lines). As we mentioned earlier, you need the Direct Selection tool to select specific points on a path.

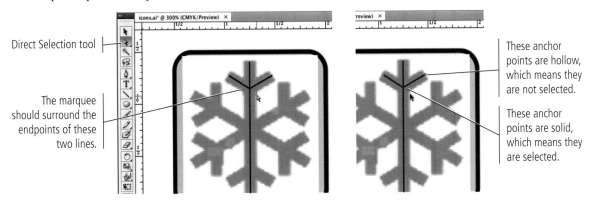

Direct Selection tool

The marquee should surround the endpoints of these two lines.

These anchor points are hollow, which means they are not selected.

These anchor points are solid, which means they are selected.

10. **Choose Object>Path>Join.**

11. **In the resulting dialog box, make sure the Corner option is selected and click OK.**

When you join the endpoints of two lines, the result is a single path with a connecting point where the two endpoints meet. If endpoints are too far apart, they can't be joined; fortunately, the Smart Guides function makes it very easy to place the end of a line exactly on top of the endpoint of an existing line, so you can join them later if necessary.

12. **Save the file and continue to the next exercise.**

REFLECT DRAWING OBJECTS

Illustrator includes four important transformation tools — Rotate, Reflect, Scale, and Shear. Each of these transformations can be applied by hand using the related tool in the Tools panel, as well as numerically using the appropriate dialog box from the Object>Transform menu.

Much of the work you do in Illustrator requires changing objects that already exist. In this exercise, you use reflection to create additional sections of the snowflake icon.

1. **With icons.ai open, choose the Selection tool in the Tools panel. Make sure the angled-branch object is selected on the Artboard.**

    Because the Selection tool is active, you can now see the bounding box of the selected object — both angled lines, which have been joined into a single object.

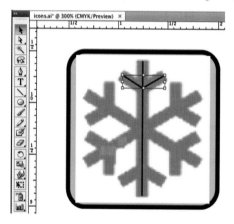

2. **Choose Object>Transform>Reflect.**

    You can reflect objects around the vertical or horizontal axis at specific degrees. In this case, you want to make the braches at the bottom of the snowflake, so you need to reflect the object around the horizontal axis.

3. **In the Reflect dialog box, activate the Preview check box.**

    The Preview option, which is available in all of the Illustrator transformation dialog boxes, allows you to see the effects of your changes before you commit them.

4. **Choose the Horizontal option and click Copy.**

    If you click OK in any of the transformation dialog boxes, the transformation directly affects the selected object. Because you want another branch for the bottom of the flake, you are using the Copy function instead of simply clicking OK.

Note:

Reflecting on the horizontal axis flips the object top over bottom. Reflecting around the vertical axis flips the object left to right.

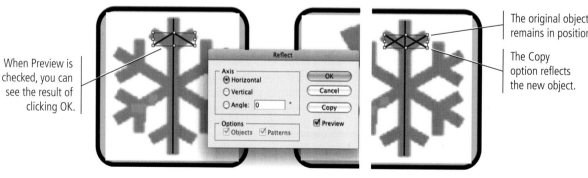

When Preview is checked, you can see the result of clicking OK.

The original object remains in position.

The Copy option reflects the new object.

5. **With the Selection tool still active, click the reflected branches and drag them to the bottom of the flake and place the object appropriately. Use the template image as a guide.**

   Again, the Smart Guides function helps you place the object; the green line and cursor feedback show the angle at which you're moving the selected object, so you can more easily maintain the same vertical position.

Use the cursor feedback to move the shape to the exact vertical position (dX = 0).

6. **Choose Object>Unlock All.**

   Remember, you locked the original vertical line to protect it while you worked with the endpoints of the angled branches. Now that you have one complete set of branches, you can use the existing objects to create the remaining icon elements — which means you need to unlock the vertical line so you can access and copy it.

7. **Choose Select>All.**

   All three objects — the vertical line and the two branch objects — are now selected.

8. **In the Control panel, change the stroke width to 7 pt.**

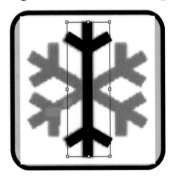

9. **Choose Object>Group.**

   Because these three objects are basically a single entity in the icon, it's a good idea to treat them as a single object.

10. **Save the file and continue to the next exercise.**

ROTATE DRAWING OBJECTS

Very few projects are entirely horizontal, making rotating objects a foundational Illustrator skill. In this exercise, you use several rotation techniques to create the rest of the snowflake artwork.

1. **With icons.ai open, make sure the grouped object is selected.**

2. **Activate the Rotate tool in the Tools panel.**

   When you select the Rotate tool, an **origin point** appears by default at the center of the selected object. This origin point is the point around which rotation occurs. If you want to rotate an object around some other point, you can single-click anywhere to define a different origin point.

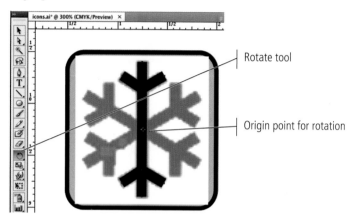

Rotate tool

Origin point for rotation

> *Note:*
>
> *All four of the Illustrator transformation tools use this same origin point concept as the basis for transformations. First, you click to define the origin point, and then you click and drag to apply the transformation.*

3. **Click near the top of the vertical line, hold down the mouse button, and then drag left and down until the line appears over the next branch in the snowflake. Release the mouse button.**

   As you can see, the rotation moved the selected objects around the origin point. Unfortunately, the vertical line is no longer there because you just rotated it.

When you drag with the Rotate tool, the cursor feedback shows the angle of rotation.

When you release the mouse button, the original object rotates.

4. **Press Command/Control-Z to undo the rotation.**

5. **Press Option/Alt, click near the top of the vertical line, hold down the mouse button and begin dragging down and left. While still dragging, press Option/Alt, and then continue dragging until the objects again match the next branch. Release the mouse button.**

Remember from the first stage of this project: Pressing Option/Alt clones the object you are dragging. The same is true when you transform a selection. By pressing Option/Alt after you begin dragging to rotate, the rotated objects become a copy of the original selection.

When you release the mouse button, the original object remains in place.

Pressing Option/Alt while you drag rotates a copy of the original.

6. **With the rotated objects selected, Option/Alt-click the origin point of the selection.**

When using the transformation tools, Option/Alt-clicking opens the related transformation dialog box, where you can make specific numeric transformations.

Transformation dialog boxes default to the last-used settings for that transformation. In this case, the last time you rotated something was Step 5, so the dialog box shows the degree of that rotation (it should be somewhere around 60°).

7. **Click Copy to implement the transformation and make the final set of snowflake branches.**

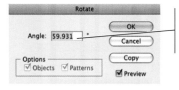

The dialog box remembers the angle of the last rotation (in this case, from Step 5).

8. **Choose Select>All. Using the Control panel, click the Vertical Align Center and Horizontal Align Center buttons.**

Because each "branch" is a group, the alignment functions work as you would expect. The three sets of branches are now exactly centered in both directions.

This step might not produce noticeable effect, depending on how precisely you placed the lines; but it's a good idea to be certain that the groups align properly.

Note:

The "click" part of the Option/Alt-click positions the transformation origin point, so you have to click the existing origin point to make the new transformation around the existing origin.

Note:

The Transform Again command applies the last-used transformation of any type to a selected object without opening a dialog box. This command might result in movement, rotation, reflection, shear, or scale, depending on the last transformation you applied.

9. **With all snowflake objects selected, choose Object>Lock>Selection.**

10. **In the Layers panel, select the Template cold.tif layer and click the Delete Selection button at the bottom of the panel. Click Yes in the confirmation message.**

    Since the snowflake drawing is complete, you no longer need the template image.

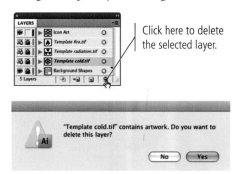

Click here to delete the selected layer.

11. **Save the file and continue to the next exercise.**

DIVIDE BASIC SHAPES INTO COMPONENT PIECES

Using the Illustrator Pathfinder panel, you can combine multiple shapes in a variety of ways, or you can use one object as a "cookie cutter" to remove or separate one shape from another. As you work with more complicated artwork in Illustrator, you will find many different ways to use the Pathfinder functions, either alone or in combination.

1. **With icons.ai open, make sure the Icon Art layer is selected in the Layers panel. Zoom into the second rectangle in the first row of background shapes.**

2. **Select the Ellipse tool (nested under the Rounded Rectangle tool) in the Tools panel. Set the fill color to black and the stroke color to None.**

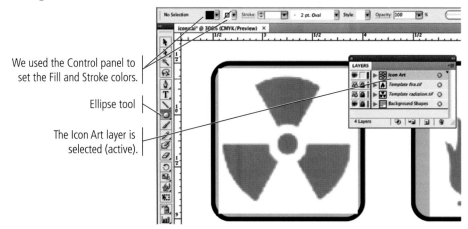

We used the Control panel to set the Fill and Stroke colors.

Ellipse tool

The Icon Art layer is selected (active).

3. Click in the center of the biohazard icon, press Option/Alt-Shift, and then drag to create a circle that covers the entire biohazard icon.

Remember, pressing Option/Alt allows you to draw a shape from the center out. Pressing Shift constrains the shape to equal height and width.

Note:

The fill color does not appear until you release the mouse button.

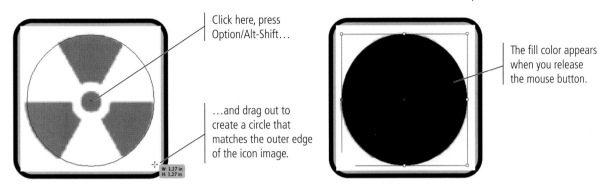

Click here, press Option/Alt-Shift…

…and drag out to create a circle that matches the outer edge of the icon image.

W: 1.27 in
H: 1.27 in

The fill color appears when you release the mouse button.

4. With the new circle selected, change the Opacity field in the Control panel to 50.

Opacity defines the transparency of the selected object. In this case, you're reducing the opacity from 100% (entirely solid or opaque) so you can see the template image behind the circle you just drew.

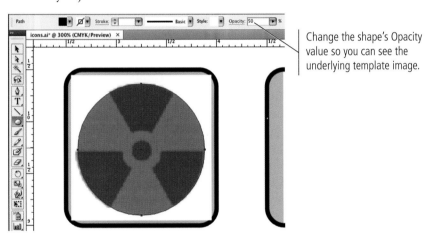

Change the shape's Opacity value so you can see the underlying template image.

Note:

You'll work with opacity as a design element in Project 6.

5. Using the Ellipse tool, click again in the center of the template image, press Option/Alt-Shift, and drag to create the smaller circle in the center of the shape.

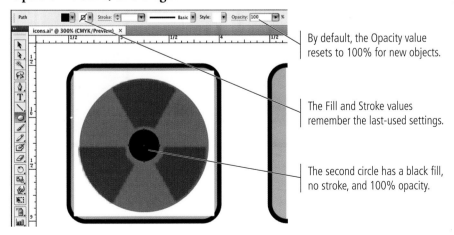

By default, the Opacity value resets to 100% for new objects.

The Fill and Stroke values remember the last-used settings.

The second circle has a black fill, no stroke, and 100% opacity.

6. **With the smaller circle selected, change the fill color to None and the stroke color to white. Change the stroke weight to 5 pt.**

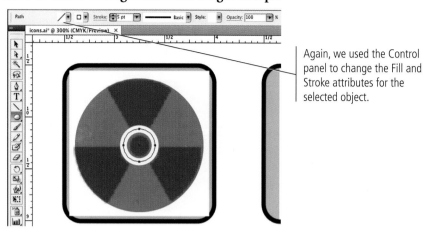

Again, we used the Control panel to change the Fill and Stroke attributes for the selected object.

7. **Press Command/Control to temporarily access the Selection tool. While holding down the mouse button, click away from the existing shapes to deselect them.**

   If you don't deselect the circle, changing the Fill and Stroke attributes in the next step will change the attributes of the selected shape.

8. **Choose the Line tool in the Tools panel, and then click the Default Fill and Stroke button at the bottom of the Tools panel.**

9. **Move the cursor below the circles you created until you see the Smart Guide connecting to the existing shape's center point. Click and drag up to create a vertical line that extends past the top edge of the outer circle.**

   Although none of the icon wedges have a vertical line, it's easier to start at vertical and rotate the objects as necessary.

   To create the vertical line, use the cursor feedback to drag a 90° line, or press Shift to automatically constrain the line to 90°.

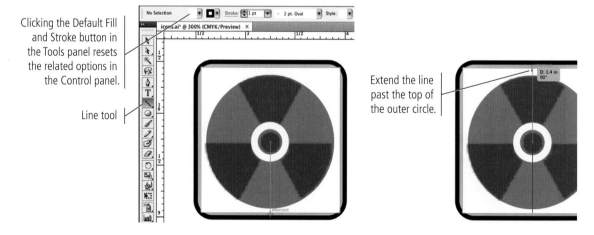

Clicking the Default Fill and Stroke button in the Tools panel resets the related options in the Control panel.

Line tool

Extend the line past the top of the outer circle.

10. Using the Selection tool, draw a marquee around the three objects you've created to select all three objects in the icon art. Use the options in the Control panel to align the selected objects horizontally and vertically.

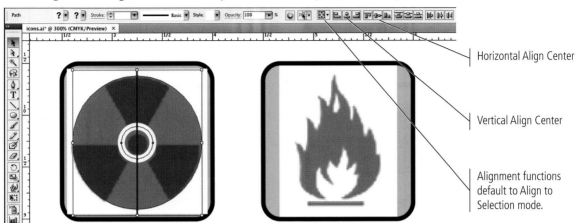

Horizontal Align Center

Vertical Align Center

Alignment functions default to Align to Selection mode.

11. Click away from the selected objects, and then select only the vertical line.

The icon has six wedges, which means each half of the circle needs to be divided into three pieces. To accomplish this, you use precise rotation to slice the larger circle into the necessary parts.

12. With the vertical line selected, choose Object>Transform>Rotate. Type **60** in the Angle field and click Copy.

A full circle has 360 degrees. You're cutting the circle into six equal pieces; one sixth of 360 is 60 — the angle you need to create the right number of pieces.

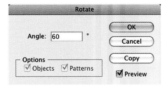

13. Choose Object>Transform>Transform Again to make a third line.

The Transform Again command applies the last-used transformation of any type to a selected object without opening a dialog box. Because you used the Rotate dialog box with the Copy button in the previous step, the Transform Again command copies the current selection and rotates it by the same angle you used in Step 12.

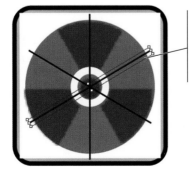

You now have all the pieces you need. The next step is to use these basic elements to create the final icon.

14. **Using the Selection tool, select the smaller circle only and choose Object>Path>Outline Stroke.**

This command changes the object stroke to a filled object. You drew the white circle to "cut out" the smaller black circle from the wedges. The Pathfinder functions recognize strokes for cutting apart shapes, but the stroke weight is not considered when the new paths are generated. To create the thick white space in the actual icon, you need to convert the heavy stroke to a filled shape.

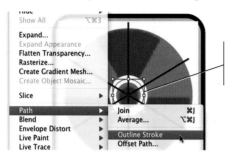

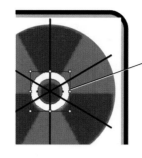

The original object had a 5-pt stroke weight.

The Outline Stroke command changes the selected object to a filled shape with no visible stroke attributes.

15. **Select all the objects in the icon, and then open the Pathfinder panel (Window>Pathfinder).**

You can drag a marquee with the Selection tool, or choose Select>All. Because you locked the snowflake artwork in the first icon, those objects are not selected.

Note:

Press Command/ Control-A to select all unlocked objects on the Artboard.

The Pathfinder Panel in Depth

In the Pathfinder panel, the top row of buttons — the Shape Modes — create complex shapes by combining the originally selected shapes. (You can press Option/Alt and click a Shape Mode to maintain the paths from the original objects.)

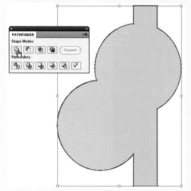

Unite combines all selected objects into a single shape.

Minus Front removes overlapping areas from the backmost shape in the selection.

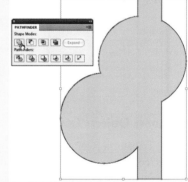

By default, the Shape options result in a single new object.

Intersect creates a shape of only areas where selected objects overlap.

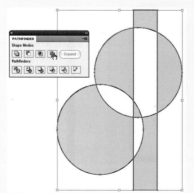

Exclude removes any areas where two objects overlap.

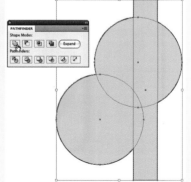

If you Option/Alt-click a shape mode button, the result maintains the original paths unless you manually expand it.

---

16. **In the Pathfinder panel, click the Divide button.**

Options in the Pathfinder panel allow you to cut shapes out of other shapes and merge multiple shapes into a single shape.

It's important to realize that many Pathfinder options can be applied in more than one way. We're using the Divide and Unite options in this exercise to give you an idea of what you can accomplish with Pathfinder.

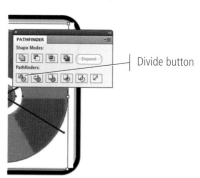

Divide button

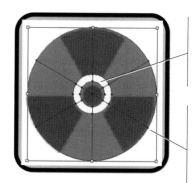

The Divide function slices apart all possible shapes of the selected objects. Everywhere two objects overlap, a new shape is created.

Because the straight lines are open shapes, they divide the circles into sixths, but the open ends of the lines (outside the area of the larger circle) are removed.

17. **Save the file and continue to the next exercise.**

The Pathfinder Panel in Depth (continued)

The second row of options — the Pathfinders — do exactly that. The resulting shapes are some combination of the paths that made up the originally selected objects.

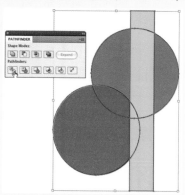

Divide creates separate shapes from all overlapping areas of selected objects.

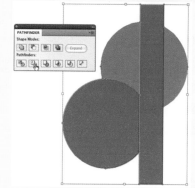

Trim removes underlying areas of overlapping objects. Objects of the same fill color are not combined.

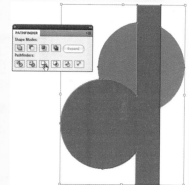

Merge removes underlying areas of overlapping objects. Objects of the same fill color are combined.

Crop returns the areas of underlying objects that are within the boundary of the topmost object.

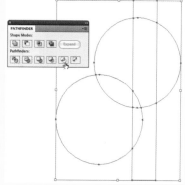

Outline divides the selected objects, then returns unfilled, open paths.

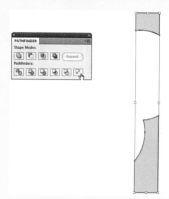

Minus Back removes the area of underlying objects from the front object.

WORK IN ISOLATION MODE

Groups can be invaluable when you need to treat multiple items as a single object. When grouped, you can move and manipulate the entire group as a single object. However, there are many times when you need to make changes to only parts of a group. Depending on the complexity of the file, this can be very difficult without first breaking apart the group ("ungrouping"). Illustrator's Isolation mode offers a convenient workspace, where you can work with grouped objects as if they were stand-alone objects.

1. **With icons.ai open, double-click any of the shapes in the biohazard icon to enter Isolation mode.**

   When you use the Pathfinder panel, the resulting shapes are automatically grouped. Because all these shapes comprise the icon artwork, it's a good idea to leave them grouped. Isolation mode allows you to work with the constituent objects without ungrouping.

2. **Using the Selection tool, click the wedge shape in the top-left area of the icon, and then press Delete.**

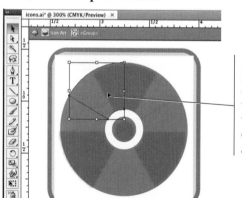

Because you're working in Isolation mode, you can use the Selection tool to select one object, even though the object is part of a group on the main Artboard.

3. **Select and delete every other wedge in the outside area of the group.**

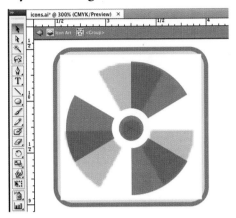

4. **Choose View>Outline.**

Outline mode allows you to see and work with the basic shapes only. This way, object fills don't obscure the shapes you need to clearly see.

5. **Click in the center set of wedges and drag a marquee that encompasses the center points of all six center wedges.**

If you tried to do this in Preview mode, clicking one of the filled shapes and dragging would actually move the shape you clicked. Because the fills are not technically present in Outline mode, you can use the click-drag method to select all six shapes instead of Shift-clicking each one individually.

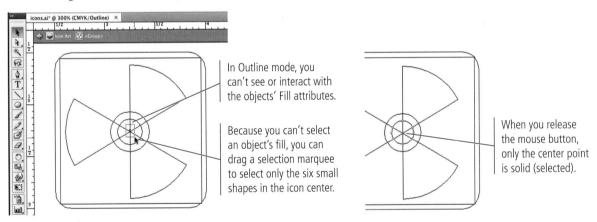

In Outline mode, you can't see or interact with the objects' Fill attributes.

Because you can't select an object's fill, you can drag a selection marquee to select only the six small shapes in the icon center.

When you release the mouse button, only the center point is solid (selected).

6. **In the Pathfinder panel, click the Unite button.**

This function merges the selected shapes into a single object.

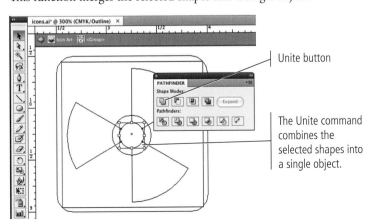

Unite button

The Unite command combines the selected shapes into a single object.

7. **Choose View>Preview to exit Outline mode and display the normal artwork.**

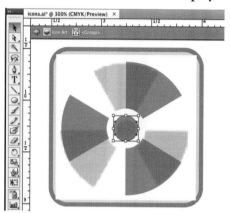

8. **Using the Selection tool, click to select any one of the black (partially transparent) objects.**

9. **In the Control panel, click the Select Similar Objects button and choose Fill Color from the menu.**

   The options in this menu (and in the Select>Same menu) are very useful for finding objects that share specific attributes.

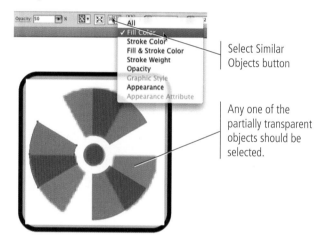

Select Similar Objects button

Any one of the partially transparent objects should be selected.

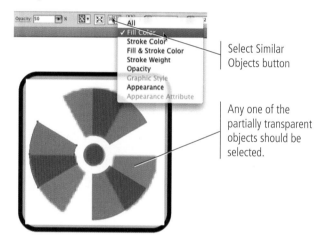

Note:

The Select Similar functions can also be accessed in the Select>Same menu.

10. **Change the Opacity value (in the Control panel) to 100 for the selected objects.**

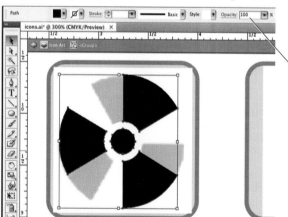

Because you no longer need to see the underlying template image, you can restore your artwork to 100% opacity.

11. **At the top of the document window, click the arrow button twice to return to the main Artboard.**

As you can see, your icon is almost complete; but you still need to rotate the shape to match the template image.

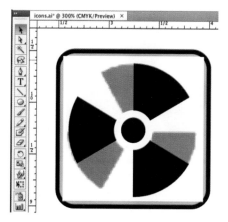

12. **Save the file and continue to the next exercise.**

USE MEASUREMENTS TO ADJUST YOUR ARTWORK

Depending on the type of work you do, Illustrator drawings can be entirely freeform, precisely measured, or a combination of the two (as in this case). You've already used a number of tools that help you create exactly what you need where you need it — Smart Guides, document rulers, the Transform panel, and even the Control panel all offer ways to precisely move and size objects on the Artboard.

You can also use the Measure tool, which evaluates different dimensional attributes of objects on the page. As you might expect from the name, the Measure tool acts like a digital tape measure. In addition to sizes and positions, the tool also measure angles — an important feature for technical drawing that requires precise detail.

1. **With icons.ai open, choose the Measure tool in the Tools panel (nested under the Eyedropper tool).**

2. **Click at the outside corner of the left wedge, and then drag down and right along the shape edge (as shown in the following image).**

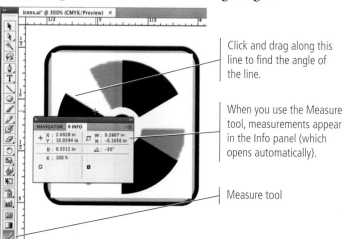

Click and drag along this line to find the angle of the line.

When you use the Measure tool, measurements appear in the Info panel (which opens automatically).

Measure tool

Note:

If you drag from the inside out, the Info panel shows an angle of 150°. This provides the same information, because 180° — your goal — minus 150° equals 30°.

The Measure tool tells you that the angle of this line is –30°. You need it to be 180° (horizontal), which means you need to rotate the shape by 30°.

3. **Select the group with the Selection tool, and then choose Object>Transform>Rotate.**

4. **Change the Angle field to 30 and click OK.**

5. **In the Layers panel, select and delete the Template radiation.tif layer.**

   After you remove the template image, you can see the remaining problem — the Divide Pathfinder function left a white ring in the shape. You need to remove these white objects.

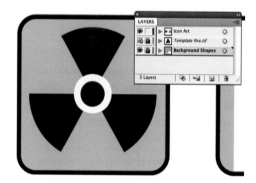

6. **Using the Direct Selection tool, click the fill of one of the white shapes to select it.**

   Remember, all of the constituent shapes are part of a group — the result of the Pathfinder Divide function — so you can't use the Selection tool. The irregular position of these small shapes also makes it difficult to individually select the six objects with the Direct Selection tool. Fortunately, Illustrator has a solution for this problem.

7. **In the Control panel, click the Select Similar Objects button and choose Fill Color from the menu.**

Note:

Be careful when you use the Select Similar functions. They select all similar objects on the entire Artboard. If the art for another icon had a white fill, for example, it would also be selected.

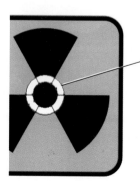

All six white-filled objects are selected because the original selection had a white fill.

8. **With all six white shapes in the icon selected, press Delete.**

9. **Select all objects in the radiation icon art and choose Object>Lock>Selection.**

   This step protects the completed icon artwork from being inadvertently changed while you work on the rest of this project.

10. **Save the file and continue to the next exercise.**

 ## DRAW WITH THE PENCIL TOOL

At this point, you have used a number of basic shapes to create finished icon artwork. As you might already realize, however, not all artwork can be created from basic shapes and lines. Illustrator includes everything you need to create artwork in any form, whether from a basic square or irregular shapes without a single visible straight edge. The Pencil tool is one method for creating custom shapes. Like a regular pencil on a piece of paper, the Pencil tool creates lines that follow the path of your cursor. (If you have a digital drawing tablet, the Pencil tool can be particularly useful for drawing custom artwork.)

Note:

In Project 2, you learn how to use the Pen tool to control every point and path of your Illustrator drawings.

1. **With icons.ai open, make sure the Icon Art layer is selected in the Layers panel. Zoom in to the third rectangle in the first row of background shapes.**

2. **Choose the Pencil tool and click the Default Fill and Stroke button in the Tools panel.**

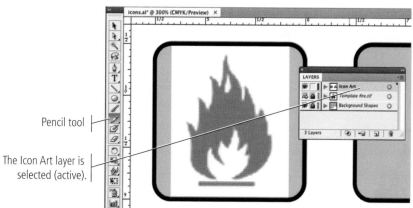

Pencil tool

The Icon Art layer is selected (active).

3. **Double-click the Pencil tool in the Tools panel.**

Double-clicking certain tools in the Tools panel opens an Options dialog box, where you can control the default behavior for the selected tool. The Pencil tool options include:

- **Fidelity.** This option determines how far apart anchor points are added as you drag. Higher values result in fewer points and smoother lines; lower values result in more anchor points, which can make the lines appear choppy.

- **Smoothness.** This option determines how closely a path follows the path of your cursor. Lower values result in more anchor points, especially if your cursor movement is choppy.

- **Fill New Pencil Strokes.** By default, pencil paths are not filled regardless of the fill color defined in the Tools panel.

- **Keep Selected.** If this option is checked, the line you draw is automatically selected when you release the mouse button.

- **Edit Selected Paths.** If this option is checked, drawing near a selected path can change the existing path. This is an important distinction (especially when Keep Selected is checked) because you can accidentally edit the first path instead of creating a second shape.

4. **Set the Fidelity value to 2.5 pixels and Smoothness to 0%.**

To draw this icon, you must make many fine movements and change direction often. Even though this icon artwork doesn't have to be exact to communicate the necessary message ("fire"), you should try to match the template as closely as possible.

5. **Make sure the Fill New Pencil Strokes and Edit Selected Paths options are unchecked, and then click OK.**

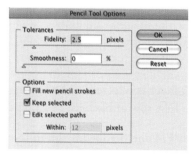

6. **Click at the bottom-left point of the fire icon, hold down the mouse button, and begin dragging around the shape of the fire. When you get near your original starting point, press Option/Alt and release the mouse button.**

As you drag, a colored line indicates the path you're drawing. Don't worry if the path isn't perfect; when you release the mouse button, Illustrator automatically smoothes the path.

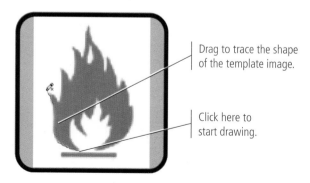

Drag to trace the shape of the template image.

Click here to start drawing.

The Pencil tool creates open-ended lines. To create a closed shape with your path, press Option/Alt before releasing the mouse button at your original starting point.

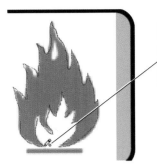

The hollow circle in the cursor icon indicates that releasing the mouse button will create a closed shape.

When you release the mouse button, the shape shows the defined stroke color but not the fill color.

7. **Click near the top point of the white flame area (inside the first path) and drag to create the white inner shape in the fire icon. Press Option/Alt before releasing the mouse button so you end up with a closed shape.**

Use the Pencil tool to draw this shape. Press Option/Alt before releasing the mouse button to create a closed shape.

8. **Using the Rectangle tool, draw the shape below the fire in the template image.**

9. **In the Layers panel, delete the Template fire.tif layer.**

10. **Use the Selection tool to select all three shapes of the icon art. Change the fill color to black and the stroke color to None.**

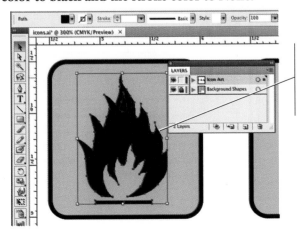

When all three objects are filled, you can't see the inner shape at the top of the flame.

11. **Choose Object>Compound Path>Make.**

This option combines all three selected shapes into a single shape; the area of the smaller shape is removed from the larger shape behind it.

As a compound path, the inner shape is removed from the outer shape.

Note:

*A **compound path** is a single shape made up of more than one path. Compound paths usually have inner "empty" areas, such as the letter O or Q.*

12. **Save the file and close it.**

Using Live Trace to Create Artwork from Images

ILLUSTRATOR FOUNDATIONS

In many cases, the basic drawing tools are often not enough to efficiently create the artwork you need. When you need to create artwork from a placed image — as in the case of the low-resolution icon bitmaps that you're using in this project — you can also use the Live Trace function to create vector graphics from placed bitmap images. When an image is selected, choose Object>Live Trace>Tracing Options to open the Tracing Options dialog box. (A number of defined presets are also available in the Live Trace menu.

When you use the Live Trace function, the result is a special type of object, which you can edit by changing the settings in the Live Trace dialog box. To access the individual paths and anchor points of the traced shape, you have to first expand the Live Trace object by choosing Object>Expand.

(Our goal in this project is to teach you the basics of drawing in Illustrator, so we don't include a complete exercise on the Live Trace feature here. You'll use it in Project 8 to create a full-color graphic from a placed photograph. However, feel free to experiment and test the results of different options. A number of additional icon bitmap files are available in the RF_Illustrator>Symbols folder.)

Original placed image

Result using the built-in Black and White Logo preset

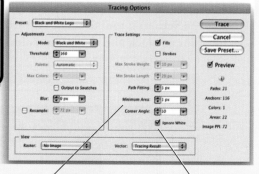

With Preview active, we adjusted the various settings to fine-tune the result.

Checking Ignore White removes the white areas of the placed image.

fill in the blank

1. _____ are composed of mathematical descriptions of a series of lines and points; they are resolution independent, can be freely scaled, and are automatically output at the resolution of the output device.

2. _____ are pixel-based, made up of a grid of individual pixels (rasters or bits) in rows and columns.

3. The _____ is a rectangle that marks the outermost edges of an object, regardless of the actual object shape.

4. _____ is the relative top-to-botom order of objects on the Artboard, or of layers in the Layer panel.

5. The _____ is used to select entire objects or groups.

6. The _____ is used to select indiivdual paths and points of a shape, or to select component pieces within a group.

7. The _____ is used to draw freeform paths defined by dragging the mouse cursor.

8. Press _____ to temporarily access the Selection tool; releasing the modifier key restores the previously selected tool.

9. The _____ is used to create complex shapes by combining multiple selected objects.

10. A(n) _____ is a single object that is made up of more than one shape.

short answer

1. Briefly explain the difference between vector graphics and raster images.

2. Briefly explain the difference between the Selection tool and the Direct Selection tool.

3. Briefly explain the difference between Shape Mode and Pathfinder operations in the Pathfinder panel.

Portfolio Builder Project

Use what you learned in this project to complete the following freeform exercise.
Carefully read the art director and client comments, then create your own design to meet the needs of the project.
Use the space below to sketch ideas; when finished, write a brief explanation of your reasoning behind your final design.

art director comments

The client is pleased with the first three icons, and they want you to complete the rest of the warning icons. They also want you to create an additional set of icons for travel and outdoor activities that they offer as benefits during their international corporate conferences.

To complete this project, you should:

❏ Complete the remaining international warning icons. The bitmap versions are in your RF_Illustrator>Symbols folder.

❏ Carefully consider the best approach for each icon and use whichever tool (or tools) you feel is most appropriate.

❏ Create a second Illustrator file for the six new recreation icons.

client comments

We host a number of large, international conventions and conferences every year, and many attendees bring their families along for a working vacation. To keep everyone happy, we've started offering different outdoor activities for the families while their spouses are atending sessions, but the international nature means that a lot of people need visual help getting to the right place.

Since you did such a good job on the first three icons, we'd like you to finish those. But first, we want you to create icons for horseback riding, sailing, swimming, hiking, rock climbing, and nature walks.

We don't have the images for these ones. Can you find something on the Internet to use as a guide? Remember, icons need to be easily recognizable in any language, so they should very clearly convey visually what each one is for.

project justification

Project Summary

In this project, you learned many skills that will serve as the foundation for most work you create in Illustrator. You learned how to place raster images as templates, from which you created scalable vector graphics that will work in virtually any printed application. You learned a number of techniques for selecting objects and component pieces of objects, as well as various options for aligning objects relative to one another and to the Artboard.

You learned how to draw primitive geometric shapes, and how to control the color of objects' fill and stroke attributes. You used a number of transformation options, including cloning methods to copy existing objects. Finally, you learned how to draw freeform shapes to suit more complex needs. As you move forward in this book, you'll build on the basic skills you learned in this project to create increasingly complex artwork.

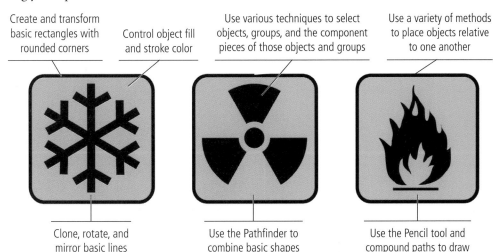

Create and transform basic rectangles with rounded corners

Control object fill and stroke color

Use various techniques to select objects, groups, and the component pieces of those objects and groups

Use a variety of methods to place objects relative to one another

Clone, rotate, and mirror basic lines

Use the Pathfinder to combine basic shapes into complex artwork

Use the Pencil tool and compound paths to draw complex shapes

Balloon Festival Artwork

Your client is the marketing director for the Temecula Hot Air Balloon Festival, which attracts thousands of tourists to the desert community throughout the three-day event. You have been hired to create the primary artwork for this year's event, which will be used in a variety of different products (ads, souvenirs, etc.).

This project incorporates the following skills:

❏ Drawing complex custom shapes with the Pen tool

❏ Drawing irregular shape outlines by painting with the Blob Brush tool

❏ Editing anchor points and handles to control the precise position of vector paths

❏ Creating a custom color scheme using saved swatches

❏ Adjusting color, both globally and in specific selections

❏ Adding interest and depth with color gradients

❏ Saving multiple file versions for various print applications

client comments

Although the festival is popular, it's an aging crowd; we hope to bring in more families so we can get more younger people interested in ballooning as a hobby. This year is the 25th anniversary of the festival, and we've added a range of entertainment and educational options for younger children.

We want this year's artwork to be very bright and colorful; we also want a "cartoon-y" look that might appeal to young kids. It will be used on everything from festival programs to glassware — we're even planning on a teddy bear who is wearing a t-shirt with the artwork silk-screened on the back.

art director comments

I sketched a mock-up of a hot air balloon that you can use as the basis for the artwork. You should use the Pen tool to draw the balloon because simple shapes won't work and the Pencil tool doesn't provide fine enough control to efficiently achieve what you need.

Temecula is on the edge of the desert in southern California, so I'm going to have your partner create a desert panorama scene to put behind the balloons.

Rather than just one balloon floating over the desert, the finished piece should actually create the effect of a whole fleet of balloons. You can just clone the first balloon a couple of times, but make sure you change the color scheme in each one so they are all a bit different.

This is going to be a complex piece of artwork, so I recommend using layers to organize the various pieces. That will make it far easier to edit specific components as necessary if the client decides to make changes.

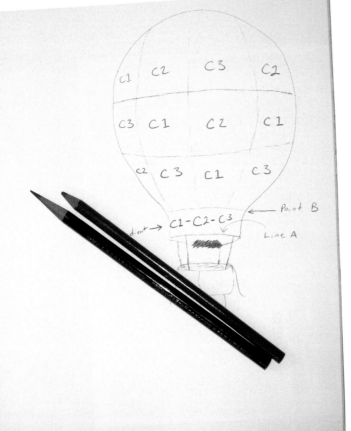

project objectives

To complete this project, you will:

❑ Use the Pen tool to draw precise curves

❑ Use the Blob Brush tool to "paint" the area of vector shapes

❑ Adjust anchor points and handles to precisely control the shape of vector objects

❑ Define custom color swatches to allow easy universal changes

❑ Create color gradients to blend multiple colors in a single object

❑ Adjust gradients in context on the Artboard

❑ Change colors in specific selected objects

❑ Save multiple file versions for use in various design applications

Stage 1 **Drawing Complex Artwork**

In Project 1, you used a number of techniques to create finished artwork from basic shapes. Of course, much of the artwork you create will require far more complexity than simple lines and geometric shapes. When you need to produce custom artwork — whether from scratch or by tracing a hand-drawn sketch or photo — Illustrator includes a powerful set of tools to create and manipulate every point and path in the illustration. In the first stage of this project, you begin exploring the Pen tool, as well as other options for building and controlling custom shapes.

PREPARE THE DRAWING WORKSPACE

As with any project, setting up the workspace is an important first step. This project requires a single Artboard to contain the entire illustration.

1. **Copy the Festival folder from the WIP folder on your Resource CD to the WIP folder where you are saving your work.**

   Save all files for this project in your WIP>Festival folder.

2. **Choose File>New.**

3. **Type balloons in the Name field, choose Letter in the Size menu, and choose Inches in the Units menu.**

4. **If the Advanced options are not visible, click the down-arrow button to show those options. Choose CMYK in the Color Mode menu and choose High (300 PPI) in the Raster Effects menu.**

   This illustration will be printed in various documents, so you should design the job in the CMYK color mode. Some Illustrator functions, such as effects and gradient meshes, will be rasterized for commercial output; the High (300 PPI) raster effects setting results in sufficient resolution for those elements.

Note:

If you use the Welcome Screen instead of the menu command to make the new file, click the Create New Print Document link.

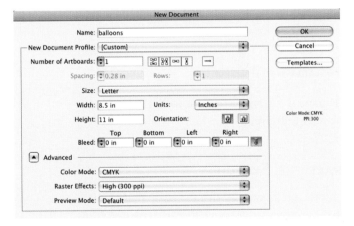

5. **Click OK to create the file.**

6. **Choose File>Place. Navigate to the file `sketch.jpg` in the RF_Illustrator>Festival folder. Make sure the Link option is not checked and the Template option is checked, and then click Place.**

You will use this client-supplied sketch to create the primary artwork for this illustration.

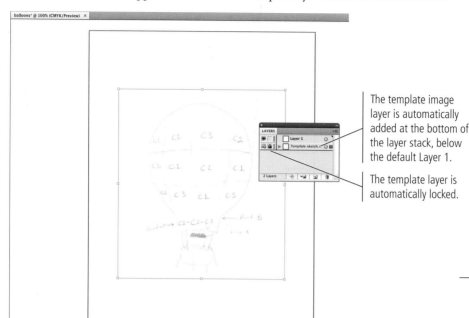

The template image layer is automatically added at the bottom of the layer stack, below the default Layer 1.

The template layer is automatically locked.

7. **Double-click Layer 1 to open the Layer Options dialog box. Rename the layer `Balloon 1` and click OK.**

8. **Click away from the placed sketch image to deselect it.**

9. **Save the file as an Illustrator file named `balloons.ai` in your WIP>Festival folder, and then continue to the next exercise.**

 ## USE THE PEN TOOL TO TRACE THE SKETCH

As you discovered in Project 1, many objects can be drawn with the basic shape tools. The true power of Illustrator, however, comes from being able to draw just as you would on a piece of paper — including freeform objects that have no basis in geometric shapes. You used the Pencil tool in Project 1 to begin working with custom artwork. In this project, you use the Pen tool, which provides far more power to control the precise position of every line in a drawing. In fact, many believe the Pen tool is the most powerful and important tool in the Illustrator Tools panel.

When you draw with the Pen tool, an anchor point marks the end of a line segment, and the point handles determine the shape of that segment. That's the basic definition of a geometric vector. Fortunately, you don't need to be a mathematician to master the Pen tool because Illustrator handles the underlying geometry for you.

Note:

The default color of a new layer is based on the order in the Color list of the Layer Options dialog box. The first layer in a file is Light Blue, the second layer is Red, the third layer is Green, and so on.

Each segment in a path has two anchoring end points and two associated handles. In the following image, we first clicked to create Point A and dragged to the right (without releasing the mouse button) to create Handle A1. We then clicked and dragged to create Point B and Handle B1; Handle B2 was automatically created as a reflection of B1 (Point B is a smooth symmetrical point).

Note:

The lines you create by connecting anchor points and pulling handles are called **Bézier curves**.

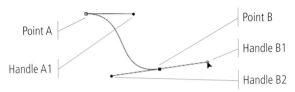

The following image shows the result of dragging Handle B1 to the left instead of to the right. Notice the difference in the curve, as compared to the curve above. When you drag the handle, the segment arcs away from the direction of the handle.

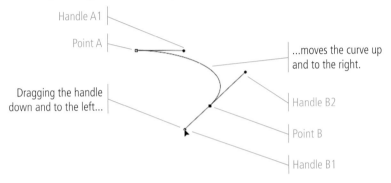

It's important to understand that a segment is connected to two handles. In this image, dragging the handle to the right pulls out the arc of the connected segment. You could change the shape of Segment A by dragging either Handle A1 or A2.

The final concept you should understand about anchors and handles (for now, at least) is that clicking and dragging to create a point creates a smooth symmetrical point. Dragging one handle of a smooth point also changes the other handle of that point. In the image shown below, dragging Handle B also moves Handle A, which affects the shape of Segment A.

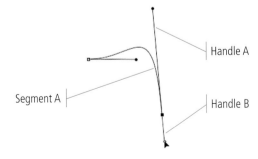

You can create corner points by simply clicking with the Pen tool instead of clicking and dragging. Corner points do not have their own handles; the connected segments are controlled by the handles of the other associated points.

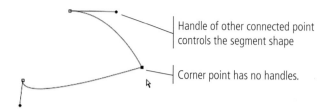

Handle of other connected point controls the segment shape

Corner point has no handles.

You can convert a symmetrical point into a corner point by clicking the point with the Convert Anchor Point tool (nested under the Pen tool). You can also add a handle to only one side of an anchor point by Option/Alt-clicking a point with the Pen tool and dragging.

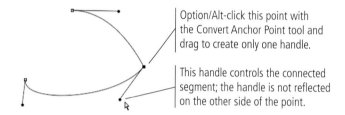

Option/Alt-click this point with the Convert Anchor Point tool and drag to create only one handle.

This handle controls the connected segment; the handle is not reflected on the other side of the point.

1. **With balloons.ai open, choose the Pen tool in the Tools panel.**

2. **Using the Control panel, set the stroke to 1-pt black and the fill to None.**

3. **Click with the Pen tool to place the first anchor point on the left side of the balloon where the round part meets the flat base.**

   We typically find it easier to start drawing at a corner (if one exists).

Note:

As you draw, zoom in as necessary to easily view the various parts of the sketch.

You should have a fill of None and a 1-pt black stroke.

Pen tool

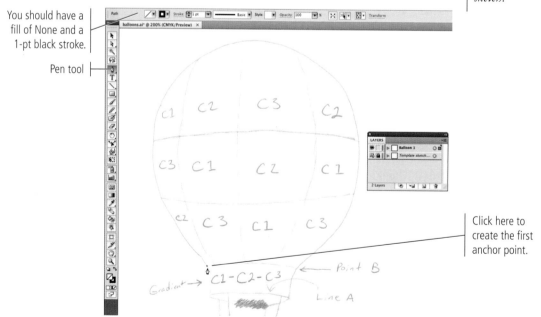

Click here to create the first anchor point.

4. **Click the right side of the balloon (at Point B in the sketch) and immediately drag right and slightly down to create handles for the second point. When the segment between the two points matches the line in the sketch, release the mouse button.**

   When you click and drag without releasing the mouse button, you create handles, which determine the shape of the segment that connects the two points.

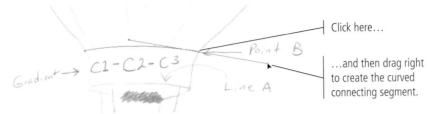

Click here…

…and then drag right to create the curved connecting segment.

5. **Click again on the second anchor point and release the mouse button without dragging.**

   Clicking a smooth point as you draw converts it to a corner point, removing the outside handle from the point; the inside handle that defines the shape of the connecting segment remains in place. This allows you to change direction as you draw.

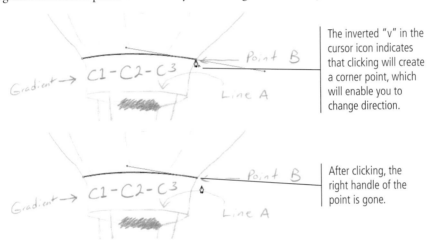

The inverted "v" in the cursor icon indicates that clicking will create a corner point, which will enable you to change direction.

After clicking, the right handle of the point is gone.

Note:

If you're editing an existing path, you can click a point with the Convert Anchor Point tool (nested under the Pen tool) to change a smooth point to a corner point. You can also click and drag to change an existing corner point to a smooth point.

6. **Option/Alt-click the second anchor point and pull slightly up and right to generate a new handle for the right side of the anchor point.**

   Pulling the new handle determines the direction of the next segment you create. The curve will bend in the direction of the new handle.

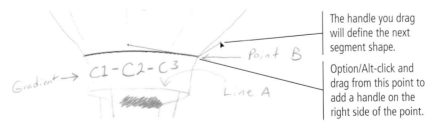

The handle you drag will define the next segment shape.

Option/Alt-click and drag from this point to add a handle on the right side of the point.

7. **Click and drag to create a new point (with handles) on the outside edge of the balloon where the C3 section meets the C1 section.**

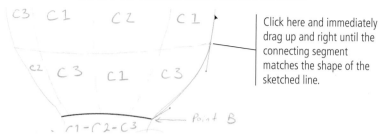

Click here and immediately drag up and right until the connecting segment matches the shape of the sketched line.

8. **Continue adding points and handles to outline the entire outside edge of the balloon.**

9. **Click the original point without dragging to close the shape.**

   When you return to the original point, the cursor shows a small hollow circle. This indicates that clicking the existing point will close the shape.

Note:

As a general rule, use as few points as necessary to create a shape with the Pen tool.

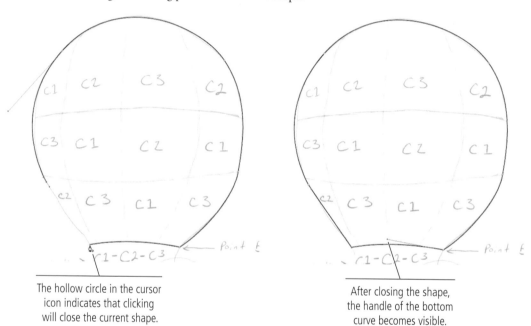

The hollow circle in the cursor icon indicates that clicking will close the current shape.

After closing the shape, the handle of the bottom curve becomes visible.

10. **Using the Direct Selection tool, click a point along the left side of the shape.**

    You can use the Direct Selection tool to edit a specific anchor point or segment.

    Depending on your precision when you dragged the handles, some curves might not match the sketch. When tracing a hand-drawn sketch, however, your shape doesn't need to be exact, but it should be close.

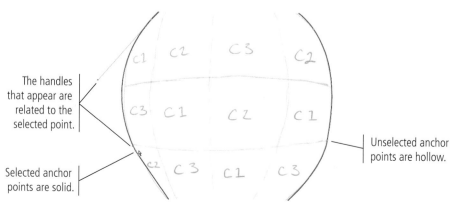

The handles that appear are related to the selected point.

Selected anchor points are solid.

Unselected anchor points are hollow.

11. Use the Direct Selection tool to make any adjustments you feel necessary. You can move specific anchor points by dragging them to a new position, and/or drag handles to adjust curve segments that connect two anchor points.

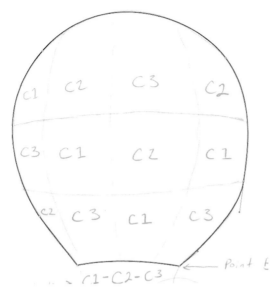

12. Save the file and continue to the next exercise.

SELECT AND EDIT COMPLEX PATHS

In Illustrator, you can manipulate and change your drawings until they precisely match your vision for the artwork. You can use numerous options to select and modify shapes — or parts of shapes — so you can create exactly what you need, regardless of what is already on the Artboard.

1. With **balloons.ai** open, choose the Direct Selection tool.

2. With nothing selected, click the horizontal segment that represents the bottom of the balloon shape.

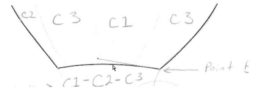

3. Choose Edit>Copy to copy the selected segment.

4. Choose Object>Hide>Selection.

The Hide command affects only the selected object(s). The object is still on the Artboard but not visible, and the layer is still visible.

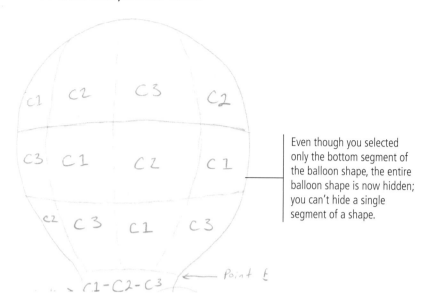

Even though you selected only the bottom segment of the balloon shape, the entire balloon shape is now hidden; you can't hide a single segment of a shape.

5. Choose Edit>Paste in Front.

The segment you copied is pasted in exactly the same place as the original. Because you selected the segment with the Direct Selection tool, only that segment (not the entire object) was copied and pasted.

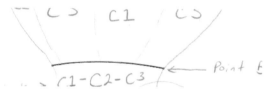

6. Choose the Pen tool in the Tools panel and move the cursor over the right open endpoint.

The diagonal line in the cursor indicates that clicking will connect to the existing opening endpoint.

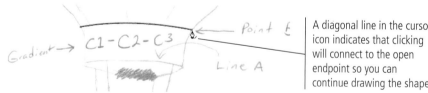

A diagonal line in the cursor icon indicates that clicking will connect to the open endpoint so you can continue drawing the shape.

Note:

If you turn on Smart Guides (View>Smart Guides), the cursor shows the word "anchor" when the cursor is over an existing anchor point. This can be helpful if you are trying to connect to an open endpoint of an existing line (as in Step 6).

7. Click to resume working from the open endpoint.

8. Click and drag to create the bottom-right point of the balloon shape. Drag the handle down and right until the connecting curve matches the shape of the line in the sketch.

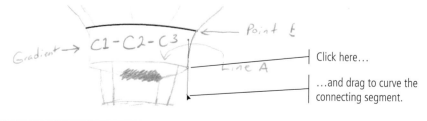

Click here...

...and drag to curve the connecting segment.

9. **Click the point from Step 8 to remove the handle from the outside of the point, and then click and drag again to create the bottom-left point.**

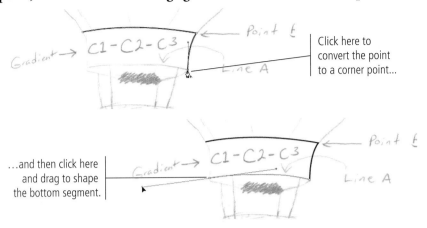

10. **Move the cursor over the open left endpoint of the top segment and click to close the shape.**

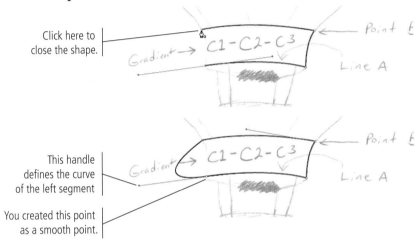

11. **Choose the Direct Selection tool in the Tools panel. Press Option/Alt, and then click and drag the outside handle of the bottom-left point. Drag the handle right until the left segment matches the shape of the line in the sketch.**

Remember, the Direct Selection tool allows you to adjust individual anchor points and handles. Option/Alt-dragging one handle of a smooth point converts the point to a corner point, but leaves both handles in place. This method allows you to change the direction of an existing point, but leave the opposite curve intact.

12. **Save the file and continue to the next exercise.**

CONTROL OBJECT VISIBILITY AND LOCKING

When multiple objects exist on the same layer, it can be difficult to work on certain objects without affecting others. As you saw in the previous exercise, Illustrator includes options to show and hide specific objects without changing layer visibility. You can also lock and unlock specific objects on a layer without unlocking an entire layer; this protects other objects on the layer from unintentional changes.

1. **With balloons.ai open, choose Object>Show All.**

   Although the Hide command affects only selected objects, the Show All command is not selective; all hidden objects become visible.

2. **Using either the Selection or Direct Selection tool, select only the bottom shape and choose Object>Lock>Selection.**

   Because the lower shape is now locked, you can't select it.

   You can't lock only part of an object, so the entire object is locked even if you only select one of the segments or anchor points using the Direct Selection tool.

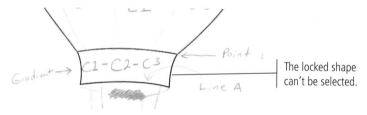

The locked shape can't be selected.

3. **Using the sketch as a guide, use the Pen tool to create the leftmost vertical line in the balloon, starting and stopping past the edges of the balloon shape (as shown in the following image).**

   You are going to use the Pathfinder to divide the balloon into the necessary shapes. For this process to work properly, the dividing lines need to be at least on top of the outside shape; to be sure, you need to extend the lines farther than they need to be.

The endpoints of the segment should extend beyond the edge of the outline shape.

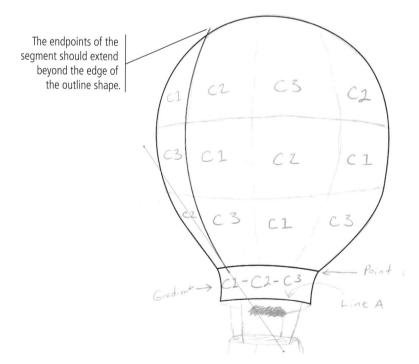

Note:

If necessary, use the Direct Selection tool to adjust the anchor points and handles of the line until they match the sketch.

4. **While the Pen tool is still active, press Command/Control to temporarily access the Selection tool and click away from the line to deselect it.**

When you release the mouse button, you return to the Pen tool. This technique allows you to easily deselect the current path and then continue to draw the next, unconnected path.

5. **Repeat Steps 3–4 to create the remaining vertical and horizontal lines of the balloon.**

If you don't deselect the path from Step 3 before clicking to draw the next line, the third click would create a segment that is connected to the last place you clicked (on the first line). In the context of this exercise, a single line with multiple anchor points is much more difficult to control than two separate lines with open endpoints.

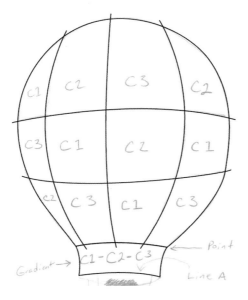

6. **Choose the Selection tool in the Tools panel, and then choose Select>All.**

Because the bottom shape is locked, it is not included in the selection.

7. **In the Pathfinder panel (Window>Pathfinder), click the Divide button.**

The result is a group of twelve shapes; ends of the lines that extended beyond the outer shape are removed.

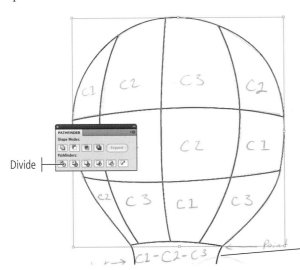

Divide

Select All does not include the bottom shape because it is locked.

8. **Deselect all objects by clicking away from the current selection.**

Note:

Press Command/Control-A to select everything in the drawing space that is not locked.

Note:

Remember, all panels can be accessed in the Window menu.

Note:

If you don't see the bounding box for the entire resulting group, you can choose View>Show Bounding Box to toggle it on. If the option is already toggled on, make sure the Selection tool is active (the bounding box won't be visible if the Pen tool is still selected).

9. **Choose the Direct Selection tool, then click the top-left segment of the balloon's outer edge (labeled C1 in the sketch).**

   Remember, clicking a segment with the Direct Selection tool reveals the handles that define the shape of the segment.

10. **If your segment includes an extra anchor point, place the Delete Anchor Point tool cursor over the point and click to delete it.**

    Your original points might have been in different places, depending on where you clicked to create the initial outline shape. When the Pathfinder divides the objects into multiple shapes, the original points are maintained, but unnecessary.

Delete unnecessary points from the outside of your balloon shape.

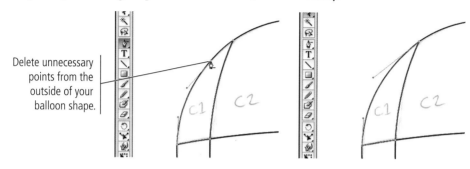

11. **Using the Direct Selection tool, click the top handle of the selected segment and drag up and left.**

    By adjusting the segment, you can create the "pillow" appearance of the panels of a hot air balloon. The point where the two shapes meet is unaffected by dragging the point handle.

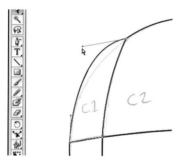

12. **Choose Object>Lock>Selection.**

    Even though only part of the object was selected, you can't lock only part of an object. The entire object becomes locked.

13. **Repeat Steps 9–12 to adjust the top edges of the top three shapes to create a similar "pillow" effect.**

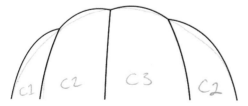

14. **Choose Object>Unlock All.**

    As with the Show All command, the Unlock All command affects all individually locked objects, regardless of when the Lock command was applied.

15. **Save the file and continue to the next exercise.**

ILLUSTRATOR FOUNDATIONS

Keep the following points in mind as you work with the Pen tool (and its four nested variations) and Bézier curves.

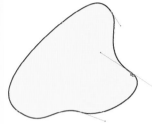

Click a specific anchor point to select it and show all handles that relate to that point.

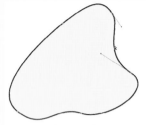

Click a specific segment to select it and show all handles that relate to that segment.

Place the Pen tool cursor over an existing point to temporarily access the Delete Anchor Point tool.

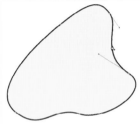

Place the Pen tool cursor over an existing segment to temporarily access the Add Anchor Point tool.

Press Option/Alt and place the Pen tool cursor over an existing point to temporarily access the Convert Anchor Point tool.

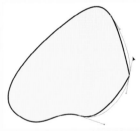

Click a corner point with the Convert Anchor Point tool, then drag to convert the point to a smooth point.

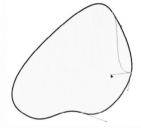

Option/Alt drag a handle of a smooth point to convert it to a corner point.

Drawing with the Pencil tool is similar to sketching with a pencil and paper. The Pencil tool is a good choice if you want to create an object that appears sketchy or hand-drawn. Illustrator adds anchor points and handles as necessary to create the path you draw; you don't have control over where the anchor points are placed, but you can edit the path however you prefer.

1. **With balloons.ai open, select the Pencil tool in the Tools panel. Set the fill to None and the stroke to 1-pt black.**

2. **Double-click the Pencil tool in the Tools panel to open the Pencil Tool Options dialog box.**

3. **Set the Fidelity value to 2 pixels and Smoothness to 1%. Make sure Keep Selected is checked and Edit Selected Paths is not checked, and then click OK.**

   Low Fidelity and Smoothness settings result in fewer anchor points, which makes it easier to edit later (especially when working with small shapes).

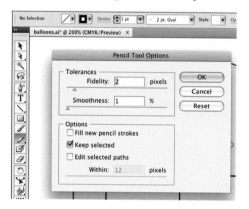

4. **Starting at the top-right corner, carefully trace the outline of the basket. As you approach the starting point, press Option/Alt and release the mouse button to close the basket shape.**

   As you drag the Pencil tool, a dotted line shows the path you traced (and thus, the shape you created). Don't worry if the shape isn't perfect; you clean up the path in the next step.

Pencil tool ⊢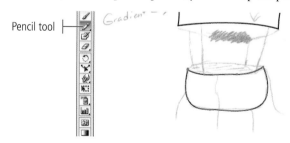

5. **Use the Direct Selection tool to adjust the anchor points and handles of the shape until you are satisfied with the result.**

6. **Deselect the basket shape, activate the Pencil tool, and change the stroke weight to 2 pt.**

7. **Trace the rope lines hanging from the basket. Start the lines on the top edge of the basket shape path.**

Note:

Remember: Simply click away from the object with the Selection or Direct Selection tool to deselect it.

You can also press Command/Control-Shift-A to deselect the current selection.

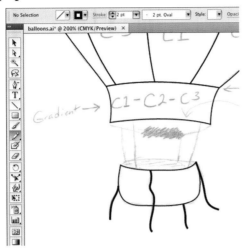

8. **Use the Line tool to draw the lines that will connect the basket shapes to the balloon shapes.**

   You could also use the Pen tool to draw these lines. However, using the Line tool, you don't need to deselect after each line.

9. **Change the Line tool stroke weight to 1 pt, and then draw crossing diagonal lines to represent a "basket weave" texture (using the following image as a guide).**

10. **Save the file and continue to the next exercise.**

CREATE SHAPES WITH THE BLOB BRUSH TOOL

The Blob Brush tool is used to paint filled shapes, which you can manipulate just as you would any other shape comprised of anchor points and handles. In this exercise, you use the Blob Brush tool to quickly create the shape for the inside areas of the balloon and basket. You work with this tool again later to add visual interest and depth to the finished illustration.

1. **With balloons.ai open, use the Selection tool to select everything on the Artboard, and the lock the selection (Object>Lock>Selection).**

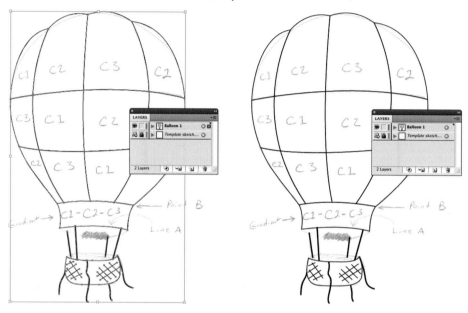

2. **Double-click the Blob Brush tool in the Tools panel to open the Blob Brush Tool Options dialog box.**

3. **Make sure the Keep Selected option is checked. Set the Fidelity value to 4 pixels and Smoothness value to 9%. In the Default Brush Options area, define a 10-pt brush size with a 0° angle and 100% Roundness. Click OK to apply the settings.**

   Like the Pencil tool, the Blob Brush tool Tolerance options determine the accuracy of the resulting shape. Higher Fidelity and Smoothness values result in finer precision, but also more anchor points on the shape. The lower half of the dialog box defines the size, angle, and roundness of the brush cursor.

Blob Brush tool

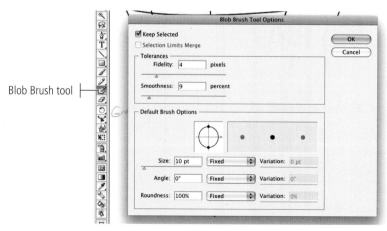

4. **Set the fill color to Black and the stroke to None.**

5. **Click at the left side of the balloon base and drag an arc that flows down and to the right, as shown in the following illustrations. Without releasing the mouse button, drag back to the left, slightly above the existing shape. Continue dragging until the entire area of the shape is painted, and then release the mouse button**

As you paint, the path might look a bit sketchy. When you release the mouse button, however, the path smoothes out based on the Smoothness option defined in the Blob Brush Tool Options dialog box.

When you draw with the Blob Brush tool, the cursor shows the size and shape of the defined brush.

When you release the mouse button, the result is a single shape that fills the entire area where you drew. Overlapping areas of the shape you paint combine to make one shape.

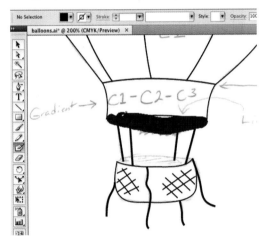

Note:

If you see odd anchors and handles in the middle of the shape, you missed painting some areas; use the Blob Brush tool to paint over those areas.

After you release the mouse button, anchor points appear along the outside edge of the shape. Your shape doesn't need to be perfect because you'll adjust it in the next exercise.

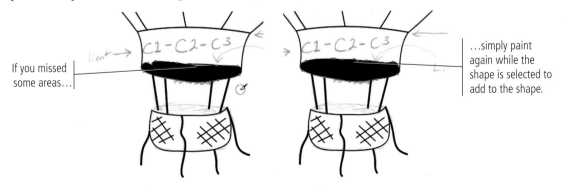

If you missed some areas…

…simply paint again while the shape is selected to add to the shape.

6. **Repeat this process to create a shape that represents the inside of the balloon basket, as shown below.**

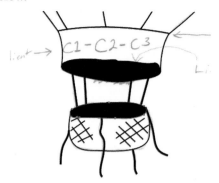

Note:

Press the right bracket key ( ]) to increase the brush size by 1 point. Press the left bracket key ([ ) to reduce the brush size by 1 point.

7. **Save the file and continue to the next exercise.**

 ## ADJUST ANCHOR POINTS AND HANDLES

As we said at the beginning of this project, practice is the best way to master Bézier curves. In this exercise, you use the techniques you already learned to adjust and fine-tune the filled shapes from the previous exercise.

1. **With balloons.ai open, select the shape that represents the inside of the balloon.**

2. **Choose the Add Anchor Point tool (nested below the Pen tool) in the Tools panel.**

3. **Click the active shape to add an anchor point near where the balloon back meets the front (use the following image as a guide).**

Add Anchor Point tool

Click here to add an anchor point.

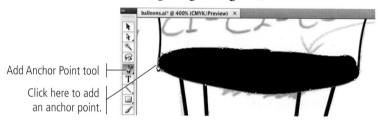

4. **Choose the Convert Anchor Point tool (nested under the Add Anchor Point tool) in the Tools panel.**

5. **Click the point you created in Step 3 to convert it to a corner point.**

Convert Anchor Point tool

Click to convert the point to a corner point.

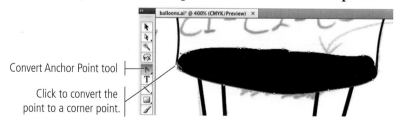

Note:

Because the other shapes are locked, none of the steps in this exercise affect the balloon front shape.

6. Repeat Steps 2–5 to add a corner point to the right side of the shape.

7. If necessary, use the Direct Selection tool to drag the corner points to match the bottom points of the balloon front shape.

The corner points should align to the corner points of the locked balloon corner.

8. Choose the Delete Anchor Point tool (nested under the Convert Anchor Point tool) in the Tools panel.

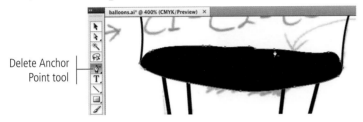

Delete Anchor Point tool

9. Click all but one anchor point on the top edge of the active shape to delete them.

10. Use the Direct Selection tool to adjust the remaining point and handles until the entire top edge of the shape is above the bottom edge of the balloon front shape.

This edge should entirely hide the bottom edge of the balloon shape.

11. Repeat Steps 8–10 to adjust the bottom edge of the shape.

The ends of these lines should be hidden by the bottom edge of the inside balloon shape.

12. Save the file and continue to the next stage of the project.

Stage 2 Coloring and Painting Artwork

The CMYK color model, also called "process color," recreates the range of printable colors by overlapping layers of cyan, magenta, yellow, and black inks in varying percentages from 0–100.

Using theoretically pure pigments, a mixture of equal parts of cyan, magenta, and yellow would produce black. Real pigments, however, are not pure; the actual result of mixing these three colors usually appears as a muddy brown. The fourth color, black (K), is added to the three subtractive primaries to extend the range of printable colors and allow much purer blacks to be printed than is possible with only the three primaries. Black is abbreviated as "K" because it is the "key" color to which others are aligned on the printing press. Using K for black also avoids confusion with blue in the RGB color model.

In the following image, the left block is printed with 100% black ink. The right block is a combination of 100% cyan, 100% magenta, and 100% yellow inks.

In process-color printing, the four process colors — cyan, magenta, yellow, and black (CMYK) — are imaged (also referred to as separated) onto individual printing plates. Each color separation is printed on a separate unit of a printing press. When printed on top of each other in varying percentages, the semi-transparent inks produce the range of colors in the CMYK gamut. Special (spot) colors are printed using specifically formulated inks as additional color separations.

 +  + 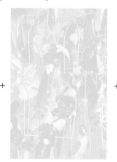 +  =

Different color models have different ranges or **gamuts** of possible colors. A normal human visual system is capable of distinguishing approximately 16.7 million different colors; color reproduction systems, however, are far more limited. The RGB model has the largest gamut of the output models. The CMYK gamut is much more limited; many of the brightest and most saturated colors that can be reproduced using light (in the RGB model) cannot be reproduced using CMYK inks.

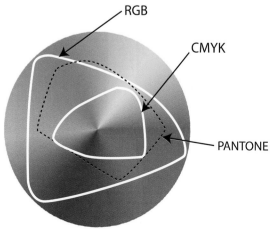

USE THE COLOR PANEL TO DEFINE CUSTOM SWATCHES

As you can see from the sketch below, the balloon in this project will be filled using three different colors (indicated as C1, C2, and C3). In the next two exercises, you use the Color panel to create the colors you need, and then save those colors as custom swatches.

1. **With balloons.ai open, choose Object>Unlock All.**

   You need to be able to select an object before you can change its color attributes. Remember, the Unlock All command unlocks all locked objects on the Artboard; it does not, however, affect layers that have been locked in the Layers panel.

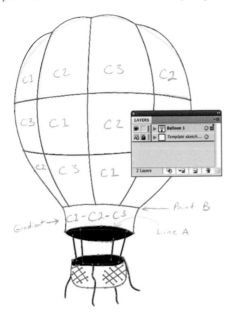

2. **Deselect everything, and then use the Selection tool to select only the basket shape path.**

   Because this object currently has no fill, you have to click the actual path to select the target object; clicking inside the shape selects nothing.

3. **Open the Color and Swatches panels.**

   Because you defined CMYK as the color mode for this document, the Color panel sliders show inks for those four primary colors.

The default Swatches panel includes a number of default swatches.

Note:

We dragged both panels out of the panel dock so we could work with both panels at once.

4. **In the Color panel, make sure the Fill icon is on top of the Stroke icon.**

   Like the options in the Tools panel, the Fill and Stroke icons determine which attribute you are currently changing. Whichever icon is on top will be affected by changes to the color values.

5. **Click the white swatch in the top row of the Swatches panel.**

   If you don't first apply some fill color to the object, changing the color values in the next step could produce strange and unpredictable results.

6. **Highlight the C (cyan) field and type 15. Press Tab to highlight the M (magenta) field and type 25. Press Tab again and change the Y (yellow) field to 45. Press Tab again and change the K (black) field to 0.**

   To define a specific ink percentage, you can either drag the color sliders or simply type in the fields. The selected object dynamically reflects the new color as you change the color values.

The Fill and Stroke icons serve the same purpose here as they do in the Tools panel.

Type directly in these fields to enter specific values.

You can also drag these sliders to adjust the component color percentages.

Or you can click in the spectrum to select a color.

7. **Select the shape that represents the inside of the basket and choose Object>Arrange>Send to Back.**

   Objects created on the same layer are arranged front-to-back in the order they were created. Because you created the "inside" shape last, it was on top of the basket shape. You can always rearrange the stacking order of objects on the same layer by using the options in the Object>Arrange menu.

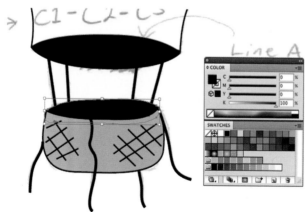

Note:

Press Shift while dragging any of the sliders in the Color panel to drag all four sliders at once. Their relative relationship (e.g., if Yellow is 20% and Cyan is 40%) to each other remains the same while you drag.

8. **Select the basket shape again. Make sure the Fill icon is active in the Color panel, and then click the New Swatch button at the bottom of the Swatches panel.**

Because the Fill icon is active, the fill color is the one that will be stored in the new swatch.

Click this button to make a new swatch from the currently active color.

9. **Click OK to accept the default options in the New Swatch dialog box.**

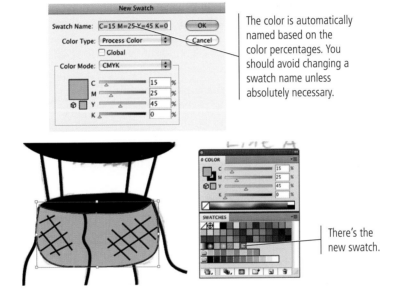

The color is automatically named based on the color percentages. You should avoid changing a swatch name unless absolutely necessary.

There's the new swatch.

10. **Open the Swatches panel Options menu and choose Select All Unused.**

As you know, the default Swatches panel includes a number of basic swatches that provide a good starting point for some artwork. However, you are creating you own swatches for this project, so the built-in ones are unnecessary. When you build custom swatches, it's a good idea to delete the default swatches you don't need.

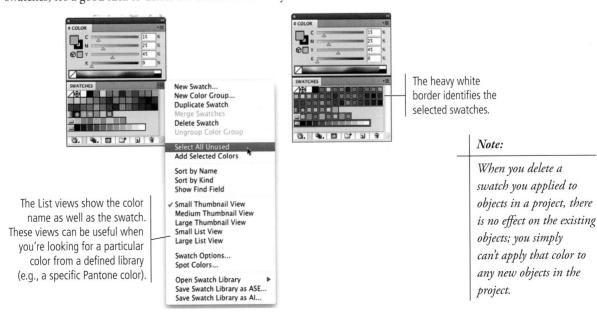

The List views show the color name as well as the swatch. These views can be useful when you're looking for a particular color from a defined library (e.g., a specific Pantone color).

The heavy white border identifies the selected swatches.

> **Note:**
>
> *When you delete a swatch you applied to objects in a project, there is no effect on the existing objects; you simply can't apply that color to any new objects in the project.*

11. Click the Swatches panel Delete button, and then click Yes in the resulting warning dialog box.

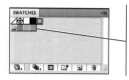

Illustrator sometimes maintains swatches that are stored in sets, even if they are not used.

Note:

The default swatches appear in every new file you create, even if you delete them from a specific file.

12. Save the file and continue to the next exercise.

Note:

The extra three swatches that remain are likely the result of a bug in the software. You know they are not used in the application, but Illustrator does not identify them as "unused."

CREATE GLOBAL SWATCHES

The basket shape is now filled with a custom swatch, which is stored in the Swatches panel for the open document. You also need three more colors to fill the various sections of the balloon. You are going to use a different method to create these colors, and then save them as swatches that can be changed at any time to dynamically modify the colors in the artwork.

1. With balloons.ai open, use the Selection tool to click the top-left section of the balloon (labeled C1 in the sketch).

If you remember from the beginning of the project, the twelve sections of the balloon were created by the Pathfinder Divide function; the results of Pathfinder functions are always grouped. To work with individual pieces of the group, you can enter into Isolation mode, use the Direct Selection tool, or ungroup the selection.

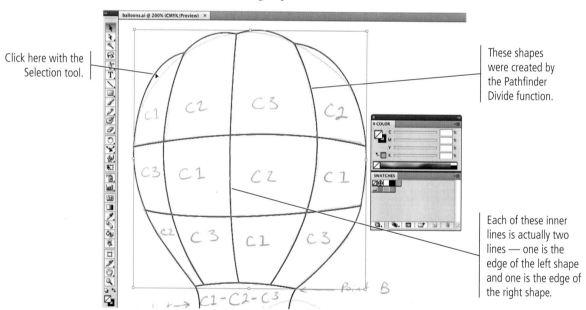

Click here with the Selection tool.

These shapes were created by the Pathfinder Divide function.

Each of these inner lines is actually two lines — one is the edge of the left shape and one is the edge of the right shape.

2. Choose Object>Ungroup.

3. **Click away from the ungrouped objects to deselect them. Use the Selection or Direct Selection tool to select and hide all but the C1 shapes.**

   These objects currently have no fill, which means you have to select the edges to select the shapes. Because of the way the Pathfinder arranges resulting objects front-to-back, however, it can be difficult to select objects whose edges overlap other objects (especially the ones that have no independent edges, such as the middle C1 and C2 segments in this balloon).

   One trick for selecting only what you want is to select what you *don't* want but can easily access — working from the outside in — and hide those objects.

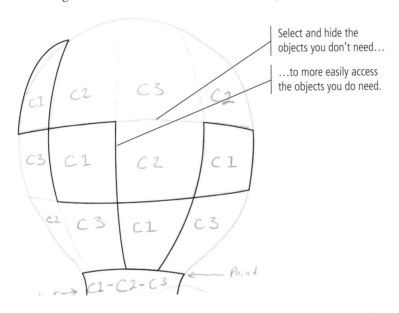

Select and hide the objects you don't need…

…to more easily access the objects you do need.

4. **Select the four C1 shapes. In the Color panel, click a green area in the color spectrum at the bottom of the Color panel.**

   All four selected objects fill with the green color you clicked.

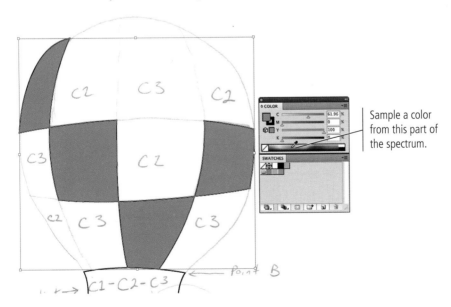

Sample a color from this part of the spectrum.

5. **With the Fill icon still active, click the New Swatch button in the Swatches panel.**

6. **Check the Global Color option in the New Swatch dialog box and click OK.**

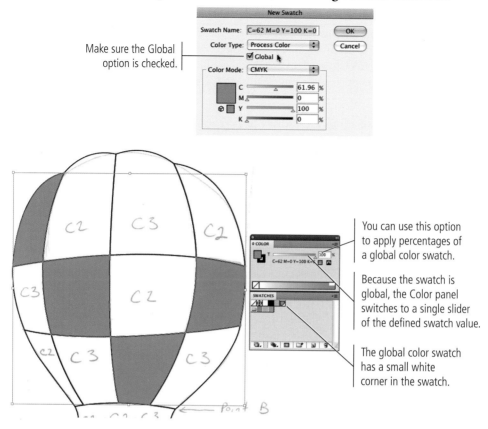

Make sure the Global option is checked.

New Swatch

Swatch Name: `C=62 M=0 Y=100 K=0`
Color Type: `Process Color`
☑ Global
Color Mode: `CMYK`

C	△	61.96 %
M		0 %
Y	△	100 %
K		0 %

You can use this option to apply percentages of a global color swatch.

Because the swatch is global, the Color panel switches to a single slider of the defined swatch value.

The global color swatch has a small white corner in the swatch.

7. **With the C1 objects selected, choose Object>Lock>Selection.**

   Locking these objects makes it easier to select the remaining objects that have adjoining paths as edges.

8. **Show all hidden objects (Object>Show All), and then select all four C2 shapes.**

9. **In the Color panel, click the green swatch below the Fill/Stroke icons to change the selected objects' fill.**

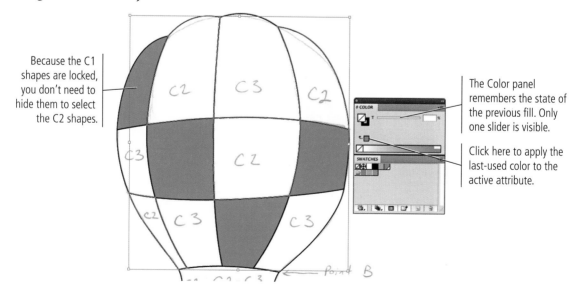

Because the C1 shapes are locked, you don't need to hide them to select the C2 shapes.

The Color panel remembers the state of the previous fill. Only one slider is visible.

Click here to apply the last-used color to the active attribute.

10. **In the Color panel, click the CMYK button to convert the color to a standard process-color build (showing all four color sliders).**

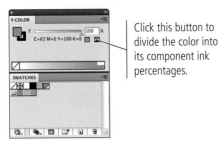

Click this button to divide the color into its component ink percentages.

11. **Click a blue color in the Color panel spectrum to change the C2 objects to blue.**

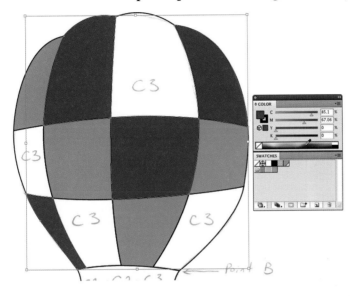

12. **Click the New Swatch button in the Swatches panel. Check the Global Color box and click OK.**

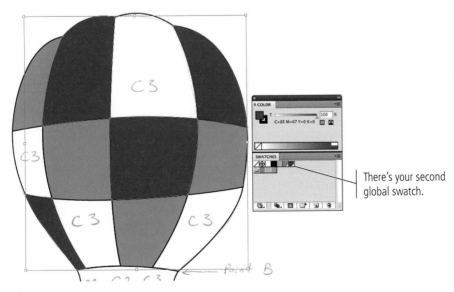

There's your second global swatch.

13. **Lock the active selection.**

14. **Repeat Steps 9–12 to fill the four C3 shapes with a purple color and create a global swatch from the fill color.**

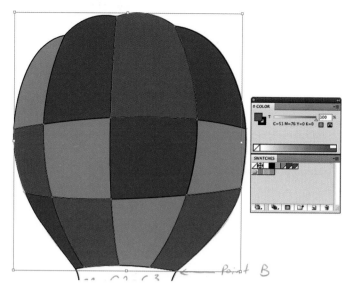

15. **Save the file and continue to the next exercise.**

 ADD A COLOR GRADIENT

The original sketch shows that the bottom of the balloon needs to be a gradient of the three colors in the balloon sections. Illustrator's Gradient tool makes it easy to create this gradient based on the three custom swatches you defined in the previous exercise.

1. **With `balloons.ai` open, select the shape that represents the bottom edge of the balloon by clicking the path with the Selection tool.**

2. **Open the Gradient panel and click the swatch in the top-left corner.**

   Clicking the swatch applies the linear gradient to the selected object.

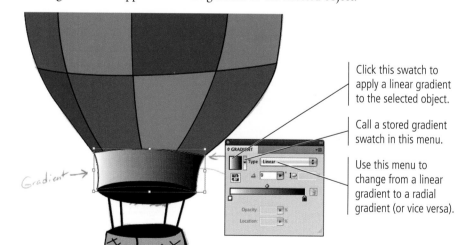

Click this swatch to apply a linear gradient to the selected object.

Call a stored gradient swatch in this menu.

Use this menu to change from a linear gradient to a radial gradient (or vice versa).

Note:

Gradients can only be applied to an object's fill; so in this instance, it doesn't matter whether the Fill icon is active in the Tools panel or Color panel.

3. **In the Gradient panel, double-click the left gradient stop on the gradient ramp.**

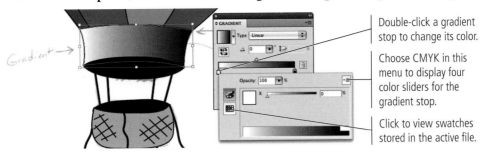

Double-click a gradient stop to change its color.

Choose CMYK in this menu to display four color sliders for the gradient stop.

Click to view swatches stored in the active file.

4. **In the pop-up panel, click the Swatches button to display the swatches stored in the current document.**

5. **Click the blue global swatch you created in the previous exercise, and then press Return/Enter to close the pop-up panel.**

The color in the artwork changes as soon as you click the swatch.

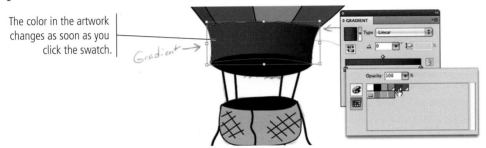

6. **Double-click the right gradient stop to open the pop-up panel. Apply the purple custom swatch to this stop.**

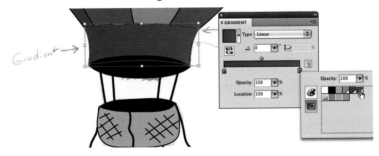

Note:

You can also drag a swatch from the Swatches panel onto a particular gradient stop to change the color of that stop.

Note:

You can remove a stop by dragging it down and off the gradient ramp.

7. **Click once below the gradient ramp to add another stop to the gradient. With the new stop selected, type 50 in the Location field.**

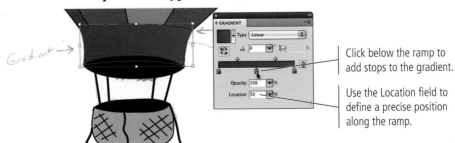

Click below the ramp to add stops to the gradient.

Use the Location field to define a precise position along the ramp.

8. **Double-click the middle stop and apply the green swatch.**

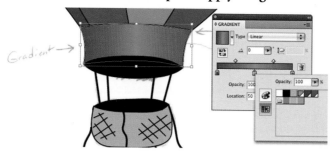

9. **Click the left gradient stop and drag right until the Location field shows approximately 10%.**

Moving this stop to the right extends the blue area of the gradient.

10. **Click the right gradient stop and drag left until the Location field shows approximately 90%.**

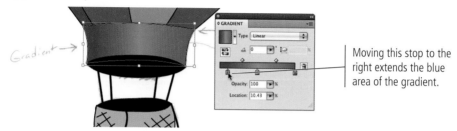

Moving this stop to the left extends the purple area of the gradient.

11. **Click the marker above the gradient ramp between the left and middle stops. Drag left until the Location field shows approximately 40%.**

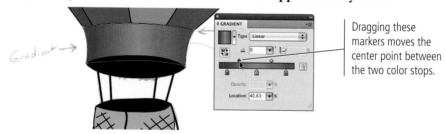

Dragging these markers moves the center point between the two color stops.

12. **Click the marker above the gradient ramp between the middle and right stops. Drag right until the Location field shows approximately 60%.**

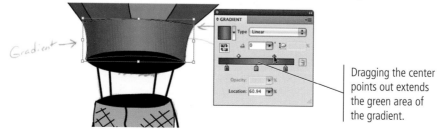

Dragging the center points out extends the green area of the gradient.

13. **Save the file and continue to the next exercise.**

EDIT GLOBAL COLOR SWATCHES

Global swatches offer a particular advantage when you need to change the colors used in your artwork. In the case of this project, the client requested a red-orange-yellow scheme for the balloon, so you need to change the custom swatches you created in the previous exercise.

1. With **balloons.ai** open, deselect all objects on the Artboard.

2. In the Swatches panel, double-click the blue custom swatch you created in the previous exercise.

3. In the resulting Swatch Options dialog box, make sure the Preview option is checked.

4. **Change the color values to C=0 M=100 Y=100 K=0, and then click OK to change the swatch definition.**

   Because this is a global color swatch, any objects that use the color — including the gradient — reflect the new swatch definition. Locked objects are also affected by the change.

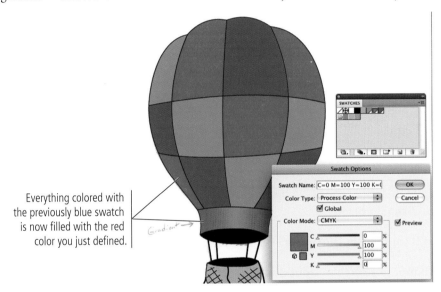

Everything colored with the previously blue swatch is now filled with the red color you just defined.

5. Repeat Steps 2–3 to change the green swatch definition to C=0 M=10 Y=100 K=0.

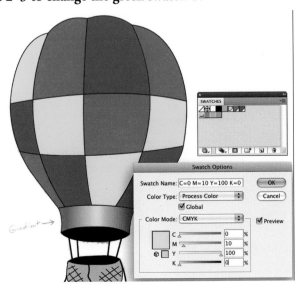

6. Repeat Steps 2–3 to change the purple swatch definition to C=0 M=60 Y=100 K=0.

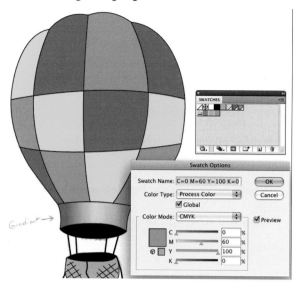

7. Unlock all objects in the file (Object>Unlock All).

8. Select all the objects on the Balloon layer and group them (Object>Group).

9. Save the file and continue to the next exercise.

 ## USE THE GRADIENT TOOL

One of the best ways to add color and depth to your illustrations is by adding gradient colors. A gradient is a smooth blend of two or more colors. You can add gradient color to your artwork with the Gradient tool. Illustrator CS4 includes an improved Gradient tool, which offers more options than ever before.

1. Open the file **desert.ai** from the RF_Illustrator>Festival folder.

2. Use the Direct Selection tool to select the front dune shape, and then fill it with the black-to-white linear gradient.

   Remember, clicking the object's fill with the Direct Selection tool selects the entire object. This allows you to work with individual objects on the main Artboard, even if they are part of a group.

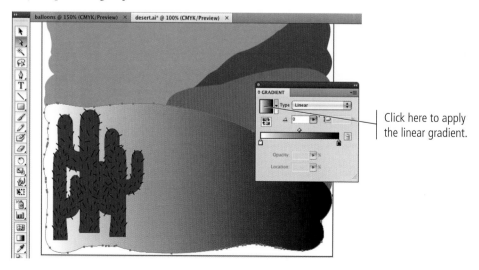

Click here to apply the linear gradient.

3. **Choose the Gradient tool in the Tools panel.**

   Windows users: Click away from the gradient-filled object to deselect it and then click the object with the Gradient tool to reveal the Gradient Annotator widget.

   There appears to be a bug in the software that requires this extra step for Windows users to access the Gradient Annotator.

   If you don't still see the Gradient Annotator on top of the object, open the View menu and make sure object bounding boxes are showing (View>Show Bounding Box).

   When a selected object is filled with a gradient, choosing the Gradient tool reveals the Gradient Annotator for that shape. The Gradient Annotator is simply a visual tool for applying most of the same options that are available in the Gradient panel. When you move your cursor over the gradient bar, it turns into a gradient slider.

Note:

You can turn off the Gradient Annotator in the View menu (View>Hide Gradient Annotator).

Note:

If the current selection is part of a group, selecting the Gradient tool does not reveal the Gradient Annotator widget. You have to first deselect the active group, and then click a specific object with the Gradient tool to show the Gradient Annotator for a specific object.

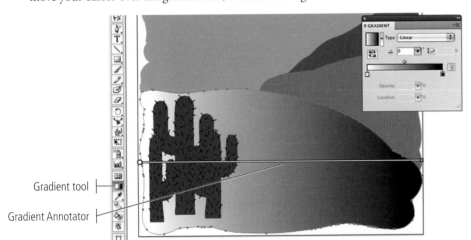

Gradient tool

Gradient Annotator

4. **Move your cursor over the Gradient Annotator to show the associated stops.**

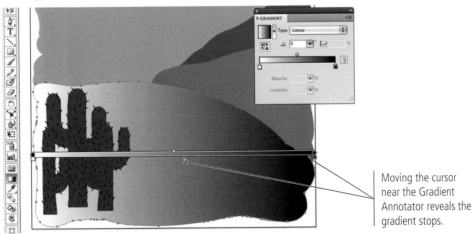

Moving the cursor near the Gradient Annotator reveals the gradient stops.

5. On the Gradient Annotator, click the white stop and drag to about the halfway point of the gradient.

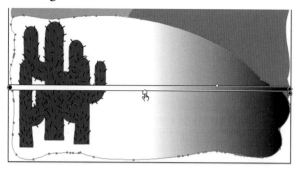

6. Place the cursor directly below the left end of the Gradient Annotator. When you see a plus sign (+) in the cursor, click to add a new stop to the gradient.

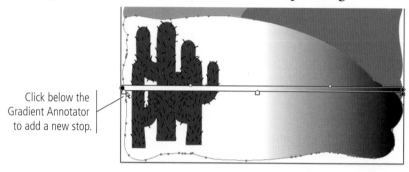

Click below the Gradient Annotator to add a new stop.

7. Double-click the new stop to open the pop-up panel. Change the stop color to the available orange swatch.

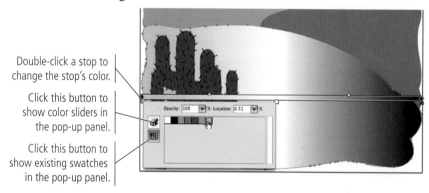

Double-click a stop to change the stop's color.

Click this button to show color sliders in the pop-up panel.

Click this button to show existing swatches in the pop-up panel.

8. Repeat Step 7 to apply the same orange swatch to the right gradient stop.

9. Click the right end of the annotator and drag left (toward the center of the Artboard), until the Annotator is about two-thirds the width of the selected object.

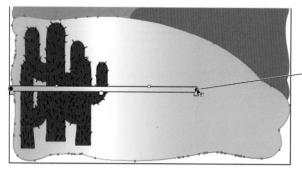

Drag the right end of the annotator to shorten or lengthen the gradient within the shape.

10. **Place the cursor near the right end of the Gradient Annotator. When the cursor changes to a rotation symbol, click and drag down to rotate the gradient clockwise.**

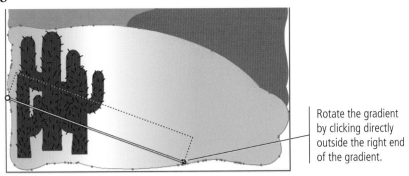

Rotate the gradient by clicking directly outside the right end of the gradient.

11. **Select the second dune shape, and then click the gradient swatch in the Gradient panel.**

The Gradient panel remembers the last-used gradient, so you can simply click the sample to apply the gradient to the new object.

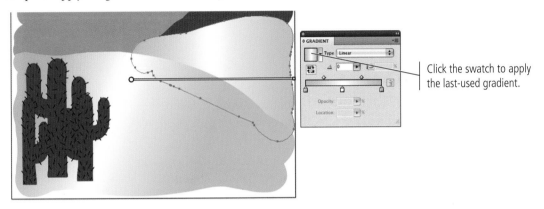

Click the swatch to apply the last-used gradient.

12. **Using the Gradient tool, click near the left edge of the selected shape and drag close to the right edge of the selected shape.**

Rather than dragging the Annotator bar, you can also click and drag with the Gradient tool to define the direction and position of the gradient within a selected object.

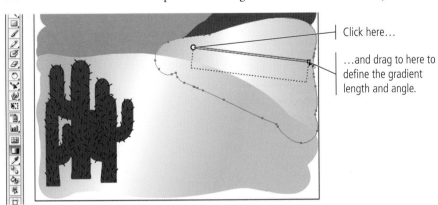

Click here...

...and drag to here to define the gradient length and angle.

13. **Use the same method from Steps 11–12 to apply the gradient to the third dune shape. Drag this gradient from the bottom-left area to the top-right area of the selected shape.**

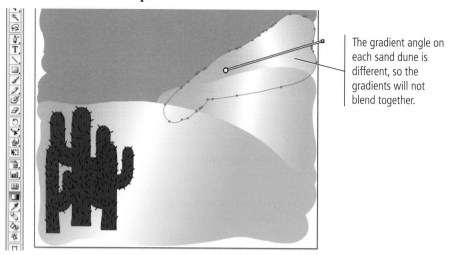

The gradient angle on each sand dune is different, so the gradients will not blend together.

14. **Save the file as `poster.ai` in your WIP>Festival folder and continue to the next exercise.**

MANAGE ARTWORK WITH LAYERS

The next step in the process is to place your finished balloon in the background illustration; you can then duplicate the balloon artwork to create a small fleet of different-colored balloons floating over the desert.

You created the entire balloon artwork on a single layer. In this exercise, you add multiple layers so you can organize and manage the additional balloon objects.

1. **With `poster.ai` open, Shift-click to select all three layers in the Layers panel.**

2. **Choose Merge Selected in the Layers panel Options menu.**

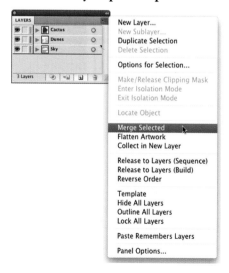

3. Double-click the new layer to open the Layer Options dialog box. Rename the layer `Desert` and click OK.

4. Activate (or open, if necessary) the `balloons.ai` file.

5. Select the Sketch layer in the Layers panel and drag it to the panel's Delete button.

Drag the template (Sketch) layer to the Delete button to remove that layer.

Note:

If you delete a non-template layer that contains artwork, Illustrator asks you to confirm that you want to delete the layer (and all artwork on the layer).

6. Select everything on the Artboard, choose Edit>Copy, save the `balloons.ai` file, and then close it.

7. With `poster.ai` active, click the New Layer button in the Layers panel. Double-click the new layer, name it `Balloon 1`, and then click OK.

8. Make sure the Balloon 1 layer is active in the Layers panel and choose Edit>Paste. Drag the pasted artwork to the approximate center of the Artboard.

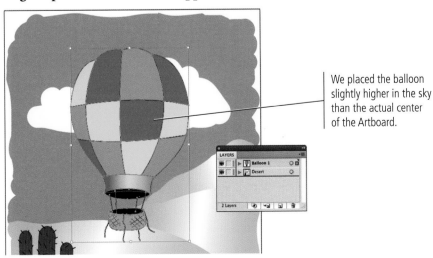

We placed the balloon slightly higher in the sky than the actual center of the Artboard.

9. **Click the Balloon 1 layer and drag it to the New Layer button at the bottom of the Layers panel.**

You now have a copy of the layer you dragged. You see no difference on the Artboard because the copy is in the exact same position as the original layer.

Drag an existing layer to the New Layer button to make an exact copy of the layer.   The copy is added directly above the original layer.

10. **Rename the Balloon 1 copy layer as** Balloon 2.

11. **Repeat Step 9 to create a third balloon layer. Rename this layer** Balloon 3.

12. **Lock all but the Balloon 2 layer, and then choose Select>All.**

Because all the other layers are locked, you selected only the artwork on the Balloon 2 layer. The difference between locking objects and locking layers depends on what you need to accomplish. In this case, it's best to place each piece of artwork on its own layer, so you can lock the layers you want to protect from change.

Note:

You can also select all objects on a specific layer by clicking the round button to the right of the layer name (in the Layers panel).

13. **Choose Object>Transform>Scale. In the Scale dialog box, type** 75% **in the Uniform Scale field. Make sure the Scale Strokes & Effects option is checked, and then click OK.**

If Scale Strokes & Effects is not checked, a 2-pt stroke will remain a 2-pt stroke, even if you reduce the selected object to 10% of its original size. With the Scale Strokes & Effects option checked, a 2-pt stroke scaled to 75% becomes a 1.5-pt stroke.

14. **Drag the scaled artwork left.**

15. **In the Layers panel, click the Balloon 2 layer and drag it below the Balloon 1 layer.**

Drag layers in the panel to rearrange the layer stacking order.

Because the Balloon 2 layer is now behind the Balloon 1 layer, parts of the scaled object are obscured.

16. **Lock the Balloon 2 layer and unlock the Balloon 3 layer.**

17. **Repeat Steps 13–15 for the artwork on Balloon 3 layer. Scale it to 50%, and then move it right to make it seem farthest back in the fleet.**

    The different scaling, position, and stacking order of the three balloons creates the illusion of depth within the illustration.

18. **Adjust the position and scale of each balloon (unlocking individual layers as necessary) until you are satisfied with the overall result.**

19. **Save the file and continue to the next exercise.**

 RECOLOR ARTWORK

Your illustration is nearly complete. The only work left to do is change the colors of the two new balloons. Although you could manually select the shapes and apply different ink percentages, Illustrator includes a sophisticated tool that makes it easy to experiment with and change all colors in a selection.

1. **With poster.ai open, lock all but the Balloon 2 layer. Choose Select>All to select everything on the unlocked Balloon 2 layer.**

2. **With the Balloon 2 objects selected, click the Recolor Artwork button in the Control panel.**

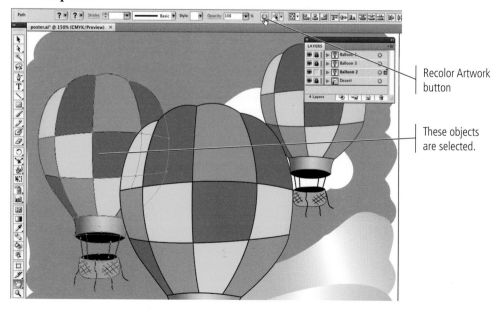

Recolor Artwork button

These objects are selected.

Many vague and technical-sounding terms are mentioned when discussing color. Is hue the same as color? The same as value? As tone? What's the difference between lightness and brightness? What is chroma? And where does saturation fit in?

This problem has resulted in several attempts to normalize color communication. A number of systems have been developed to define color according to specific criteria, including Hue, Saturation, and Brightness (HSB); Hue, Saturation, and Lightness (HSL); Hue, Saturation, and Value (HSV); and Lightness, Chroma, and Hue (LCH). Each of these models or systems plots color on a three-dimensional diagram, based on the elements of human color perception — hue, colorfulness, and brightness.

Hue is what most people think of as color — red, green, purple, and so on. Hue is defined according to a color's position on a color wheel, beginning from red (0°) and traveling counterclockwise around the wheel.

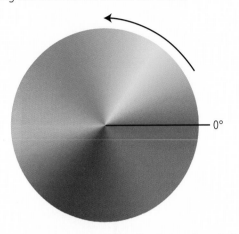

Saturation (also called "intensity") refers to the color's difference from neutral gray. Highly saturated colors are more vivid than those with low saturation. Saturation is plotted from the center of the color wheel. Color at the center is neutral gray and has a saturation value of 0; color at the edge of the wheel is the most intense value of the corresponding hue and has a saturation value of 100.

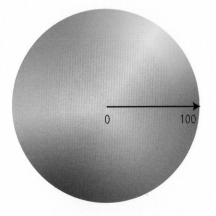

If you bisect the color wheel with a straight line, the line creates a saturation axis for two complementary colors. A color is dulled by the introduction of its complement. Red, for example, is neutralized by the addition of cyan (blue and green). Near the center of the axis, the result is neutral gray.

−100   0   +100

Chroma is similar to saturation, but chroma factors in a reference white. In any viewing situation, colors appear less vivid as the light source dims. The process of chromatic adaptation, however, allows the human visual system to adjust to changes in light and still differentiate colors according to the relative saturation.

Brightness is the amount of light reflected off an object. As an element of color reproduction, brightness is typically judged by comparing the color to the lightest nearby object (such as an unprinted area of white paper).

Lightness is the amount of white or black added to the pure color. Lightness (also called "luminance" or "value") is the relative brightness based purely on the black-white value of a color. A lightness value of 0 means there is no addition of white or black. Lightness of +100 is pure white; lightness of −100 is pure black.

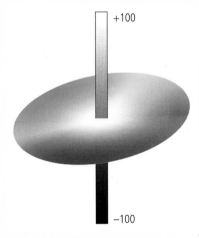

All hues are affected equally by changes in lightness.

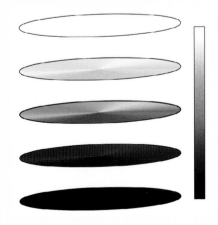

The Recolor Artwork dialog box shows all colors used in the selection. You can edit or replace individual colors, or you can apply global changes that affect the entire selection.

All colors in the active selection are listed here.

Use the options to select and change individual colors.

Use this area to redefine the selected color.

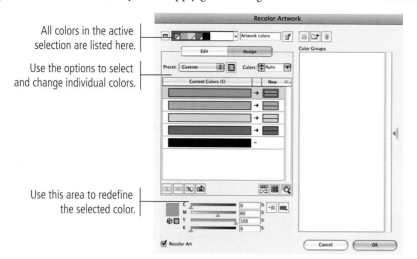

Note:

You can also choose Edit>Edit Colors>Recolor Artwork to open the dialog box.

3. **Click the Edit button to show the active colors on a color wheel.**

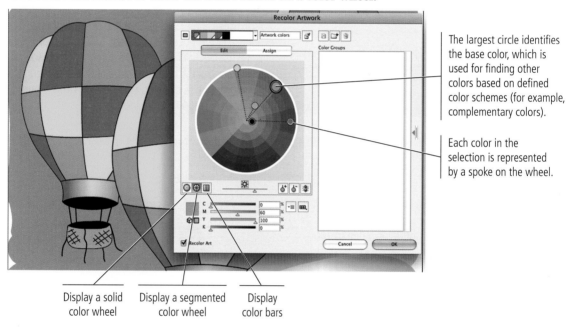

The largest circle identifies the base color, which is used for finding other colors based on defined color schemes (for example, complementary colors).

Each color in the selection is represented by a spoke on the wheel.

Display a solid color wheel

Display a segmented color wheel

Display color bars

4. **Make sure the Recolor Art option is checked, and then click the Display Segmented Color Wheel button.**

5. **Click the orange circle and drag it to a middle-blue area on the color wheel.**

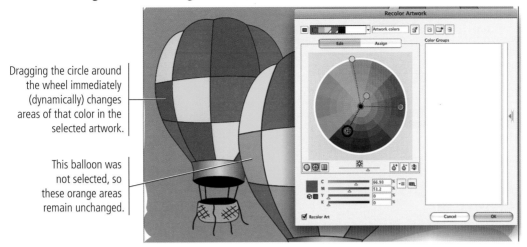

Dragging the circle around the wheel immediately (dynamically) changes areas of that color in the selected artwork.

This balloon was not selected, so these orange areas remain unchanged.

6. **Click the yellow circle and drag it to a medium-dark green.**

7. **Click the red circle and drag it to a medium-dark purple.**

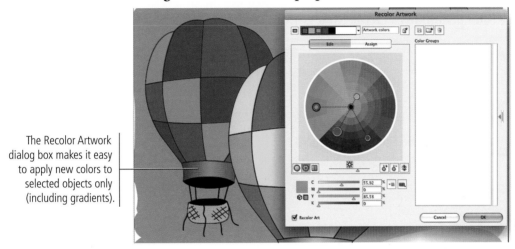

The Recolor Artwork dialog box makes it easy to apply new colors to selected objects only (including gradients).

8. **Click OK to return to the Artboard.**

9. **Lock the Balloon 2 layer and unlock the Balloon 3 layer. Select everything on the unlocked layer, and then click the Recolor Artwork button in the Control panel.**

10. **With the dialog box in Assign mode, make sure the first color is selected in the list.**

11. **Click the button to the right of the color sliders and choose CMYK from the menu.**

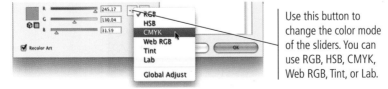

Use this button to change the color mode of the sliders. You can use RGB, HSB, CMYK, Web RGB, Tint, or Lab.

12. **Use the sliders to change the color definition to C=0 M=100 Y=0 K=0.**

This color is selected.

This swatch reflects the new color definition.

Use these sliders to define different component values for the selected color.

Because Recolor Art is checked, the selected artwork immediately reflects the change.

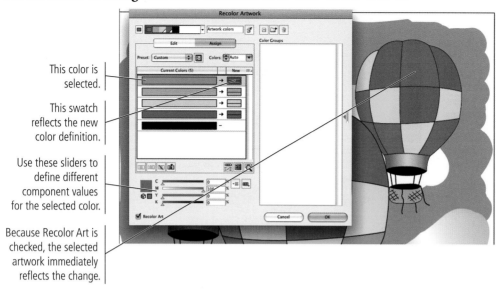

13. **Click the red color in the Current Colors list, and then use the sliders to change the color definition to C=100 M=0 Y=15 K=0.**

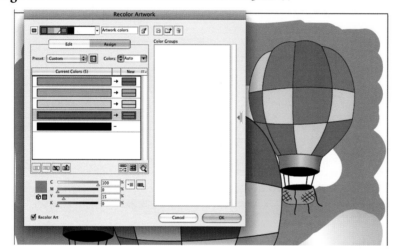

Note:

If you are working with global color swatches, you can also use the Tint slider you saw earlier when you worked with the global color swatches.

14. **Click the yellow color in the Current Colors list, and then use the sliders to change the color definition to C=0 M=0 Y=60 K=0.**

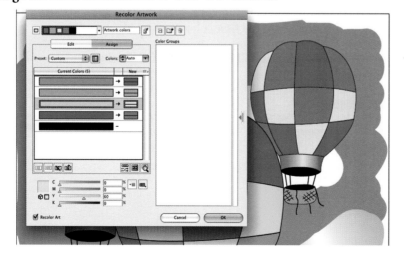

The Recolor Artwork dialog box has dozens of options for changing colors, and the sheer number of choices can be intimidating. However, you already used two of the most important options in this dialog box, so you should feel confident in your ability to use it — especially when experimenting with colors to use in a particular piece of artwork. In addition to the functions you already used, the Recolor Artwork dialog box also enables global color changes.

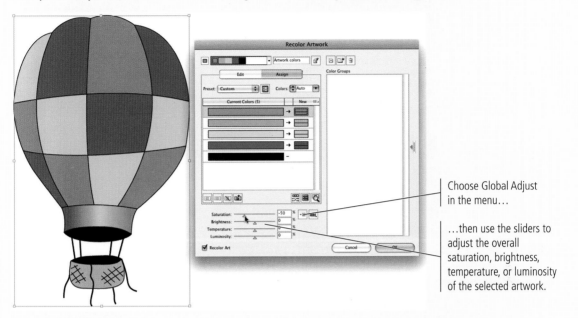

Choose Global Adjust in the menu...

...then use the sliders to adjust the overall saturation, brightness, temperature, or luminosity of the selected artwork.

You should also understand that you aren't required to do a 1-to-1 replacement. You can replace multiple colors with the same new color by simply dragging one current color onto another. (This is especially useful if you are converting four-color artwork to a two-color or one-color job.)

Drag one current color onto another to replace both colors with the same new color.

When you release the mouse button, both colors appear in the same row.

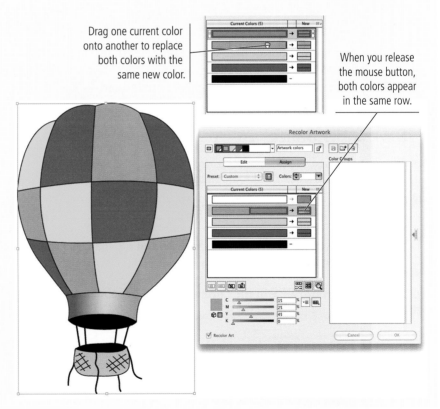

15. Click OK to return to the Artboard.

16. Save the file and continue to the final stage of the project.

Stage 3 Exporting EPS and PDF Files

Although most current versions of page-layout software can manage the native Illustrator file format, some older applications — which are still in common use — can't interpret Illustrator files. For those applications, you need to save files in formats that can be used — namely, EPS and PDF.

SAVE AN EPS FILE

The EPS (Encapsulated PostScript) file format was designed for high-quality print applications. The format can store both raster and vector elements, and it supports transparency. Before page-layout applications were able to support native Illustrator files (or PDF), EPS was the most common format used for files created in Illustrator.

1. With poster.ai open, choose File>Save As and navigate to your WIP>Festival folder as the target location.

2. Choose Illustrator EPS in the Format/Save As Type menu.

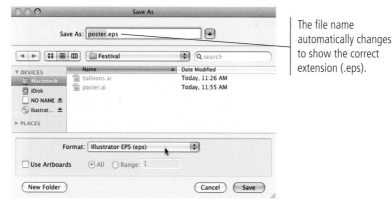

The file name automatically changes to show the correct extension (.eps).

Note:

If you have more than one Artboard in a file, you can check the Use Artboards option to export each Artboard as a separate EPS file.

3. **Click Save.**

4. **In the resulting EPS Options dialog box, choose TIFF (8-bit Color) in the Format menu and click the Transparent radio button. Make sure Embed Fonts is checked.**

5. **Click OK to create the EPS file.**

6. **Continue to the next exercise.**

EPS Options

When you save a file in the EPS format, you can define a number of format-specific options.

Version allows you to save a file to be compatible with earlier versions of Illustrator. Be aware that features not available in earlier versions will be lost in the saved file.

Format defines the type of preview that will be saved in the file (these previews are used for applications that can't directly read the EPS file format). Be aware that Windows users cannot access Macintosh-format previews; if you're working in a Windows-based or cross-platform environment, use one of the TIFF preview options.

Another advantage of the TIFF preview is the ability to save the preview with a transparent background or opaque background. When you choose TIFF (8-bit Color) in the Preview menu, you can choose the **Transparent** option to save a preview that will show background objects through the empty areas of the artwork; the **Opaque** option creates the preview with a solid white background.

Transparency options control the output settings for transparent and semi-transparent objects, including drop shadows and other effects. (These options will be explained in depth in Project 6.)

Embed Fonts (for other applications) embeds used fonts into the EPS file. This option ensures that the type displays and prints properly when the file is placed into another application such as Adobe InDesign or QuarkXPress.

Include Linked Files embeds files that are linked to the artwork.

Include Document Thumbnails creates a thumbnail image of the artwork that displays in the Illustrator Open and Place dialog boxes.

Include CMYK PostScript in RGB Files allows RGB color documents to be printed from applications that do not support RGB output. When the EPS file is reopened in Illustrator, the RGB colors are preserved.

Compatible Gradient and Gradient Mesh Printing is necessary for older printers and PostScript devices to print gradients and gradient meshes; those elements (explained in Project 4) are converted to the JPEG format.

Adobe PostScript® determines what level of PostScript is used to save the artwork. PostScript Level 2 represents color as well as grayscale vector and bitmap images. PostScript Level 3 includes the ability to print mesh objects when printing to a PostScript 3 printer.

SAVE A FILE AS PDF

The **Adobe PDF** (or simply PDF) format has become a universal method of moving files to virtually any digital destination. One of the most important uses for the PDF format is the ability to create perfectly formatted digital documents, exactly as they would appear if printed on paper. You can embed fonts, images, drawings, and other elements into the file so all the required bits are available on any computer. The PDF format can be used to move your artwork to the Web as a low-resolution RGB file or to a commercial printer as a high-resolution CMYK file.

Note:

PDF stands for Portable Document Format.

1. **With `poster.ai` open, choose File>Save As. If necessary, navigate to your WIP>Festival folder as the target location.**

2. **Choose Adobe PDF in the Format/Save As Type menu and click Save.**

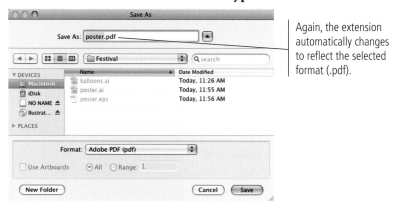

Again, the extension automatically changes to reflect the selected format (.pdf).

3. **Review the options in the General pane.**

    Read the description area to see what Adobe has to say about these options.

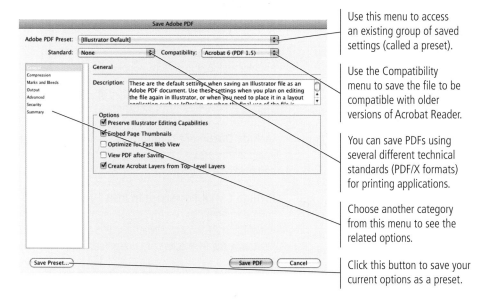

Use this menu to access an existing group of saved settings (called a preset).

Use the Compatibility menu to save the file to be compatible with older versions of Acrobat Reader.

You can save PDFs using several different technical standards (PDF/X formats) for printing applications.

Choose another category from this menu to see the related options.

Click this button to save your current options as a preset.

4. **Click Compression in the list of categories on the left and review the options.**

   These options allow you to reduce the resulting file size by compressing color, grayscale, and/or monochrome bitmap (raster) images. You can also compress text and line art by clicking the check box at the bottom.

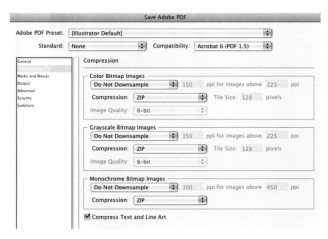

5. **Review the Marks and Bleeds options.**

   These options add different types of marks to the output page:

   - **Trim marks** indicate the edge of the page, where a page printed on a larger sheet will be cut down to its final size. You can also define the thickness (weight) of the trim marks, as well as how far from the page edge the lines should appear (offset).

   - **Registration marks** resemble a small crosshair. These marks are added to each ink unit on a printing press to make sure the different inks are properly aligned to one another.

   - **Color bars** are rows of small squares across the sheet, used to verify press settings for accurate color reproduction.

   - **Page information** adds the file name, date, and time of output. You can also define what font to use for page information

   - **Bleeds** define how much of elements outside the page boundaries will be included in the final output. Most printers require at least a 0.125″ bleed on each side, but you should always ask before you create the final file.

Note:

Most printers require trim marks to be created outside the bleed area. Always check with your service provider when saving a PDF for commercial output.

Note:

The Output, Advanced, and Security options are explained in later projects that discuss transparency and color management.

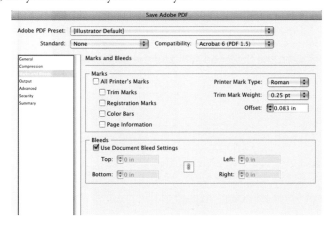

6. **Choose Illustrator Default in the Adobe PDF Preset menu and click Save PDF.**

7. **Close the file.**

1. The _____ tool is used to place anchor points that are connected by line segments.

2. The _____ tool is used to change a smooth anchor point to a corner anchor point (and vice versa).

3. The _____ tool is used to edit individual anchor points (and their related handles) on a vector path.

4. _____ is the range of possible colors within a specific color model.

5. _____ are the four component colors in process-color output.

6. The _____ panel includes value sliders for each component in the defined color model.

7. The _____ is used to paint shapes of solid color based on the defined brush size and the area you drag with a single mouse click.

8. The _____ appears over a gradient-filled object when selected with the Gradient tool; you can use it to control the position and direction of color in the gradient-filled object.

9. Changes made to a _____ color swatch are reflected in all elements where that color is applied.

10. The _____ dialog box can be used to change individual colors in an entire file, or make global changes to all colors in the file.

1. Briefly explain three ways to deselect the current selection on the Artboard.

2. Briefly explain the difference between the Selection tool and the Direct Selection tool.

3. Briefly explain the significance of "process color" related to Illustrator artwork.

Portfolio Builder Project

Use what you learned in this project to complete the following freeform exercise.
Carefully read the art director and client comments, then create your own design to meet the needs of the project.
Use the space below to sketch ideas; when finished, write a brief explanation of your reasoning behind your final design.

art director comments

The former marketing director for the Temecula Balloon Festival recently moved to Florida to be the director of the annual Miami Jazzfest. She was pleased with your work on the balloon festival project, and would like to hire you to create the advertising for next year's jazz festival event.

To complete this project, you should:

❏ Develop artwork that will be the primary image for posters and print advertisements, as well as shirts and other souvenirs.

❏ Create the primary artwork to fit onto the festival program cover, which is 8×10″.

client comments

Jazzfest is one of the longest running and well-known music festivals in the southeastern part of the United States. In addition to the music, the festival also features food from prominent restaurants; the food is almost as big of an attraction as the music — maybe even moreso for some people.

We want artwork that appeals to a 40-something, middle- and upper-class audience; tickets to this event are fairly expensive, but we always have some very well-known acts that make it worth the price.

Finally, we want the artwork to be an appealing aspect of our ad campaign, but we want it to be artwork in its own right. The artwork gets printed as posters that are hung in some very exclusive establishments around the Miami area, and they weren't happy with the cartoon style of art from previous years.

project justification

_____
_____
_____
_____
_____
_____
_____
_____
_____
_____
_____
_____

Project Summary

This project built on the skills you learned in Project 1, incorporating more advanced drawing techniques that allow you to exercise precise control over every point and path in a file. The Pen tool is arguably one of the most important tools you will use throughout your career as an illustrator; although it can be difficult at first, practice is the best way to master this skill.

The second half of this project explored color in Illustrator: applying color, saving global color swatches to make changes more efficiently, using gradients to add visual interest, and making changes to specific colors throughout a selection.

Finally, you explored two different file formats that are commonly used to share Illustrator artwork with other applications. EPS and PDF formats are invaluable parts of design workflows using software applications that can't import native Illustrator files.

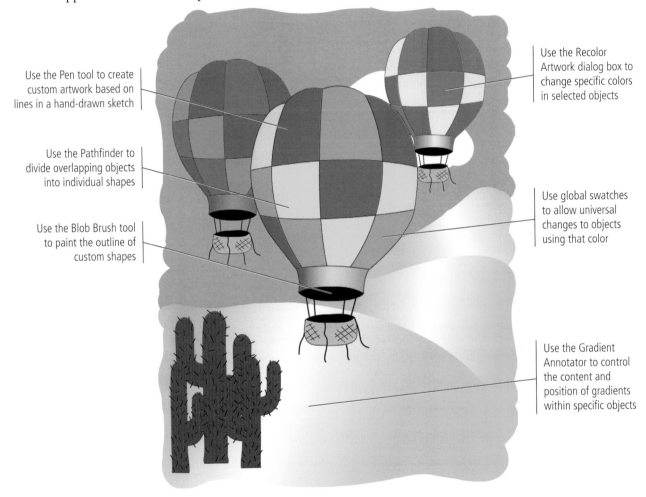

Use the Pen tool to create custom artwork based on lines in a hand-drawn sketch

Use the Pathfinder to divide overlapping objects into individual shapes

Use the Blob Brush tool to paint the outline of custom shapes

Use the Recolor Artwork dialog box to change specific colors in selected objects

Use global swatches to allow universal changes to objects using that color

Use the Gradient Annotator to control the content and position of gradients within specific objects

Identity Package

Your client, Graham Apple, owns an organic orchard in Central Florida. He hired you to create a corporate identity package so he can begin branding his products to reach a larger consumer base in gourmet groceries throughout the southeast. He asked you to first develop a logo, and then create the standard identity pieces (letterhead and envelope) that he will use for business promotion and correspondence.

This project incorporates the following skills:

❏ Developing custom logo artwork based on an object in a photograph

❏ Using a gradient mesh to create realistic color blends

❏ Building various logo versions to meet specific output requirements

❏ Saving EPS files for maximum flexibility

❏ Converting type to outlines and manipulating letter shapes to create a finished logotype

❏ Using layers to easily manage complex artwork

❏ Creating multiple Artboards to contain specific projects and layouts

❏ Printing desktop proofs of individual Artboards

It's just a coincidence that my last name is apple and I own an organic orchard, but I might as well take advantage where I can. I want my logo to be — surprise! — an apple, with some creative type treatment for the name of the farm (Apple Organics).

Once the logo is complete, I want you to use it to create letterhead and envelopes that I will have preprinted; I want a more professional feel than I can create using my laser printer. The printer I spoke with said I could do this for less money if I go "4-color" for the letterhead, but "2-color" for the envelope; I really don't know what that means — I'm hoping you do.

The logo is the first part of this project because you'll use it on the other two pieces. The client told you exactly what he wants, so that part is taken care of. I had our photographer take a good apple picture; use that as the basis for the one you draw in the logo art.

The client wants to print the letterhead in four-color and the envelope in two-color, so you'll have to create two different versions of the logo. Since logos are used on far more than just these two jobs in this one application, you'll also create a one-color version because the client will inevitably ask for it at some point.

To complete this project, you will:

❏ Draw the logo artwork using the Pen tool to trace the outline in a photograph

❏ Create a gradient mesh

❏ Use Smart Guides to manage a gradient mesh

❏ Use effects to add object highlights

❏ Create and control point-type objects

❏ Convert text to outlines so you can manipulate the letter shapes.

❏ Apply spot-color inks for special printing applications

❏ Use the Appearance panel to revert gradient mesh objects back to regular paths

❏ Create versions of the final logo for 1-color, 2-color, and 4-color printing

❏ Print desktop proofs of the completed identity pieces

Stage 1 Working with Gradient Meshes

The first part of this project is to create the client's logo. There are several important points to keep in mind when you design a logo.

First, logos need to be scalable. A company might place its logo on the head of a golf tee or on the side of a building. (This is a strong argument for using the simpler line art approach instead of photography.) Vector graphics — the kind you typically create in Illustrator — can be scaled as large or small as necessary without losing quality; photographs are raster images, and they can't be greatly enlarged or reduced without losing quality. That's why you're converting the client's photograph (a raster image) into a vector graphic.

Second, you almost always need more than one version of any given logo — very often in more than one file format. Different kinds of output require different formats (specifically, one set of files for print and one for the Web), and some types of jobs require special options saved in the files — such as the 4-color, 2-color, and 1-color versions of the logo you create in this project.

Note:

Logos are perhaps the most versatile type of graphic. They have to work in a wide variety of applications, from printed in one color on a box to printed in full color on a billboard, from being placed on a company's Web site to appearing on a television commercial, and virtually anything else in between.

SET UP THE WORKSPACE

Your client needs several versions of a new logo, including one with realistic color. Illustrator includes a number of tools ideally suited for creating lifelike illustrations. In this project, you work from a photograph to create a vector-based apple graphic that will be part of your client's logo. You start with the full-color version, and then work from there to create the other variations that are part of a typical logo package.

1. **On your desktop, drag the Organics folder from the WIP folder on your Resource CD to the WIP folder where you're saving your work.**

2. **In Illustrator, choose File>New.**

3. **Type apple in the Name field, choose Letter as the page size, and choose Inches as the unit of measurement.**

   At this point, you are simply using the Artboard as a drawing space, so you only need to make it large enough to draw. Later, you will adjust the Artboard to meet the specific needs of the finished logo.

4. **Make sure the Number of Artboards field is set to 1.**

   Later in this project, you will add multiple Artboards to hold various versions of the logo. For now, you only need one Artboard, which will serve as a drawing board.

5. **In the Advanced options, choose CMYK in the Color Mode menu and choose High (300 ppi) in the Raster Effects menu.**

   Because the CMYK gamut is smaller than the RGB gamut, you are starting with the smaller gamut to avoid the color shift that could occur if you started with RGB and converted the colors to CMYK. You are also creating the file to meet the high-resolution requirements of commercial printing. While not part of this project, you can easily use the Save For Web utility to export low-resolution RGB versions of the file for digital media.

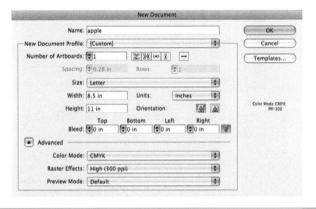

6. **Click OK to create the new file.**

7. **Choose File>Place. Navigate to the file `apple.jpg` in the RF_Illustrator> Organics folder. Make sure the Link and Template options are not checked, and then click Place.**

Choosing the Template option places an image onto a template layer that is automatically dimmed. That's not what you want to do here; you want the photograph to remain at full visibility so you can extract colors from the photo.

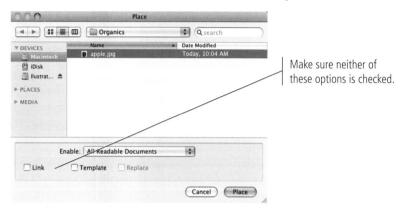

Make sure neither of these options is checked.

8. **Center the photo to the horizontal and vertical center of the Artboard.**

9. **Rename Layer 1 Apple Photo, and then lock the layer.**

For most of the drawing process, you use the Apple Photo layer as the basis of your artwork. You will draw on other layers, and then delete the photo layer when your apple graphic is complete.

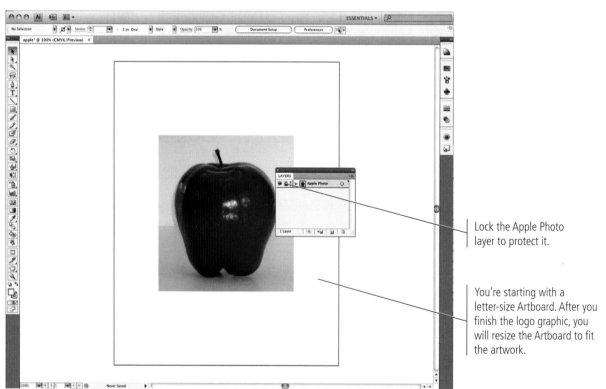

Lock the Apple Photo layer to protect it.

You're starting with a letter-size Artboard. After you finish the logo graphic, you will resize the Artboard to fit the artwork.

10. **Save the file as `apple.ai` in your WIP>Organics folder, and then continue to the next exercise.**

DRAW THE APPLE SHAPES

In Project 2, you used the Pen tool to create custom shapes. The apple shape in this logo is another example of a custom shape comprised of lines and paths. In Project 2, you used a hand-drawn sketch as your template, but now you're using a photograph. The first step is to determine what shapes you need to create.

1. **With apple.ai open, create a new layer at the top of the layer stack and rename it Apple Front.**

2. **Using the Pen tool with a 1-pt black stroke and no fill, draw the outline for the front part of the apple. Follow the shape of the apple as it curves in front of the stem.**

   We started our contour line at the bottom part of the apple where there is a sharp corner because starting a contour line on a curve often creates less than perfect results. You can start your outline wherever you feel most comfortable.

Pen tool

Skip over the area that wraps behind the stem.

If you start drawing here....

...you can continue your outline along the curve of the apple.

3. **If necessary, use the Direct Selection tool to adjust the anchor points and handles until the outline matches the shape of the apple.**

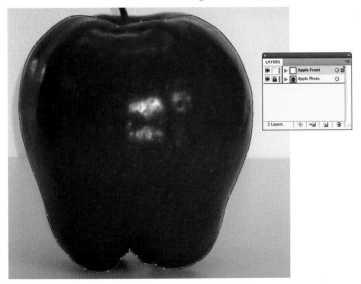

4. **Create another new layer and rename it Apple Back. In the Layers panel, drag this layer below the Apple Front layer.**

5. **On the Apple Back layer, use the Pen tool to draw the shape of the back part of the apple (where the apple curves behind the stem).**

   Be sure to overlap this shape with the Apple Front shape so no blank space will show between the two elements later.

Overlap this line to ensure complete coverage when you start adding color.

6. **Create a new layer and rename it Stem.**

   Since you were just working on the Apple Back layer, the new Stem layer should automatically reside between the Apple Front and Apple Back layers in the Layers panel (which is where you want it to reside). If not, drag the Stem layer to the correct position before continuing.

7. **Draw the outline of the stem on the active Stem layer. Again, overlap the bottom of the Stem shape with the Apple Front shape.**

   You now have all the outlines for the apple, with each outline on its own layer. When you start adding gradient meshes in the next stage of the project, you will see how important it is to use a different layer for each element.

The Stem shape overlaps the Apple Front shape.

8. **Save the file and continue to the next exercise.**

CREATE A GRADIENT MESH

A gradient mesh is basically a special type of fill. Each point in the mesh can have a different color value; the colors of adjacent mesh points determine the colors in the gradient between the two points. When you paint objects with a mesh, it's similar to painting with ink or watercolor. It takes considerable practice to become proficient with gradient meshes.

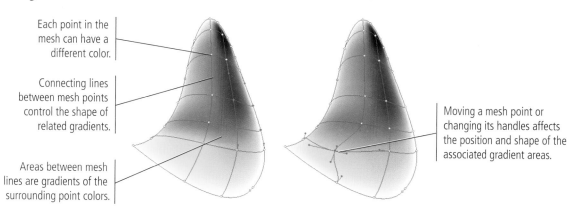

Each point in the mesh can have a different color.

Connecting lines between mesh points control the shape of related gradients.

Areas between mesh lines are gradients of the surrounding point colors.

Moving a mesh point or changing its handles affects the position and shape of the associated gradient areas.

One of the techniques you apply in this project is Illustrator's Outline mode. Outline mode allows you to see the points and paths of an object without the colors and fills. This viewing mode can be very useful when you need to adjust anchor points of one shape while viewing the underlying objects.

1. **With apple.ai open, lock and hide the Apple Back and Stem layers, and then select the Apple Front layer.**

2. **Using the Selection tool, select the outline shape on the Apple Front layer.**

3. **Using the Eyedropper tool, click a medium-red color in the apple image to fill the selected apple shape with the sampled color.**

   You can add a gradient mesh to a path without filling it with color first; but if you don't choose a color, the mesh will automatically fill with white. It's easier to create a good mesh if you start with a fill that colors most of the object.

Note:

When you convert a path to a mesh, the shape is no longer a path. You cannot apply a stroke attribute to a gradient mesh object.

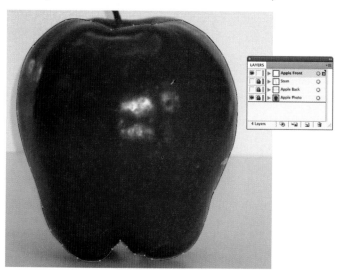

4. **Choose Object>Create Gradient Mesh and make sure the Preview option is checked.**

5. **In the Create Gradient Mesh dialog box, set the Rows value to 8 and the Columns value to 9, and make sure the Appearance menu is set to Flat.**

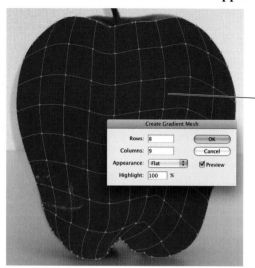

The Rows and Columns settings determine how many lines will make up the resulting mesh.

6. **Click OK to create the mesh.**

Gradient Mesh Options

When creating a gradient mesh, the numbers of rows and columns you create depends on the size and shape of the object you want to create. You might want to experiment with these settings before you click OK and create the mesh. If you add too many mesh points, the colors blend incorrectly and take a long time to paint; if you add too few mesh lines, it can be difficult — if not impossible — to add enough depth to the illustration. (Even though you can use the Mesh tool to add and delete mesh lines later, it's more efficient to create a mesh as close as possible to what you need as the final result.)

The Appearance option in the Create Gradient Mesh dialog box determines how colors affect the mesh you create:

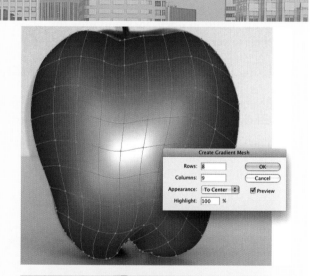

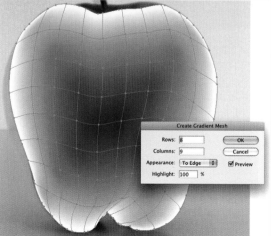

- The **Flat** option, which you used in this exercise, spreads a single color to all points in the mesh. If you don't fill the shape with a color before creating the mesh, the mesh object will fill with solid white.

- The **To Center** option (right top) creates a white highlight at the center of the mesh and gradually spreads highlight color outward toward the edges of the object. The Highlight (%) field controls the strength of the white highlight in the resulting mesh.

- The **To Edge** option (right top) is essentially the opposite of the To Center option; the white highlight appears around the edges of the mesh, blending to the solid color in the center of the mesh object.

7. Choose View>Outline.

In Outline mode, you see only the edges or **wireframes** of the objects in the file.

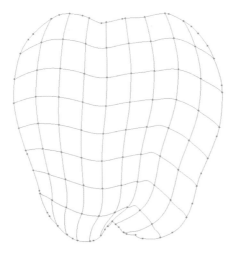

Note:

In our screen shots, we have the bounding box turned off to better show only the mesh points. You can turn off the bounding box by choosing View>Hide Bounding Box.

8. Command/Control-click the eye icon next to the Apple Photo layer to return it to Preview viewing mode.

You can now see the mesh wireframe and the actual pixels of the apple image, enabling you to sample colors directly from the apple image, and then use those colors to paint the mesh points.

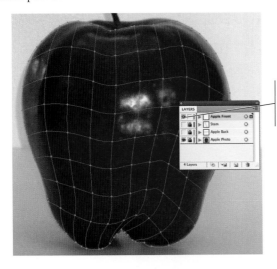

The iris in the icon is hollow when a layer displays in Outline mode.

Note:

When working in Outline mode, Command/Control-clicking a layer's visibility icon (the eye icon) returns only that layer to Preview mode.

9. Using the Direct Selection tool, click the top-left point on the inside of the mesh object to select only that mesh point.

Don't select one of the mesh points on the outside edge of the shape.

10. **With the mesh point selected, choose the Eyedropper tool in the Tools panel, and then click next to the selected mesh point to sample the color from the apple photo.**

Because the mesh object is still displayed in Outline mode, you can't see the effect of the color sampling.

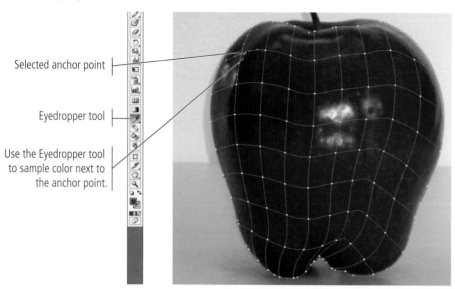

Selected anchor point

Eyedropper tool

Use the Eyedropper tool to sample color next to the anchor point.

11. **Press Command/Control to temporarily access the Direct Selection tool, and then click the next mesh point on the same vertical mesh line.**

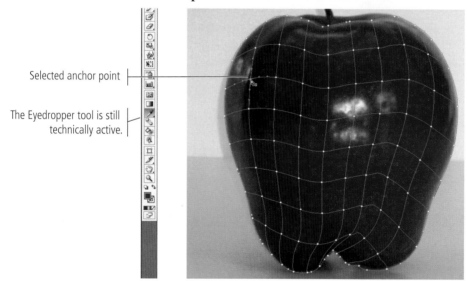

Selected anchor point

The Eyedropper tool is still technically active.

12. **Release the Command/Control key to return to the Eyedropper tool, and then sample the color next to the selected mesh point.**

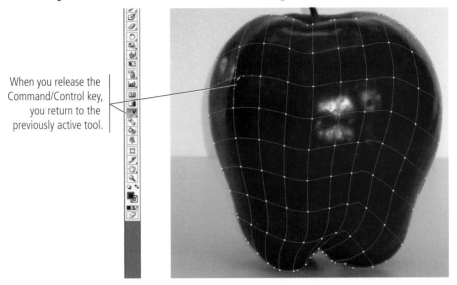

When you release the Command/Control key, you return to the previously active tool.

13. **Continue this process to change the color of the mesh points in the first three columns of the mesh.**

14. **Choose View>Outline to see the actual content of the visible layers.**

This highlights a bug in the application.

The View>Outline command is typically a toggle, which changes to View>Preview when you are already in Outline mode. However, displaying one layer in Preview mode when already in Outline mode seems to break the command. You have to choose View>Outline to return all layers to Preview mode. The menu command then reverts to its correct behavior, toggling between View>Outline and View>Preview.

15. **Deselect everything on the page and review your progress.**

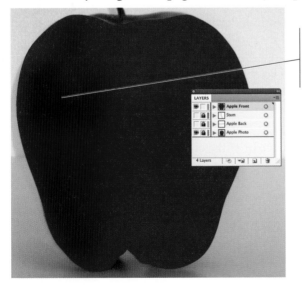

After painting only three columns of the mesh, you can already see how the shadows and highlights are starting to blend naturally.

16. **Command/Control-click the eye icon for the Apple Front layer to change only that layer to Outline mode.**

17. **Using the same technique from the previous steps, finish painting all the mesh points in the mesh object.**

    Ignore the bright highlights for now; you will add the proper highlights later.

    This task might seem tedious because there are so many points in the mesh; but with this process, you can create realistic depth in a flat vector object in a matter of minutes. To accomplish the same result using manual techniques would require many hours of time and a high degree of artistic skill.

18. **Command/Control-click the Apple Front layer eye icon to return the layer to Preview mode, and then deselect the mesh object and review your results.**

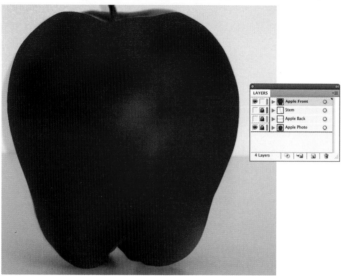

19. **Save the file and continue to the next exercise.**

 ## WORK WITH A MESH USING SMART GUIDES

It is difficult (at best) to select and manipulate points in a mesh in Preview mode because you can't see the actual mesh lines and points until the mesh object is selected. You could move your cursor around until you located the exact mesh point you wanted to work with; or you could continue switching back and forth between Preview and Outline modes. Both methods, however, can be time consuming (and frustrating).

Fortunately, Smart Guides solve this problem. Using Smart Guides, you can see the entire mesh wireframe as soon as your cursor touches any part of the object — providing a temporary outline/preview combination.

1. **With apple.ai open, choose View>Smart Guides to make sure that option is turned on.**

2. **Make sure the Snap to Point option is toggled off in the View menu.**

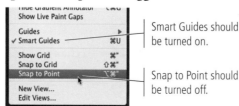

Smart Guides should be turned on.

Snap to Point should be turned off.

Note:

When using Smart Guides, make sure the Snap to Point option is toggled off. If Snap to Point is active, Smart Guides will not work (even if you have the command selected in the menu).

3. **Make sure everything in the file is deselected, and then roll the Direct Selection tool over the apple shape.**

You can now see the mesh points and lines, as well as the precise location of the Direct Selection tool.

With Smart Guides turned on you can easily view and select specific anchors in the mesh.

Using Smart Guides

In addition to being the best tool to view and select gradient mesh points, Smart Guides are also temporary snap-to guides that help you create, align, and transform objects.

Smart Guides show you when the cursor is at a precise angle relative to the original position of the object or point you're moving. When a Smart Guide is visible, it acts as a temporary snap-to guide so you can more easily maintain the correct angle (such as exactly horizontal, vertical, or 45 degrees from the origin).

You can change the appearance and behavior of Smart Guides in the Smart Guides pane of the Preferences dialog box. The Display options determine what is visible when Smart Guides are active:

- When **Alignment Guides** is active, Smart Guides show when a new or moved object aligns to the center or edge of a nearby object.a

- When **Object Highlighting** is active, moving the mouse over any part of an unselected object shows the anchors and paths that make up the object.

- When **Transform Tools** is active, Smart Guides display when you scale, rotate, or shear objects.

- When **Anchor/Path Labels** is active, Smart Guides include labels that show the type of element (path or anchor) under the cursor.

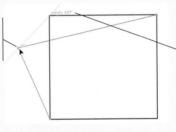

This anchor is being dragged with the Direct Selection tool.

The Smart Guide shows that the anchor is being moved at a 45-degree angle from the original position.

- When **Measurement Labels** is active, Smart Gudies show the distance and angle of movement.

- When **Construction Guides** is active, Smart Guides appear when you move objects in the file at or near defined angles (0°, 45°, 90°, and 135° are the default angles). A number of common angle options are built into the related menu, or you can type up to six specific angles in the available fields.

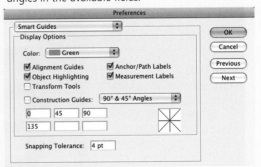

4. **Command/Control-click the visibility icon for the Apple Front layer so you can see the photo behind the mesh object.**

5. **Using the Eyedropper tool, sample the highlight color on the top-left side of the apple shape.**

   You're going to use the Mesh tool to create the rest of this highlight. By choosing a color from the existing highlight on your mesh object, rather than taking a sample from the photo, the highlight you create will blend more naturally with the highlight already in the top part of the mesh object.

   Sample the color from this highlight.

6. **Command/Control-click the visibility icon for the Apple Front layer to restore that layer to Preview mode.**

7. **Choose the Mesh tool from the Tools panel.**

   The Mesh tool adds new gridlines to an existing mesh, or it creates a mesh if you click inside a basic shape that doesn't currently have a mesh.

8. **Click the third horizontal mesh line, between the first and second vertical mesh lines, to create a new vertical mesh line (as shown in the following image).**

   The mesh is visible because the cursor is hovering over the object and Smart Guides are active.

   Mesh tool cursor

   Mesh tool

   The highlight color sampled in Step 5 is active in the Fill box.

   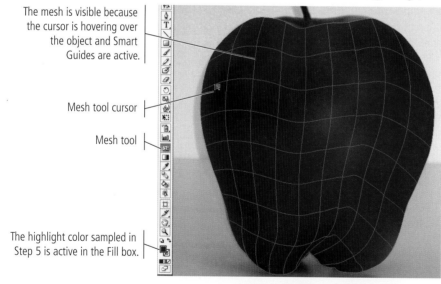

   Note:

   Clicking a horizontal mesh line with the Mesh tool creates a new vertical mesh line. To add a horizontal mesh line, click the Mesh tool on a vertical mesh line.

   Clicking this horizontal mesh line with the Mesh tool adds a new vertical mesh line, already colored with the highlight color you sampled in the previous step.

9. Press Command/Control and click away from the mesh object to deselect it.

10. Change the Apple Front layer to Outline mode, then use the Eyedropper tool to sample the highlight along the top-front curve of the apple photo.

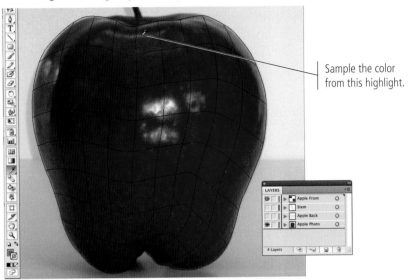

Sample the color from this highlight.

11. Select the Mesh tool. Click twice on the vertical mesh line directly below the stem to add two horizontal mesh lines between the first two rows of the existing mesh.

It isn't necessary to return the layer to Preview mode before adding lines to the mesh.

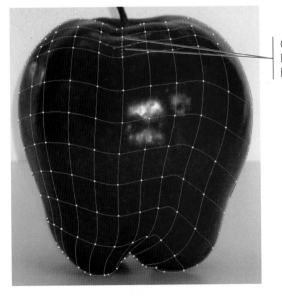

Click this vertical mesh line twice to add two horizontal mesh lines.

Note:

It might be helpful to deselect the mesh after adding the first new mesh line, and then click again to add the second mesh line.

12. Using the Direct Selection tool, select the point on the (now) second horizontal mesh line, directly below the stem.

This is one of the mesh lines you created with the Mesh tool in the previous step.

13. **With the mesh point selected, use the Eyedropper tool to sample the light red of the apple's highlight to change the color of the point.**

When you change the color of a mesh point, you change the way surrounding colors blend into that point's color. By changing this point to a medium red, you reduce the distance over which the highlight color (in the lower point) can blend — effectively shortening the highlight area.

Changing this anchor point to a lighter red adds a highlight to the apple graphic, more closely matching the highlight in the original image.

Note:

Remember, pressing Command/Control with another tool selected temporarily accesses the Direct Selection tool.

14. **Command/Control-click to select the mesh point to the immediate left of the point where you placed the highlight.**

15. **Release the mouse button to return to the Eyedropper tool, and then sample the highlight color again to spread the highlight horizontally across the apple.**

16. **Repeat Steps 14–15 for the point to the right of the one you changed in Step 13.**

By filling these two anchors with the highlight color, you extend the highlight horizontally along the mesh line.

17. **Deselect the mesh object, return the Apple Front layer to Preview mode, and review your work.**

The highlight adds depth, but it spreads a bit too far (compared to the original image).

18. **Using the Direct Selection tool, drag up the three mesh points immediately below the highlight points.**

Reducing the distance between the points shortens the distance of the blended highlight-colored area.

Moving the anchors below the highlight shortens the height of the blended highlight.

As soon as you move the cursor over the object, the mesh lines become visible.

19. **Continue adjusting the colors of the mesh points until you are satisfied with the result.**

20. **Choose View>Smart Guides to toggle off the Smart Guides.**

21. **Save the file and continue to the next exercise.**

 ## COLOR THE REMAINING OBJECTS

Building and coloring the shape for the apple's front should have given you a good idea of how mesh points control color blending from one point to another. Because you set up the file using layers for the individual shapes that comprise the apple, it will be fairly easy to create additional meshes for the remaining pieces of the apple.

1. **With apple.ai open, lock and hide the Apple Front layer, and then show and unlock the Apple Back layer.**

2. **Using the Selection tool, select the shape on the Apple Back layer.**

3. **Using the Eyedropper tool, click a darker part of the apple to fill the selected shape with the sampled color.**

4. **Choose Object>Create Gradient Mesh and add a 3-row, 5-column mesh with the Appearance menu set to Flat.**

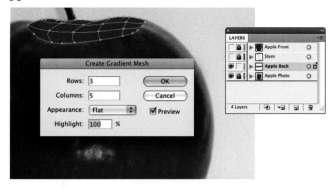

5. **Use the same method you learned in the previous exercise to color the mesh points for the Apple Back shape.**

    Switch the Apple Back layer to Outline mode, and then use the Eyedropper tool to sample colors from the photo for each point in the mesh.

6. **Show the Apple Front layer and review your work.**

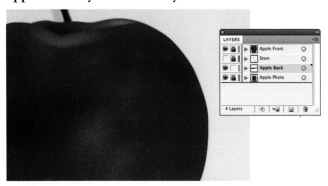

7. **Lock the Apple Back layer, and show and unlock the Stem layer.**

8. **Select the stem shape and fill it with a color sampled from the lightest color near the top of the stem.**

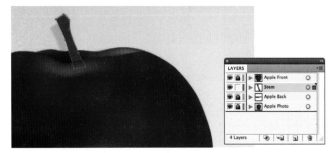

9. **Change the Stem layer to Outline mode.**

10. **Deselect all objects, and then use the Eyedropper tool to sample the dark color of the stem.**

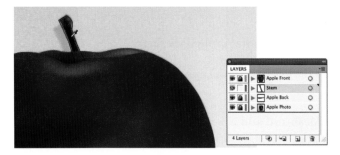

11. **Return the Stem layer to Preview mode.**

12. **Using the Mesh tool, click in the middle of the stem shape to create a mesh.**

The stem shape is converted to a mesh, and a new mesh point (with the color you sampled in Step 10) is added where you click.

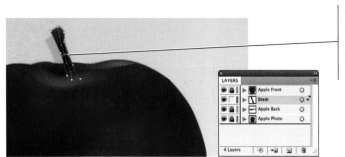

Clicking with the Mesh tool converts the stem shape to a mesh object and adds a point (and the associated lines) where you click.

13. Deselect everything, and then hide the Apple Photo layer to review your work.

14. Show the Apple Photo layer again, save the file, and continue to the next exercise.

USE FILTERS TO ADD OBJECT HIGHLIGHTS

As with any illustration, painting, or drawing, the details separate good work from great work. In this exercise, you add the highlights on the front and left sides of the apple to finish the illustration.

1. With **apple.ai** open, hide and lock the Apple Front, Apple Back, and Stem layers.

2. Create a new layer named **Highlights** and move this layer to the top of the stack in the Layers panel.

3. Using the Pen tool with a 1-pt black stroke and no fill, create the shapes of the highlights on the front and left side of the apple.

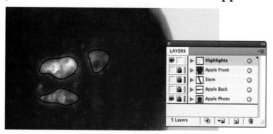

4. Select all the highlight shapes you drew in Step 3 and fill them with a color sampled from the highlights in the photo.

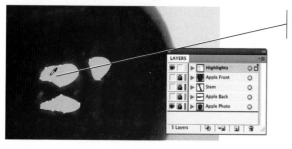

We sampled the image here to fill the selected objects.

5. **Deselect all objects. Select one of the larger highlight shapes and choose Effect>Stylize>Feather.**

   Make sure you choose from the Illustrator Effects list (at the top of the menu) and not the Photoshop Effects list. (You will learn more about these effects, including the difference between the two sets, in Project 6.)

6. **Activate the Preview option in the Feather dialog box, and then set the Feather Radius to 0.2 in.**

   The Feather effect softens the edges of the shape, blending from fully opaque to fully transparent. A higher Feather Radius value extends the distance from opaque to transparent color in the effect.

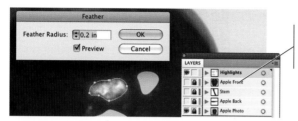

It is difficult to evaluate the actual results while the Apple Front layer is hidden.

7. **Click OK, and then show the Apple Front layer.**

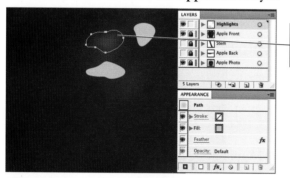

With the Apple Front layer showing, the large feather radius appears weak.

Using the Appearance Panel

ILLUSTRATOR FOUNDATIONS

The Appearance panel (Window>Appearance) allows you to review and change the appearance attributes of objects, including stroke, fill, transparency, and applied effects.

As you know, the last-used settings for fill color, stroke color, and stroke weight are applied to new objects. Other attributes, such as the applied brush or effects, are not automatically applied to new objects. If you need to create a series of objects with the same overall appearance, you can turn off the **New Art Has Basic Appearance** option in the Appearance panel Options menu.

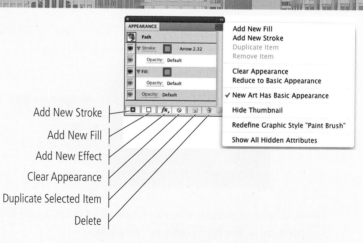

Add New Stroke
Add New Fill
Add New Effect
Clear Appearance
Duplicate Selected Item
Delete

Clicking the **Clear Appearance** button reduces the selected object to a fill and stroke of None. Choosing **Reduce to Basic Appearance** in the panel Options menu resets an object to only basic fill and stroke attributes; fill color and stroke weight and color are maintained, but all other attributes are removed.

You can also use the **Duplicate Selected Item** button to create multiple versions of the same attribute for a single object, such as two different stroke weights and colors. This option allows you to compound the effect of different attributes without layering multiple objects on top of one another. If you want to remove a specific attribute from an object, simply select that item in the panel and click the panel's Delete button.

8. **With the feathered object selected, open the Appearance panel.**

Effects in Illustrator are non-destructive attributes, which means they do not permanently change the object being styled. Because these effects are stored as object attributes, you can change the settings for any effect at any time.

9. **In the Appearance panel, click the Feather hot text to open the dialog box for that appearance attribute.**

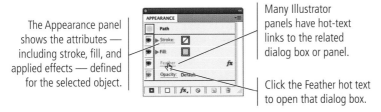

The Appearance panel shows the attributes — including stroke, fill, and applied effects — defined for the selected object.

Many Illustrator panels have hot-text links to the related dialog box or panel.

Click the Feather hot text to open that dialog box.

10. **Make sure the Preview option is checked, and then experiment with the Feather Radius setting until you are satisfied with the highlight.**

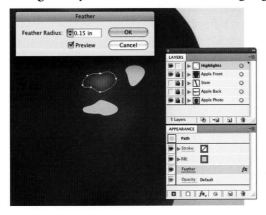

11. **Apply the Feather effect to all highlight areas, changing the Feather Radius value as appropriate for each object.**

12. **Delete the Apple Photo layer, and then show and unlock all remaining layers.**

13. Select everything on the Artboard and drag all objects to the top-left corner of the Artboard. Lock all layers.

14. Save the file and continue to the next stage of the project.

Type Terminology

Before you jump into the exercises in this stage of the project, you should understand the terms that are commonly used when people talk about type. Keep the following terms in mind as you work through the following exercises.

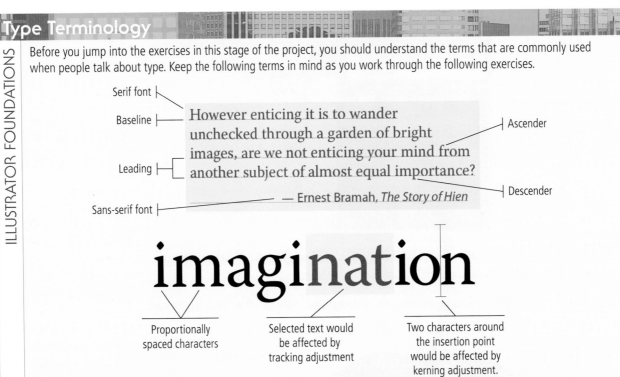

Serif font
Baseline
Leading
Sans-serif font

Ascender
Descender

However enticing it is to wander unchecked through a garden of bright images, are we not enticing your mind from another subject of almost equal importance?
— Ernest Bramah, *The Story of Hien*

imagination

Proportionally spaced characters

Selected text would be affected by tracking adjustment

Two characters around the insertion point would be affected by kerning adjustment.

Type is typically divided into two basic categories: serif and sans serif. **Serif type** has small flourishes on the ends of the letterforms; **sans-serif** has no such decorations (**sans** is French for "without"). There are other categories of special or decorative fonts, including script, symbol, dingbat, decorative, and image fonts.

The actual shape of letters is determined by the specific **font** you use; each character in a font is referred to as a **character** or **glyph**. Fonts can be monospaced or proportionally spaced. In a monospace font, each character takes up the same amount of space on a line; in other words, a lowercase i and m occupy the same horizontal space. In a proportionally spaced font, different characters occupy different amounts of horizontal space as necessary.

The **x-height** of type is the height of the lowercase letter x. Elements that extend below the baseline are called **descenders** (as in g, j, and p); elements that extend above the x-height are called **ascenders** (as in b, d, and k).

The size of type is usually measured in **points** (there are approximately 72 points in an inch). When you define a type size, you determine the distance from the bottom of the descenders to the top of the ascenders (plus a small extra space above the ascenders called the **body clearance**).

When you set type in a digital application, it rests on a non-printing line called the **baseline**. If a type element has more than one line in a single paragraph, the distance from one baseline to the next is called **leading** (pronounced "ledding"). Most applications set the default leading as 120% of the type size.

Stage 2 Working with Type

To create a complete logo, you pair logo artwork with text that makes up the corporate brand (the company name and tagline, if there is one). Illustrator includes sophisticated tools for controlling type — from changing the font and size to controlling the appearance of quotes and using styles to format long blocks of text.

In this stage of the project, you use some of the basic type formatting options to set your client's company name. You also use illustration techniques to manipulate the individual letter shapes in the company name to create the finished logotype.

CREATE POINT-TYPE OBJECTS

Creating type in Illustrator is fairly simple; simply click with the Type tool and type. Many advanced options are also available, such as importing type from an external file, using type areas to control long blocks of text, and so on. In this project, you concentrate on the basic type-formatting controls.

1. **With apple.ai open (from your WIP>Organics folder), create a new layer named Logotype at the top of the layer stack.**

2. **Choose the Type tool in the Tools panel, and then click the empty area of the Artboard to the right of the apple graphic.**

   There are two basic kinds of type (or text) objects you can create in Illustrator: **point-type objects** (also called **path type**), where the text usually resides on a single line or path; and **area-type objects,** where the text fills a specific shape, usually a rectangle.

   When you single-click with the Type tool, you create **point type**. You'll see a flashing **insertion point** where text will appear when you begin typing.

3. **With the insertion point flashing, type apple.**

   When you add a new type object (whether point type or area type) without changing anything in Illustrator, the type is automatically set in the last-used font and type settings, which will probably be different from one computer to the next.

Note:

If you want to add another type object, you have to first deselect the one where the insertion point is flashing. To accomplish this, you can Command/Control-click away from the currently active type object. Remember: Pressing Command/Control temporarily switches to the Selection tool; when you release the Command/Control key, you return to the previously active tool — in this case, the Type tool.

You can also choose Select>Deselect, and then click again with the Type tool to create a new type object.

Use these swatches to change the color of text fill and strokes.

When working with text, the Control panel includes the most common text formatting options.

When you click the Type tool, Illustrator automatically switches to a black fill and no stroke (unless you define different defaults).

Type tool

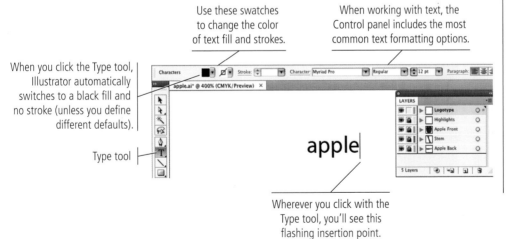

Wherever you click with the Type tool, you'll see this flashing insertion point.

4. **Choose the Direct Selection tool in the Tools panel.**

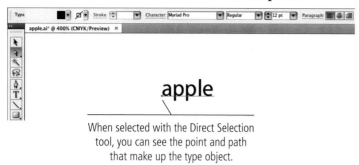

When selected with the Direct Selection tool, you can see the point and path that make up the type object.

5. **With the type object selected, click the Paragraph Align Center button in the Control panel.**

Individual characters do not need to be selected to change text formatting. Changes made while a type *object* is selected apply to all text in that type object.

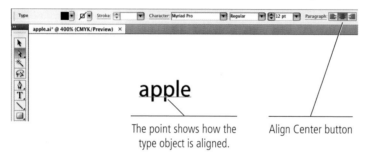

The point shows how the type object is aligned.

Align Center button

6. **Click the arrow to the right of the Font menu. Scroll through the list of available fonts and choose ATC Oak Normal.**

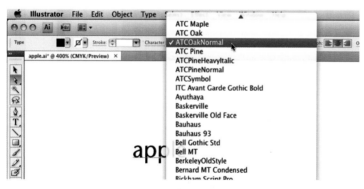

Note:

You can simply type in the Font field to find a specific font. As you type in the field, Illustrator skips to the first available font with the characters you type (for example, typing "Aar" would automatically find an installed font named Aardvark).

7. **Click the Selection tool in the Tools panel.**

When the Selection tool is active, you can see the bounding box of the type object. Like any other object, you can use the bounding box handles to stretch, scale, or rotate the type object (including the characters in the type object).

8. **Click any of the type object's corner handles and drag out to make the type larger.**

   We turned Smart Guides on (View>Smart Guides) to show the cursor feedback in our screen shots.

9. **In the Control panel, click the Character hot text to open the Character panel directly below the hot text.**

   In addition to the font and size values available in the main Control panel, the Character panel provides access to all the character-formatting options that can be applied in Illustrator.

The size menu shows the new size that results from resizing the object by dragging its bounding box handles.

If you do not constrain the resizing process, you might have a horizontal or vertical scale other than 100% of the font size.

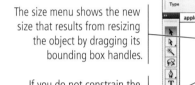
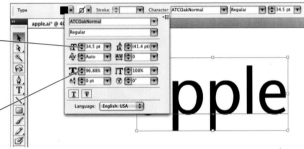

   Some argue that you should never artificially scale type horizontally or vertically (as you did in Step 8) because it distorts the spacing and shape of characters, and requires more processing time for an output device to accurately output the non-standard type sizes.

   However, this type will eventually be converted to vector outlines so artificially scaling the type will cause no problems.

10. **In the Character panel, change the Size field to 72. Make sure both the horizontal and vertical scale values are set to 100%.**

   Pressing Tab moves through the panel fields; as soon as you move to a new field, your changes in the previous field are reflected in the document. You can also press Return/ Enter to apply a change and collapse the Character panel back into the Contol panel.

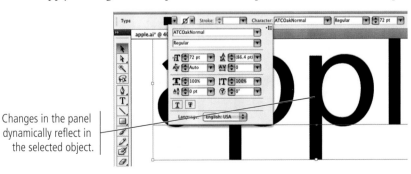

Changes in the panel dynamically reflect in the selected object.

11. **Using the Type tool, double-click the word "apple" to select all the letters in the word, and then open the Character panel (from the Control panel or the Window menu).**

Tracking and kerning are two terms related to the same value — the horizontal spacing between characters in a line of text. Remember: kerning is the spacing between two specific characters; tracking refers to the spacing between all characters in a selection.

Most industrial-quality font families come with built-in kern and track values. Smaller type does not usually pose tracking and kerning problems; when type is very large, however, spacing often becomes an issue. To fix spacing problems, you need to adjust the kerning and/or tracking values.

Note:

Kerning and tracking are largely a matter of personal preference. Some people prefer much tighter spacing than others.

12. **Change the Tracking field to –25 to tighten the space between all selected letters.**

You can change the field manually, choose a pre-defined value from the Tracking menu, or click the up- or down-arrow button to change the tracking by 1 unit with each click.

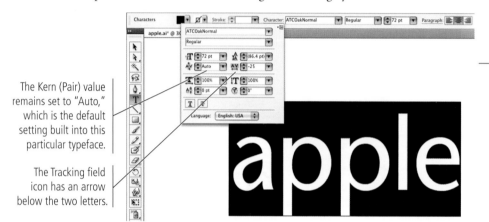

The Kern (Pair) value remains set to "Auto," which is the default setting built into this particular typeface.

The Tracking field icon has an arrow below the two letters.

Note:

If you use the panel's arrow buttons or menus to make changes, you don't need to press Return/Enter to apply the change.

13. **Click with the Type tool to place the insertion point between the "a" and the "p".**

This is a good example of a **kern pair** that needs adjustment. The Auto setting built into the font leaves a little too much space between the two characters — even after you've tightened the tracking considerably.

14. **Change the Kerning value to –20.**

Like tracking, you can change this value manually, choose a value from the pop-up menu, or use the Kerning field buttons to change kerning by 1 unit.

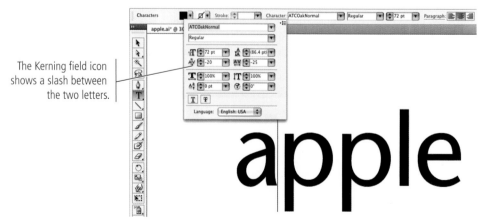

The Kerning field icon shows a slash between the two letters.

Note:

These slight modifications to tracking and kerning improve the overall appearance and readability of the headline. Later in the project, you will use a different technique to adjust letter spacing. For now, however, you should become familiar with making this type of manual adjustment.

15. **Save the file and continue to the next exercise.**

ILLUSTRATOR FOUNDATIONS

The Character panel, accessed either from the Control panel hot text or as an independent panel by choosing Window>Type>Character, includes all the options you can use to change the appearance of selected text characters.

If these options are not visible, choose Show Options in the panel Options menu.

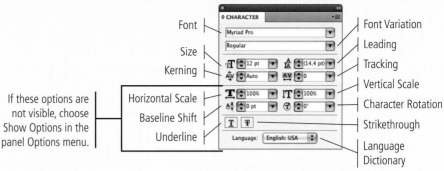

Font
Size
Kerning
Horizontal Scale
Baseline Shift
Underline

Font Variation
Leading
Tracking
Vertical Scale
Character Rotation
Strikethrough
Language Dictionary

- **Leading** is the distance from one baseline to the next. Adobe applications treat leading as a character attribute, even though leading controls the space between lines of an individual paragraph. (Space between paragraphs is controlled using the Space Before option in the Paragraph panel.) To change leading for an entire paragraph, you must first select the entire paragraph. This approach means you can change the leading for a single line of a paragraph by selecting any character(s) in that line; however, changing the leading for any character in a line applies the same change to the entire line that contains those characters.

- **Kerning** increases or decreases the space between pairs of letters. Kerning is used in cases where particular letters in specific fonts need to be manually spread apart or brought together to eliminate a too-tight or too-spread-out appearance. Manual kerning is usually necessary in headlines or other large type elements. (Many commercial fonts have built-in kerning pairs, so you won't need to apply much hands-on intervention with kerning. Adobe applications default to the kerning values stored in the **font metrics**.)

- **Tracking**, also known as "range kerning," refers to the overall tightness or looseness across a range of characters. Tracking and kerning are applied in thousandths of an **em** (or the amount of space occupied by an uppercase "M," which is usually the widest character in a typeface).

- **Vertical Scale** and **Horizontal Scale** artificially stretch or contract the selected characters. This scaling is a quick way of achieving condensed or expanded type if those variations of a font don't exist. (Type that has been artificially condensed or expanded too much looks bad because the scaling destroys the type's metrics; if possible, use a condensed or expanded version a font before resorting to horizontal or vertical scaling.)

- **Baseline Shift** moves the selected type above or below the baseline by a specific number of points. Positive numbers move the characters up; negative values move the characters down.

- **Character Rotation** rotates only selected letters, rather than rotating the entire type object.

- **Underline** places a line below the selected characters.

- **Strikethrough** places a line through the middle of selected characters.

- In addition to these options, several artificial type styles (**All Caps**, **Small Caps**, **Superscript**, and **Subscript**) can be applied using the panel Options menu.

Point Type vs. Area Type

Clicking with the Type tool creates a point-type object. Clicking and dragging with the Type tool creates an area-type object. **Point type** (or path type) starts at a single point and extends along or follows a single path. **Area type** fills up an area (normally a rectangle). The following images show point type on the left and area type on the right.

The difference between the two kinds of type becomes obvious when you try to resize them or otherwise modify their shapes using the Selection tool. Area type is contained within an area. If you resize that area, the type doesn't resize; it remains within the area but simply flows (or wraps) differently. If you scale or resize point type by dragging a bounding box handle, the type within the object resizes accordingly.

This point-type object is selected with the Direct Selection tool. You can see the paths that comprise the single type object.

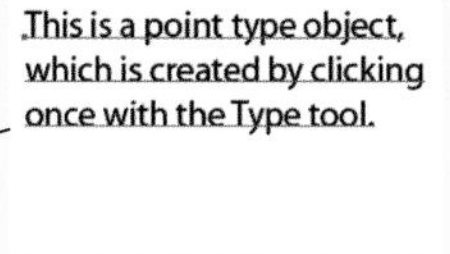

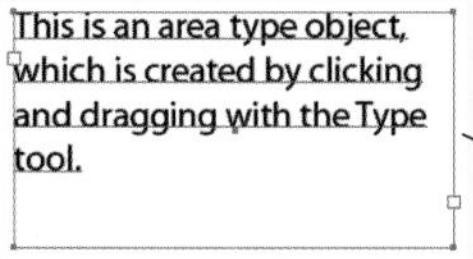

This is a point type object, which is created by clicking once with the Type tool.

This is an area type object, which is created by clicking and dragging with the Type tool.

This area-type object is selected with the Direct Selection tool. You can see the edges of the type object, but no bounding box handles appear.

The object is selected with the Selection tool. You can now see the object's bounding box handles.

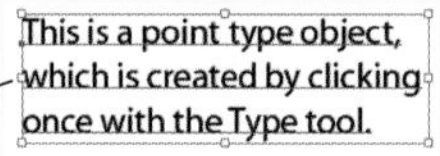

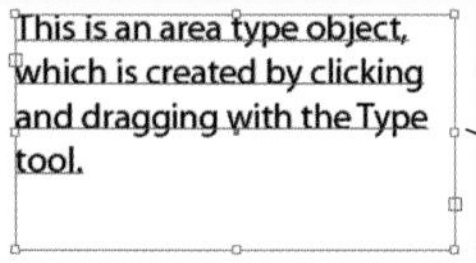

This is a point type object, which is created by clicking once with the Type tool.

This is an area type object, which is created by clicking and dragging with the Type tool.

The object is selected with the Selection tool. You can see the edges of the type object, as well as the object's bounding box handles.

Resizing the bounding box with the Selection tool resizes the text in the point-type object.

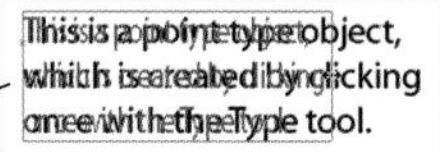

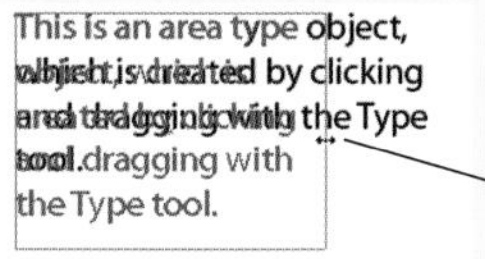

This is a point type object, which is created by clicking once with the Type tool.

This is an area type object, which is created by clicking and dragging with the Type tool.dragging with the Type tool.

Resizing the bounding box with the Selection tool resizes the object; the text rewraps inside the new object dimensions.

Another consideration is where the "point" sits on the type path. When you change the paragraph alignment of point type, the point remains in the same position; the text on the point moves to the appropriate position, relative to the fixed point.

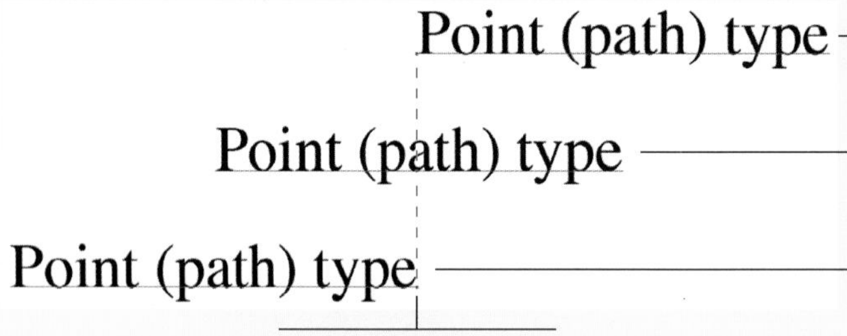

Point (path) type — Left-aligned text

Point (path) type — Center-aligned text

Point (path) type — Right-aligned text

The point for path type is determined by where you click to place the object.

(When you're working with type, it can be easier — at least at first — to work with bounding boxes turned off. You can turn off the bounding boxes for all objects — including type objects — by choosing View>Hide Bounding Box.)

MANIPULATE TYPE OBJECTS

When you work with type in Illustrator, you need to be aware of a few special issues that can affect the way you interact with the application. This exercise explores some common problems that can arise when you work with type, as well as some tricks you can use to work around them.

1. **With apple.ai open, select the Type tool in the Tools panel. Click at the end of the existing type object to place the insertion point.**

2. **Move the Type tool cursor below the existing type object and click.**

When the insertion point is already flashing, you can't click with the Type tool to create a new point-type object.

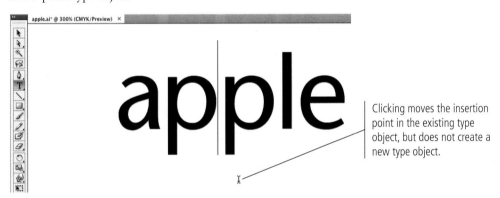

Clicking moves the insertion point in the existing type object, but does not create a new type object.

3. **With the insertion point flashing, press Command/Control.**

As you know, this modifier key temporarily switches the active tool to the Selection tool. The bounding box of the type object remains visible as long as you hold down the Command/Control key.

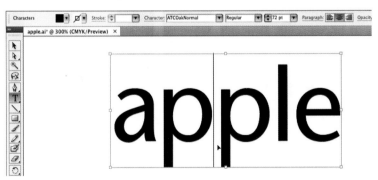

Note:

When the insertion point is flashing in a type object, you can't use the keyboard shortcuts to access tools. Because the insertion point is flashing, pressing a key adds that letter to the current type object, at the location of the insertion point.

4. **While still holding down the Command/Control key, click within the bounding box of the type object.**

When you click, you select the actual type object. The point and path become active, and the insertion point no longer flashes. You can use this method to move or modify a type object without switching away from the Type tool.

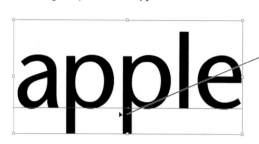

Clicking to select the type object reveals the type path and alignment point.

Note:

While working in a type object, you can simply Command/Control-click away from the object to deselect it (and effectively turn off the insertion point). You can then release the Command/Control key to return to the Type tool, and then click the Artboard to create a new type object.

5. **Release the Command/Control key to return to the Type tool.**

6. **Click below the existing type object to create a new type object.**

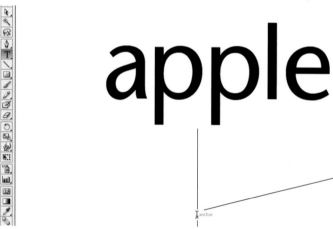

Because the insertion point was not flashing, you can click with the Type tool to create a new type object.

7. **Type** organics.

When you add a new type object, the type is automatically set using the last-used formatting options.

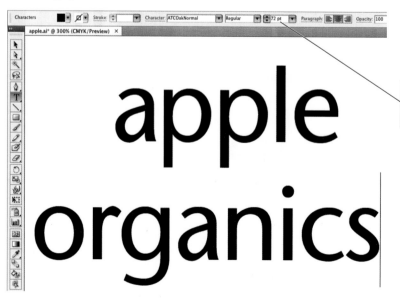

The new type object has the same formatting as the last-used settings.

8. **Press Command/Control. Click the new type object and drag it up until the descender of the second "p" in apple aligns with the stem of the "g" in the word "organics."**

Leave approximately 0.1" between the baseline of "apple" and the x-height of the letters in "organic."

Note:

Remember: Turn Rulers on by choosing View>Show Rulers.

The layer color shows the position of the type object.

9. **Release the mouse button to reposition the type object, and then release the Command/Control key to return to the Type tool.**

10. **Save the file and continue to the next exercise.**

CONVERT TYPE TO OUTLINES

In Illustrator, fonts — and the characters that comprise them — are like any other vector object. They are comprised of anchors and paths, which you can modify just as you would any other vector object. To access the anchor points, however, you must first convert the text to outlines.

1. **With `apple.ai` open, use the Selection tool to select both type objects in the file.**

2. **Choose Type>Create Outlines.**

When you convert the type to outlines, the anchor points and paths that comprise the letter shapes appear.

3. **Click away from the objects to deselect them, and then click the word "apple."**

4. **In the Layers panel, click the arrow to the left of the Logotype layer name to expand the layer.**

   In addition to arranging layers, you can use the expanded lists in the Layers panel to review and manage the individual objects on each layer (called **sublayers**).

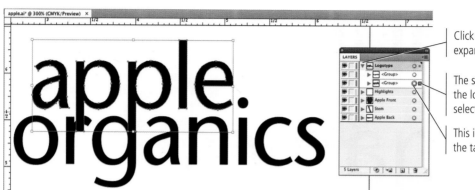

Click this arrow to expand the layer.

The square identifies the location of the selected object(s).

This icon indicates the target object.

5. **In the Layers panel, expand the apple group.**

6. **Click the Target icon for the first (lowest) "p" to select only that object.**

   By expanding the individual layers, you can use the Layers panel to access and work with individual objects in a group, without ungrouping the objects.

Click the Target icon to select or deselect a specific object within a group.

7. **Press the Right Arrow key to nudge the selected object right (narrowing the space between the letter shapes).**

   You could have fine-tuned the letter spacing with the tracking and kerning controls. Since you're working with these letters as graphics, however, it's easier to adjust the letters as shapes relative to the overall logotype.

Note:

*Open the General pane of the Preferences dialog box to change the distance an object moves when you press the arrow keys (called the **keyboard increment**).*

Note:

Press Shift and an arrow key to move an object 10 times the default keyboard increment.

8. Repeat Step 7 to move the "a" shape right, and again to move the "l" and "e" shapes left.

9. In the Layers panel, collapse the apple group and expand the organics group.

10. Click the Target icon for the "s" shape, and then Shift-click the Target icons for the "c", "i", "n", and "a" shapes.

   Just as Shift-clicking objects selects multiple objects, Shift-clicking the Target icons allows you to easily select multiple objects within a group.

11. Press the Left Arrow key to nudge the selected shapes left.

12. In the Layers panel, shift-click the Target icon for the selected "a" letter shape.

   Shift-clicking a selected object (Target icon) deselects that object only.

13. Press the Left Arrow key to nudge the remaining selection left.

14. Continue selecting and nudging the letter shapes to reduce the spacing between all letters in the word "organics." Use the following image as a guide.

15. Save the file and continue to the next exercise.

CREATE CUSTOM GRAPHICS FROM LETTER SHAPES

The logo text is no longer type, so you can apply your drawing skills to create a unique logotype. Remember: You can use the Add Anchor Point tool to add points to a vector path, use the Delete Anchor Point tool to remove points from a vector path, and use the Convert Anchor Point tool to convert smooth points to corner points (and vice versa). All three of these tools are nested below the Pen tool in the Tools panel.

1. With **apple.ai** open, use the Direct Selection tool to adjust the anchor points at the bottom of the "p" to follow the same arch as the lowercase "r".

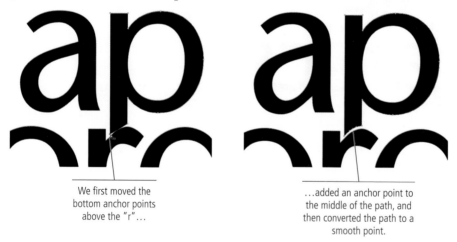

We first moved the bottom anchor points above the "r"...

...added an anchor point to the middle of the path, and then converted the path to a smooth point.

2. Using the Direct Selection tool, click the second "p" in the word "apple". Press Shift, and then click the "g" in the word "organics".

3. **Using the Pathfinder panel (Window>Pathfinder), unite the two selected shapes into a single shape.**

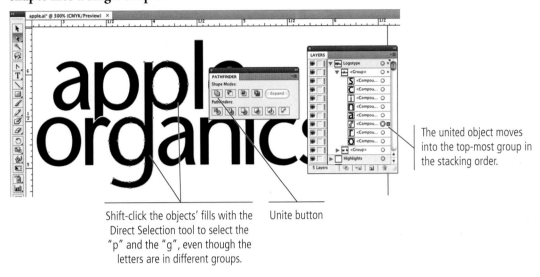

The united object moves into the top-most group in the stacking order.

Shift-click the objects' fills with the Direct Selection tool to select the "p" and the "g", even though the letters are in different groups.

Unite button

4. **Using the Direct Selection tool, click the edge of the dot (above the letter "i") to show the anchor points of that shape. Use what you know about points and handles to change the dot to a leaf shape.**

5. **In the Layers panel, click the Target icon for the "i" shape to select the entire compound path. Change the fill color of the selected object to a medium green from the built-in swatches.**

6. **Select both groups of type shapes and group them.**

7. **Zoom out so you can see the apple artwork and the logotype graphics.**

8. **In the Control panel, click the Transform hot text to open the Transform panel. Make sure the W and H fields are linked, and type 250% in the W panel.**

When you press Return/Enter (or simply click away from the Transform panel), the logotype group is scaled proportionally to 250% of its original size.

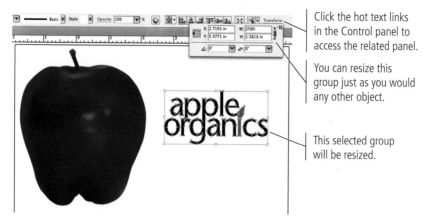

Click the hot text links in the Control panel to access the related panel.

You can resize this group just as you would any other object.

This selected group will be resized.

Note:

The appearance of the Transform hot text depends on the width of your Application frame/ monitor; if you have enough vertical screen space, the Transform hot text is replaced by individual X, Y, W, and H fields. In that case, you can click any of those field names to open the Transform panel.

9. **Drag the logotype group so the "a" and "o" closely align with the bottom contour of the apple shape. Use the following image as a guide.**

10. **Save the file and continue to the next stage of the project.**

ILLUSTRATOR FOUNDATIONS

When the Artboard tool is active, the Control panel presents a number of options for adjusting the active Artboard.

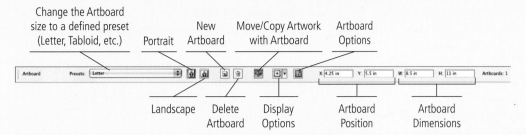

Change the Artboard size to a defined preset (Letter, Tabloid, etc.) · Portrait · New Artboard · Move/Copy Artwork with Artboard · Artboard Options

Landscape · Delete Artboard · Display Options · Artboard Position · Artboard Dimensions

Clicking the Artboard Options button opens a dialog box where you can further manage and control the selected Artboard.

Most of these options (Preset, Width, Height, Orientation, and Position) are the same as those available in the Control panel. The remaining choices are explained here:

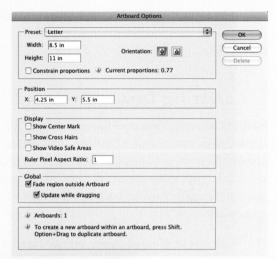

- **Constrain Proportions** maintains a consistent aspect ratio (height to width) if you resize the Artboard.

- The Display options (also available in the Display menu of the Control panel) determine what is visible when the Artboard tool is active. **Show Center Mark** displays a point in the center of the crop area. **Show Cross Hairs** displays lines that extend into the artwork from the center of each edge of the crop area. **Show Video Safe Areas** displays guides that represent the areas that fall inside the viewable area of video.

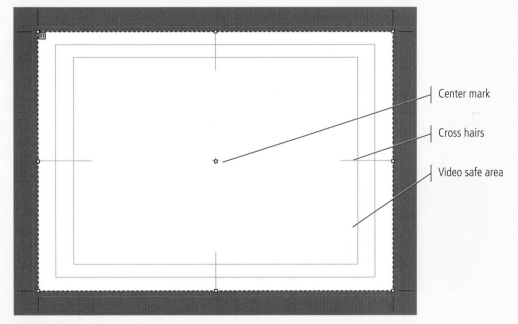

Center mark

Cross hairs

Video safe area

- **Ruler Pixel Aspect Ratio** specifies the pixel aspect ratio used for Artboard rulers.
- **Fade Region Outside Artboard** displays the area outside the Artboard darker than the area inside the Artboard.
- **Update While Dragging** keeps the area outside the Artboard darker as you move or resize the Artboard.

Stage 3 Working with Multiple Artboards

For all intents and purposes, the Apple Organics logo is now complete. However, you still need to create the alternate versions that can be used in other applications. You need a two-color version for jobs that will be printed with spot colors, and you need a one-color version for jobs that will be printed with black ink only.

Before Illustrator CS4, creating multiple variations of a logo meant generating multiple files, with each variation residing in a separate file. This process could result in dozens of logo files that needed to be maintained and tracked for a single client. In Illustrator CS4, however, you can streamline the process by creating a single file that includes multiple Artboards, with each Artboard containing one variation of the logo.

In this stage of the project, you adjust the Artboard to fit the completed logo. You then duplicate the artwork on additional Artboards, and adjust the colors in each version to meet the specific needs of different color applications.

 ### ADJUST THE DEFAULT ARTBOARD

When you place an Illustrator file into another file (for example, a page-layout file in InDesign or even another Illustrator file) you can decide how to place that file — based on the artwork boundaries (the outermost bounding box), on the Artboard boundaries, or on other specific dimensions. To make the logo artwork more placement-friendly, you should adjust the Illustrator Artboard to fit the completed logo artwork.

1. **With apple.ai open, make sure all layers are unlocked.**

2. **Select everything on the Artboard, and then review the W and H values in the Control panel.**

   You created this file with a letter-size Artboard. As you can see, the size is both too narrow and too high for the finished artwork. (Your W and H values might be slightly different than what you see in our screen shots, but they should be in the same general ballpark.)

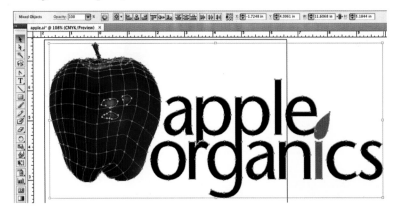

3. **Select the Artboard tool in the Tools panel.**

When the Artboard tool is active, the Artboard edge is surrounded by marching ants; you can drag the side and corner handles to manually resize the Artboard in the workspace.

The Control panel shows information about the active Artboard.

Artboard center point

Artboard tool

Drag the handles to manually resize the Artboard.

4. **In the Control panel, change the Artboard width to 11.9″ and the height to 5.4″.**

These dimensions are large enough to entirely encompass the logo artwork. If your dimensions are different than ours, use whatever values you need to fit your artwork and leave a bit of white space on all four sides.

You don't have a reference-point option when you resize the Artboard; it automatically resizes around the center point.

5. **In the Control panel, click the Move/Copy Artwork with Artboard button to turn off that option.**

   If the Move/Copy Artwork button is active, dragging the Artboard also moves the artwork. In this case, you want to move the Artboard to surround the artwork, so you need to toggle off this button, enabling you to move the Artboard independently.

6. **Click inside the resized Artboard area and drag the Artboard to surround the logo artwork.**

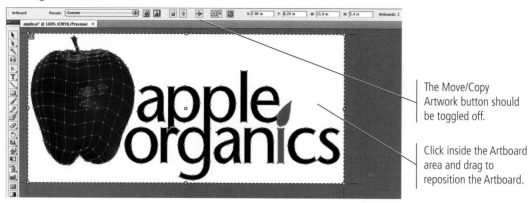

The Move/Copy Artwork button should be toggled off.

Click inside the Artboard area and drag to reposition the Artboard.

7. **Click the Selection tool to restore the Artboard to its normal state.**

8. **Save the file and continue to the next exercise.**

USE THE LAYERS PANEL TO ORGANIZE ARTWORK

Your goal is to create three separate versions of the logo — the four-color version that's already done, a two-color version for spot-color applications, and a one-color version that will be used in jobs that are printed black-only.

As you created the artwork, you used five layers to manage the arrangement and stacking order of the various elements. The Apple Back layer is behind the Stem layer, which is behind the Apple Front layer, which is behind the Apple Highlights layer. This precise order produces the effect you need to create a realistic illustration.

Now that the drawing is complete, however, you will use layers for a different purpose — to create, isolate, and manage multiple versions of the logo in a single file.

1. **With apple.ai open, make sure all layers are unlocked in the Layers panel.**

2. **Click the Target icon of the Stem layer to select the objects on that layer.**

The Selected Art icon indicates what is selected in the file.

3. **Click the Selected Art icon to the right of the Target icon and drag down to the Apple Back layer.**

   Dragging the Selected Art icon is an easy way to move objects from one layer to another without manually cutting and pasting.

4. **Expand the Apple Back layer.**

The mesh object that was on the Stem layer is now on the Apple Back layer, at the top of the sublayer stack.

The stem object guides now show the color of the Apple Back layer instead of the color of the Stem layer.

5. **Repeat Steps 2–3 for the Apple Front, Highlights, and Logotype layers.**

6. **Delete the four empty layers from the Layers panel.**

7. **Rename the Apple Back layer Four Color.**

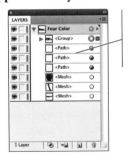

You can access the sublayers, so you can still use the panel to select, arrange, and manage individual objects.

8. **Collapse the Four Color layer to hide the sublayers.**

9. **Save the file and continue to the next exercise.**

Now that all the logo artwork resides on a single layer, the final step is to create the two alternate versions of the logo. This process is largely a matter of cloning the existing Artboard and artwork — but you need to complete a few extra steps to convert the mesh objects to standard filled paths.

1. **With apple.ai open, choose the Artboard tool in the Tools panel.**

2. **In the Control panel, click the Move/Copy Artwork with Artboard button to toggle on that option.**

3. **Place the cursor inside the Artboard area. Press Option/Alt-Shift and then click and drag down to clone the existing Artboard.**

   You might want to zoom out so you can see the entire original Artboard and the empty space below it.

The Move/Copy Artwork option should be toggled on.

Because the Move/Copy Artwork option is toggled on, the logo artwork and the Artboard are both cloned at the same time.

Pressing Option/Alt allows you to clone the existing Artboard, just as you would clone a regular drawing object.

4. **When the new Artboard/artwork is entirely outside the boundaries of the first Artboard, release the mouse button.**

The Control panel shows that the file has two Artboards.

5. **Add a new layer to the file. Change the new layer's name to Two Color.**

6. **Using the Selection tool, drag a marquee to select all the objects on the second Artboard.**

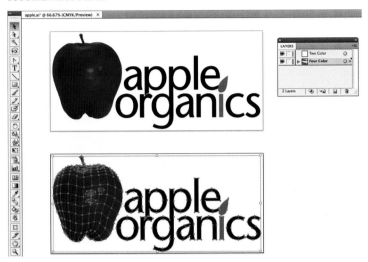

7. **In the Layers panel, drag the Selected Art icon from the Four Color layer to the Two Color layer.**

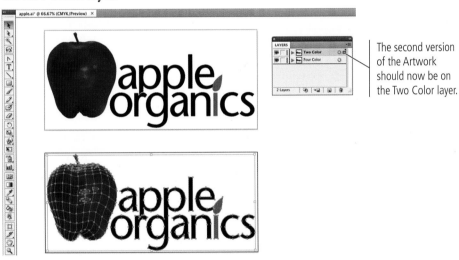

The second version of the Artwork should now be on the Two Color layer.

8. **Save the file and continue to the next exercise.**

CONVERT MESH OBJECTS TO REGULAR PATHS

When you created the gradient meshes in the first stage of this project, you saw that adding the mesh removed the original path you drew. When you worked on the mesh, you might have noticed that the Control panel showed that the selected object was transformed from a path object to a mesh object.

To create the flat two-color version of the logo, however, you need to access the original paths you drew to create the mesh objects. There is no one-step process to convert the mesh object back to a flat path object, so you need to take a few extra steps to create the flat version of the logo.

1. **With apple.ai open, expand the Two Color layer in the Layers panel.**

2. **Use the Layers panel to select the mesh object that represents the Front Apple shape, and then open the Appearance panel.**

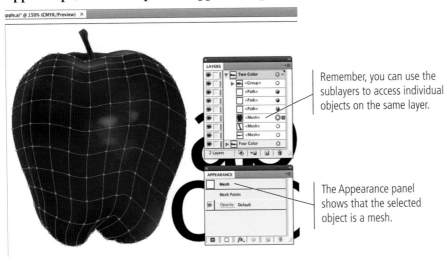

Remember, you can use the sublayers to access individual objects on the same layer.

The Appearance panel shows that the selected object is a mesh.

3. **With the mesh object selected, click the Add New Stroke button at the bottom of the Appearance panel.**

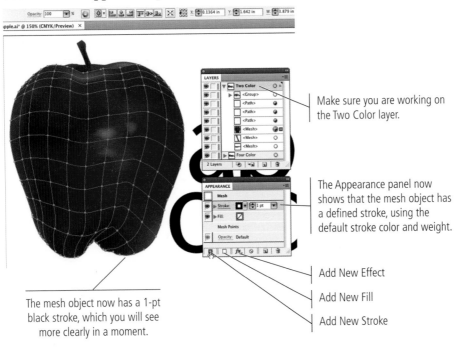

Make sure you are working on the Two Color layer.

The Appearance panel now shows that the mesh object has a defined stroke, using the default stroke color and weight.

Add New Effect

Add New Fill

Add New Stroke

The mesh object now has a 1-pt black stroke, which you will see more clearly in a moment.

Note:

Because the black-only version of the logo is also flat, you are going to create the flat two-color version first, and then clone it. Doing so avoids unnecessary repetition of the process presented in this exercise.

Note:

When working with a mesh object, it can be helpfu to turn off object bounding boxes (View>Hide Bounding Box), as you can see in these screen shots.

Note:

In addition to changing the existing attributes of an object, you can also use the Appearance panel to compound effects and attributes. In other words, you can add a new stroke to any object, including an object that already has a defined stroke.

4. **With the mesh object still selected, choose Object>Expand Appearance.**

   This command converts the selected object into separate constituent objects — one path for the shape's stroke attribute and one for the object's mesh fill — which are automatically grouped together.

5. **In the Layers panel, expand the new group.**

6. **Use the Layers panel to select only the mesh object in the group.**

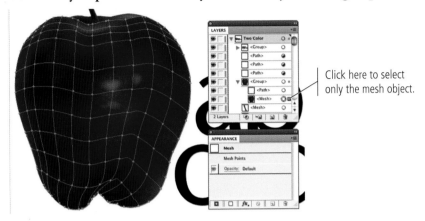

Click here to select only the mesh object.

7. **Press Delete/Backspace to remove the selected mesh object.**

   You now have a simple path object that is essentially the Apple Front shape. However, you need to complete one more step because the path is still part of the group that was created by the Expand Appearance command.

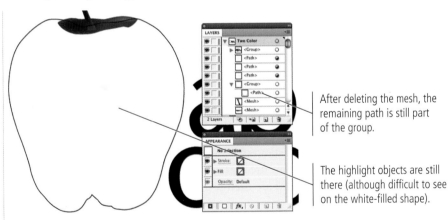

After deleting the mesh, the remaining path is still part of the group.

The highlight objects are still there (although difficult to see on the white-filled shape).

8. **Use the Layers panel to select the path in the group, and then choose Object>Ungroup.**

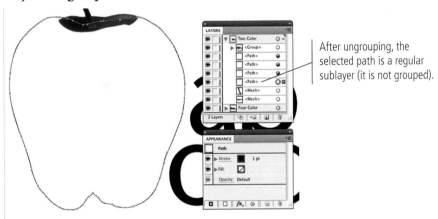

After ungrouping, the selected path is a regular sublayer (it is not grouped).

9. **Repeat this process to convert the other two mesh objects (the Stem shape and the Apple Back shape) back into standard paths with the default stroke attributes.**

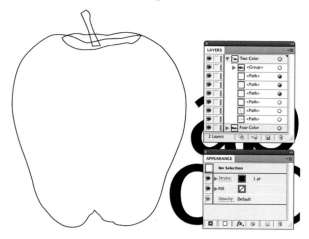

10. **Save the file and continue to the next exercise.**

 ## ADD SPOT COLOR TO THE TWO-COLOR LOGO

Spot colors are created with special premixed inks that produce a certain color with one ink layer; spot colors are not built from the standard process inks used in CMYK printing. When you output a job with spot colors, each spot color appears on its own separation. Spot inks are commonly used to reproduce colors you can't get from a CMYK build, in two- and three-color documents, and as additional separations in a process color job when an exact color (such as a corporate color) is needed.

Even though you can choose a spot color directly from the library on your screen, you should look at a swatch book to verify that you're using the color you intend. Special inks exist because many of the colors can't be reproduced with process inks, nor can they be accurately represented on a computer monitor. If you specify spot colors, and then convert them to process colors later, your job probably won't look exactly as you expect.

In the United States, the most popular collections of spot colors are the Pantone Matching System (PMS) libraries. TruMatch and Focoltone are also used in the United States. Toyo and DICColor (Dainippon Ink & Chemicals) are used primarily in Japan.

1. **With apple.ai open, choose Window>Swatch Libraries>Color Books>Pantone Solid Coated.**

    Illustrator includes swatch libraries of all the common spot color libraries. You can open any of these libraries to access the various colors available in each collection.

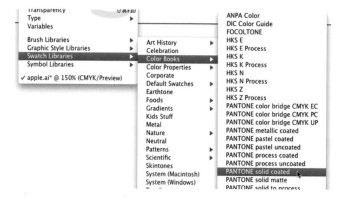

2. **In the Pantone Solid Coated library Options menu, choose Small List View to show the color names for each swatch.**

It is often easier to view swatches with their names and samples, especially when you need to find a specific swatch (as in this exercise).

Note:

The View options in the panel Options menu are available for all swatch panels, including colors, patterns, and brushes. You use many types of swatches in Project 4.

3. **On the Artboard, select the shape that represents the apple front (on the Two Color layer).**

4. **Scroll through the Pantone swatch Library panel until you find Pantone 188 C.**

5. **Make sure the Fill icon is active in the Tools panel, and then click Pantone 188 C in the swatch Library panel.**

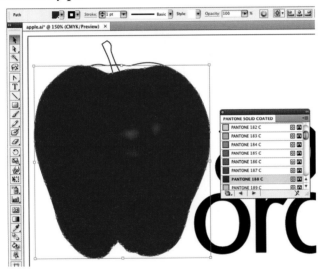

6. **Review the Swatches panel (Window>Swatches).**

When you apply a color from a swatch library, that swatch is added to the Swatches panel for the open file.

This is the Pantone color swatch.

7. **Using whichever method you prefer, change the stroke color of the selected object to None.**

8. **Select and delete the three highlight shapes.**

In a flat logo, the highlight shapes are unnecessary. In fact, the technical aspects involved in reproducing the feather effect applied to those shapes can cause output problems.

9. Select the Apple Back shape. Apply Pantone 188 C as the fill color and None as the stroke color.

10. Select the stem shape. Swap the current stroke and fill colors so the shape is filled with black and has no stroke.

Note:

Keep in mind that the swatch libraries are not the same as the Swatches panel for the open file.

11. Select the shape that comprises the "p" and "g" in the logotype and change the fill color to Pantone 188 C.

12. Select the "i" shape. Change the fill color to white (not None) and change the stroke to 2-pt Pantone 188 C.

Because our leaf overlaps the "e", we used white as the fill color instead of None.

13. Choose the Artboard tool. With the Move/Copy Artwork option still active, press Option/Alt and then click and drag down to clone the flat version.

14. Move the artwork on the third Artboard to a new layer named `One Color`. Change all Pantone 188 C elements in the third version to black.

Change all Pantone 188 C elements in this version to black.

15. Save the file, close it, and then continue to the final stage of the project.

Stage 4 **Combining Text and Graphics**

The final stage of this project requires two additional layouts: a letterhead and a business envelope. Rather than addding more Artboards to the logo file, you are going to create a new file that will contain both pieces of stationery. This means you must place the logos from the original apple.ai file, and understand how to work with objects that are placed from external files.

WORK WITH PLACED GRAPHICS

Some production-related concerns dictate how you design a letterhead. In general, there are two ways to print a letterhead: commercially in large quantities or one-offs on your desktop laser or inkjet printer. (The second method includes a letterhead template, which you can use to write and print your letters from directly within a page-layout program. While this method is quite common among designers, it is rarely done using Illustrator.)

If your letterhead is being printed commercially, it's probably being printed with multiple copies on a large press sheet, from which the individual letterhead sheets will be cut. (In fact, most commercial printing happens this way.) This type of printing typically means that design elements can run right off the edge of the sheet, called **bleeding**. If you're using a commercial printer, always ask the output provider whether it's safe (and cost-effective) to design with bleeds, and find out how much bleed allowance to include.

If you're designing for a printer that can only run letter-size paper, you need to allow enough of a margin area for your printer to hold the paper as it moves through the device (called the **gripper margin**); in this case, you can't design with bleeds.

Note:

Older desktop printers typically have a larger minimum gripper margin; you're usually safe with 3/8" margins. Newer inkjet printers often have the capability to print 8.5×11" sheets with full bleed. In either case, consult your printer documentation before you design your document.

1. **Open the New Document dialog box (File>New). Name the new file stationery, with 1 Artboard that is letter-size in portrait orientation. Define 0.125" bleeds on all four sides, CMYK color mode, and 300 PPI raster effects.**

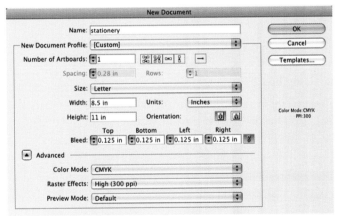

2. **Click OK to create the new file.**

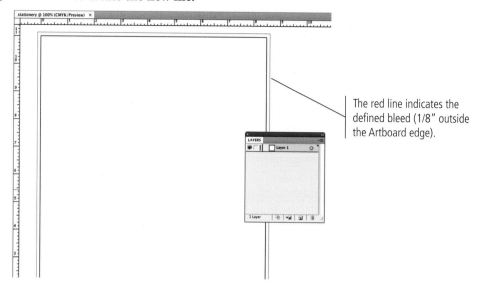

The red line indicates the defined bleed (1/8″ outside the Artboard edge).

3. **Choose File>Place. Navigate to the file apple.ai in your WIP>Organics folder, make sure Link and Template are both unchecked, and then click Place.**

Until now, you have placed raster images in the JPEG format. Different types of files, however, have different options that determine what is imported into your Illustrator file.

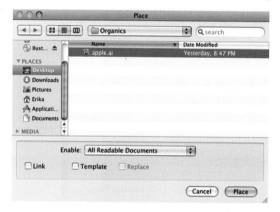

4. **Review the options in the Place dialog box.**

Although you're placing a native Illustrator (.ai) file, the dialog box shows options for placing PDF files. Illustrator files use PDF as the underlying structure (which is what enables multiple Artboard capability), so the options are the same as the ones you would see if you were placing a PDF file.

5. **Make sure Media is selected in the Crop To menu, and then click OK to place the logo artwork.**

6. **If you get a warning about an unknown image construct, click OK to dismiss it.**

For some reason, gradient mesh objects *created in Illustrator* are unrecognized *by Illustrator* when the logo file is placed into another Illustrator file. Gradient meshes are imported into the new file as "non-native art" objects that can't be edited in the new file unless you use the Flatten Transparency command to turn them into embedded raster objects.

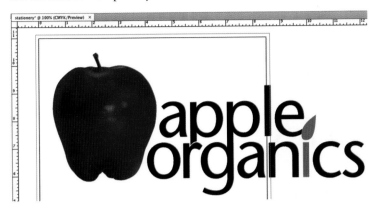

Note:

Because you set the logo file's raster effects to 300 ppi at the beginning of this project, the resulting gradient mesh object should still output properly.

7. **Open the General pane of the Preferences dialog box. Make sure the Scale Strokes & Effects option is checked, and then click OK.**

If this option is checked, scaling an object also scales the applied strokes and effects (including the Feather effect you used to create the front highlight objects) proportionally to the new object size. For example, reducing an object by 50% changes a 1-pt stroke to a 0.5-pt stroke. If this option is unchecked, a 1-pt stroke remains a 1-pt stroke, regardless of how much you reduce or enlarge the object.

Note:

On Macintosh, open the Preferences dialog box in the Illustrator menu. On Windows, open the Preferences dialog box in the Edit menu.

8. **With the placed artwork selected, transform the artwork to 3″ wide (constrained). Use the Selection tool to move the placed logo to the top-left corner of the Artboard, approximately 1/8″ from the top and left edges (as shown in the following image).**

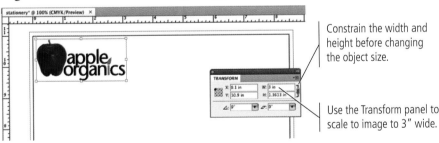

Constrain the width and height before changing the object size.

Use the Transform panel to scale to image to 3″ wide.

Note:

Remember, your original artwork might be a slightly different size than ours, so your resized height might also be slightly different than what is shown here.

9. **Open the Layers panel. Expand the sublayer groups until you see the individual shapes in the sublayer thumbnails.**

When the file is imported, certain objects (such as meshes and other raster effects) are rasterized and clipped, enabling Illustrator to replicate the artwork in the original file.

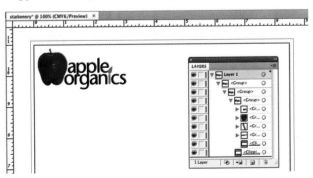

Note:

When you create a new file, the Raster Effects setting determines the resolution of raster objects that are created by Illustrator to output effects like gradient meshes and feathering.

10. Using the Type tool, click to create a new point-type object. Type 564 Orchard Way. Format the type as 10-pt ATC Oak Normal with right paragraph alignment, and apply a medium-red swatch as the type fill color.

11. Using the Selection tool, position the type object directly to the left of the "g" descender (use the following image as a guide).

12. Clone the type object (Option/Alt-click-drag) immediately to the right of the "g" descender. Change the cloned object to left paragraph alignment, and then change the type to Orange, FL 35682.

Note:

Press Shift while cloning the type object to move the clone exactly horizontal from the original.

13. Choose File>Place. Navigate to the file leaves.eps in the RF_Illustrator> Organics folder and click Place.

EPS stands for Encapsulated PostScript. This format is commonly used for vector-based images such as those you create in Illustrator — especially when saving files for older page-layout applications that do not support the native Illustrator format. In this case, you do not have additional options when you place the file into Illustrator; it is **parsed** (processed) and placed onto the Illustrator Artboard.

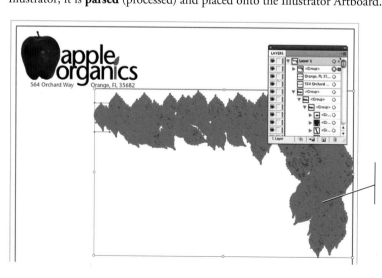

When processed and placed, vector artwork in the file becomes accessible.

14. **Drag the placed graphic so the edges of the artwork bleed past the edge of the Artboard area. Use the following image as a guide.**

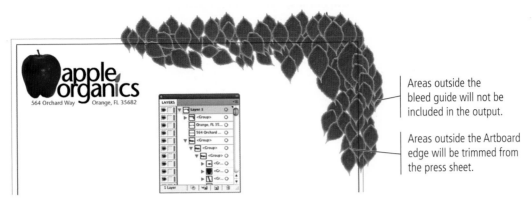

Areas outside the bleed guide will not be included in the output.

Areas outside the Artboard edge will be trimmed from the press sheet.

15. **Save the file as an Illustrator file named** stationery.ai **in your WIP>Organics folder, and then continue to the next exercise.**

CREATE THE ENVELOPE LAYOUT

In general, printed envelopes can be created in two ways. You can create and print the design on a flat sheet, which will be specially **die cut** (stamped out of the press sheet), and then folded and glued into the shape of the finished envelope. Alternatively (and usually at less expense), you can print on pre-folded and -glued envelopes.

Both of these methods for envelope design have special printing requirements, such as ensuring no ink is placed where glue will be applied (if you're printing on flat sheets), or printing far enough away from the edge (if you're printing on pre-formed envelopes). Whenever you design an envelope, consult with the output provider that will print the job before you get too far into the project.

In this case, the design will be output on pre-folded #10 business-size envelopes (4-1/8″ by 9-1/2″). The printer requires a 1/4″ gripper margin around the edge of the envelope where you cannot include any ink coverage.

Note:

*The **live area** is the "safe" area inside the page edge, where important design elements should remain. Because printing and trimming are mechanical processes, there will always be some variation, however slight. Elements too close to the page edge run the risk of being accidentally trimmed off.*

1. **With** stationery.ai **open, zoom out until you can see the entire Artboard and an equal amount of space to the right.**

2. **Choose the Artboard tool. In the Control panel, click the New Artboard button.**

3. **Place the cursor over the area right of the existing Artboard.**

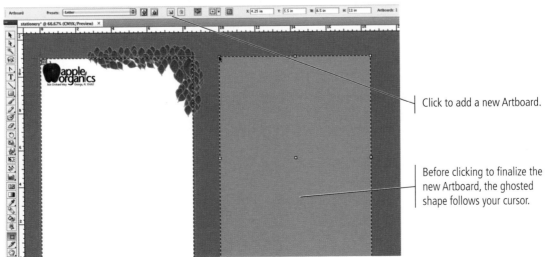

Click to add a new Artboard.

Before clicking to finalize the new Artboard, the ghosted shape follows your cursor.

4. **Click to create a second Artboard.**

5. **With the second Artboard active, use the fields in the Control panel to change the Artboard dimensions to W: 9.5″, H: 4.13″.**

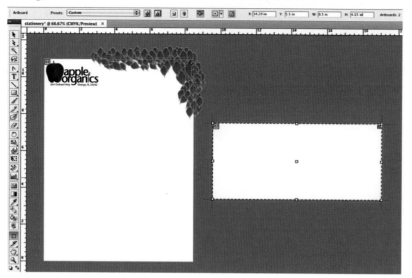

6. **Choose File>Place. Navigate to the file apple.ai in your WIP>Organics folder and click Place.**

7. **In the Place PDF dialog box, click the right-arrow button to show 2 of 3, then click OK.**

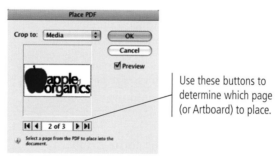

Use these buttons to determine which page (or Artboard) to place.

8. **Select the placed object with the Selection tool. Scale it to 2.5″ wide (constrained) and place it 0.25″ from the top and left edges of the envelope Artboard.**

We repositioned the zero point to the Artboard's top-left corner, which makes it easier to position the artwork.

9. Copy the type objects from the letterhead layout and paste them onto the envelope layout. Change the size of the type in the pasted objects to 8 pt and change the fill to the same Pantone color you used in the two-color logo artwork.

10. Save the file and continue to the next exercise.

Understanding Placed-Image Bounding Boxes

The **Crop To** option determines exactly what is placed into an Illustrator file. (If you are placing an Illustrator file, many of these options produce the same result).

- The **Bounding Box** setting places the file's bounding box, or the minimum area that encloses the objects on the page or Artboard.

- The **Art** setting crops incoming files relative to the size and position of any objects selected at the time of the cropping. For example, you can create a frame and use it to crop an incoming piece of artwork.

- Use the **Crop** setting when you want the position of the placed file to be determined by the location of a crop region you drew on the page (when placing an Illustrator file, this refers to the defined Artboard).

- The **Trim** setting identifies the place where the final page will be physically cut in the production process, if trim marks are present.

- The **Bleed** setting places only the area within bleed margins (if a bleed area is defined). This information is useful if the page is being output in a production environment. (The printed page may include page marks that fall outside the bleed area.)

- The **Media** setting places the area that represents the physical paper size of the original PDF document (for example, the dimensions of an A4 sheet of paper), including printers' marks.

PRINT DESKTOP PROOFS OF MULTIPLE ARTBOARDS

Before you send a file to a commercial output provider, it's a good idea to print a sample to see how the artwork looks on paper. Illustrator provides a large number of options for outputting files, including the ability to define the area that comprises the actual artwork.

There are two important points to remember about using inkjet and laser proofs. First, inkjet printers are usually not PostScript driven; because the commercial output process revolves around the PostScript language, proofs should be created using a PostScript-compatible printer if possible (if not, the proofs might not accurately represent what will appear in final output). Second, inkjet and laser printers typically do not accurately represent color.

1. **With stationery.ai open, choose File>Print.**

   The Print dialog box is divided into eight sections or categories, which display in the window on the left side of the dialog box. Clicking one of the categories in the list shows the associated options in the right side of the dialog box.

2. **In the Printer menu, choose the printer you want to use, and then choose the PPD for that printer in the PPD menu (if possible).**

   If you are using a non-PostScript printer, complete as much of the rest of this exercise as possible based on the limitations of your output device.

3. **With the General options showing, choose the Range radio button and type 1 in the field.**

   By default, all Artboards in the file are output when you click Print.

   If your printer can only print letter-size paper, you need to tile the letterhead Artboard to multiple sheets so you can output a full-size proof. Tiling is unavailable when printing multiple Artboards, so in this exercise you are printing each Artboard separately.

4. **In the Options section, make sure the Do Not Scale option is selected.**

   As a general rule, proofs — especially final proofs that would be sent to a printer with the job files — should be output at 100%.

5a. **If your printer is capable of printing oversize sheets, choose Tabloid/A3/11×17 in the Media menu. Choose the Portrait orientation option.**

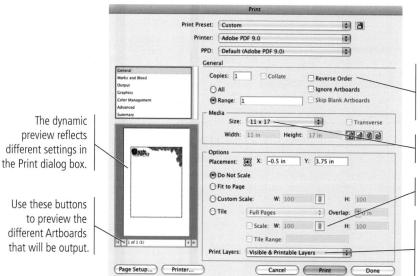

The dynamic preview reflects different settings in the Print dialog box.

Use these buttons to preview the different Artboards that will be output.

Use these options to print more than one copy and reverse the output order of the multiple Artboards (last to first).

Define the paper size used for the output.

Use these options to scale the output (if necessary).

Use this menu to output visible and printable layers, visible layers, or all layers.

5b. If you can only print to letter-size paper, choose the landscape paper orientation option, and then activate the Tile check box.

To output a letter-size page at 100% on letter-size paper, you have to tile to multiple sheets of paper; using the landscape paper orientation allows you to tile to 2 sheets instead of 4 (as shown in the preview area).

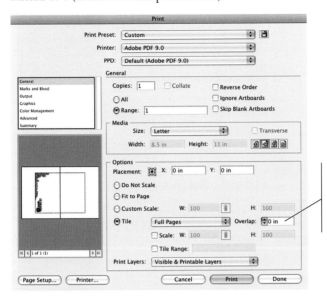

Note:

A print preset is a way to store many different settings in a single menu choice. You can create a print preset by making your choices in the Print dialog box, and then clicking the Save Preset button.

When tiling a page to multiple sheets, you can define a specific amount of space that will be included on both sheets.

6. Click the Marks and Bleed option in the list of categories on the left. Activate the All Printer's Marks option, and then change the Offset value to 0.125".

7. In the Bleeds section, check the Use Document Bleed Settings option.

When you created the stationery file, you defined 1/8" bleeds on all four sides of the Artboard. Checking this box in the Print dialog box includes that same 1/8" extra on all four sides of the output.

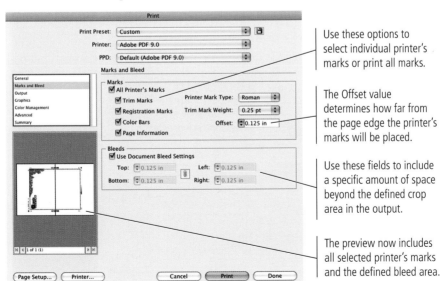

Use these options to select individual printer's marks or print all marks.

The Offset value determines how far from the page edge the printer's marks will be placed.

Use these fields to include a specific amount of space beyond the defined crop area in the output.

The preview now includes all selected printer's marks and the defined bleed area.

Note:

Some printers require printer's marks to stay outside the bleed area, which means the offset should be at least the same as or greater than the defined bleed area.

8. **Click the Output option in the list of categories on the left. Choose Composite in the Mode menu.**

   You can print all colors to a single sheet by choosing Composite, or you can print each color to an individual sheet by choosing Separations (Host-based). The third option — In-RIP Separation — allows the file data to be separated by the output device instead of by the software.

Note:

The other options in this dialog box (Emulsion and Image) are reserved for high-end commercial output to a filmsetter or imagesetter.

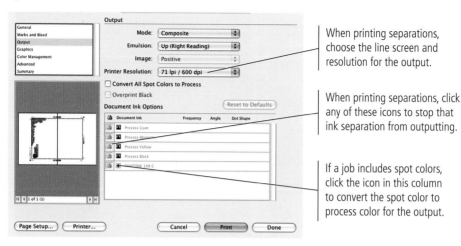

When printing separations, choose the line screen and resolution for the output.

When printing separations, click any of these icons to stop that ink separation from outputting.

If a job includes spot colors, click the icon in this column to convert the spot color to process color for the output.

9. **Click Print to output the artwork.**

10. **Choose File>Print again. Choose the Range radio button and type 2 in the field to print the envelope layout.**

11. **Choose Letter/US Letter in the Size menu and choose the Landscape orientation option. Make sure the Do Not Scale option is checked.**

   In this case, a letter-size sheet is large enough to print the envelope Artboard without scaling. (Some of the printer's marks might be cut off by the printer's gripper margin, but that is fine for the purpose of a desktop proof.

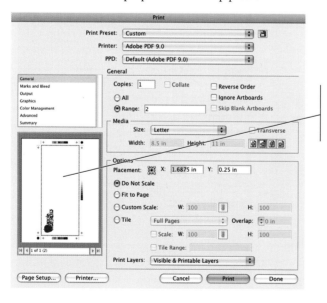

The preview area shows that the envelope Artboard will fit on a letter-size page at 100% if you use landscape orientation.

12. **Click Print to output the envelope proof.**

13. **When the document comes back into focus, save and close it.**

1. The _____ can be used to draw a new Artboard in the current file.

2. Press _____ and click the Eye icon on a specific layer to switch only that layer between Preview and Outline mode.

3. When _____ are active, moving your cursor over an unselected object reveals the paths that make up that object.

4. The _____ tool is used to sample colors from an object already placed in the file.

5. The _____ is used to monitor and change the individual attributes (fill, stroke, etc.) of the selected object.

6. The _____ is the imaginary line on which the bottoms of letters rest.

7. _____ is the spacing between specific pairs of letters (where the insertion point is placed).

8. The _____ command makes the vector shapes of letters accessible to the Direct Selection tool.

9. A _____ is a special ink used to reproduce a specific color, typically used for one- or two-color jobs.

10. Click the _____ in the Layers panel to select a specific sublayer.

1. Explain the advantages to using a gradient mesh, compared to a regular gradient.

2. Briefly explain two primary differences between point-type objects and area-type objects.

3. Explain the potential benefits of using multiple Artboards rather than different files for different pieces.

Use what you learned in this project to complete the following freeform exercise.
Carefully read the art director and client comments, then create your own design to meet the needs of the project.
Use the space below to sketch ideas; when finished, write a brief explanation of your reasoning behind your final design.

art director comments

Your client, Tracey Dillon, is a local architect. She has hired you to create a corporate identity package so she can begin marketing her services to local land development companies. She has asked you first to develop a logo, and then to create the standard identity pieces that she can use for business promotion and correspondence.

To complete this project, you should:

❑ Develop a compelling logo that suggests the agency's purpose (architectural services).

❑ Incorporate the agency's name (TD Associates) into the logo.

❑ Build the letterhead and envelope with the same technical specs that you used to design the Apple Organics pieces.

client comments

I've decided to open my own architectural services firm, and I need to start advertising. That means I need to brand my business so companies who need an architect will recognize and remember my name. I'm calling my business TD Associates.

I want a logo that really says 'architect', and I want the central color in my logo to be blue — like the blue you'd see on a blueprint.

Once the logo is finished, I need you to use the logo on business cards, letterhead, and envelopes that I will have preprinted; I want a more professional feel than I can create using my laser printer. The printer I spoke with said I could do this for less money if I go 4-color for the letterhead, but 2-color for the envelope.

Eventually, I'll be incorporating my logo into all kinds of advertising — newspaper, local magazines, and even the Internet; I'd like you to create whatever versions you think I'll need for any purpose.

project justification

Logos are one of the most common types of artwork that you will create in Illustrator. These can be as simple as text converted to outlines, or as complex as a line drawing based on an object in a photograph. Most logos will actually be some combination of drawing and text-based elements. As you learned throughout this project, one of the most important qualities of a logo is versatility — the ability to use it in many different types of projects and output it in many different types of print processes. To accomplish this goal, logos should work equally well in grayscale, four-color, and spot-color printing.

By completing this project, you worked with complex gradients to draw a realistic apple, then added creative type treatment to build the finished logotype. After completing the initial logo, you converted it to other variants that will work with different output processes (two-color and one-color). Finally, you incorporated the logo artwork into completed stationery to help solve your client's communication needs as he expands his business.

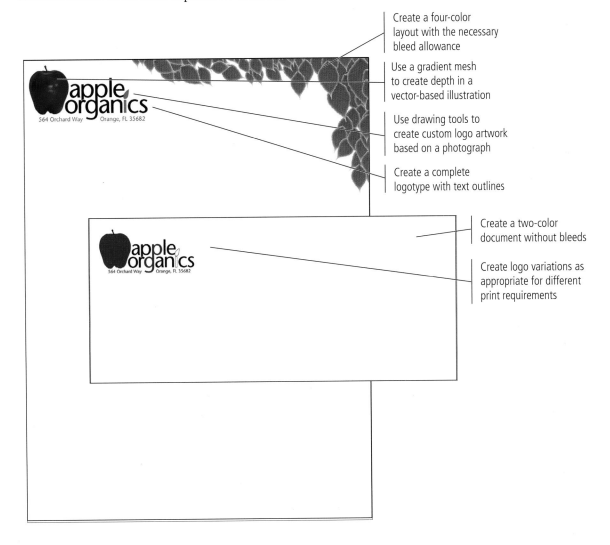

Create a four-color layout with the necessary bleed allowance

Use a gradient mesh to create depth in a vector-based illustration

Use drawing tools to create custom logo artwork based on a photograph

Create a complete logotype with text outlines

Create a two-color document without bleeds

Create logo variations as appropriate for different print requirements

Realty Development Map

Your client is a real estate developer who needs an illustrated map of a new community development. Phase I of the development is already complete; Phase II is getting underway. The developer wants the map to show the overall property, available and sold homes in Phase I, and available and sold home sites in Phase II.

This project incorporates the following skills:

❏ Accessing and managing built-in libraries of swatches, brushes, and symbols

❏ Defining custom art and pattern brushes for specific applications

❏ Applying and controlling brush strokes in relation to paths

❏ Saving user-defined libraries of custom assets

❏ Opening and using symbol libraries created by other users

❏ Understanding and creating symbols and symbol instances

❏ Transforming symbol instances and editing symbol artwork

❏ Swapping symbols in placed instances

❏ Creating a clipping mask

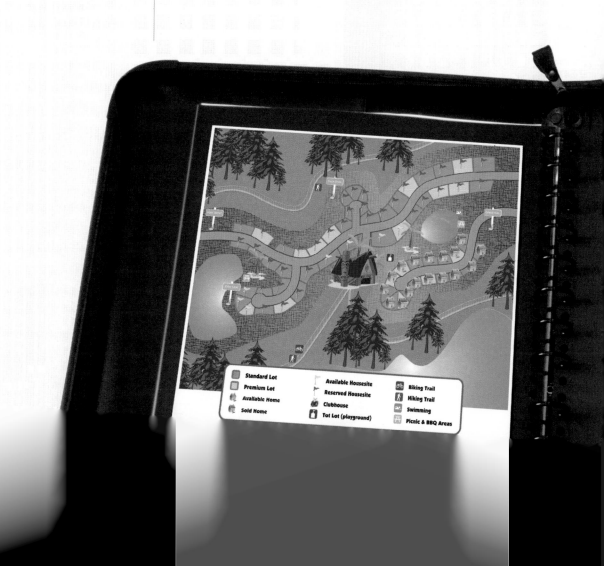

Project Meeting

We're ready to launch a big marketing push on Phase II of our housing development, and we want to include an illustrated map in marketing materials and newspaper advertisements. I sent a sketch of the property to your art director, and I already approved the icons she showed me when we first met about this project.

I want to be able to change the map every time we sell a home in Phase I and reserve a lot or complete a building in Phase II. I forgot to bring the current sale information, but I will send it to you as soon as I get back to my home office next week.

We advertise in many places and we never know what formats will be required. We need you to create different types of files that can be used by anyone doing print design work.

When I first met with the client, I showed him some ideas for icons we can use for the map. We also discussed the importance of creating a legend for the finished map so potential buyers can make sense of the various icons.

The client approved the icons I suggested, so I created the legend with those icons. I also created the artwork for the lot spaces because I needed to include "Standard Lot" and "Premium Lot" identifiers in the legend. I created a library where you can pull all of the various elements.

One of the most important aspects of this project for us is versatility. The client needs to be able to make changes frequently — as soon as a home is sold, a home site is reserved, or a new house is built in Phase II. As the client said, he didn't bring the current status report, so you can't mark the sold spaces right away. You can build the file, however, and mark the sales as soon as you have that information.

Anything you can do to make revisions easier will be well worth the effort later.

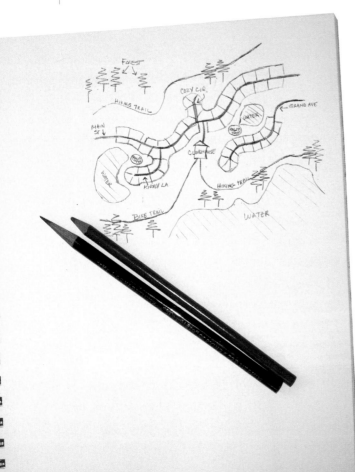

To complete this project, you will:

- ❏ Open and use built-in swatch libraries
- ❏ Define custom gradient swatches
- ❏ Create a new pattern swatch based on a built-in pattern
- ❏ Define custom art brushes to paint roads and paths
- ❏ Define a pattern brush to paint roads with cul de sac endings
- ❏ Save a custom brush library so it can be accessed again later
- ❏ Open and use an external symbol library
- ❏ Place and control symbol instances
- ❏ Edit symbols to change all placed instances
- ❏ Break the link from placed instances to the original symbols
- ❏ Swap symbols in placed instances
- ❏ Create a clipping mask to hide unwanted parts of the artwork

Stage 1　Swatches, Gradients, and Patterns

The default Swatches panel (Window>Swatches) includes a seemingly random collection of swatches from the various built-in libraries.

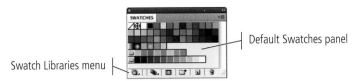

Default Swatches panel

Swatch Libraries menu

Illustrator also includes a large number of built-in swatch libraries, many of which contain thematic color schemes (such as Earthtone, Metal, and Nature). These libraries are accessed by choosing Window>Swatch Libraries or by opening the Swatch Libraries menu at the bottom of the Swatches panel.

If you open more than one swatch library from the Window>Swatch Libraries menu, each library opens as a new panel, grouped by default with other open swatch libraries. If you open a different library using the menu at the bottom of an open library panel, the new library replaces the one that was active when you opened the new library.

Note:

You can drag any library panel out of the group to manage it independently.

Opening the Neutral library from the Window>Swatch Libraries menu adds the Neutral library to the panel group with the Metal library.

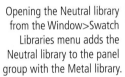

Click this button to open a different swatch library in place of the active one.

Opening the Textiles library from the panel's Swatch Libraries menu replaces the Neutral library.

The Swatches panel appears by default in Thumbnail mode. If you choose List View from the panel Options menu, you see the name of the color, as well as an icon that indicates the type of the color. Viewing swatches by name can be useful because the swatch name indicates the components of the associated color.

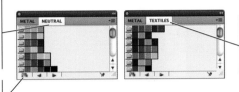

Thumbnail mode shows only the swatch.

CMYK color icon

List mode shows the swatch and the color name (based on the color components).

Note:

When a library displays in Thumbnail mode, you can roll the mouse over a specific swatch to see the swatch name in a tool tip. The same option is available for brush libraries, graphic style libraries, and symbol libraries.

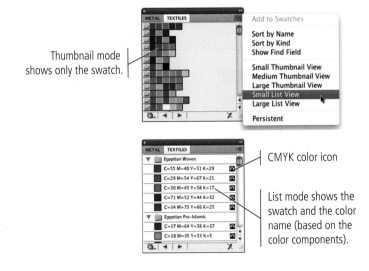

OPEN BUILT-IN SWATCH LIBRARIES

Before you begin drawing and painting, you need to prepare the workspace and import the client's sketch to use as a template. You use the sketch to create the shape of the roads, the location of the water, and the position of the various amenities available in the development. The sketch also shows the location of the clubhouse and other amenities, which you create using symbols in the second stage of this project.

1. **On your desktop, drag the Realty folder from the WIP folder on your Resource CD to the WIP folder where you will save your work.**

    Use this folder to save all files in this project.

2. **Create a new letter-size CMYK document using landscape orientation. Type map in the Name field, choose Inches as the unit of measurement, and then click OK.**

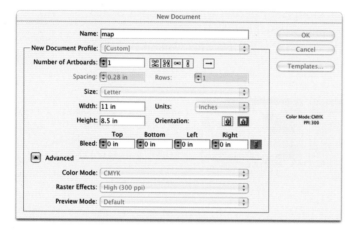

3. **Place the file sketch.jpg from the RF_Illustrator>Realty folder. Make sure the file is not linked when you place it.**

4. **Using the Align panel, align the sketch horizontally and vertically to the center of the Artboard.**

5. **Rename the default layer Sketch and convert it to a template layer.**

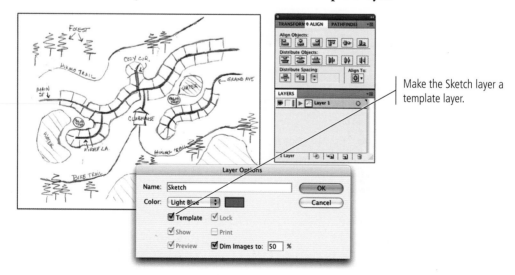

Make the Sketch layer a template layer.

6. **Choose Window>Swatch Libraries>Nature>Landscape.**

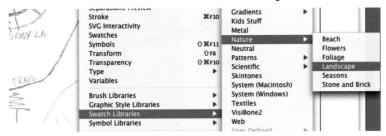

When you open the first swatch library, the library appears in its own panel.

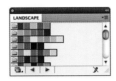

Note:

Library panels open in the same location and state as the last time they were used. If a panel is not automatically grouped with other library panels, it was already used and repositioned.

7. **Repeat Step 6 to open the Stone and Brick swatch library from the Nature collection.**

   Don't click the button at the bottom of the library panel to open the new library. Doing so would replace the Landscape library with the Stone and Brick library.

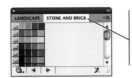

The Stone and Brick library is added to the panel group with the Landscape library.

Note:

You might want to drag this panel group to the dock and save a custom workspace so you can easily access the same libraries later.

8. **Save the file as a native Illustrator file named `map.ai` in your WIP>Realty folder, and then continue to the next exercise.**

 ## DEFINE GRADIENT SWATCHES

As you learned in Project 2, a gradient smoothly merges one color into another color. Illustrator supports both linear gradients, which move in a line from one color to another; and radial gradients, which move from one color at the center of a circle to another color at the outer edges.

Illustrator also includes a number of built-in pattern and gradient swatches, several of which are available in the default Swatches panel. You can even use the panel to only display swatches of a specific kind.

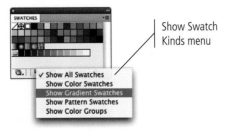

Show Swatch Kinds menu

The options in the default Swatches panel are quite limited, making that panel alone insufficient for most Illustrator jobs. To overcome this limitation, you can use other gradient and pattern swatch libraries from the Swatch Libraries menu (or from the Window>Swatch Libraries submenus).

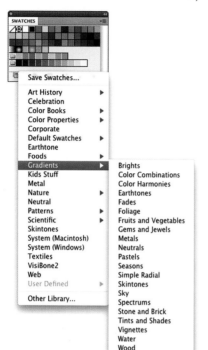

Note:

Gradient and pattern libraries, as with any other kind of swatch library, open in their own panels.

In this exercise, you create two custom gradient swatches to fill the primary areas of the map (the lake and ponds, and the grass surrounding the houses).

1. **With map.ai open, create two new layers named Water and Grass.**

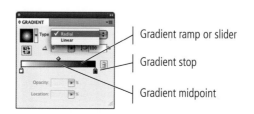

2. **Make sure the Landscape swatch library is visible. If it is not, choose Window>Swatch Libraries>Nature>Landscape.**

3. **Open the Gradient panel (Window>Gradient).**

4. **If you see only a gradient sample in the panel, open the panel Options menu and choose Show Options.**

5. **Choose Radial in the Type menu.**

If you don't see the gradient stops under the ramp, click the ramp once to show the stops.

Gradient ramp or slider

Gradient stop

Gradient midpoint

Note:

You can use the Gradient panel to define a gradient, save a specific gradient by dragging the gradient into the Swatches panel, and use the Gradient tool to apply a gradient swatch to an object on the Artboard.

6. **Drag a medium-blue swatch from the Landscape swatch library onto the right stop of the gradient ramp (in the Gradient panel).**

The stop color changes from black to blue, and the sample swatch now shows the effect of the new stop color.

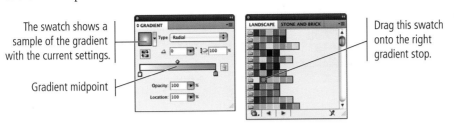

The swatch shows a sample of the gradient with the current settings.

Gradient midpoint

Drag this swatch onto the right gradient stop.

Note:

You can double-click a gradient stop to open the Color panel, where you can change the stop color without using existing swatches.

7. **Drag the gradient midpoint left until the Location field shows 30%.**

This point indicates where the colors of the two surrounding stops are equally mixed. Dragging the point extends the gradient on one side of the point and compresses the gradient on the other side.

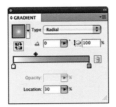

Note:

You can also simply drag a swatch to any place under the gradient ramp to add a new stop of the dragged swatch color.

8. **Open the main Swatches panel (Window>Swatches).**

9. **Click the sample swatch in the Gradient panel and drag it into the main Swatches panel.**

10. **Double-click the new swatch in the Swatches panel to open the Swatch Options dialog box. Change the swatch name to** Water Gradient **and click OK.**

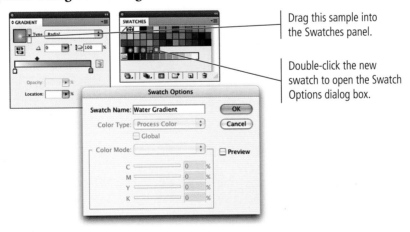

Drag this sample into the Swatches panel.

Double-click the new swatch to open the Swatch Options dialog box.

11. **In the Gradient panel, change the Type menu to Linear.**

12. **Drag a light green color to the left gradient stop, and drag a dark green color to the right gradient stop.**

By default, the midpoint retains the location from the last gradient you created.

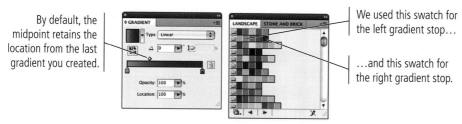

We used this swatch for the left gradient stop...

...and this swatch for the right gradient stop.

13. **Drag the gradient midpoint to 50%.**

14. **Drag the left gradient stop until the Location field shows approximately 60%.**

As you can see in the gradient ramp, most of the gradient (left of the leftmost stop) will be filled with the lighter green color.

15. **Click below the gradient ramp near the left end of the ramp.**

You can create additional stops on the gradient, each of which can have a different color.

16. **Drag the dark green swatch onto the new leftmost gradient stop.**

Your gradient should now go from dark to light and back to dark.

Note:

Delete specific stops from the gradient by dragging the stops down and away from the gradient ramp.

17. **Create a new swatch from this linear gradient. Name the swatch Grass Gradient.**

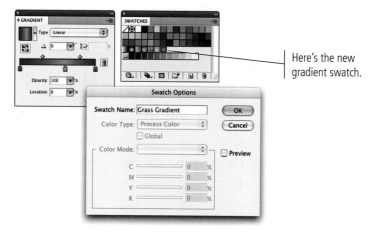

Here's the new gradient swatch.

18. **Save the file and continue to the next exercise.**

APPLY AND CONTROL GRADIENTS

Once you have created gradient swatches, you can apply them by simply selecting an object and clicking the appropriate swatch. You can also use the Gradient tool to control the position of a gradient.

1. **With the Grass layer of the map.ai file selected, change the fill to None and the stroke to 0.5-pt black.**

2. **Use the Pen tool to create a closed shape for the grass. Use the following image as a rough guide for positioning the shape's edges.**

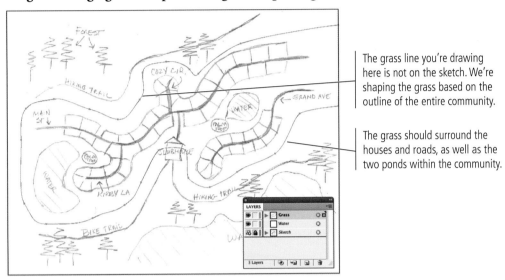

The grass line you're drawing here is not on the sketch. We're shaping the grass based on the outline of the entire community.

The grass should surround the houses and roads, as well as the two ponds within the community.

3. **Make sure the shape you drew in Step 2 is selected, and then click the Grass Gradient swatch in the Swatches panel to fill the shape with the defined gradient.**

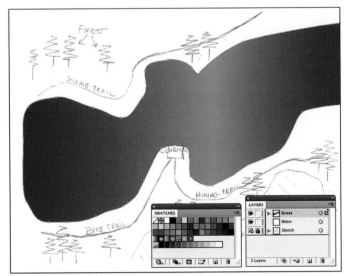

4. **Choose the Gradient tool in the Tools panel, and then choose View>Hide Gradient Annotator.**

The Gradient Annotator appears by default when you select the Gradient tool. When you turn it off, you can still drag with the Gradient tool to orient the gradient inside the shape.

5. **Click in the left side of the shape and drag up toward the right edge.**

When working with a linear gradient, the first place you click with the Gradient tool defines the location for the starting color of the gradient; where you release the mouse button marks the location for the ending color of the gradient. Any areas beyond the two ends fill with the end-stop colors of the gradient.

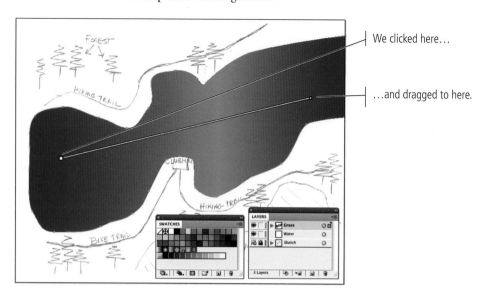

We clicked here…

…and dragged to here.

Dragging with the Gradient tool defines the direction and position of the gradient.

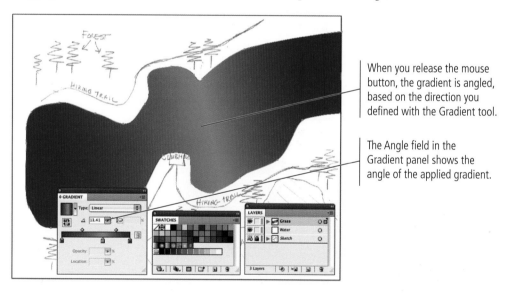

When you release the mouse button, the gradient is angled, based on the direction you defined with the Gradient tool.

The Angle field in the Gradient panel shows the angle of the applied gradient.

6. **In the Layers panel, drag the Grass layer to the bottom of the layer stack (directly above the Sketch layer). Hide and lock the Grass layer.**

7. **Select the Water layer to make it active. Use the Pen or Pencil tool with a black stroke and no fill to draw the three shapes for the lake and ponds.**

8. **Select all three water shapes and apply the Water Gradient swatch.**

9. **Use the Gradient tool to determine the position of the gradient center for each body of water.**

To modify each body of water separately, you must first deselect all three objects, and then select the one you want to modify with the Gradient tool. If you leave all three objects selected when you drag with the Gradient tool, the single gradient will extend across all three selected objects.

When working with a radial gradient, the first place you click with the Gradient tool defines the center point (the starting color) of the applied gradient. The location where you release the mouse button marks the outer edge of the radial gradient. The area beyond the outer edge of the gradient fills with the end-stop color of the gradient.

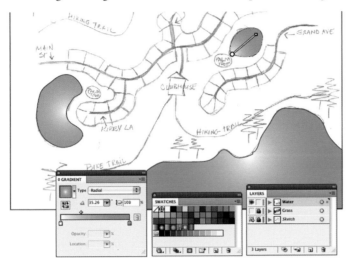

10. **Create a new layer named Undeveloped, arranged in the layer stack below the Grass layer.**

11. **On the Undeveloped layer, draw a rectangle that covers the entire Artboard. Fill it with a light brown swatch from the Landscape swatch library.**

12. **Show all layers and unlock all but the Sketch layer.**

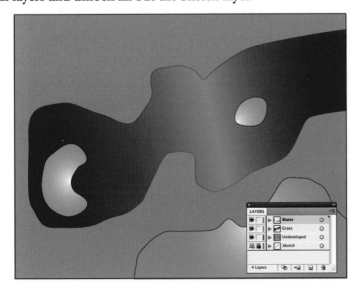

13. **Choose Select>All. Change the stroke for all selected objects to None.**

14. Deselect all objects and review your work.

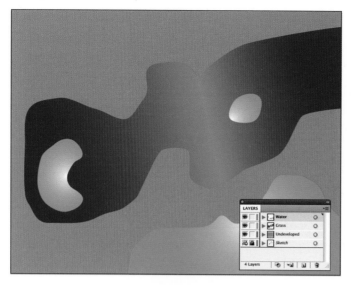

15. Save the file and continue to the next exercise.

Using Spot Colors in Gradients

If you create a gradient that blends a spot color into a process color build, the results will be unpredictable at best and disastrous at worst. In short, we highly recommend that you do not do this.

It is fairly common to create a gradient that blends from a spot color to white. This can be problematic too, but there is an easy solution for this type of gradient.

The accompanying images show the components of a basic linear gradient that blends from white to Pantone 7455. When you click a gradient stop, the Color panel shows the color values of the selected stop.

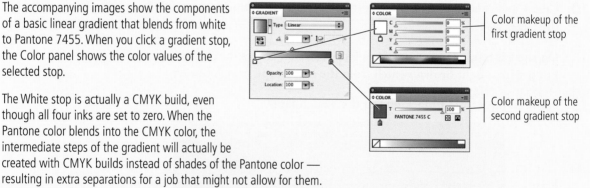

Color makeup of the first gradient stop

Color makeup of the second gradient stop

The White stop is actually a CMYK build, even though all four inks are set to zero. When the Pantone color blends into the CMYK color, the intermediate steps of the gradient will actually be created with CMYK builds instead of shades of the Pantone color — resulting in extra separations for a job that might not allow for them.

To solve the problem, you can apply the same spot color to both stops, and use the Color panel to apply 0% of the spot color for the stop where you want the gradient to be white. When both stops in the gradient are colored with a Pantone color (regardless of the defined tint for the stop), the intermediate shades of the gradient will be created as shades of the Pantone color instead of CMYK percentages.

CREATE PATTERNS

The final step in creating the background artwork is to add texture to the grassy areas in the main community. This will clearly differentiate the grass from the surrounding "land" area and the backyards of the individual properties.

1. **With map.ai open, duplicate the Grass layer and name the duplicate** Grassy Texture. **Hide all but the Sketch and Grassy Texture layers, and lock all but the Grassy Texture layer.**

2. **Choose Window>Swatch Libraries>Patterns>Basic Graphics>Basic Graphics_Textures. Change the panel display to one of the List views (small or large, whichever you prefer).**

3. **With nothing selected, click the Burlap swatch and drag it onto the empty area to the right of the Artboard.**

   When you drag a pattern or brush from a library panel, you place a copy of the artwork used to make that pattern or brush.

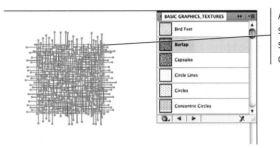

Although difficult to see, a square shape with no fill or stroke value marks the edge of the pattern tile.

4. **Deselect all the pattern elements, and then use the Direct Selection tool to select only one of the interior lines.**

   It doesn't matter which line you select, as long as it's not the square tile shape.

5. **Choose Select>Same>Fill & Stroke.**

   Because all other layers are locked, and the grass shape on this layer has a gradient fill, this command selects all the lines in the pattern artwork, but nothing else.

6. **With all the lines selected, change the stroke color for all selected lines to a light green from the Landscape swatch library.**

   To change the stroke color, remember to make the Stroke icon active at the bottom of the Tools panel before clicking the swatch in the Swatches panel.

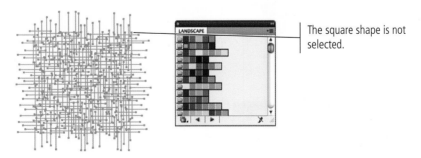

The square shape is not selected.

7. **Using the Selection tool, drag a marquee to select the entire pattern artwork — including the square tile shape.**

8. **Drag the selected art into the Swatches panel to create a new pattern swatch.**

This time the square shape is selected.

There's the new pattern swatch.

9. **Double-click the new pattern swatch to open the Swatch Options dialog box. Name the pattern Grassy Texture, and then click OK.**

10. **To the right of the Artboard, delete the Burlap objects you used to create the pattern.**

11. **Select the grass area shape on the Artboard and make sure the Fill color is active in the Tools panel. Change the shape's fill to the new Grassy Texture pattern.**

Unlike gradients, patterns can be applied to the stroke of an object; make sure the fill color is active before applying the pattern.

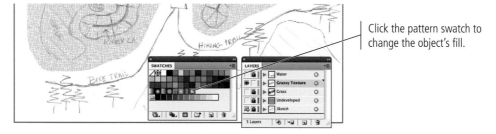

Click the pattern swatch to change the object's fill.

12. **Show the Grass layer.**

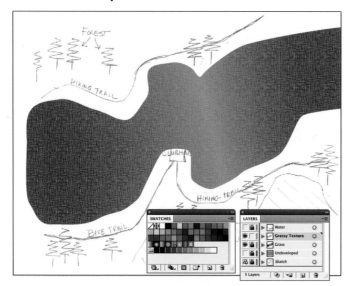

13. **Save the file and continue to the next stage of the project.**

Stage 2 Using Brushes and Brush Libraries

Brushes enhance or (as Adobe puts it) decorate paths. The default Brushes panel (Window>Brushes) includes several basic brushes of different types. You can use the Brushes panel Options menu to change the panel display, manage brushes, and load different brush libraries.

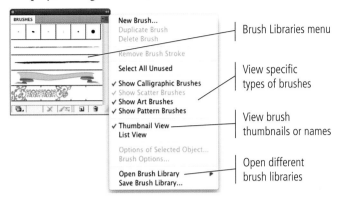

Brush Libraries menu

View specific types of brushes

View brush thumbnails or names

Open different brush libraries

Illustrator includes a number of different types of brushes, divided into four categories:

- **Calligraphic brushes** create strokes that resemble what you would draw with the angled tip of a calligraphic pen.

- **Scatter brushes** scatter copies of an object along a path.

- **Art brushes** apply a brush stroke or object shape across the length of a path.

- **Pattern brushes** paint a pattern of defined tiles along the length of a path. You can define different tiles for straight edges, inner and outer corners, and the beginning and end of a path.

The Brushes panel appears by default in Thumbnail mode. If you choose List View from the panel Options menu, you see the name of the brush, as well as an icon that indicates the type of the brush. Viewing brushes by name can be useful — especially when working with the built-in brushes — because the brush names indicate what each brush creates.

Note:

We added the 3D Geometric 1 brush to the default panel so we could show you the icon for a scatter brush. This brush is not included in the default Brushes panel.

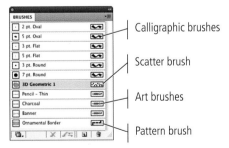

Calligraphic brushes

Scatter brush

Art brushes

Pattern brush

Beyond the few brushes in the default Brushes panel, you can also open a number of built-in brush libraries using the Brush Libraries menu at the bottom of the Brushes panel or at the bottom of the Window menu.

When you open the first brush library, the library appears in its own panel. If you open more than one brush library using the Window>Brush Libraries menu, each library opens as a new panel, grouped by default with other open brush libraries. You can drag any library panel out of the group to manage it independently.

Note:

Library panels open in the same location and state as the last time they were used. If a panel is not automatically grouped with other library panels, it was already used and repositioned.

If you open a library using the menu at the bottom of an open library panel, the new library replaces the one that was active when you opened the new library.

Multiple brush libraries are automatically combined into a single panel group when you open them from the Window>Brush Libraries menu.

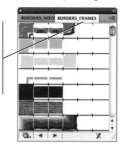
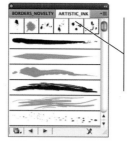

Opening a new library from the menu at the bottom of the panel replaces the active library with the new one.

 CREATE A NEW ART BRUSH

To complete this project, you need to create two custom art brushes: one to make the main roads in the development resemble brick with darker brick edges, and one to paint the hiking and bike trails. As we explained at the beginning of this stage of the project, an art brush applies an object across the length of a path. To create an art brush, you must first create the object you want to use as the brush stroke.

1. **With map.ai open, lock all layers, and then hide all but the Sketch layer. Create a new layer at the top of the stack named Roads.**

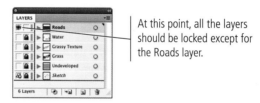

At this point, all the layers should be locked except for the Roads layer.

2. **With the Roads layer selected, create a rectangle that is 1″ wide by 0.5″ high.**

3. **Change the rectangle's stroke to None. Use one of the dark red swatches from the Stone and Brick Swatch library as the rectangle's fill color.**

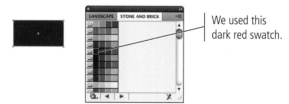

We used this dark red swatch.

4. **Use the Selection tool to select the rectangle, and then copy the rectangle.**

5. **Choose Edit>Paste in Front to paste a copy of the rectangle directly on top of the original.**

6. **In the Transform panel, make sure the Constrain option is turned off. Select the center reference point and change the object height to 0.45″.**

Note:

Press Command/ Control-F to apply the Paste in Front command.

Press Command/ Control-B to apply the Paste in Back command.

7. **Change the fill color of the top rectangle to one of the lighter brick colors.**

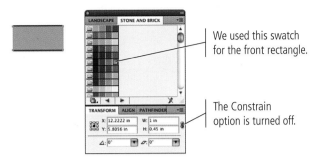

We used this swatch for the front rectangle.

The Constrain option is turned off.

Note:

Depending on what you (or other users) did before beginning this project, your Brushes panel might have fewer or more default brushes than what you see in our screen shots. It doesn't matter in this case, because you will only use the brushes that you create.

8. **Select both rectangles and group them (Object>Group or Command/Control-G).**

9. **Make sure the basic Brushes panel is open (Window>Brushes).**

10. **Drag the grouped rectangles into the Brushes panel.**

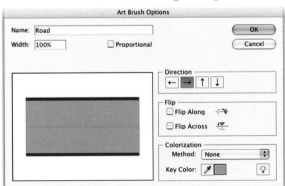

11. **In the New Brush dialog box, click the New Art Brush radio button and click OK.**

Note:

You can't create an art brush from objects that use gradients, meshes, bitmap elements, masks, or type.

12. **Type Road in the Name field of the resulting dialog box, and then click OK.**

After you click OK in the dialog box, the new brush appears in the Brushes panel.

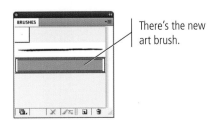

There's the new art brush.

13. **Using the Direct Selection tool, drag the top edge of the top rectangle down so it occupies less than half the height of the back rectangle.**

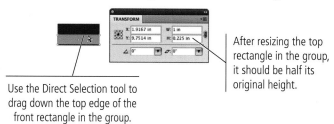

Use the Direct Selection tool to drag down the top edge of the front rectangle in the group.

After resizing the top rectangle in the group, it should be half its original height.

14. **Change the fill color of the front rectangle to a light gray, and change the fill color of the back rectangle to a light brown.**

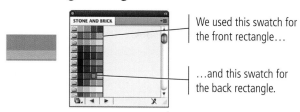

We used this swatch for the front rectangle…

…and this swatch for the back rectangle.

Note:

We're still using the Stone and Brick swatches we loaded in the first part of this project.

Changing and Deleting Brushes

You could have changed the size for the entire brush by double-clicking the Road brush in the Brushes panel. When you change the options for a specific brush, you can determine what to do for strokes where the brush has already been applied.

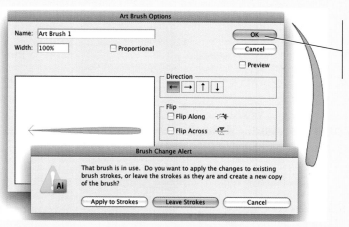

Clicking OK opens the Brush Change Alert if the brush has already been applied in the artwork.

- If you click **Apply to Strokes**, the changes will be applied to any path where the brush has been applied.
- If you click **Leave Strokes**, existing paths are unaffected; a copy of the changed brush is added to the Brushes panel.
- If you click **Cancel**, the Brush Options dialog box closes without applying the new brush options.

If you try to delete a brush that has been used in the open file, you again have to decide what to do with the strokes where the brush has already been applied.

- If you click **Expand Strokes**, the applied brush strokes are converted to filled objects.
- If you click **Remove Strokes**, objects that include the deleted brush strokes are reduced to their basic appearance (fill color, stroke color, and weight).
- If you click **Cancel**, your artwork is unaffected and the brush remains in the Brushes panel.

ILLUSTRATOR FOUNDATIONS

Art brush options control how the object is applied as a brush stroke. This dialog box opens automatically when you create a new art brush. You can also double-click an existing art brush to change the options for that brush.

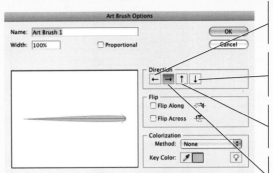

The left side of the artwork is the end of the stroke.

The bottom of the artwork is the end of the stroke.

The top of the artwork is the end of the stroke.

The right side of the artwork is the end of the stroke.

The **Direction** options control the direction of the artwork in relation to the path. The direction of the active button matches the direction of the arrow in the preview; both of these indicate which side of the original artwork will be the end of the stroke.

The **Width** field adjusts the width of the applied brush stroke relative to the width of the original art. The **Proportional** option preserves proportions in scaled art.

Flip Along and **Flip Across** reverse the orientation of the art in relation to the path.

Brush Colorization

The **Colorization** menu allows you to control how the colors in a brush (art, scatter, or pattern) interact with the currently defined stroke color.

Select **None** to use only the colors defined in the brush.

Select **Tints** to apply the brush stroke in tints of the current stroke color. (Black areas of the brush become the stroke color, other areas become tints of the stroke color, and white remains white.)

Select **Tints and Shades** to apply the brush stroke in tints and shades of the stroke color. Black and white areas of the brush remain unaffected; all other areas are painted as a blend from black to white through the stroke color.

Select **Hue Shift** to change the defined key color in the brush artwork to the defined stroke color when the brush is applied; other colors in the brush are adjusted to be similar to the stroke color. (Black, white, and gray areas remain unaffected). The key color defaults to the most prominent color in the brush art. To change the key color, click the eyedropper in the brush preview to select a different color.

Click the Tips button in the bottom-right corner to see a preview of the colorization options.

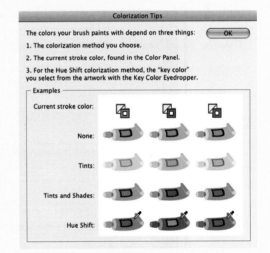

15. **Create a new art brush named Hike and Bike from the group of two modified rectangles.**

16. **Delete the grouped rectangles from the Artboard.**

17. **Save your work and continue to the next exercise.**

 ## CONTROL AN ART BRUSH STROKE

Applying a brush stroke is simple — draw a path (or select an object) and click the brush you want to apply (either in the Brushes panel or in the Control panel menu). Once a brush stroke is applied, however, you should also understand how to control it.

1. **With map.ai open, change the fill to None and the stroke to 1-pt black.**

2. **Using the Pen tool, draw a path that follows Main Street in the map sketch.**

3. **Click the Road brush in the Brushes panel.**

   The road immediately takes on the appearance of the brush you created earlier.

   You created the original rectangle with a height of 0.5″. When you created a brush from the grouped rectangles, you left the Width field (in the Brush Options dialog box) at the default 100%.

   The width of the path stroke is important when using brushes. When you apply artistic brush strokes, the width of the path's stroke actually defines the percentage of the brush width that will be applied.

   In this case, the width of the path stroke is 1 pt, so the applied brush stroke is 100% of the brush size. In other words, applying the brush to a 1-pt path results in a brush stroke with a 0.5″ width.

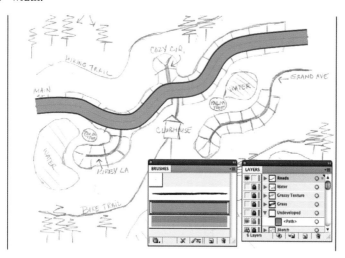

4. **With the brushed path selected, click the Options of Selected Object button at the bottom of the Brushes panel.**

5. **In the Stroke Options (Art Brush) dialog box, change the Width field to 50% and click OK.**

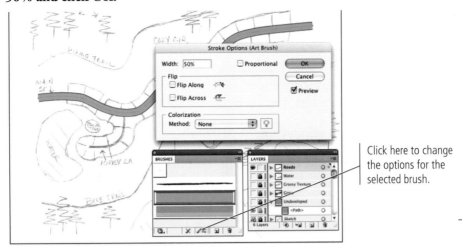

Note:

Changing the path width to 0.5 pt would reduce the brush stroke to 50% of the brush size; changing the path width to 2 pt would enlarge the brush stroke to 200% of the brush size.

Click here to change the options for the selected brush.

6. **Create another new layer named Bike Paths.**

7. **Use the Pen tool with a 1-pt black stroke and no fill to draw the hiking trails and bike path.**

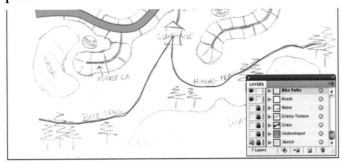

Note:

You could have accomplished the same result by changing the path stroke to 0.5 pt. Every job has different requirements, so it's important to understand your options.

8. **Apply the Hike and Bike art brush to the paths you drew in Step 7.**

9. **Adjust the paths' stroke width so the trails seem proportionate to the roads.**

   We changed the strokes to 35% of the brush size.

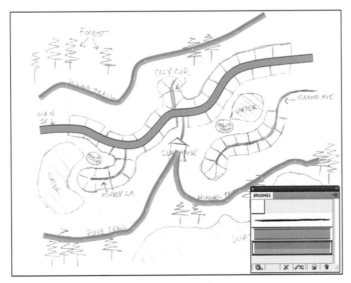

10. **Save the file and continue to the next exercise.**

The art brush you created earlier is basic, but it suits its purpose — painting the main road. According to the client, the side roads (Cozy Circle, Kirby Lane, and Grand Avenue) are actually cul de sacs with circles at the ends of the roads.

You could manually create and align these "lollipop" road endings, but you can use a pattern brush to more easily complete the task. Before you can create a pattern brush, however, you need to first create the pattern tiles that will be used in the brush.

1. **With map.ai open, make sure nothing is selected on the Artboard.**

2. **Drag the Road brush from the Brushes panel onto the Artboard outside the main map area.**

   You can always access the basic brush art by dragging the brush from the Brushes panel onto the Artboard.

   Dragging the brush from the Brushes panel onto the Artboard creates a group with the basic brush art.

3. **Choose the Ellipse tool from the Tools panel. Click once to the right of the brush art and define a circle with a 0.8″ diameter.**

   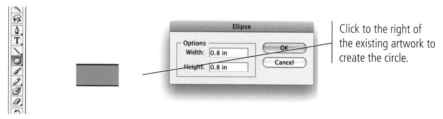

   Click to the right of the existing artwork to create the circle.

4. **Copy the circle and paste a copy in front of the original.**

5. **Using the Control or Transform panel, change the diameter of the pasted circle to 0.75″, based on the center reference point.**

   To change the circle's diameter, constrain the height and width and change either field in the Control or Transform panel.

6. **Fill the top circle with the same color as the center road color, and fill the back circle with the same color as the road edges. Make sure both circles have a stroke of None.**

7. **Select the two circles and group them.**

8. **Align the vertical centers of the two groups, and make sure the circle group completely obscures the right end of the rectangles.**

9. **Ungroup both groups of objects, and then select only the back rectangle and back circle (the darker objects).**

10. **In the Pathfinder panel, click the Unite button.**

    Using the Pathfinder panel can have unexpected effects on the object stacking order. Because you created both circles after the two rectangles, the back circle lies in front of the top rectangle. When the two darker objects are united by the Pathfinder operation, the back rectangle is brought forward to the same stacking level as the darker circle — in front of the lighter rectangle.

11. **Send the united shape to the back of the stacking order (Object>Arrange>Send to Back).**

12. **Repeat Steps 9–10 to create a single shape for the two lighter shapes that comprise the inner road (you don't need to ungroup again).**

    When you create pattern brush elements, you should simplify the shapes as much as possible. Using the Pathfinder options, you have simplified the overall shape from four objects to two.

13. **Select and group the two objects that comprise the road ending (the cul de sac).**

14. **Drag the Road brush from the Brushes panel to create another group of the original Road artwork.**

    These two groups will be the tiles for your pattern brush.

15. **Save the file and continue to the next exercise.**

CREATE A NEW PATTERN BRUSH

Now that you have the two objects you need to create the pattern brush, you have to convert those objects to patterns, and then define the pattern brush.

1. **With map.ai open, open the Swatches panel. Use the Show Swatch Kinds menu at the bottom of the panel to show only pattern swatches.**

2. **Using the Selection tool, click the cul de sac group and drag it into the Swatches panel. Deselect the artwork on the Artboard.**

3. **In the Swatches panel, double-click the new swatch, name it Cul De Sac, and then click OK to close the Swatch Options dialog box.**

Note:

If the roads in this project had sharp corners, you would also need to define shapes for both inside and outside corners.

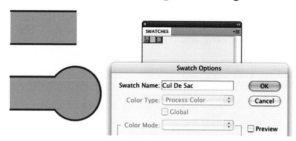

4. **Drag the straight road segment from the Artboard onto the Swatches panel. Deselect the artwork on the Artboard. Double-click the new swatch in the Swatches panel, name the new swatch Straight Road, and click OK.**

5. **Delete the two grouped elements from the Artboard and make sure nothing is selected.**

6. **In the Brushes panel, click the New Brush button at the bottom of the panel.**

7. **Select the New Pattern Brush option and click OK.**

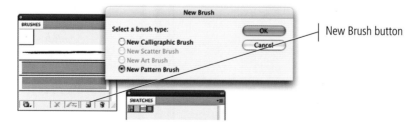

New Brush button

Note:

If anything had been selected when you clicked the New Brush button, Illustrator would have tried to create a new brush based on the current selection.

8. **In the Pattern Brush Options dialog box, name the brush Cul De Sac Roads.**

9. **Click the Side Tile icon, and then choose Straight Road from the list of available pattern swatches.**

Pattern brush tiles must be saved as patterns so you can access them in the Pattern Brush Options dialog box.

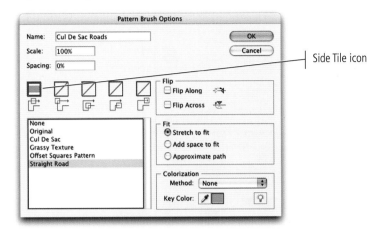

Side Tile icon

Note:

Pattern brushes can consist of five possible tiles: side, outer corner, inner corner, start, and end. You can define different patterns for any or all of these tiles.

10. **Click the End Tile icon, and then click Cul De Sac in the list of patterns.**

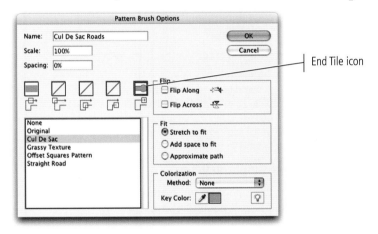

End Tile icon

Note:

The arrow in the End Tile icon shows why you moved the circle group to the right side instead of the left side of the rectangle group.

The end tile of a pattern brush should always be created with the path end pointing to the right. If the "end" of the end tile points to the left, you could end up with unexpected results such as this:

This direction has no effect on the stroke that will be applied in the artwork. If you draw a path from right to left, the end tile of the applied pattern brush will point to the left:

11. **Click OK to create the brush.**

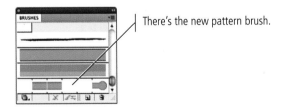

There's the new pattern brush.

12. **Select the Roads layer as the active layer.**

13. **Using the Pen tool with a fill of None and a 1-pt black stroke, draw the four side roads.**

   - **For the three lines that connect to the main road, start those lines at the main road and work out.**

   - **For the road that is not connected to the others, start at the right side of the line and end on the left side.**

14. Select all four of the paths from Step 13 and click the Cul De Sac Roads pattern brush in the Brushes panel.

Depending on how you create the road paths, the cul-de-sac shapes might be distorted on your various lines (especially at 100% of 1-pt lines). You can correct some of the distortion by manipulating the anchor points and handles that make up the line, as shown in the following images.

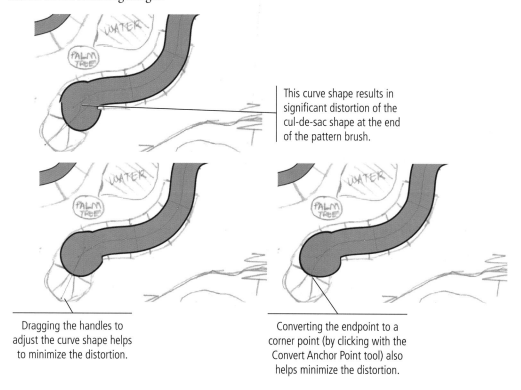

This curve shape results in significant distortion of the cul-de-sac shape at the end of the pattern brush.

Dragging the handles to adjust the curve shape helps to minimize the distortion.

Converting the endpoint to a corner point (by clicking with the Convert Anchor Point tool) also helps minimize the distortion.

15. With all four paths selected, change the stroke weight to 0.5 pt.

As we mentioned earlier, changing the stroke size for the applied art brush and changing the stroke width of the path achieves the same result. The half-point (0.5) stroke width means the applied stroke is half the width of the defined brush.

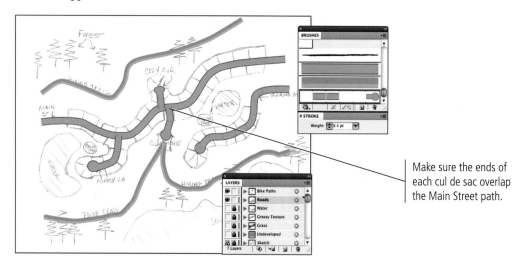

Make sure the ends of each cul de sac overlap the Main Street path.

16. Send the four selected paths to the back of the stacking order.

The main road should appear in front of the other roads.

17. Save the file and continue to the next exercise.

As with art brushes, you can control the settings for pattern brushes when you first create them or by double-clicking an existing pattern brush in the Brushes panel.

The **Tile buttons** allow you to apply different patterns to different parts of the line.

The **Scale** option adjusts the size of tiles relative to their original size.

The **Spacing** option adjusts the space between tiles in the applied stroke.

The Flip Along and **Flip Across** options reverse the orientation of the art in relation to the path.

The **Fit** options define how the pattern fits on the path. Stretch to Fit adjusts the length of the pattern tiles to fit the path. Add Space to Fit adds blank space between pattern tiles to maintain proportions in the applied pattern. Approximate Path fits tiles to the closest approximate path without changing the tiles.

The **Colorization** options are the same for pattern brushes as for art brushes.

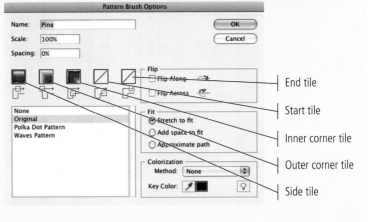

- End tile
- Start tile
- Inner corner tile
- Outer corner tile
- Side tile

EXPAND BRUSH STROKES INTO OBJECTS

If you look at the map as it is now, you might notice a problem where the road paths connect — the intersections don't have curbs running through them. To more accurately reflect the appearance of real road intersections, you need to convert the road path strokes to regular objects so you can manipulate selected parts of the roads (i.e., where the paths intersect).

1. **With map.ai open, select the Main Street road path.**

2. **Open the Appearance panel.**

   The Appearance panel shows the properties of the selected objects, including the applied stroke and fill attributes. You can see here that the stroke attribute is Road.

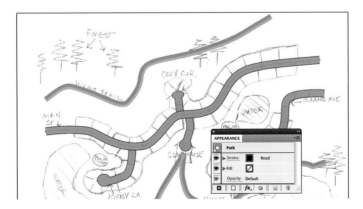

3. Choose View>Outline.

In Outline mode, you can see the basic paths without the applied stroke.

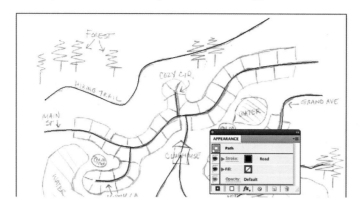

Note:

Press Command/ Control-Y to toggle between Outline and Preview modes.

4. Choose View>Preview to return to the full-color version of your work.

5. With the path still selected, choose Object>Expand Appearance.

In the Appearance panel, you now see that the selection is a group. When you expand the appearance of a selection, Illustrator simplifies the selection (as much as possible) into basic filled and stroked shapes; the resulting shapes are grouped.

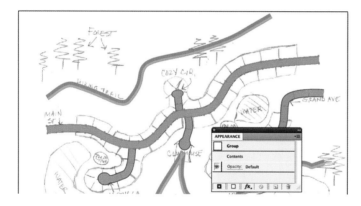

Note:

Art brushes can produce unexpected results on sharp corners and closed paths.

Pattern brushes are the best choices for creating borders on closed paths or for other paths that have sharp corners.

6. Choose View>Outline.

In this case, expanding the stroked path results in two filled objects — the inner road bed (with the lighter fill color) and the outer road bed (with the darker fill). The original path (called the "spine" of the brush stroke) is also maintained, with a fill and stroke of None.

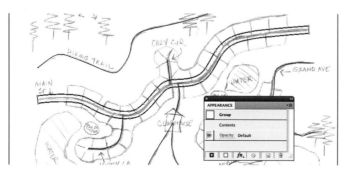

7. **Return to Preview mode (View>Preview) and select the three road paths that intersect Main Street.**

8. **With all three paths selected, choose Object>Expand Appearance.**

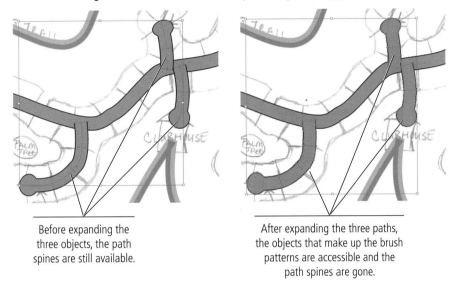

Before expanding the three objects, the path spines are still available.

After expanding the three paths, the objects that make up the brush patterns are accessible and the path spines are gone.

9. **Shift-click to select the expanded Main Street group.**

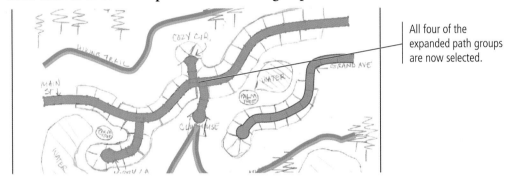

All four of the expanded path groups are now selected.

10. **Choose Object>Ungroup two times.**

   You have to ungroup twice to remove the different groupings created by the Expand Appearance command.

11. **Deselect everything, and then select one of the dark-red-filled objects (the back part of the road).**

   You might have to zoom in to select the dark-red objects. Watch the Appearance panel to make sure you select the correct color.

12. **Choose Select>Same>Fill Color to select all objects that have the dark-red fill.**

   Notice that the Grand Avenue path is unaffected because you didn't expand the appearance of that path.

13. **In the Pathfinder panel, click the Unite button.**

All the selected shapes are now a single object filled with the dark-red color.

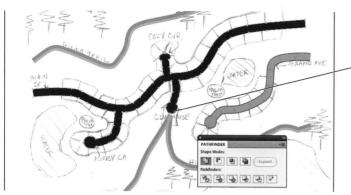

As we mentioned previously, using the Pathfinder panel can have unexpected effects on the stacking order. The dark-red areas of the three cul de sacs are brought to the front of the stacking order within their groups.

14. **Send the selected object to the back of the stacking order.**

15. **Repeat Steps 11–13 to combine all the light-red-filled objects into a single shape at the top of the stacking order.**

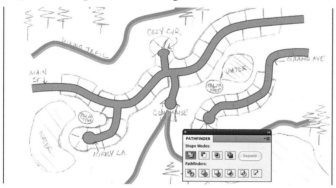

16. **Save the file and continue to the next exercise.**

 SAVE CUSTOM BRUSHES

When you create custom brushes, swatches, or other elements, they are only available in the file where you create them. To access those assets in other files, you have to save your own custom libraries.

1. **With map.ai open, show the Brushes panel.**

2. **Open the panel Options menu and choose Select All Unused.**

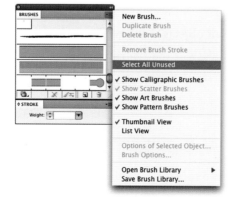

Everything but the Hike and Bike art brush and the Cul De Sac Roads pattern brush should be selected. (Remember, you expanded the appearance of Main Street, so the Road art brush is not currently applied in the file.)

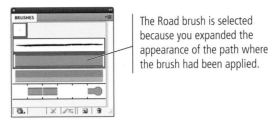

The Road brush is selected because you expanded the appearance of the path where the brush had been applied.

3. **Command/Control-click the Road art brush to deselect it, and then click the panel's Delete button. Click Yes in the dialog box asking if you want to delete the brush selection.**

   You are not permanently deleting the brushes from the application; you are only deleting them from the Brushes panel for this file. However, Illustrator still asks you to confirm the deletion.

4. **Open the panel Options menu and choose Save Brush Library.**

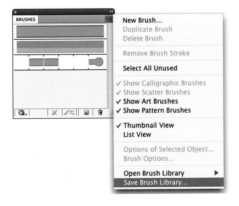

5. **In the resulting dialog box, name the library `map brushes.ai` and click Save.**

   If you're working on your own computer, the application defaults to a Brushes folder created when the application was installed.

Note:

Brush, symbol, and swatch libraries are saved with the extension ".ai." You can also save swatch libraries in the Adobe Swatch Exchange format (using the extension ".ase") if you want to use a swatch library in another Adobe application such as Photoshop.

If you are using a shared computer, you might not be able to save files in the application's default location. If this is the case, navigate to your WIP>Realty folder to save the map brushes.ai file.

6. Close the Brushes panel.

7. Create a new document using the default settings, and then open the Brushes panel.

8. Choose Window>Brush Libraries>User Defined>map brushes.

If you saved the brush library file in your WIP folder (in Step 5), choose Other Library from the bottom of the submenu, navigate to your WIP>Realty folder, and open the map brushes.ai file.

The map brushes panel opens, grouped with the other open brush libraries. The panel contains only the three brushes that were available when you saved the library.

9. Close the new file without saving.

10. Save the map.ai file and continue to the next stage of the project.

Stage 3 Using Symbols

Symbols are graphic elements you draw once, and then use as many times as necessary in a drawing. The advantage to using symbols is that if you change the symbol, all placed instances of that symbol can reflect the same changes (you have a choice when you change the symbol). You can also isolate specific instances of a symbol, which separates them and breaks the link to the original symbol (and other instances). Once the link is broken, changes to the original symbol have no effect on the isolated instances.

As with brushes and swatches, symbols are managed in panels. The default Symbols panel (Window>Symbols) has a few randomly selected symbols from various built-in symbol libraries. You can also open other symbol libraries by choosing from the menu at the bottom of the Window menu.

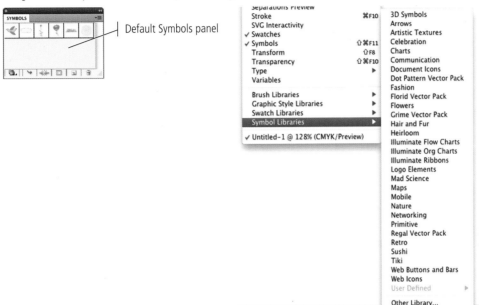

Default Symbols panel

If you open a symbol library from the Window menu, the first library opens in its own panel. Successive panels open in separate panels that are automatically grouped with other open symbol libraries. If you open a symbol library using the Symbol Libraries Menu at the bottom of a library panel, the new library replaces the active library.

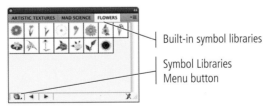

Built-in symbol libraries

Symbol Libraries
Menu button

OPEN CUSTOM SYMBOL LIBRARIES

Several elements of this project will benefit from the use of symbols. Many of the symbols for this project have already been created and saved in a custom library, which you can easily load so you don't have to recreate work that has already been completed.

1. **With map.ai open, open the Symbols panel (Window>Symbols).**

2. **Click the Symbol Libraries Menu button at the bottom of the default Symbols panel.**

3. Choose Other Library at the bottom of the menu.

You can load custom symbol libraries that were created on another computer by choosing Other Library from the menu and navigating to the file that contains the library you want to use.

Note:

If you create a custom library on your computer, it appears in the User Defined submenu of the main Libraries menu. If a custom library was created on another computer, you have to use the Other Library option to load the new custom library on your computer.

Note:

As with the Brushes panel, your default Symbols panel might have more options than what you see in our screen shots. Again, you will only be using the symbols you create (or import), so the default symbols don't matter in this project.

4. Navigate to the file named map symbols.ai in the RF_Illustrator>Realty folder and click Open.

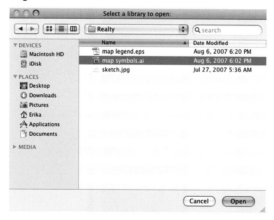

Note:

The same options are also available for loading swatch libraries and brush libraries that were created on another computer.

The new symbol library appears in its own panel (possibly grouped with other library panels if other symbol libraries are also open).

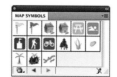

5. **Open the Options menu for the Map Symbols library panel and choose Large List View.**

6. **Continue to the next exercise.**

Note:

Symbols in loaded libraries are not connected to the current file unless you place an instance of a symbol from the loaded library into the file. When you place a symbol instance from a loaded library, the symbol is added to the default symbol library for the file. (The same is true when working with brush libraries.)

CONTROL SYMBOL INSTANCES

In addition to loading built-in or custom symbol libraries, you can also create new symbols by drawing the art and dragging it into the default Symbols panel. In this exercise, you create a custom symbol to identify the roads on the map — namely, a road sign. You need four different signs for the various roads.

1. **With map.ai open, lock and hide all layers. Create a new layer named Street Signs at the top of the layer stack.**

2. **Using the Rounded Rectangle tool, create a rounded rectangle 2″ wide and 0.75″ high with a 0.15″ corner radius. Change the object to a medium-blue fill and a 3-pt white stroke.**

3. **Deselect the rounded rectangle you just created.**

4. **Choose the basic Rectangle tool (not the Rounded Rectangle tool) and click the Default Fill and Stroke button in the Tools panel.**

5. **Draw a post for the sign, and then center the post behind the blue rounded rectangle.**

6. **Click the Grass symbol in the Map Symbols panel and drag it onto the Artboard (in front of the signpost).**

   You're going to use several of these symbols to add decorative elements to the road sign.

Note that the post has square corners and the sign has rounded corners.

A symbol instance is a single object. You can't directly access the individual shapes that make up the symbol.

7. **Drag the bounding box handles to resize the grass instance so it's appropriately sized in relation to the sign.**

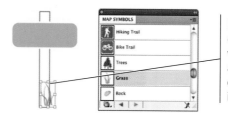

Because an instance is an object, you can transform the instance as you would any other object. Transforming an instance has no effect on the original symbol, nor on other placed instances of the same symbol.

8. **Clone (Option/Alt-click-drag) the Grass instance several times. Resize and arrange the instances to create a thick cluster of grass at the base of the post.**

Each symbol instance is an object, which means it can be modified — transformed, rotated, stretched, etc. — as you would modify any other object. Transforming a placed instance has no effect on other placed instances of the same symbol.

9. **Drag an instance of the Rock symbol onto the Artboard.**

10. **Use the Selection tool to resize and rotate the Rock instance as appropriate for the surrounding artwork.**

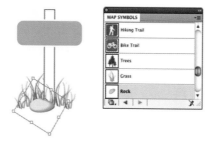

11. **Select the placed Rock instance and click the Break Link to Symbol button at the bottom of the main Symbols panel.**

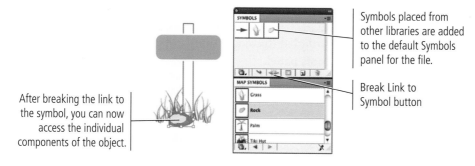

Symbols placed from other libraries are added to the default Symbols panel for the file.

Break Link to Symbol button

After breaking the link to the symbol, you can now access the individual components of the object.

12. **Break the links of all placed symbol instances.**

In this case, you're only using the symbols to access the artwork; you don't need to maintain the link to the original symbols.

13. **Select all the objects on the Street Signs layer and group them.**

14. **Drag the grouped road sign onto the main Symbols panel. In the resulting dialog box, name the symbol** Street Signs **and click OK.**

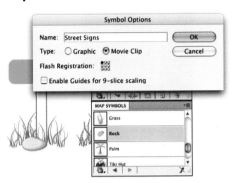

Note:

The Type options are relevant for files that will be exported for Adobe Flash. If your symbols will remain in Illustrator, you can use either the Graphic or Movie Clip option.

When you create a symbol from objects on the Artboard, the original objects are automatically converted to an instance of the new symbol.

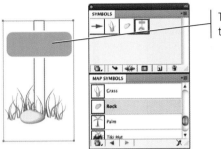

This group is now an instance of the new Street Signs symbol.

15. **Save the file and continue to the next exercise.**

 PLACE SYMBOL INSTANCES

Now that you've created the custom symbol, it will be fairly easy to place instances where you need them.

1. **With map.ai open, show the Sketch and Roads layers. Make sure the Street Signs layer is selected as the active layer.**

2. **Resize the existing instance of the Street Signs symbol so it is an appropriate size for the overall map.**

   We used the Transform panel to scale the instance to 25% of its original size.

3. **Drag the instance onto the left end of Main Street (where the street name is already sketched).**

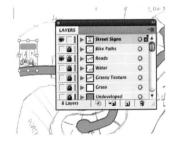

4. **Clone three instances of the scaled instance. Place an instance where each street name is indicated on the sketch.**

   Cloning an instance results in an additional instance of the symbol. All instances are linked to the original symbol.

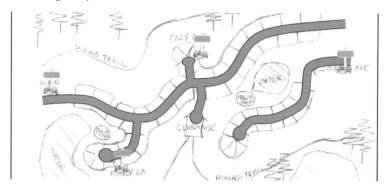

5. **In the Symbols panel, double-click the Street Signs symbol.**

   This opens a new Artboard, called **Symbol Editing mode**. The symbol artwork is the only visible item.

6. **Create a point-type object with the text Street Name, using 24-pt ATC Maple Medium colored white with centered paragraph alignment.**

7. **Center the type object in the rounded rectangle of the sign artwork.**

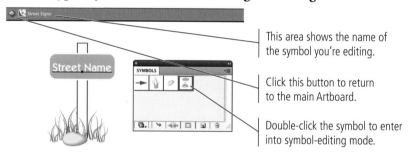

   This area shows the name of the symbol you're editing.

   Click this button to return to the main Artboard.

   Double-click the symbol to enter into symbol-editing mode.

8. **In the top-left corner of the screen, click the left arrow button to exit symbol-editing mode and return to the main Artboard.**

   Notice that the new type element has been added to all four placed instances. As we mentioned, the advantage of using symbols is that all linked symbol instances — whether 4 or 400 — reflect changes you make only once.

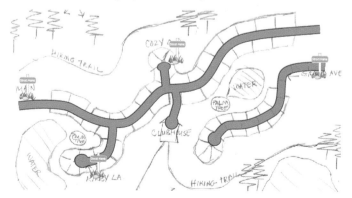

   The problem, of course, is that the streets are not all named "Street Name". To change the text on each individual road sign, you have to break the link from each instance to the original symbol.

9. **Break the link between the main Street Signs symbol and each placed instance.**

   Once the links are broken, all the elements of the symbol artwork become a group in the main file.

10. **Change the text of each former symbol instance to identify the names of the roads, as identified in the sketched map.**

    Abbreviate the name if necessary ("Ave." instead of "Avenue", for example) to make the road names fit on the signs.

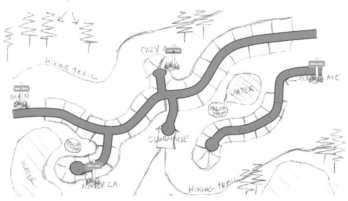

11. **Save the file and continue to the next exercise.**

Editing Symbols in Place

You can double-click any placed instance to enter a modified symbol-editing mode, called **editing in place**. Instead of seeing only the symbol artwork, you can see the entire file behind the instance you are editing. Changing an instance in this manner has the same effect as changing the original symbol — all other linked instances reflect the changes when you return to the main Artboard.

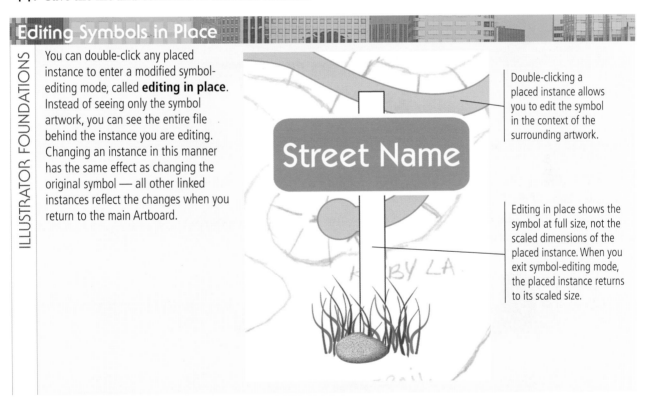

Double-clicking a placed instance allows you to edit the symbol in the context of the surrounding artwork.

Editing in place shows the symbol at full size, not the scaled dimensions of the placed instance. When you exit symbol-editing mode, the placed instance returns to its scaled size.

SPRAY SYMBOLS

The next task is to create the hiking path and surrounding forest. The path requires another custom brush. Once the path is finished, you can use built-in nature symbols to create an entire forest with just a few clicks.

1. **With map.ai open, lock the Street Signs layer. Create a new layer named** Forest **at the top of the layer stack.**

2. **Choose the Symbol Sprayer tool from the Tools panel.**

   The Symbol Sprayer tool is used to spray multiple symbol instances onto the Artboard. Other tools nested under the Symbol Sprayer in the Tools panel can be used to squeeze, spread, pinch, and otherwise modify the sprayed symbol instances.

3. **Click the Trees symbol in the Map Symbols library panel.**

4. **Press the left bracket key ([ ) to decrease or right bracket key ( ]) to increase the size of the tool (and its cursor).**

   Brush size affects the results of the Symbol Sprayer tool; larger brush size results in larger symbol instances. We're using a large brush size to create the forest.

Note:

The Symbol Sprayer tool defaults to the last-used size.

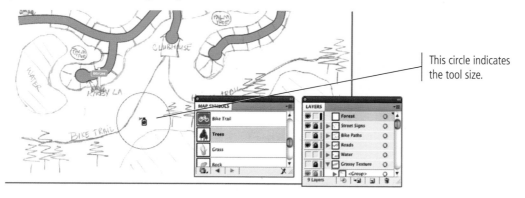

This circle indicates the tool size.

5. **Click directly above the top hiking trail and drag right, roughly following the shape of the hiking trail.**

   When you click and drag with the Symbol Sprayer tool, you create a **symbol set** — multiple instances of a single symbol that are treated as a single, cohesive unit.

As you spray the symbols, you can see wireframe outlines of the shapes that will be added.

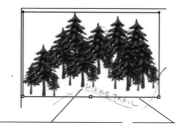

When you release the mouse button, the full-color symbol instances appear on the Artboard.

This boundary shows the edge of the symbol set.

6. **Without deselecting the symbol set, add a few instances near the right side of the path.**

   By leaving the set selected, the new instances are added to the existing set.

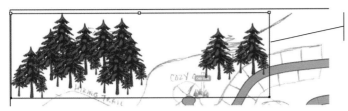

   The set expands to include the new instances.

7. **Press Command/Control to temporarily access the Selection tool and click away from the symbol set to deselect it.**

   If you don't deselect the active symbol set, clicking again adds more instances to the selected symbol set. In this case, you want to create a second symbol set, so you have to deselect the first set before clicking again with the Symbol Sprayer tool.

   Note:

   Pressing Command/ Control temporarily switches to the Selection tool; when you release the Command/Control key, the Symbol Sprayer tool is again active.

8. **Click the Symbol Sprayer tool below the lower bike path and drag right to the lake area of the sketch.**

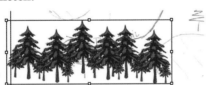

9. **Without deselecting the set, add several additional instances in front of the lower path.**

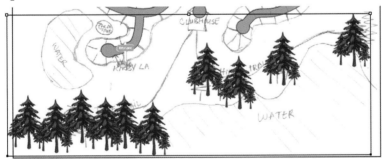

   Note:

   Press Option/Alt and drag with the Symbol Sprayer tool to delete symbol instances from a symbol set.

10. **If necessary, use the Symbol Shifter tool (nested under the Symbol Sprayer tool) to move the instances within the sets. Make sure no trees are sprouting from the water.**

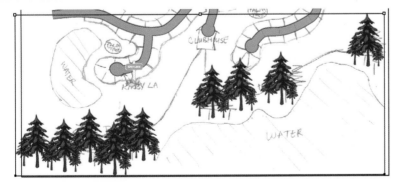

    Note:

    If you click and hold the mouse button without dragging, symbol instances pile on top of one another (just as spray paint builds up if you hold the can in one place).

11. **Save the file and continue to the next exercise.**

When using sprayed symbols, many designs call for adjustments to individual components or instances within a symbol set. Without breaking the links between individual instances and the original symbol, you can use a number of tools to modify symbols within a set.

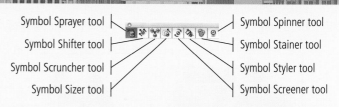

Symbol Sprayer tool — Symbol Spinner tool
Symbol Shifter tool — Symbol Stainer tool
Symbol Scruncher tool — Symbol Styler tool
Symbol Sizer tool — Symbol Screener tool

The **Symbol Shifter** tool pushes instances around the Artboard. The tool only affects instances touched by the tool cursor.

The **Symbol Scruncher** tool causes the cursor to act as a magnet; all instances in the set are drawn toward the cursor when you click. Pressing Option/Alt reverses the effect, pushing instances away from the cursor.

The **Symbol Sizer** tool changes the size of instances within a set. Clicking causes instances under the cursor to grow. Option/Alt-clicking causes instances under the cursor to shrink.

The **Symbol Spinner** tool rotates instances under the cursor where you click. Dragging indicates the direction of the rotation.

The **Symbol Stainer** tool changes the hue of instances under the cursor using the defined fill color.

The **Symbol Screener** tool increases the opacity of instances under the cursor. Press Option/Alt to decrease instance opacity.

The **Symbol Styler** tool allows you to apply a graphic style to symbol instances.

ADD THE REMAINING SYMBOLS

Much of the remaining artwork can be created using symbols. After you place these components, you can finish the artwork.

1. **With map.ai open, lock and hide the Forest and Street Signs layers. Create a new layer named Amenities at the top of the layer stack.**

2. **Using the symbols in the Map Symbols library:**

   - **Place an instance of the Tiki Hut symbol where the sketch indicates the club house.**
   - **Place instances of the Palm symbol where the sketch indicates.**
   - **Place an instance of the Playground symbol to the immediate right of the clubhouse.**
   - **Place an instance of the Swimming symbol near the smallest pond.**
   - **Place instances of the Hiking Trail symbol on the upper and lower trails.**
   - **Place an instance of the Bike Trail symbol somewhere along the lower trail.**
   - **Place instances of the Picnic Area symbol near the two ponds.**

ILLUSTRATOR FOUNDATIONS

Symbolism Tool Options

Double-clicking any of the symbolism tools in the Tools panel opens the Symbolism Tools Options dialog box.

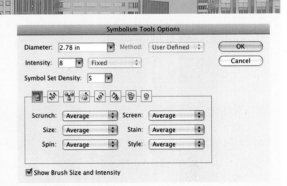

Diameter reflects the tool's current brush size.

Intensity determines the rate of change for modifying instances.

Symbol Set Density creates more tightly packed (higher values) or loosely packed (lower values) instances in the symbol set.

Method determines how the symbol modifier tools (all but the Symbol Sprayer and Symbol Shifter) adjust symbol instances:

- **Average** smoothes out values in symbol instances.
- **User Defined** adjusts instances in relation to the position of the cursor.
- **Random** modifies instances randomly under the cursor.

If the Symbol Sprayer tool is selected in the middle of the dialog box, you can control a variety of options related to how new symbol instances are added to symbol sets; each option has two possible choices:

- **Average** adds new symbols with the average value of existing symbol instances within the brush radius. For example, in an area where the average existing instance is rotated by 10°, new instances will be rotated by 10°.
- **User Defined** applies specific values for each parameter, primarily based on the original symbol size, mouse direction, and current color settings.

If the Symbol Sizer is selected, you have two additional options:

- **Proportional Resizing** maintains a uniform shape for each symbol instance as you resize.
- **Resizing Affects Density** moves symbol instances away from each other when they are scaled up, and moves symbol instances toward each other when they are scaled down.

If the **Show Brush Size and Intensity** option is checked, the cursor reflects the tool diameter.

3. Create another new layer named Properties and position the layer below the Roads layer in the layer stack.

4. Place an instance of the Home Lots symbol on the Properties layer. Use the Sketch layer as a guide for correctly positioning the symbol.

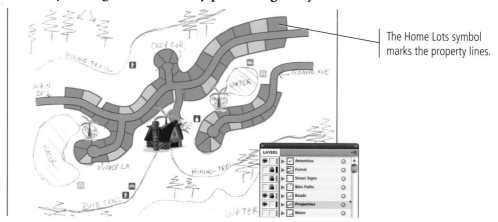

The Home Lots symbol marks the property lines.

5. Create a new layer named Houses at the top of the layer stack.

6. Place an instance of the House Blue Roof symbol on each lot along Grand Avenue.

7. Place instances of the Red Flag symbol on each lot along Main Street and the connecting roads.

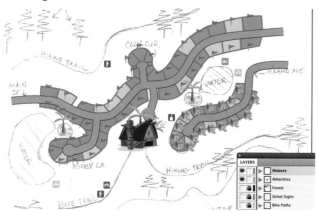

Note:

You might want to lock the Properties layer while you place the house and flag instances.

8. Save the file and continue to the next exercise.

 ## REPLACE SYMBOLS

Your clients stated that they want to be able to easily update the map as additional houses are sold and properties are reserved. Symbols make this task easy because you can quickly change the symbol associated with individual placed instances.

1. With **map.ai** open, make sure nothing is selected in the layout.

2. Using either selection tool, Shift-click to select the Red Flag instances on the four lots nearest the clubhouse and the three lots at the end of Kirby Lane.

3. In the Map Symbols panel, click the Yellow Flag symbol once to copy it into the Symbols panel for the map file.

4. **Click the House Red Roof symbol in the Map Symbols panel to add it to the main Symbols panel.**

5. **In the Control panel, open the Replace menu and click the Yellow Flag symbol.**

   As soon as you select the new symbol, the selected instances change to the new symbol.

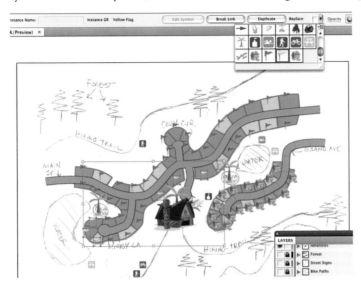

Note:

The Replace menu only shows symbols in the current file's symbol library.

6. **Select the first five house symbols on the north end of Grand Avenue, and the two instances on the tan lots on the south side of the road (see the screen shot following Step 7).**

7. **In the Replace menu on the Control panel, choose the House Red Roof symbol to replace the selected instances.**

   Again, the selected symbol instances immediately change to reflect the new symbol you chose in the Replace menu. If you have multiple variations of an object — such as houses available and houses sold — the ability to replace symbol instances is a tremendous time saver, enabling you to revise the file quickly and easily.

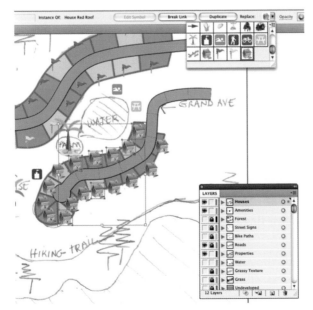

8. **Save the file and continue to the next exercise.**

CREATE A CLIPPING MASK

The final step of this project is to save the file so it can be used in other applications. Part of this process requires "finishing off" the edges so that no objects — such as trees or road ends — hang past the artwork edges. Rather than manually cutting your artwork, you can square off the design by creating a mask to hide the elements you don't want to see. Once you've created the mask, you can save the file in several different formats so it can be used in a variety of applications.

A **clipping mask** is an object that masks other artwork; only those areas within the clipping mask shape remain visible. To create a clipping mask, however, all the objects you want to clip should be part of the same layer as the masking object. Before you flatten the artwork, however, you should make all necessary changes in the final file, and save an archive copy of the layered file so you can more easily make changes later.

Note:

*The clipping mask and the masked objects are called a **clipping set**.*

Note:

*You can create a clipping mask for objects on different layers, as long as the layers are visible and unlocked. When you apply the Clipping Mask>Create command, however, all affected objects are automatically copied to the layer that contains the mask object (called **flattening**).*

1. **With map.ai open, delete the Sketch layer. Make sure all other layers are unlocked and visible.**

2. **Create a new layer named Mask at the top of the layer stack.**

3. **With the Mask layer selected, draw a rectangle that is 9″ wide by 7″ high, with a black stroke and no fill.**

4. **Align the rectangle to the horizontal and vertical centers of the Artboard.**

   After you create a clipping mask with this rectangle, objects outside the rectangle's edges will no longer be visible.

5. **Make sure all pieces of your artwork are positioned correctly:**

   • **If necessary, extend the ends of the road and path artwork so they all end outside the rectangle edges.**

   • **Make sure the street signs fall entirely within the boundaries of the rectangle on the Mask layer.**

   • **Make sure none of the red or yellow flag instances obscures a street sign.**

   • **Make sure enough trees fall inside the rectangle's edge to create the illusion of a forest. If not, use the Symbol Sprayer tool to add more instances of the Trees symbol to the existing symbol sets.**

   • **If any trees appear to grow out of the water, use the Symbol Shifter tool to move them to solid ground.**

6. **Create another layer named** Legend **at the top of the layer stack (above the Mask layer).**

7. **Place the file** map legend.eps **(from the RF_Illustrator>Realty folder) onto the Legend layer. Center the artwork horizontally to the Artboard, and align the vertical center of the placed artwork to the rectangle on the Mask layer.**

   You can easily use the Selection tool to drag the legend group into the correct position if Smart Guides are turned on.

Note:

When you place the map legend file, make sure the Link option is not checked in the Place dialog box.

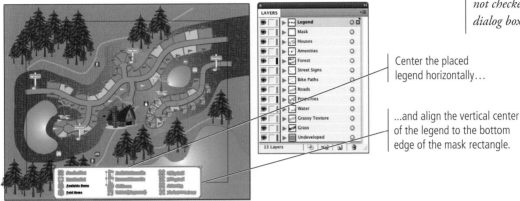

Center the placed legend horizontally…

…and align the vertical center of the legend to the bottom edge of the mask rectangle.

8. **Choose File>Save As. Save the file as** map_layered_unmasked.ai **in your WIP>Realty folder.**

   If you see a message asking you about saving spot colors containing transparencies, click OK and accept the default settings. (You learn about transparency in Project 6.)

   You're saving the file at this point because the next few steps are going to flatten the multiple layers, which will make later revisions more difficult. The map_layered_unmasked file is essentially your archive file before you make some relatively destructive changes.

9. **In the Layers panel, select all but the Legend layer.**

   The map legend is not going to be clipped by the mask, so it can remain on its own layer.

10. **In the Layers panel Options menu, choose Merge Selected.**

    You can merge only selected layers, or you can use the Flatten Artwork command to combine all layers in the selected file.

11. Lock the Legend layer, and then choose Select>All.

When you create a clipping mask, the topmost selected object is the masking shape; all selected objects below the mask shape are masked.

When you merge (or flatten) layers, the objects on each layer are combined into a single layer; the relative stacking order from the previous layer stack is maintained. In this case, the Mask layer was at the top of the layer stack, so the rectangle on the previous Mask layer is still the topmost object on the combined layer.

12. Choose Object>Clipping Mask>Make.

When you make a clipping mask, the masking object automatically converts to having no fill and no stroke. You can change these attributes after making the mask; if you apply a fill to a masking shape, the fill is added behind the objects that are masked.

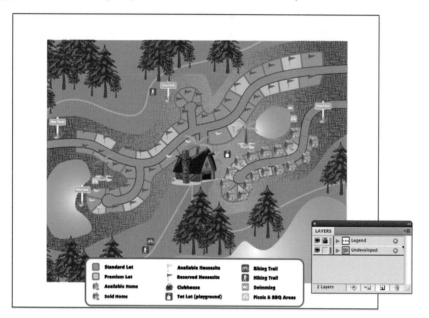

Note:

Clipping masks do not permanently affect the artwork. You can remove the mask by selecting the mask shape and choosing Object>Clipping Mask>Release.

13. Choose File>Save As. Save the file as `map_final_flat.ai` in your WIP>Realty folder.

Native Illustrator files can be placed into Adobe InDesign layouts, as well as into other Illustrator files.

Note:

In this workflow, any future changes would be made to the map_layered_unmasked file, and then Steps 9–13 would need to be repeated. It is far easier to redo these few steps than to make necessary changes when all the artwork is mashed onto a single layer.

14. Choose File>Save As. Save another version of the map file using the Adobe PDF format for high-resolution printing requirements. Name this file `map_final_flat.pdf`.

In case you run into an application that can't manage native Illustrator files, PDF is almost universally accepted.

Note:

Refer to Project 2 for information on the options in the PDF Options dialog box.

15. Close the file.

fill in the blank

1. The _____ panel provides access to colors, patterns, and gradients that have been saved in the active file.

2. _____ brushes scatter copies of an object along a path.

3. _____ brushes apply a brush stroke or object shape across the length of a path.

4. _____ brushes paint a pattern of defined tiles along the length of a path. You can define different tiles for straight edges, inner and outer corners, and the beginning and end of a path.

5. After choosing _____ in the Object menu, you can no longer access a path spine, but you can access the outlines of the resulting shapes.

6. The _____ is used to add multiple copies of a symbol with a single mouse click. When you release the mouse button, added symbol instances are contained within a group.

7. Use the _____ format to export an Illustrator swatch library for use in Photoshop.

8. After clicking the _____ button for a specific symbol instance, editing a symbol's content has no effect on that instance.

9. Double-clicking a symbol instance on the Artboard, or double-clicking a symbol in the Symbols panel, enters into _____.

10. A(n) _____ is an object that masks other artwork; only those areas within the _____ shape remain visible.

short answer

1. Briefly explain the potential problem caused by using spot colors in gradients.

2. Briefly explain possible solutions to the problem caused by shapes such as the cul de sac end tile in pattern brushes.

3. Briefly explain two advantages of using symbols.

Portfolio Builder Project

Use what you learned in this project to complete the following freeform exercise.
Carefully read the art director and client comments, then create your own design to meet the needs of the project.
Use the space below to sketch ideas; when finished, write a brief explanation of your reasoning behind your final design.

art director comments

The Los Angeles parks and recreation director has hired you to create an illustrated, user-friendly map of the Griffith Park recreation complex.

❏ Download the park map from the master plan document (see the client's comments to the right) to use as a template.

❏ Use drawing techniques to create the basic park layout, including roads, trails, and defined paths.

❏ Create or find symbols to identify the different facilities and services.

❏ Add artwork, images, and color however you prefer to identify the different venues and attractions throughout the park.

client comments

Griffith Park is one of the largest public green spaces in the Western United States. The park is home to a number of famous attractions, including the Griffith Observatory, Greek Theater, and the L.A. Zoo. It also offers equestrian trails, bike and hiking trails, and golf courses, as well as swimming, camping, concerts, and a host of other activities.

As you can guess from all of these available activities and attractions, the park is a very large place. We currently have a detailed topographic map from our master plan document, but I'd like something that is more attractive to tourists. I want to create an attractive, colorful, printed brochure that visitors can purchase for a nominal fee at park entrances and facilities, so they can easily find what they're looking for.

I don't have the actual map file. Can you access it on the Internet? I can't remember the address, but if you do a Google search on "Griffith Park Map", it comes up as one of the first results.

project justification

Project Summary

As you completed this map project, you learned a wide range of important new skills — including managing many types of assets (swatches, patterns, and brushes), accessing built-in and custom libraries, and creating your own custom assets. You can apply these skills at any stage of an Illustrator project, saving significant amounts of time and effort.

Some of the planning work for this project was completed by the art director — including creating the icons for different elements of the artwork — and approved by the client in an earlier project meeting. Rather than taking the time to recreate those elements, you streamlined the design process by accessing that artwork as symbols that can be easily updated as necessary.

Using symbols, you created a file that can be easily modified to indicate new home sales and reservations — one of the primary requirements of the project.

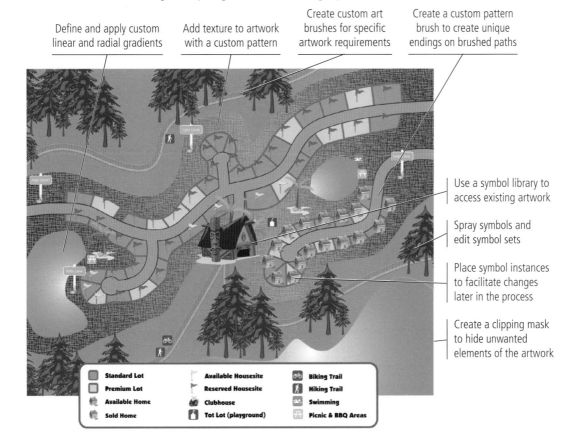

Define and apply custom linear and radial gradients

Add texture to artwork with a custom pattern

Create custom art brushes for specific artwork requirements

Create a custom pattern brush to create unique endings on brushed paths

Use a symbol library to access existing artwork

Spray symbols and edit symbol sets

Place symbol instances to facilitate changes later in the process

Create a clipping mask to hide unwanted elements of the artwork

Standard Lot · Premium Lot · Available Home · Sold Home · Available Housesite · Reserved Housesite · Clubhouse · Tot Lot (playground) · Biking Trail · Hiking Trail · Swimming · Picnic & BBQ Areas

Letterfold Brochure

Your client is a real estate developer specializing in affordable homes in gated suburban communities. The developer wants to create a mailing brochure that can be sent to real estate agents and prospective buyers, announcing a new community being built in central Florida.

This project incorporates the following skills:

❏ Creating a template for a letterfold brochure that meets folding production requirements

❏ Importing client-supplied text and controlling the flow of text across multiple frames

❏ Working with styles to automate repetitive text-formatting tasks

❏ Correcting typographic problems such as baseline alignment, smart punctuation, orphans, and widows

❏ Checking for and correcting spelling errors in the context of a specific layout

❏ Placing images to suit the unique needs and possibilities of a folding brochure

client comments

I really don't have that much input on what the flyer should look like — you know better then I what an effective brochure should look like. I have the text and a few pictures I want to include; you can modify those pictures as necessary to better fit the overall project.

art director comments

A lot of people design folding documents incorrectly. Some people use a six-page layout with each page the size of the final folded job; other people use two pages, each one divided into three equal "columns." In both cases, all panels on the job are the exact same width — which is wrong.

Paper has inherent thickness; any panel that folds "in" to the other panels needs to be smaller than the other panels. In the case of a folding brochure, the inside panel needs to be 1/16″ smaller than the other panels.

Different types of folding documents also have different facing- or non-facing-page requirements. For a letterfold, the job needs to be set up on two separate Artboards with guides and margins that mirror each other. One page has the front panel, back panel, and the outside of the folding flap; the other page has the three inside panels.

The last item to remember is that the brochure will be a self-mailer; the back panel needs to be left blank, with only the return address in the upper-left corner.

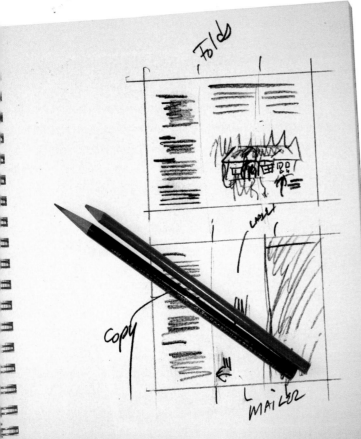

project objectives

To complete this project, you will:

❏ Define folding guides and margins as required for a folding document

❏ Create an Illustrator template file so you can access common layouts again later

❏ Import client-supplied copy into an existing text area

❏ Manage the flow of copy across multiple text frames

❏ Define paragraph and character styles to simplify formatting across multiple text elements

❏ Replace standard punctuation with smart punctuation

❏ Control hyphenation and line spacing

❏ Check spelling in a layout

❏ Place images based on the panel position in the final folded piece

When you design entire pages, you need to be aware of several important measurements. **Trim size** is the size of the flat page (for example, a letter-size piece of paper has a trim size of 8.5 × 11″). When pages are printed on a commercial output device, they are typically combined with other pages (possibly multiple copies of the same page) on a large press sheet. After the ink is dry, the individual pages are cut or trimmed from the press sheets to end up with the final job.

Because commercial printing is a mechanical process, there is inherent variation in the output from one page to another and in the accuracy of any given device (including the cutters that cut apart pages). **Bleed allowance** is the distance objects should extend beyond the trim. Using a bleed ensures that no unwanted white space appears around the edges of the final trimmed output (if there is variation in the cutting process). Most printers require at least a 1/8″ bleed allowance, but you should always check with the output provider who is producing a specific job.

Live area is the space within the trim area where it is safe to place important content. Live area is essentially the opposite of bleed allowance; content within the live area remains untouched during the trimming process.

When working with folding (multi-panel) documents, the trim size of the job is the size it appears before folding. Folding documents add another mechanical variable — the folder — to the process. To compensate for potential variation in the folding stage, you should also understand the concept of folding allowance.

There are two basic principles to remember when dealing with documents that fold:

- Paper has thickness. The thicker the paper, the more allowance you need to plan for the fold.

- Paper sometimes shifts as it flows through the machine's paper path.

In the following illustration, a document has one fold — a smaller panel that folds over to cover half of the inside of the brochure. Fold marks on the outside layout must mirror the inside of the brochure so that, when folded, the two sides align properly.

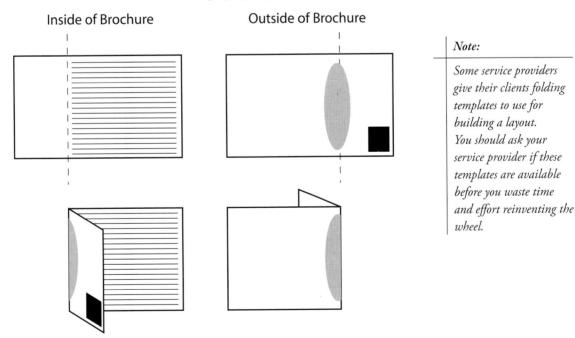

Inside of Brochure   Outside of Brochure

Note:

Some service providers give their clients folding templates to use for building a layout. You should ask your service provider if these templates are available before you waste time and effort reinventing the wheel.

ILLUSTRATOR FOUNDATIONS

There are several standard types of folded documents, each with specific formulas for setting up the layout.

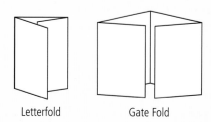
Letterfold   Gate Fold

Accordion Fold

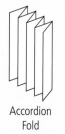
Double Parallel Fold

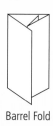
Barrel Fold

Letterfold (often incorrectly called "trifold" because it results in three panels) brochures can be printed at any size. There are three panels to a side and two folds; letterfold brochures should be created with facing pages because the two sides of the sheet need to mirror each other.

The formula for creating a letterfold brochure typically requires the panel that folds in to be 1/16″ narrower than the two outside panels. (Ask your service provider if 1/16″ allowance is enough based on the type of paper you're using.) Half of the area removed from the inside panel (1/32″) is added to each of the outside two panels.

> Trim size ÷ 3 = Starting panel size
>
> Fold-in panel = Starting panel size − 1/16″
>
> Outside panels = Starting panel size + 1/32″

Gate folds result in a four-panel document. The paper is folded in half, and then each half is folded in half toward the center so the two ends of the paper meet at the center fold. The formula for creating a gate fold is similar to the formula for the letterfold brochure; the panels that fold in are 1/16″ narrower than the two outside panels. Gate-fold brochures can be created with non-facing pages.

> Trim size ÷ 4 = Starting panel size
>
> Fold-in panels = Starting panel size − 1/32″
>
> Outside panels = Starting panel size + 1/32″

Accordion folds — a comparatively unusual format — can have as many panels as you prefer. When it has six panels (three on each side), it's often referred to as a "Z-fold" because it looks like the letter Z. Because the panels don't fold into one another, an accordion-fold document has panels of consistent width. Accordion-fold brochures can be created with non-facing pages.

> Paper size ÷ Number of panels = Panel size

Double-parallel folds are commonly used for eight-panel rack brochures (such as those you often find in a hotel or travel agency). Again, the panels on the inside are 1/16″ narrower than the outside panels. This type of fold uses facing pages because the margins need to line up on the front and back sides of the sheet. Double parallel-fold brochures should be created with facing pages.

> Trim size ÷ 4 = Starting panel size
>
> Outside panels = Starting panel size + 1/32″
>
> Fold-in panels = Starting panel size − 1/32″

Barrel folds (also called **roll folds**) are perhaps the most common fold for 14 × 8.5″ brochures. The two outside panels are full size, and each successive panel is 1/16″ narrower than the previous one. Barrel-fold brochures should be created with facing pages.

> Trim size ÷ 4 = Starting panel size
>
> Outside panels = Starting panel size + 1/32″
>
> Fold-in panel 1 = Starting panel size − 1/32″
>
> Fold-in panel 2 = Starting panel size − 3/32″

CREATE MARGIN AND BLEED GUIDES

On the outside of a letterfold brochure, the left panel is the fold-in panel; it is slightly narrower than the other two panels. On the inside of the brochure, the right panel is the fold-in panel. Because the panels for a letterfold brochure are different sizes, the inside of the brochure must be a reflection of the outside. In this exercise, you create a single Illustrator file with multiple Artboards to manage both sides of the brochure.

1. **Copy the Estates folder from the WIP folder on your resource CD to the WIP folder where you are saving your work.**

2. **Open the New Document dialog box and type letterfold in the Name field.**

3. **Choose Letter in the Size menu, select the Landscape page orientation option, and choose Inches as the default units.**

4. **Change the Number of Artboards field to 2 and choose the Arrange by Row option. Set the Spacing field to 1″.**

   The arrangement options determine how the multiple Artboards appear in the new document.

   The Grid options place multiple Artboards left-to-right, top-to-bottom, based on the defined number of rows. The Arrange options place all Artboards in a single row or column.

   By default, the top-left Artboard is Artboard 1, then Artboard 2, and so on. If you select the Change to Right-to-Left Layout option, Artboard 1 automatically appears as the top-right Artboard, then Artboard 2, and so on.

5. **In the Bleed area, make sure the chain icon is active (dark gray). Type 0.125 in the Top Bleed field and press Tab to highlight the next bleed field.**

   With the chain icon active, the bleed fields are constrained; in other words, changing one bleed value changes all four bleed values to the same measurement.

6. **In the Advanced options, choose CMYK in the Color Mode menu and choose High (300 ppi) in the Raster Effects menu.**

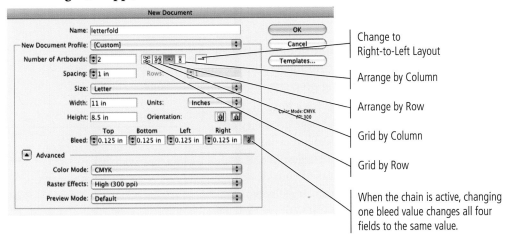

7. **Click OK to create the new file.**

The red line is the bleed guide.

The black line is the Artboard edge.

8. **Save the file as a native Illustrator file named `letterfold.ai` in your WIP>Estates folder.**

9. **Continue to the next exercise.**

 ## DEFINE PAGE AND FOLDING GUIDES

If you look at a flat representation of each side of the brochure, the fold-in (short) panel is on opposite sides of the layout. Because of this positioning, the two sides of a letterfold brochure need to mirror each other — and the folding guides for the outside short panel need to be in the correct locations relative to the inside short panel.

It's important to consider the output process when planning a job with documents that have multiple pages folded one or more times, or other non-standard page sizes. The mechanics of printing require specific allowances for cutting, folding, and other finishing processes.

You should note that the issues presented here have little to do with the subjective elements of design. Layout and page geometry are governed by specific variables, including mechanical limitations in the production process. These principles are rules, not suggestions. If you don't leave adequate margins, for example, elements of your design will be cut off or will misalign from one page to the next. It really won't matter how good a design looks on your monitor if it's cut off the edge of a printed page.

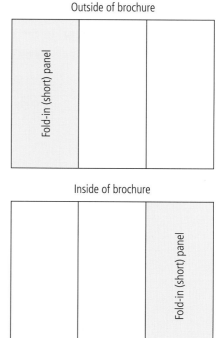

Outside of brochure

Fold-in (short) panel

Inside of brochure

Fold-in (short) panel

1. **With letterfold.ai open, use the Rectangle tool to create a rectangle with 10.5″ width and 8″ height on the left Artboard.**

2. **Choose View>Guides>Lock Guides to toggle off that feature.**

   You are going to use the Control panel to place precise guides. For this to work correctly, guides must be unlocked.

If the menu command does not show a checkmark, the guides are already unlocked in the file.

3. **Using the Align options in the Control panel, choose the Align to Artboard option, and then align the center of the rectangle both vertically and horizontally.**

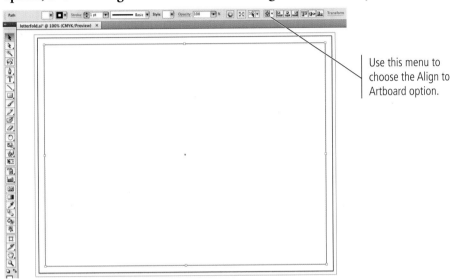

Use this menu to choose the Align to Artboard option.

Note:

Choose View>Guides> Release Guides to convert a guide object into a regular object; the object's original fill and stroke (before you converted it to a guide) are restored. (This is an all-or-nothing action. You can't release a single custom guide; you have to release all of them at once.)

4. **With the rectangle selected, choose View>Guides>Make Guides to turn the rectangle into a guide.**

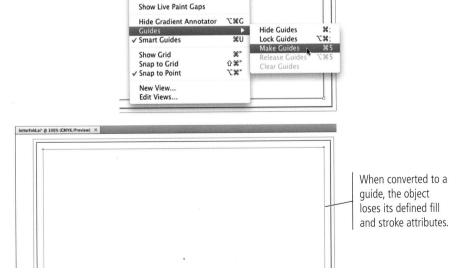

When converted to a guide, the object loses its defined fill and stroke attributes.

Note:

Press Command/ Control-5 to create a guide from any selected object. Add the Shift key to release all guides that have been created from objects.

Note:

View>Guides>Clear Guides removes all guides from the page. If you want to remove only a single guide, you can select it (as long as it's unlocked) and press Delete.

5. **With the rulers visible (View>Show Rulers), click the vertical ruler and drag a guide onto the left Artboard.**

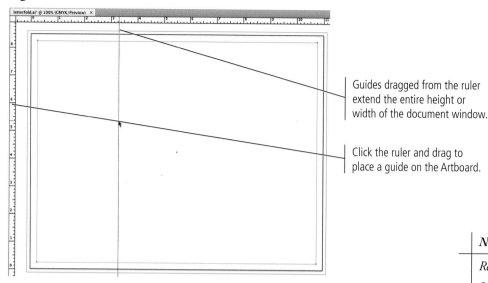

Guides dragged from the ruler extend the entire height or width of the document window.

Click the ruler and drag to place a guide on the Artboard.

6. **Use the Control panel to position the guide exactly 3.687″ from the left edge of the Artboard.**

This left Artboard represents the inside of the brochure, so the right panel is the fold-in panel. It needs to be slightly narrower than the other two panels. This guide is the first of the two fold guides, positioned exactly where it needs to be in relation to the overall trim size.

The X value defines the position of the vertical guide.

Because guides are unlocked, you can select the placed guide and modify its position, just as you would a regular object on the Artboard.

7. **Drag another vertical guide onto the left Artboard, and use the Control panel to position it at X: 7.375″.**

These two guides result in a right panel (the one that folds in) of 3.625″ and the other two panels at 3.687″.

Note:

Remember, if you have a small monitor or Application frame, the X and Y fields in the Control panel might be condensed into a "Transform" hot-text link that opens the Transform panel, where you can define the guide positions.

Note:

Remember, each Artboard requires folding guides in different positions. Because the guides extend the entire height of the document window, this method of using guides to mark fold lines wouldn't work if the Artboards were stacked in a column. To successfully use this method with vertically stacked Artboards, you have to use lines converted to guides as the folding guides.

8. **Click the intersection of the two rulers and drag the zero point onto the left folding guide on the left Artboard.**

When you release the mouse button, the zero point changes to reflect the new position you defined by dragging.

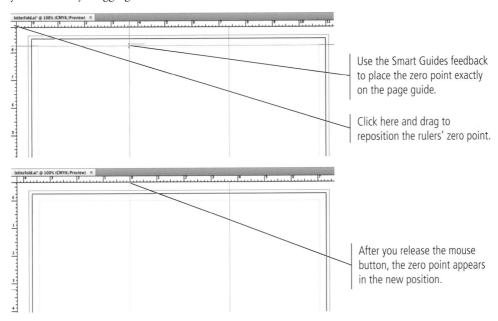

Use the Smart Guides feedback to place the zero point exactly on the page guide.

Click here and drag to reposition the rulers' zero point.

After you release the mouse button, the zero point appears in the new position.

9. **Using the Line tool with a 1-pt black stroke, draw a vertical line that extends from the top margin guide to the bottom margin guide.**

Remember that you can use the Shift key while drawing with the Line tool to constrain the line to be exactly vertical.

10. **Use the Control panel to position the new line at X: –0.25″.**

This places the line 1/4″ from the folding guide — effectively creating a right margin guide for the left panel.

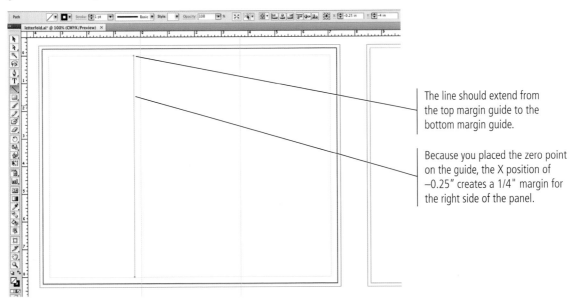

The line should extend from the top margin guide to the bottom margin guide.

Because you placed the zero point on the guide, the X position of –0.25″ creates a 1/4″ margin for the right side of the panel.

11. **Press Option/Alt-Shift and drag the vertical line to clone it exactly right; position the clone at X: 0.25″.**

This second line serves as the left margin guide of the center panel.

12. **Select both lines and convert them to guides.**

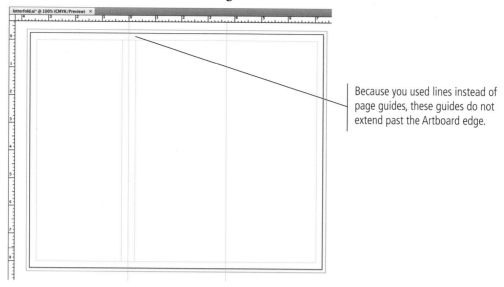

Because you used lines instead of page guides, these guides do not extend past the Artboard edge.

13. **Move the zero point to the second folding guide, and then use the same technique from Steps 9–12 to create margin guides 0.25″ away from both sides of the second folding guide.**

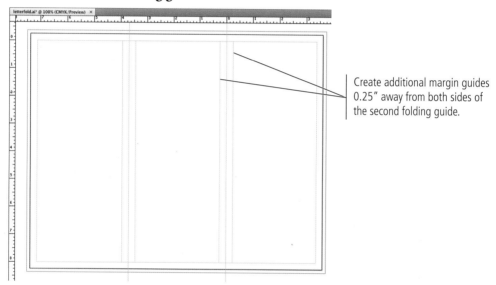

Create additional margin guides 0.25″ away from both sides of the second folding guide.

14. **Using the Selection tool, click the right Artboard to activate it.**

15. **Click the zero-point origin and drag until Smart Guides show you have dragged to the top-left corner of the right Artboard.**

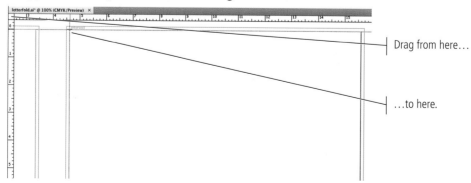

Drag from here…

…to here.

16. **Using the same methods you used to create guides on the left Artboard, create folding and margin guides on the right Artboard.**

> Folding Guide 1   X: 3.625″
>
> Folding Guide 2   X: 7.312″

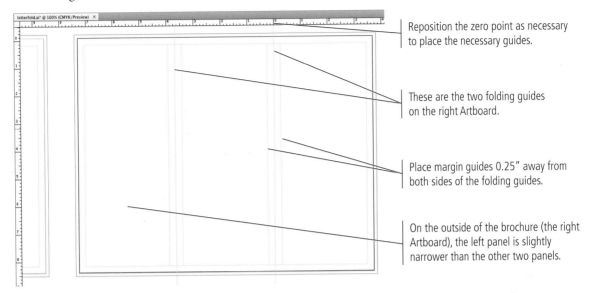

Reposition the zero point as necessary to place the necessary guides.

These are the two folding guides on the right Artboard.

Place margin guides 0.25″ away from both sides of the folding guides.

On the outside of the brochure (the right Artboard), the left panel is slightly narrower than the other two panels.

17. **Using the Selection tool, click anywhere within the boundaries of the left Artboard, and then double-click the zero-point crosshairs to restore the zero-point to it original position (the bottom-left corner of the left Artboard).**

If you have only one Artboard, double-clicking the zero-point crosshairs resets the zero-point crosshairs to the original position. If you have more than one Artboard, double-clicking resets the zero-point to the bottom-left corner of the active Artboard.

By clicking the left Artboard first, you define the Artboard where Illustrator will reset the zero point.

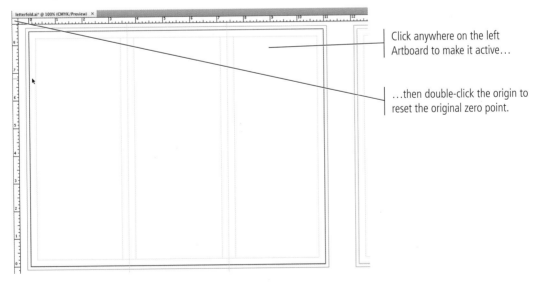

Click anywhere on the left Artboard to make it active…

…then double-click the origin to reset the original zero point.

18. **Choose View>Guides>Lock Guides to toggle that option on.**

Now that all guides are in place, locking them protects them from being accidentally moved or deleted.

19. **Save the file and continue to the next exercise.**

Now that the folds and margins are marked, you need to add slugs (identifying or informational text that appears entirely outside the trim area) to remind you which panel plays what role in the finished piece.

1. **With `letterfold.ai` open, click with the Type tool to create a point-type object above the first panel and outside the bleed guide of the left Artboard. Type** Inside Panel 1.

   These text areas are for your information while designing the piece. They will not be included in the output, and they should not interfere with the actual design area.

   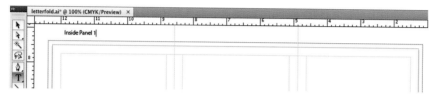

2. **Using the Selection tool, clone (Option/Alt-drag) the type object, and place the clone above the second panel. Change the text above the second panel to** Inside Panel 2.

3. **Clone the type object again, and place the third copy above the right panel. Change the text to** Inside Panel 3 - fold in.

   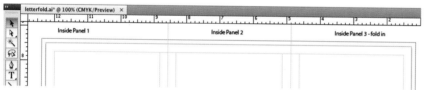

Note:

You can press Shift while cloning to constrain the clone's movement to 45° increments.

4. **Using the Line tool, create a 1-pt black vertical line, about 1/2″ high. Position the line above the first folding guide, directly outside the bleed guide.**

5. **In the Stroke panel, check the Dashed Line option.**

   Choose Window>Stroke to open the standard Stroke panel, or click the Stroke hot text in the Control panel to open the Stroke panel attached to the Control panel. If you don't see the Dashed Line check box, choose Show Options in the panel Options menu.

6. **Type** 3 **in the first Dash field, press Tab, and type** 3 **in the first Gap field.**

   The dash and gap fields define the specific appearance of dashed lines.

   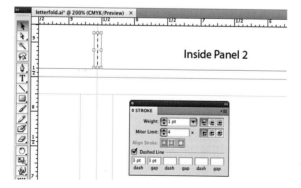

7. **Clone the fold mark and place the clone above the second folding guide.**

8. **Select both dashed lines. Clone the lines and place the clones directly below the bleed guide at the bottom of the page.**

   If you press Shift while cloning the lines, you can drag down to position the clones exactly below the original lines (at the same X position).

9. **Choose View>Guides>Hide Guides to review the current Artboard.**

Note:

Press Command/Control-; (semicolon) to toggle guide visibility.

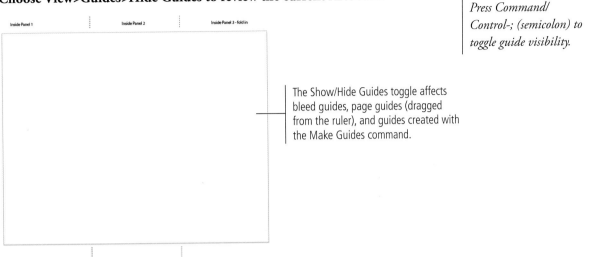

The Show/Hide Guides toggle affects bleed guides, page guides (dragged from the ruler), and guides created with the Make Guides command.

10. **Choose View>Guides>Show Guides to make the guides visible again.**

The Stroke Panel in Depth

ILLUSTRATOR FOUNDATIONS

The default Stroke panel shows only the Stroke Weight field. If you choose Show Options in the panel Options menu, you see a number of other choices for defining custom strokes.

The **Cap** options define the appearance of a stroke beyond the endpoint of the line.

The **Join** options define the appearance of corners where two lines meet. When Miter Join is selected, you can define a miter limit in the Miter field. A miter limit controls when the corner switches from a pointed joint to a beveled joint, as a factor of the stroke weight. If you define a miter limit of 2 for a 2-point line, the corner is beveled if the pointed corner extends beyond 4 points (2 × 2).

The **Align** options determine where the stroke is placed relative to the actual path.

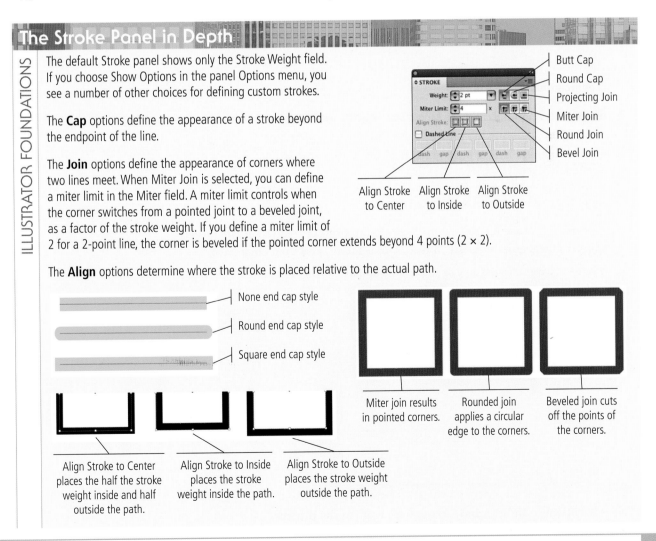

Butt Cap
Round Cap
Projecting Join
Miter Join
Round Join
Bevel Join

Align Stroke to Center   Align Stroke to Inside   Align Stroke to Outside

None end cap style
Round end cap style
Square end cap style

Miter join results in pointed corners.
Rounded join applies a circular edge to the corners.
Beveled join cuts off the points of the corners.

Align Stroke to Center places the half the stroke weight inside and half outside the path.

Align Stroke to Inside places the stroke weight inside the path.

Align Stroke to Outside places the stroke weight outside the path.

11. **Select and clone all three text slugs (type objects). Move the clones into position above the right Artboard. Change the text in each slug as follows:**

Left slug	Outside Panel 1 - fold in
Center slug	Outside Panel 2 - mail info
Right slug	Outside Panel 3 - front cover

12. **Add 1-pt dashed folding marks above and below the right Artboard at the position of the folding guides.**

13. **Toggle guides off and review your work.**

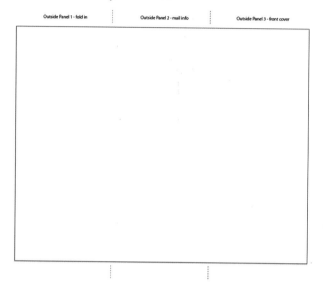

14. **Toggle guides back on.**

15. **In the Layers panel, rename Layer 1 as Guides and lock the layer.**

None of the existing elements are part of the layout "design." By placing each element on its own locked layer, it will be easier to hide them as a group while you work on the aesthetic elements of the job.

16. **Save the current file (File>Save).**

17. **Choose File>Save As. With your WIP>Estates folder selected as the target, choose Illustrator Template in the Format menu, and then click Save.**

Since you have taken the time to properly set up these folding guides, you are saving your work as a template so you can access these same folds whenever you need them.

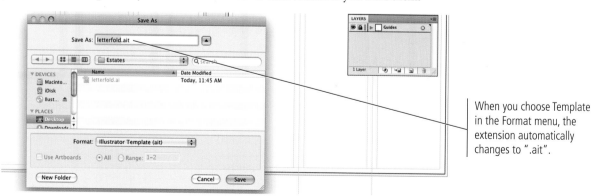

When you choose Template in the Format menu, the extension automatically changes to ".ait".

18. **Close the file and continue to the next stage of the project.**

Stage 2 Managing Imported Text

Completing this project involves combining a number of client-supplied images and text files into the layouts you defined in the first stage of the project.

IMPORT TEXT FOR THE INSIDE PANELS

Preparing for the text elements simply means bringing in the two text files the client gave you, and then dividing them so you can place the correct pieces of text in the correct columns on the templates.

1. **Choose File>Open. Navigate to letterfold.ait in your WIP>Estates folder and click Open.**

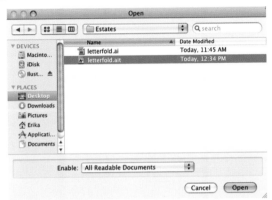

Note:

You can overwrite a template by manually typing the same file name as the original template when you save the file. You will be asked to confirm that you're sure you want to replace the existing file.

When you open a template file, you are actually opening a copy of the template with the name "Untitled." This prevents you from accidentally overwriting the original template.

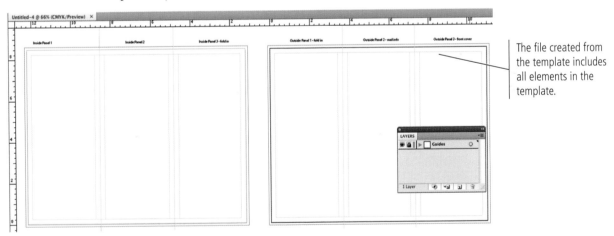

The file created from the template includes all elements in the template.

2. **Add new layers named Text and Graphics above the existing Guides layer.**

3. **Select the Text layer to make it active, and choose the Type tool in the Tools panel.**

4. **On the left Artboard, click at the top-left margin guide and drag to the bottom-right corner of Inside Panel 1.**

When you click and drag with the Type tool, you create an area-type object (also simply called a type area, and commonly referred to as a text frame).

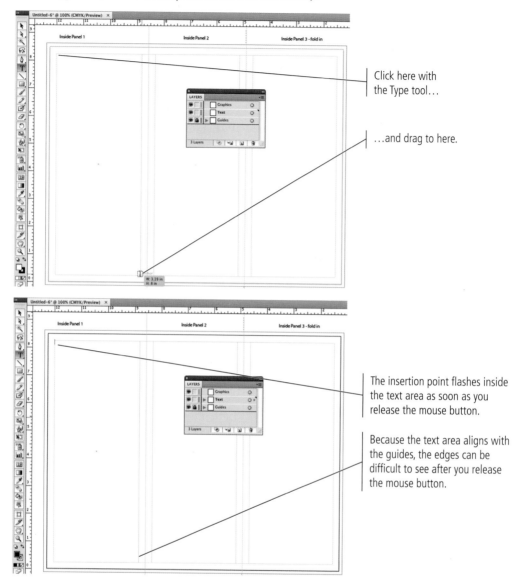

Click here with the Type tool…

…and drag to here.

The insertion point flashes inside the text area as soon as you release the mouse button.

Because the text area aligns with the guides, the edges can be difficult to see after you release the mouse button.

5. **With the insertion point flashing in the new type area, choose File>Place. Navigate to inside.doc in the RF_Illustrator>Estates folder and click Place.**

When you import a Microsoft Word file into Illustrator, the application asks how you want to handle formatting in the file. In addition to the basic text, you can also choose to include special options such as a table of contents, footnotes, and an index.

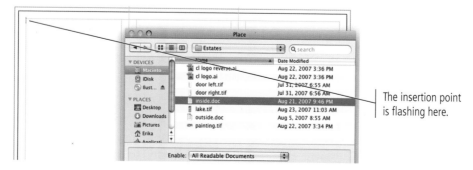

The insertion point is flashing here.

6. **In the Microsoft Word Options dialog box, make sure the Remove Text Formatting option is not checked and click OK.**

If the Remove Text Formatting option is checked, the imported copy will be formatted with the Illustrator default type settings only. Although you will typically reformat most imported text, it's a good idea to import text with formatting so you can review the editorial priority of the copy (i.e., where titles and headings appear).

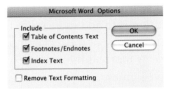

7. **Review the information in the Font Problems dialog box, and then click OK.**

For the text to display properly with the formatting that was applied in the Word file, Illustrator needs access to the same fonts that were used in the Word file. If you don't have the same fonts available on your system, you might see a Font Problems dialog box listing the missing fonts. This dialog box appears more often than not when you import a Microsoft Word file. In many cases, you can simply dismiss it because you will replace the original fonts with ones more suited to professional graphic design.

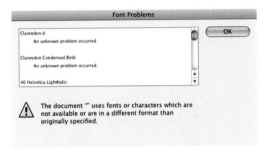

The text from the Word file flows into the type area where the insertion point was flashing. The small red symbol at the bottom of the object is called the overset text icon; this icon tells you the story includes more text than will fit in the available space.

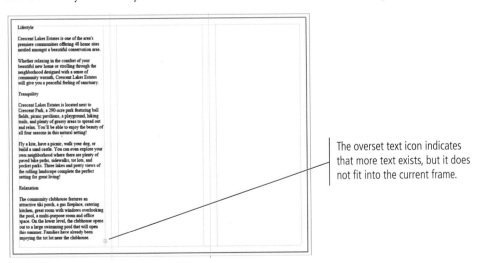

The overset text icon indicates that more text exists, but it does not fit into the current frame.

8. **Save the file in your WIP>Estates folder as a native Illustrator file named** estates.ai**.**

Now that you are incorporating project-specific content, you are saving the file as a document, rather than a template.

9. **Continue to the next exercise.**

THREAD MULTIPLE TYPE AREAS

When a story includes more text than the current type area can accommodate, you have to decide how to solve the problem. In some cases, when only one or two words are overset, minor changes in formatting will create the additional space you need. If you can edit the text (which you usually can't), changing a word or two might also help.

When you can't edit the client-supplied text, and when you have a considerable amount of overset text (as in this project), the only solution is to add more space for the leftover text. Here again, you have two alternatives: cut some of the text and paste it into another type area, or link the existing area to one or more additional type areas (called threading) so the story can flow through multiple frames.

The story you're working with in this project is intended to fill the first panel, as well as the top of the second and third panels. In this case, it's better to thread multiple text frames instead of dividing the story into multiple pieces.

1. **With estates.ai open, click the overset text icon with the Selection tool.**

   The overset text icon appears in a small rectangle, which is the out port of the selected text frame. By clicking the out port of an area (regardless of whether overset text exists), you can direct the flow of text into another type area.

   When you click an out port with an overset text icon, the cursor changes to the loaded text cursor. You can use that cursor to click any other text frame, or click and drag to create a new frame in the same thread.

Note:

You can use the out ports to link empty frames so that when you place text into the frame, it automatically flows from one to another in the chain.

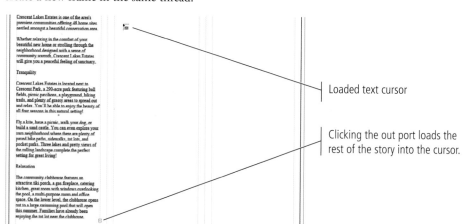

Loaded text cursor

Clicking the out port loads the rest of the story into the cursor.

Using the Find Font Dialog Box

ILLUSTRATOR FOUNDATIONS

You can use the Find Font dialog box (Type>Find Font) to replace one font with another throughout a layout. The top half of the dialog box lists every font used in the file; missing fonts are surrounded by chevrons in the list.

The lower half of the dialog box defaults to show the same list as the top half. You can also choose System in the menu to list all active fonts on your computer.

If you click the Change or Change All button, the font selected in the top list will be replaced with the font selected in the bottom list. You can also use the Find button to locate instances of the font selected in the top list.

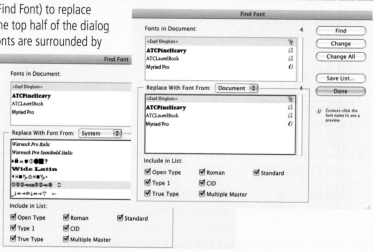

2. **Using the loaded text cursor, click and drag to create a new type area approximately 1″ high at the top of panels 2 and 3.**

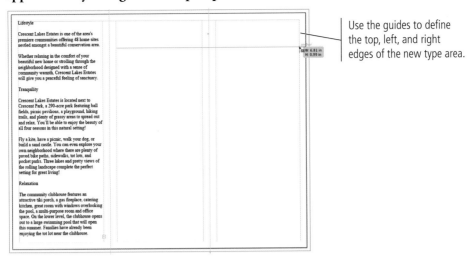

Use the guides to define the top, left, and right edges of the new type area.

When you release the mouse button, the new frame automatically fills with the text that is loaded into the cursor.

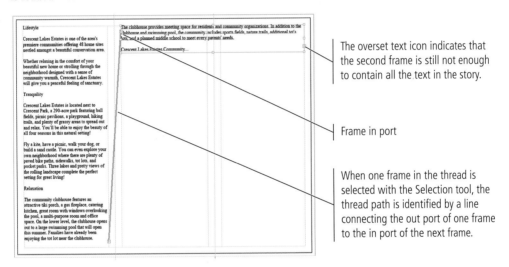

The overset text icon indicates that the second frame is still not enough to contain all the text in the story.

Frame in port

When one frame in the thread is selected with the Selection tool, the thread path is identified by a line connecting the out port of one frame to the in port of the next frame.

3. **Click the second frame's out port to load the cursor with the rest of the story. Click in the second panel below the existing type area, and drag to create a third type area in the second panel, approximately 2.5″ high.**

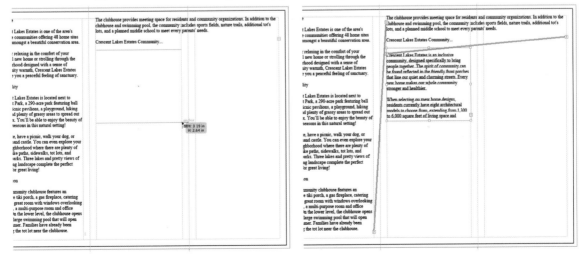

4. **Click the third frame's out port to load the overset text into the cursor. Click and drag to create a fourth type area in the third panel of the layout.**

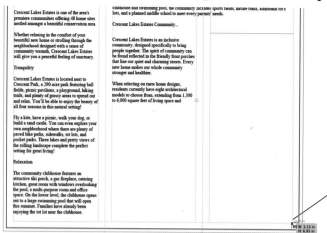

Draw the area to fill the space in the panel so it will be large enough to show the rest of the text.

Note:

If you've had prior experience with page layout software such as Adobe InDesign or QuarkXPress, you might already be familiar with the concept of threading text from one frame to another.

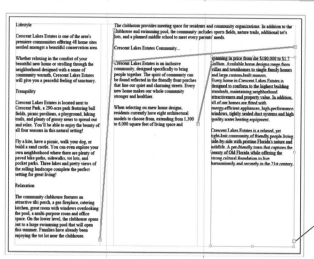

The overset text icon is gone, so the entire story is now visible.

5. **Open the Transform panel. Using the Selection tool, select the lower frame in panel 2. Drag the bottom-center handle until the frame height is approximately 3″.**

Unfortunately, you can't use the Transform panel to change the height of the type area. If you do, you will artificially scale the height of the text within the area to match the new dimensions. This is counter to what you might expect (especially if you are used to working in Adobe InDesign). However, you can drag the type area's handles to resize the area. In this case, the text is not scaled; it reflows to fit the new dimensions of the area.

Note:

If you don't see bounding-box handles for the text area, choose View>Show Bounding Box.

Note:

If you use the Transform panel to change the dimensions of a text area, type in the area is artificially scaled based on the new dimensions you define.

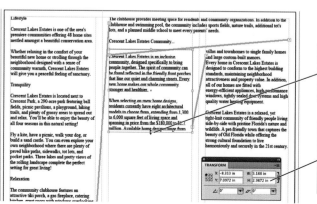

Drag the area handles to resize the area and reflow text to fit the new dimensions.

Even though you can't use it to change the area height, the Transform panel allows you to monitor the new dimensions.

6. **Save the file and continue to the next exercise.**

WORK WITH HIDDEN CHARACTERS

Your layout now includes a story that threads across four separate text frames. The only obvious formatting is extra space between paragraphs. You can identify the intended headings (the short paragraphs), but the layout lacks the polish and finesse of a professional design.

1. **With `estates.ai` open, choose Type>Show Hidden Characters.**

   Hidden characters identify spaces, paragraph returns, and other non-printing characters. It can be helpful to view these hidden characters, especially when you are working with long blocks of text.

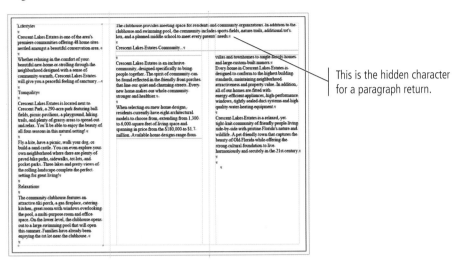

This is the hidden character for a paragraph return.

   When you work with client-supplied text, you will frequently find each paragraph separated by two (or more) paragraph returns. This kind of formatting creates the visual effect of space between paragraphs, but it also adds an unnecessary element that needs to be controlled in the story. Because Illustrator's typographic controls allow you to easily change the spacing of paragraphs, these double paragraph returns are unnecessary and should be deleted.

   Unfortunately, Illustrator's Find and Replace function is very limited. Unlike InDesign, you can't use the utility to search for a paragraph return character — you have to manually delete the extra paragraph returns.

2. **Using the Type tool, click to place the insertion point in the first empty paragraph in the left panel, and then press Delete/Backspace.**

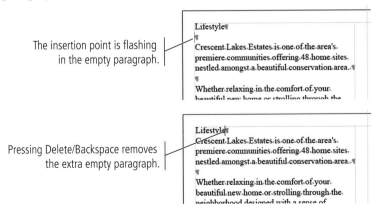

The insertion point is flashing in the empty paragraph.

Pressing Delete/Backspace removes the extra empty paragraph.

3. **Using the same method, remove all extra empty paragraphs in the story.**

In the next exercise, you use paragraph formatting options to control the space between individual paragraphs.

4. **Save the file and continue to the next exercise.**

Using the Find and Replace Dialog Box

Finding and replacing text is a function common to many applications, including Illustrator. Illustrator's Find and Replace utility (Edit>Find and Replace) is fairly straightforward, offering the ability to search for and change text in a layout, including a limited number of special characters and options.

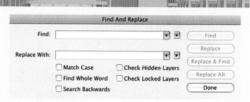

The check boxes below the Replace With field are toggles for specific types of searches:

- When **Match Case** is active, a search only finds text with the same capitalization as the text in the Find What field. For example, a search for "Illustrator" does not identify instances of "illustrator" or "ILLUSTRATOR."

- When **Find Whole Word** is active, a search only finds instances where the search text is an entire word (not part of another word). For example, a search for "old" as a whole word does not include the words "gold," "mold," or "embolden."

- When **Search Backwards** is selected, Illustrator searches from the current insertion point to the beginning of the story. (This option is irrelevant if the insertion point is not placed in a document.)

- When **Check Hidden Layers** is active, the search includes text frames on layers that are not visible. In this case, the hidden layer remains visible until you close the Find and Replace dialog box

- When **Check Locked Layers** is active, the search locates text on locked layers.

You also have limited ability to search for and replace special characters that cannot be typed directly into the dialog box fields. The menus associated with the Find and Replace With fields list the special characters that can be identified and replaced.

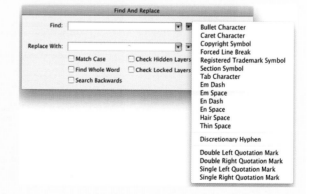

CREATE PARAGRAPH STYLES

In its present state, the brochure text appears as a long block of hard-to-read text. Using Illustrator's typographic controls, you can turn this block of lackluster text into a professional-looking layout.

Of course, when you work with long blocks of text, many of the same formatting options are applied to different text elements throughout the story (such as headings). To simplify the workflow, you can use styles to store and apply multiple formatting options in a single click.

1. **With estates.ai open, click with the Type tool to place the insertion point anywhere in the text and choose Select>All.**

   When you use the Select All command, you select the entire story in all threaded frames.

2. **Using the Character panel, change the selected text to 10-pt ATC Laurel Book with 12-pt leading.**

Note:

You might think that it would make more sense to start with the smaller of the two types of styles (character styles), but that doesn't really follow conventional workflows. In on-the-job situations, you use paragraph styles far more often than character styles.

The black highlighting identifies the selected text.

The new formatting fits all text into the first two text frames.

3. **Using the Paragraph panel, change the Left Indent and Right Indent fields to 5 pt, and change the Space After Paragraph field to 6 pt.**

   If you don't see the Space Before and Space After fields in the Paragraph panel, open the panel Options menu and choose Show Options.

   Attributes that affect the entire paragraph — such as alignment, indents, and space before and after paragraphs — can be controlled in the Paragraph panel. Unlike character formatting, paragraph formatting applies to the entire paragraph in which the insertion point is placed. If text is selected, paragraph formatting applies to any paragraph that is entirely or partially selected.

Note:

To open the Character panel, choose Window> Type>Character, or click the Character hot text in the Control panel.

Note:

To open the Paragraph panel, choose Window> Type>Paragraph, or click the Paragraph hot text in the Control panel.

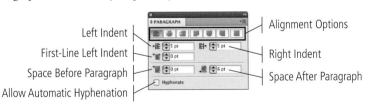

Left Indent
First-Line Left Indent
Space Before Paragraph
Allow Automatic Hyphenation
Alignment Options
Right Indent
Space After Paragraph

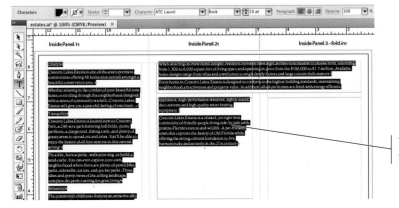

The new Space After Paragraph value forces text into the third threaded frame.

4. **With all text still selected, open the Paragraph Styles panel (Window>Type>Paragraph Styles).**

   A style is a convenient method for storing and applying multiple formatting options with a single click. The Paragraph Styles panel shows two available options:

   - Normal Paragraph Style. By default, every Illustrator document includes the Normal Paragraph Style option. The formatting applied in this style is the default formatting for new text areas created in the file. You can edit this style to change the default settings for new text areas in the existing file.

   - Normal. This is Microsoft Word's version of Normal Paragraph Style. When you imported the Word file in an earlier exercise, you also imported the text formatting — including the Normal style that was applied in the Word file.

5. **Make sure Normal+ is selected in the panel.**

   The plus sign (+) next to the Normal style name indicates that some formatting has been applied other than what is defined in the style. This can cause problems later, so you are going to redefine Normal to match the formatting you defined for the selected text.

   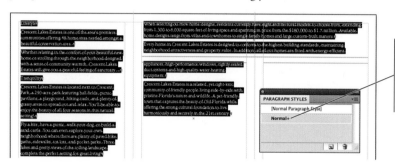

   The selected text is formatted with the Normal style, but some options have been modified locally. The + indicates that some formatting in the selected text is different than what is defined by the style.

6. **Open the Paragraph Styles panel Options menu and choose Redefine Paragraph Style.**

   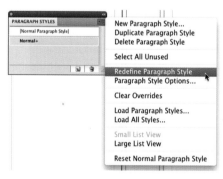

   Note:

   You can choose Clear Overrides in the Paragraph Styles panel Options menu to restore the selected text to the defined formatting in the applied style.

   This option changes the selected style formatting to match the formatting of the current text selection (in the document).

   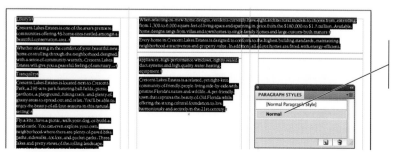

   Because the style definition now matches the text formatting, the "+" no longer appears in the style name.

7. **In the Paragraph Styles panel, double-click the Normal style.**

   Double-clicking a style opens the Paragraph Style Options dialog box for that style, where you can edit the settings stored in the style.

8. **Change the Style Name field to** `Body Copy` **and click OK.**

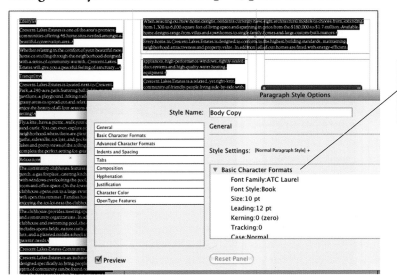

The style contains the formatting attributes of the text that was selected when you redefined the style (in Step 6).

9. **Select only the first paragraph in the story (Lifestyle).**

10. **Change the selected text to 14-pt ATC Pine Heavy. Change the indents to 0 pt, and change the Space After Paragraph value to 2 pt. Change the text color to one of the brown swatches in the default Swatches panel.**

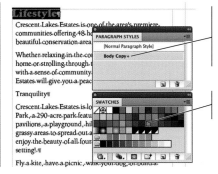

The selected text is formatted with the Body Copy style, but some formatting has been changed from the style's original settings.

We applied this swatch as the text fill color.

Note:

You can also edit a style by single-clicking it in the panel, and then choosing Paragraph Style Options in the panel Options menu.

11. **Using the Type tool, click anywhere in the word "Lifestyle" to place the insertion point, but remove the highlight from the paragraph.**

12. **Click the Create New Style button in the Paragraph Styles panel.**

When you create a new style, it defaults to include all formatting options applied to the currently selected text (or to the location of the insertion point if no characters are selected).

The insertion point is placed in the word "Lifestyle".

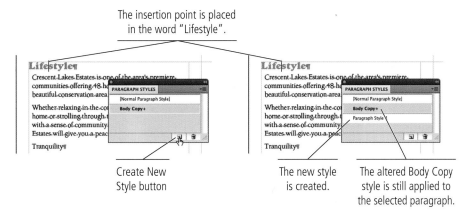

Create New Style button

The new style is created.

The altered Body Copy style is still applied to the selected paragraph.

Note:

Paragraph styles relate to entire paragraphs — anything between two paragraph return (¶) characters. When you define or apply paragraph styles, the actions relate to any paragraph even partially selected (including where the insertion point is flashing).

13. Double-click the new Paragraph Style 1 to edit it. Change the style name to Heading 1 and click OK.

If you double-click a style to edit it, the first click of that double-click applies the style to any selected text. To edit a style without applying it, make sure no text is selected in the layout before double-clicking the style in the panel.

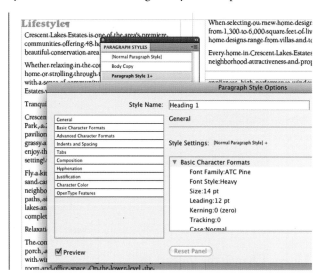

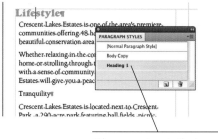

When you return to the layout, the Heading 1 style has been applied to the active paragraph, even though no actual characters are selected.

14. Place the insertion point in the second heading (Tranquility) and click the Heading 1 style in the Paragraph Styles panel.

Applying a paragraph style is as simple as placing the insertion point and clicking a style.

Note:

To apply a style, simply select the text you want to format, and then click the style name in the panel.

15. Using the same method, apply the Heading 1 style to the remaining headings in the story.

16. Choose Type>Show Hidden Characters to toggle off their visibility.

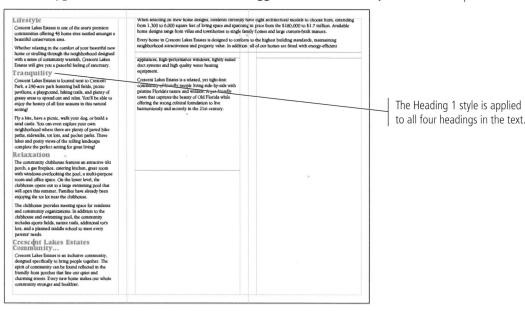

The Heading 1 style is applied to all four headings in the text.

17. Save the file and continue to the next exercise.

EDIT STYLE DEFINITIONS

As you have seen, a style applies multiple formatting options with a single click — which makes styles very useful when you need to apply the same formatting to multiple layout elements.

Styles also have another, more powerful benefit when you're designing layouts. When you change the options applied in a style, any text formatted with the style reflects the newly defined options. In other words, you can change multiple instances of non-contiguous text in a single process, instead of selecting each block and making the same changes repeatedly.

1. **With estates.ai open, make sure nothing is selected in the layout.**

2. **Double-click Heading 1 in the Paragraph Styles panel to open the Paragraph Style Options dialog box.**

3. **Make sure the Preview option is checked in the bottom-left corner of the dialog box.**

   When the Preview option is turned on, your changes dynamically reflect in the layout (behind the dialog box). This allows you to experiment with the changes before you click OK to change the style definition.

Note:

You do not have to select text to change the definition of a style. In fact, you don't even need to select a text frame for this process to work.

4. **Click Indents and Spacing in the list of formatting categories.**

   Different options are available in the right side of the dialog box, depending on what is selected in the list of categories.

Note:

A paragraph style can store character formatting options as well as paragraph formatting options.

5. **Change the Space Before field to 8 pt and press Tab to highlight the next field.**

   To see the effects of your changes, you have to click away from the active field to apply the new value. You can either tab to another field, or click an empty area of the dialog box to preview the results.

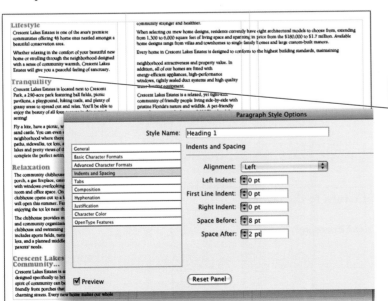

With the Preview option active, you can see the result of changing the space before and after headings before you finalize the change.

6. **Click OK to change the style definition.**

7. **Double-click Body Copy in the Paragraph Styles panel to open the Paragraph Style Options dialog box.**

8. In the Indents and Spacing options, choose Left Justify in the Alignment menu, change the Left Indent to 12 pt, and change the Right Indent to 0 pt.

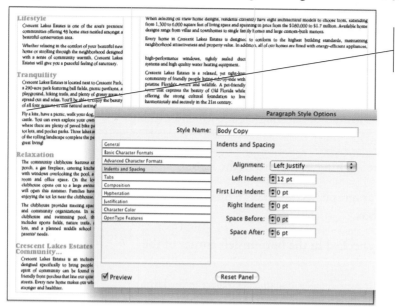

By changing the style definition, you are changing all text formatted with that style.

Note:

You can delete a style by dragging it to the panel Delete button. If the style had been applied, you would see a warning message, asking you to confirm the deletion (you do not have the opportunity to replace the applied style with another one, as you do in Adobe InDesign).

9. Click Basic Character Formats in the list of options. Change the Size to 11 pt and change the Leading to 13.5 pt.

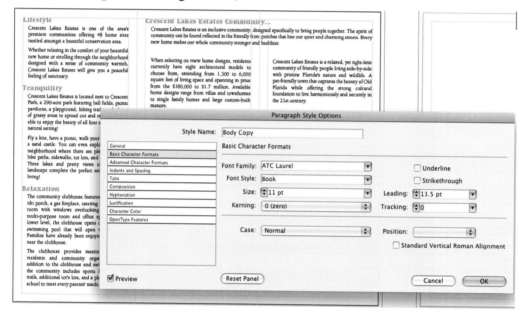

10. Click OK to redefine the style and return to the layout.

11. Save the file and continue to the next exercise.

WORK WITH A CHARACTER STYLE

As with paragraph styles, a character style can be used to store and apply multiple character formatting options with a single click. The primary difference is that character styles apply to selected text only, such as italicizing a specific word in a paragraph or adding a few characters in a different font.

1. With **estates.ai** open, place the insertion point at the very beginning of the story.

2. Type **ʋ** and then press the Spacebar.

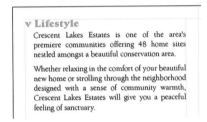

3. Highlight only the letter "v" and change the font to Zapf Dingbats or Wingdings.

   These are standard fonts on most computers, and you should have one or the other. If you have neither font, try Webdings, but change the "v" to a lowercase "l."

   Most of the heading paragraph is formatted with one set of instructions, but a single character is formatted with a different font. This is a perfect use for a character style.

4. With the single alternate character selected, open the Character Styles panel (Window>Type>Character Styles).

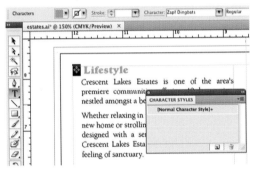

5. Click the Create New Style button at the bottom of the panel.

   The process for creating a character style is essentially the same as creating a paragraph style.

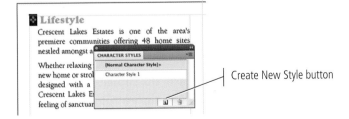

Create New Style button

6. **Double-click the new Character Style 1 item in the Character Styles panel. In the Character Style Options dialog box, change the Style Name field to** Heading Bullet **and click OK.**

As with paragraph styles, when you return to the layout, the selected character has been formatted with the Heading Bullet style.

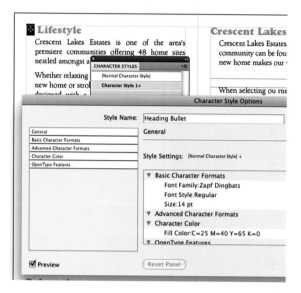

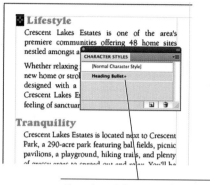

The selected character is formatted with the Heading Bullet style. The + indicates that some non-style formatting has been applied.

7. **With the bullet character selected in the layout, choose Clear Overrides in the Character Styles panel Options menu.**

If you click away from the bullet and then highlight the bullet again, the Heading Bullet style name shows a plus sign. In this case, you know the style matches the character formatting because you created the style based on a single selected character — which you formatted. However, the Character Styles panel still shows that some formatting does not match the style definition.

This is an issue that you should be aware of; if you do not clear the overrides, later changes to the style might not correctly reflect in text formatted with the style. Whenever you work with styles — whether imported or ones you create — check the applied styles to see if a plus sign appears where you know it shouldn't.

Note:

Not every instance of a plus sign next to a style name is a bug or error, but you should always be sure that what you have is really what you want.

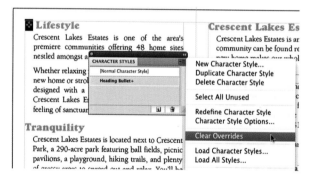

Note:

Styles can easily be imported into another document by choosing Load in the panel Options menu. This allows you to maintain consistency from one file to another without tedious note-taking, copying, or pasting.

8. **Copy the bullet and the space directly after it, and then paste the copied characters at the beginning of the next two headings. Do not paste a copy at the beginning of the fourth heading (Crescent Lakes).**

9. **Deselect everything in the layout.**

10. **In the Character Styles panel, double-click Heading Bullet to open the Character Style Options dialog box.**

11. **Make sure the Preview option is active, and then select Character Color in the list of categories. Scroll through the list of available swatches and click CMYK Blue to select it.**

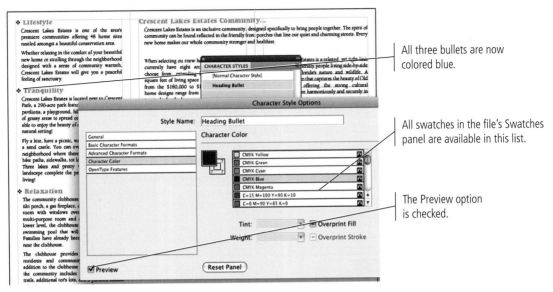

All three bullets are now colored blue.

All swatches in the file's Swatches panel are available in this list.

The Preview option is checked.

12. **Click OK to close the dialog box and change the style definition.**

13. **Using the Selection tool, click the top text frame in the second and third panels to show the frame's bounding box handles. Drag the bottom-center handle up until only the heading appears in the frame.**

Because the four text frames are linked, changing the size of one frame causes the story to reflow within the linked frames.

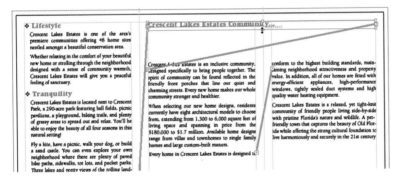

14. **For the lower text frames in panels 2 and 3, change the frames' Y position to 8″ (based on the top-left reference point).**

As we mentioned in a previous exercise, you can't use the Transform panel to resize a text frame. You can, however, use it to change the position of a text frame.

15. **Save the file and continue to the next exercise.**

PLACE TEXT FOR THE OUTSIDE ARTBOARD

Earlier versions of Illustrator (before CS4) did not offer multiple-Artboard capabilities, which meant designers had to create separate files for the inside and outside of two-page brochures. With Illustrator CS4, you can now create multiple Artboards in one file. Once you place and format text on one Artboard (as you already did for the inside of your brochure), you can quickly and easily format the text on the other Artboard (the outside of the brochure).

1. **With `estates.ai` open, use the Type tool to create an area-type object that fills the left panel area on Artboard 2 (the one on the right).**

2. **Place the file `outside.doc` (from the RF_Illustrator>Estates folder) into the type area, including formatting. Click OK when you see the Font Problems dialog box.**

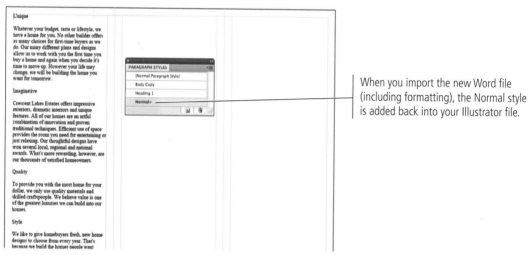

When you import the new Word file (including formatting), the Normal style is added back into your Illustrator file.

3. **Show hidden characters (Type>Show Hidden Characters) and delete all extra paragraph returns from the story. When you're finished, hide hidden characters.**

4. **Select all text in the story and apply the Body Copy paragraph style.**

   Styles apply to the entire document, which means you can apply them in any type object (point or area) in the file — including type objects on different Artboards.

5. **Using the Paragraph Styles panel Options menu, clear the style overrides in the selected text.**

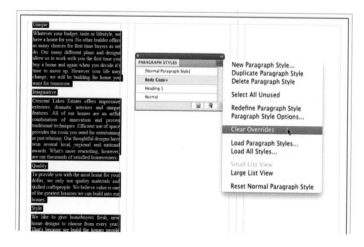

6. **Command/Control-click away from the active text area to deselect it. In the Paragraph Styles panel, click the Normal style, hold down the mouse button, and drag it to the panel Delete button.**

If you keep the mouse button pressed while dragging Normal to the panel Delete button, it isn't necessary to first deselect the highlighted text. However, deselecting the text first prevents you from accidentally applying Normal to the highlighted text if you inadvertently release the mouse button before dragging the style to the Delete button.

The Glyphs Panel in Depth

ILLUSTRATOR FOUNDATIONS

ASCII is a text-based code that defines characters with a numeric value between 001 and 256. The standard alphabet and punctuation characters are mapped from 001 to 128. Extended ASCII characters are those with ASCII numbers higher than 128; these include symbols (copyright symbols, etc.) and some special formatting characters (en dashes, accent marks, etc.). Some of the more common extended characters can be accessed in the Type>Insert submenu.

OpenType fonts offer the ability to store more than 65,000 glyphs (characters) in a single font — far beyond what you could access with a keyboard (even including combinations of the different modifier keys). The large glyph storage capacity means that a single OpenType font can replace separate "Expert" fonts that contain variations of fonts (Minion Swash, for example, is no longer necessary when you can access the Swashes subset of the Minion Pro font).

Unicode fonts include two-bit characters that are common in some foreign language typesetting (e.g., Cyrillic, Japanese, and other non-Roman or pictographic fonts).

The Glyphs panel (Type>Glyphs) provides access to every glyph in a font, including basic characters, extended ASCII and OpenType character sets, and even pictographic characters in Unicode fonts.

Using the Glyphs panel is simple: make sure the insertion point is flashing where you want a character to appear, and then double-click the character you want to place. You can view the character set for any font by changing the menu at the bottom of the panel. By default, the panel shows the entire font, but you can show only specific character sets using the Show menu.

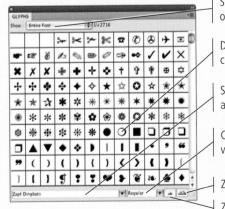

Show all characters of a font, or display only specific types of characters.

Double-click any glyph to insert it at the current location of the insertion point.

Show the characters of a different font.

Change to a different variation of the selected font.

Zoom out

Zoom in

7. Using the same technique as in the previous exercise, apply the Heading 1 paragraph style to the appropriate text, and place the Heading Bullet character at the beginning of each heading. Be sure to clear overrides where necessary.

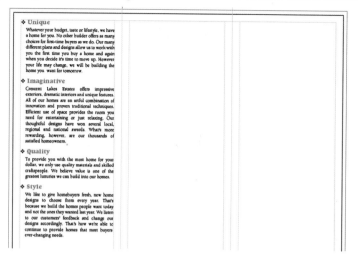

8. Make sure nothing is selected in the layout, and then double-click the Body Copy paragraph style to open the Paragraph Style Options dialog box.

9. In the Indents and Spacing options, change the Left Indent value to 15.5 pt. Click OK to redefine the style.

   Here you see the true power of using styles. By changing the style definition, you adjusted all body copy to align properly with the preceding headings. The change applies to both Artboards.

The new indent value aligns the left indent of the body copy to the first character in the headings.

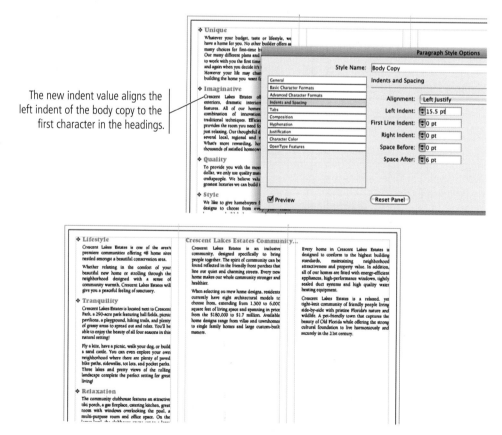

10. Save the file and continue to the next stage of the project.

Stage 3 Fine-Tuning Text

For all intents and purposes, you could say that the text for the inside of the brochure is complete — everything is visible and the headings and body copy are formatted. There are, however, a number of typographic issues that should be addressed so the layout looks professional and well polished, instead of appearing just "good-enough."

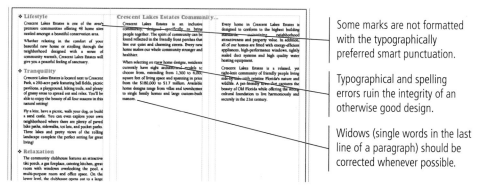

Some marks are not formatted with the typographically preferred smart punctuation.

Typographical and spelling errors ruin the integrity of an otherwise good design.

Widows (single words in the last line of a paragraph) should be corrected whenever possible.

Some of these problems can be solved using Illustrator's built-in tools and utilities. Others require manual adjustment to make sure the text appears exactly how and where you want it to appear.

APPLY SMART PUNCTUATION

Straight double quotes are actually inch marks, and straight single quotes are foot marks. To be typographically correct, these straight marks must be converted to true quotation marks or apostrophes (also called smart quotes or curly quotes).

1. **With estates.ai open, make sure nothing is selected in the layout.**

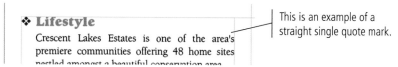

This is an example of a straight single quote mark.

2. **Choose Type>Smart Punctuation.**

This dialog box makes it very easy to search for and change common characters to their typographically correct equivalents. You can affect selected text only, or you can affect the entire document at once.

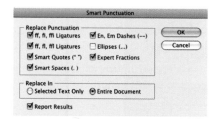

- **ff, fi, ffi Ligatures** converts these letter combinations to the replacement ligatures.
- **ff, fl, ffl Ligatures** converts these letter combinations to the replacement ligatures.
- **Smart Quotes** converts straight quotation marks into true (curly) quotes.
- **Smart Spaces** eliminates multiple space characters after a period.
- **En, Em Dashes** converts a double keyboard dash to an en dash and a triple keyboard dash to an em dash.
- **Ellipses** converts three keyboard periods to a single-character ellipsis glyph.
- **Expert Fractions** converts separate characters used to represent fractions to their single-character equivalents.

Note:

Two spaces after a period is a common text problem; it is a relic from a time when manual typewriters placed every character in the same amount of space (called monospace type). To more clearly identify a new sentence, convention called for the typist to enter two spaces after typing a period. This convention still survives today, even though most people never use manual typewriters.

3. **In the Replace Punctuation area, check all options but Ellipses.**

The actual ellipsis character is usually lighter and narrower than three sequential periods. In this project, the ellipsis in the heading should remain prominent, so you will not convert this character.

4. **Make sure the Entire Document option is selected and the Report Results box is checked, and then click OK.**

5. **Review the information in the report dialog box, and then click OK.**

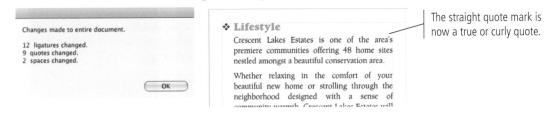

The straight quote mark is now a true or curly quote.

6. **Save the file and continue to the next exercise.**

CONTROL HYPHENATION AND LINE SPACING

The text in the second and third panels has a number of potential problems, some of which are typographically incorrect and others that are more subjective. Some problems, such as widows and orphans, should be fixed whenever possible. For other issues, you must make choices about the best way to present information, such as whether to allow hyphenation.

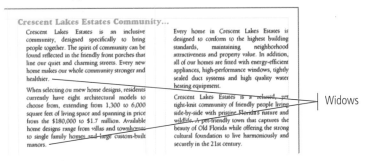

Widows

Note:

*A **widow** is a very short line — usually one or two words — at the end of a paragraph.*

*An **orphan** is a heading or the first line of a paragraph at the end of a column or the last line of a paragraph at the beginning of a column.*

1. **With estates.ai open, use the Type tool to select all four paragraphs in the second and third panels on the left Artboard. Using the Paragraph panel (Window>Type> Paragraph, or by clicking the Paragraph hot text in the Control panel), change the Left Indent value to 0 pt.**

There is no need for these paragraphs to be indented; since the indent resulted in widows at the end of two paragraphs, the first logical choice is to simply remove the indent.

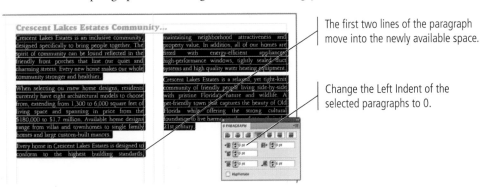

The first two lines of the paragraph move into the newly available space.

Change the Left Indent of the selected paragraphs to 0.

2. Drag up the bottom edge of the second frame so the "Every home" line is forced into the third panel.

Note:

Illustrator does not include automatic orphan control (the "Keep With" options that InDesign users might be familiar with). You have to correct this problem manually by adjusting the frame size.

Although two lines of a paragraph is not technically an orphan, the two columns were badly unbalanced. The paragraphs are now in the correct frames, and the widows have been fixed. However, the right frame has one more line than the left column, which should be fixed if possible.

The first paragraph in the right frame has a line with large gaps between words, which is often the result of justified paragraph alignment. You can try to fix this problem by changing the Justification settings or by allowing hyphenation in the affected paragraphs.

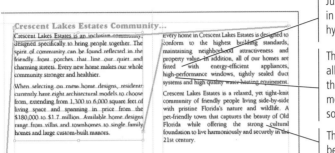

Justified alignment often results in large gaps, especially when hyphenation is turned off.

This word is hyphenated; if you allow hyphenation, the first half of the hyphenated word will probably move up to the previous line and solve the spacing problem.

This paragraph might also benefit from hyphenation.

3. Select any part of the two paragraphs in the right frame. In the Paragraph panel, activate the Hyphenation check box.

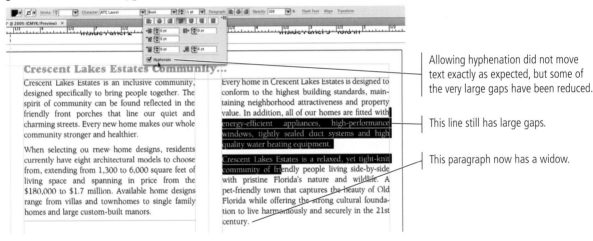

Allowing hyphenation did not move text exactly as expected, but some of the very large gaps have been reduced.

This line still has large gaps.

This paragraph now has a widow.

4. Place the insertion point anywhere in the last paragraph of the story. In the Paragraph panel Options menu, choose Hyphenation.

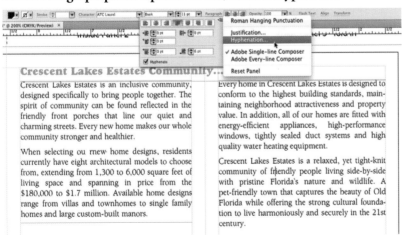

Note:

You can also apply and control hyphenation in a paragraph style definition. In this exercise, you are affecting the two selected paragraphs only (called local formatting).

5. **In the Hyphenation dialog box, activate the Preview check box, and then drag the slider all the way to the left.**

The Hyphenation options allow you to control the way Illustrator applies hyphenation.

- **Words Longer Than _ Letters** defines the minimum number of characters that must exist in a hyphenated word.

- **After First _ Letters** and **Before Last _ Letters** defines the minimum number of characters that must appear before or after a hyphen.

- **Hyphen Limit** defines the maximum number of hyphens that can appear on consecutive lines. (Remember, you are defining the limit here, so zero means there is no limit — allowing unlimited hyphens.)

- **Hyphenation Zone** defines the amount of white space allowed at the end of a line of unjustified text before hyphenation begins.

- If **Hyphenate Capitalized Words** is checked, capitalized words (proper nouns) can be hyphenated.

The Hyphenation slider allows Illustrator to determine the best spacing, depending on the location of the slider. Dragging to the left allows more hyphens, but typically results in better overall line spacing. Dragging to the right reduces the number of hyphens in a paragraph, but might produce less-pleasing results in line spacing.

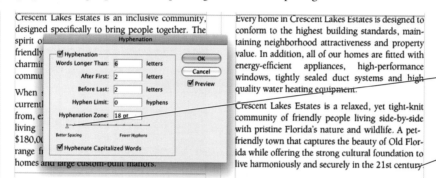

Drag this slider left so Illustrator will place more importance on line spacing than the number of hyphens in a paragraph.

Adjusting the Hyphenation slider fixes the remaining widow.

6. **Click OK to close the Hyphenation dialog box and apply the change.**

7. **Place the insertion point in the first paragraph of the frame and choose Justification in the Paragraph panel Options menu.**

A paragraph does not have to be entirely selected to change the hyphenation and justification settings. Any paragraph partially selected — including the one where the insertion point is placed — will be affected.

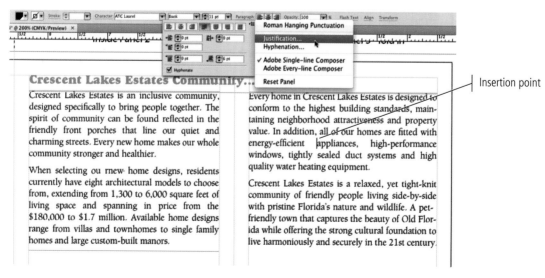

Insertion point

8. **Activate the Preview option, and then change the Minimum Word Spacing field to 100%.**

The Justification dialog box allows you to control the minimum, desired, and maximum spacing that can be applied to create justified paragraph alignment.

- **Word Spacing** defines the space that can be applied between words (where spaces exist in the text). At 100% (the default Desired amount), no additional space is added between words.

- **Letter Spacing** defines the space that can be added between individual letters within a word. All three values default to 0%, which allows no extra space between letters; at 100%, an entire space would be allowed between characters (making the text very difficult to read).

- **Glyph Scaling** determines how much individual character glyphs can be scaled (stretched or compressed) to justify the text. At 100%, the default value for all three settings, characters are not scaled.

- In narrow columns, single words sometimes appear on a line by themselves. If the paragraph is set to full justification, a single word on a line might appear to be too stretched out. You can use the **Single Word Justification** menu to center or left-align these single words instead of leaving them fully justified.

Note:

Issues such as paragraph and word spacing are somewhat subjective. Some of your clients will break all other typographic rules to reduce loosely fitted lines, while others will absolutely refuse to allow widows, and still others will disallow hyphenation of any kind.

The specific way you solve problems will be governed by your client's personal typographic preferences.

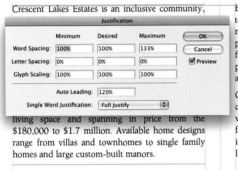

By enlarging the value in the Minimum Word Spacing field, the spaces between words in the second line are enlarged. Basically, you are telling Illustrator, "Do not reduce the amount of word spacing below 100% of the normal spacing that would be applied by pressing the spacebar."

This reflows the rest of the paragraph and results in larger word spaces throughout. However, because the entire paragraph now has larger word spacing, the paragraph appears to be more balanced than when some lines had tight spacing and others had loose spacing.

9. **Click OK to apply the change and return to the layout.**

10. Using whichever method you prefer, fix the remaining widow in the first panel of the file.

We activated automatic hyphenation for the paragraph, and dragged the spacing slider all the way to the left in the Hyphenation dialog box

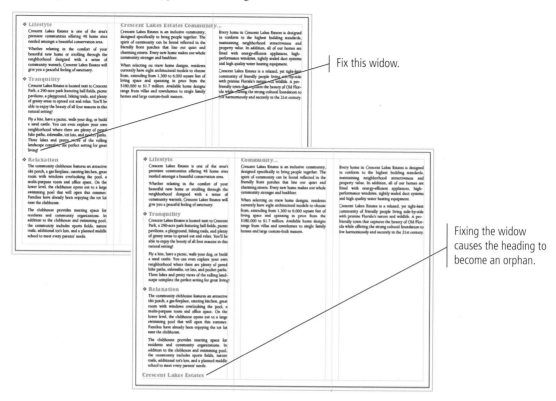

Fix this widow.

Fixing the widow causes the heading to become an orphan.

11. Using the Selection tool, drag up the bottom edge of the type area in the left panel to force the heading back into the frame over the middle and right panels.

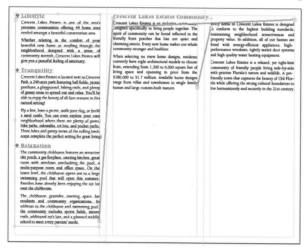

12. Save the file and continue to the next exercise.

CHECK SPELLING

Misspellings and typos creep into virtually every job, despite numerous rounds of content proofs. These errors can ruin an otherwise perfect job. As with most desktop applications, Illustrator allows you to check the spelling in a document. It's all too common, however, to skip this important step, which could result in spelling and typing errors in the final output.

You might not (and probably won't) create the text for most design jobs, and you aren't technically responsible for the words your client supplies. However, you can be a hero if you find and fix typographical errors before a job goes to press; if you don't, you will almost certainly hear about it after it's too late to fix. You simply can't brush off a problem by saying, "That's not my job" — at least, not if you want to work with that client again.

1. **With `estates.ai` open, make sure nothing is selected in the layout.**

2. **Choose Edit>Check Spelling.**

Note:

Illustrator checks spelling based on the language defined for the text. You can change the default language in the Hyphenation pane of the Preferences dialog box, or you can assign a specific language to selected text using the Character panel.

3. **In the Check Spelling dialog box, click Start.**

   Illustrator locates the single letter "v" used to add the bullet at the beginning of each heading in the left column. In this case, the single letter is not an error.

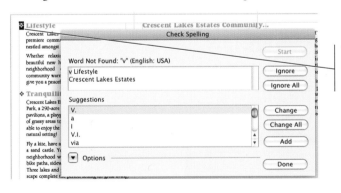

The suspect word is highlighted in the layout so you can review it in context.

4. **Click Ignore All.**

   There are three instances of the "v" bullet. If you click Ignore instead of Ignore All, the Spell Check process will identify each of the "v" bullets as a possible error.

5. Evaluate the next potential error.

The hyphenated phrase "290-acre" is not in the dictionary. However, this compound noun is correct in the context of the surrounding content.

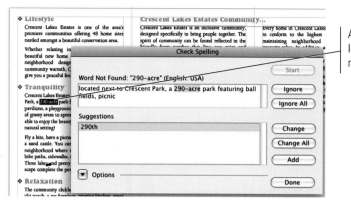

As soon as you click Ignore or Ignore All, Illustrator shows the next suspected error.

Note:

Never simply click Change when you check spelling. Carefully evaluate the suspect word in the context of the layout.

6. Click Ignore, and then evaluate the next potential problem.

The next problem is actually a typo — the client typed the space in the wrong place. Instead of "our new," the text reads "ou rnew." Fortunately, Illustrator found the problem.

7. Make sure "our" is selected in the Suggestions list and click Change.

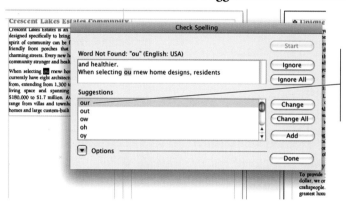

Always make sure the option you want is selected in this list. The software tries to identify the best replacement, but only you can decide if it's the right choice.

8. With the second half of the typo identified, make sure "new" is selected in the list of suggestions and click Change.

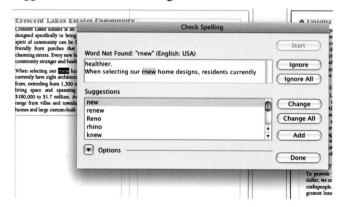

9. **Review the next suspected error, and then click Ignore.**

The word "townhomes" can be a single word or two separate words. In this case, you are assuming your client typed it the way he prefers.

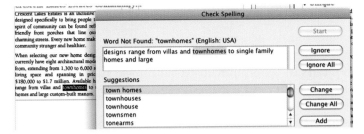

10. **Review the next suspected error, and then click Ignore.**

The Check Spelling function checks all text objects on all Artboards in the file.

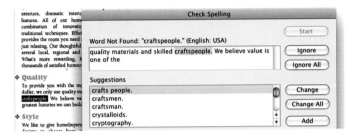

11. **Review the next suspected error. Make sure "home buyers" (2 words) is selected in the list of suggestions and click Change.**

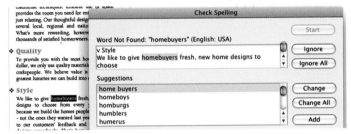

12. **Click Done to close the Check Spelling dialog box.**

When Illustrator can't find any more potential problems, the dialog box shows that the Spell Checker utility is complete.

13. **Save the file and continue to the next exercise.**

Check Spelling Options

If you click the Options button at the bottom of the Check Spelling dialog box, you see a number of choices to refine the evaluation.

- The Find section allows the spell checker to identify repeated words (e.g., "the the") and non-capitalized starts of sentences (i.e., lowercase words immediately following a period and space).

- In the Ignore section, you can force Illustrator to skip words that are all uppercase, words with numbers, and Roman numerals.

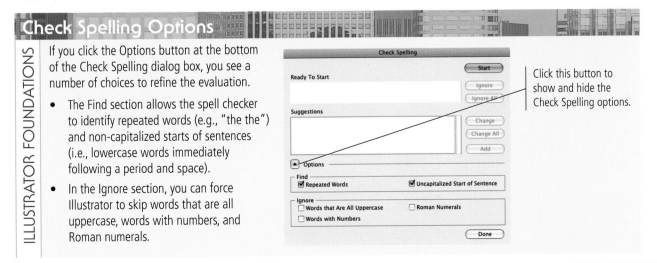

Click this button to show and hide the Check Spelling options.

PLACE LAYOUT IMAGES

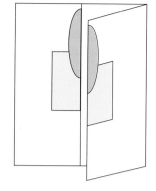

The text for both sides of the brochure is now complete. The only remaining elements to place are the images and logos. Most of this step is simply a matter of placing and positioning the external images.

When you design a letterfold brochure, you should consider the overall design — including folds — when you place images. Consider the schematic for a letterfold brochure. The way the document folds creates an opportunity to extend a single image across the two panels that are visible after the front cover is opened.

1. **With `estates.ai` open, make sure the Graphics layer is selected, and make sure it appears below the Text layer in the layer stack.**

   You are going to place images on the inside and outside of the brochure so that when the brochure cover is opened, the two halves of the image appear next to each other on the appropriate panels.

2. **Choose File>Place. Select `door left.tif` in the RF_Illustrator>Estates folder, check the Link option, and click Place.**

Note:

You might want to lock the Text layer, but it isn't necessary as long as you remember to work only on the Graphics layer.

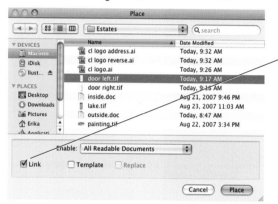

When this box is checked, the placed file will be a link to the actual file; its contents will not be embedded into your document.

3. **Drag the placed image so it fills the left panel (including the bleed area) on the inside of the brochure.**

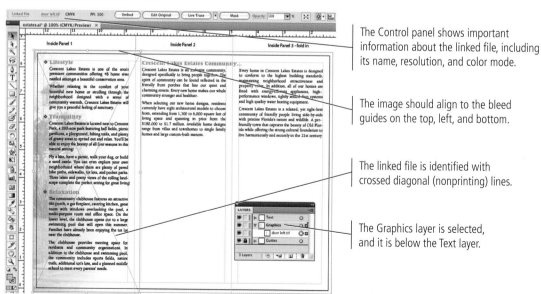

The Control panel shows important information about the linked file, including its name, resolution, and color mode.

The image should align to the bleed guides on the top, left, and bottom.

The linked file is identified with crossed diagonal (nonprinting) lines.

The Graphics layer is selected, and it is below the Text layer.

4. **Choose File>Place. Select `painting.tif` in the RF_Illustrator>Estates folder, uncheck the Link option, and click Place.**

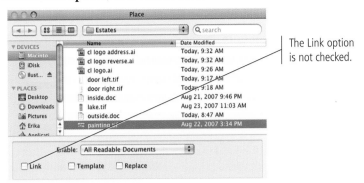

The Link option is not checked.

5. **Drag the painting image to align directly below the text in panels 2 and 3, and align the left edge to the left margin guide of panel 2.**

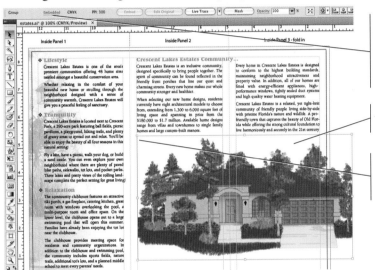

The Control panel shows that the placed image is embedded in the Illustrator file. You can still see color mode and resolution information for the embedded file.

The embedded file does not show crossed diagonal lines.

The image should align to the bottom of the text frame and the margin guide in the middle panel.

6. **Using the Selection tool, click the bottom-right corner of the painting image, press Shift, and drag left until the image fits to the right margin guide of panel 3.**

The painting.tif file is a raster image, which means it has a defined resolution. When you resize a raster image, the number of pixels per inch is stretched or reduced to fit into the new object dimensions. The result of factoring physical size into an image's resolution is called effective resolution.

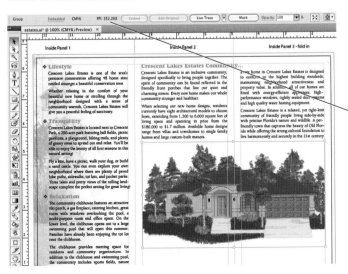

Resizing a raster image affects its resolution proportionally.

Note:

Pressing Shift proportionally scales the selected image.

7. **Choose File>Place. Select cl logo.ai and click Place. In the Place PDF dialog box, choose the Art option in the Crop To menu, and then click OK.**

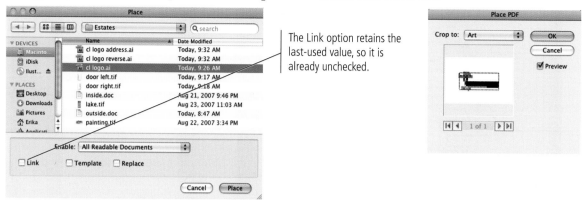

The Link option retains the last-used value, so it is already unchecked.

8. **Using the Selection tool, drag the placed group into the empty area at the bottom of the third panel.**

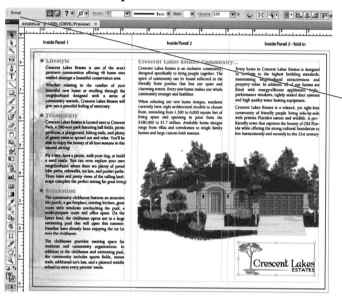

The Control panel shows that the placed image is a group, based on the artwork in the Illustrator file you placed.

9. **On Artboard 2 (the outside of the brochure), place the file door right.tif as a linked image, positioned in the left panel.**

10. **Place the file lake.tif as an embedded image in the right panel.**

11. **Place the file cl logo reverse.ai as an embedded file based on the Crop To Art option, and position it in the lake area of the right panel.**

12. **Place the file ci logo address.ai as a linked file based on the Crop To Art option. Rotate the placed graphic 90° counterclockwise, reduce it 75% proportionally, and position it at the margin guides of the middle panel (as shown in the following image).**

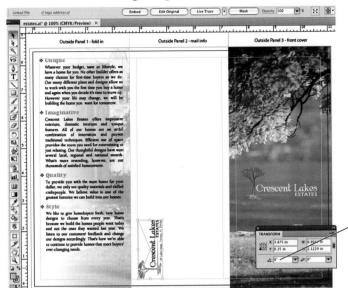

Use the Transform panel to rotate the object 90° counterclockwise.

13. **Save the file and continue to the next exercise.**

 ## MANAGE LINKED AND EMBEDDED FILES

As you have seen, you have the option to either place a link to an external file or embed the external file data directly in your Illustrator file. There are advantages and disadvantages to each method, so you should consider what you need to accomplish before you choose. (There is very little reason to use both methods in a single file. We have done so simply for the sake of teaching you how to manage the different options.)

When you create a link to an external file, the external file needs to be available when the Illustrator file is output. If the file is moved or changed in any way since being linked to the Illustrator file, you have to update the linked file before outputting the Illustrator file.

If you embed the external file into the Illustrator file, the physical file data becomes part of the file. This eliminates the potential problem of missing required files, but it can add significantly to the size of your Illustrator file.

1. **With estates.ai open, open the Links panel (Window>Links).**

2. **Select door right.tif in the Links panel and click the Go To Link button at the bottom of the panel.**

   When you click the Go To Link button, the file is selected in the layout and centered in the current workspace.

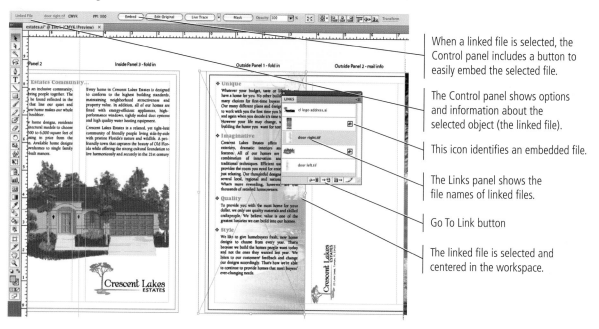

When a linked file is selected, the Control panel includes a button to easily embed the selected file.

The Control panel shows options and information about the selected object (the linked file).

This icon identifies an embedded file.

The Links panel shows the file names of linked files.

Go To Link button

The linked file is selected and centered in the workspace.

3. **In the Control panel, click the Embed button.**

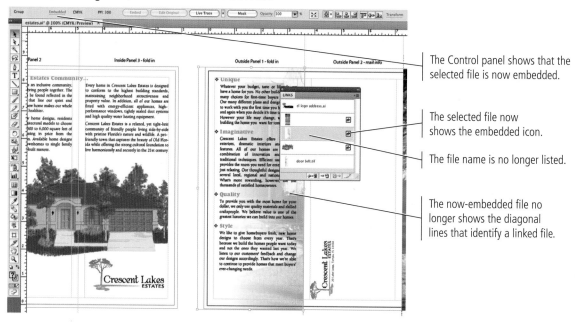

The Control panel shows that the selected file is now embedded.

The selected file now shows the embedded icon.

The file name is no longer listed.

The now-embedded file no longer shows the diagonal lines that identify a linked file.

4. **Repeat Steps 2–3 to embed the linked door left.tif file.**

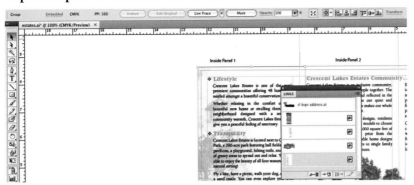

5. **Select ci logo address.ai in the Links panel and click the Go To Link button.**

6. **Click the Embed button in the Control panel.**

   When you place and embed one Illustrator file into another, it is placed as a group of the objects that make up the placed file. When you embed a previously linked Illustrator file, it is converted to a group of artwork objects, just as if you had placed it without linking.

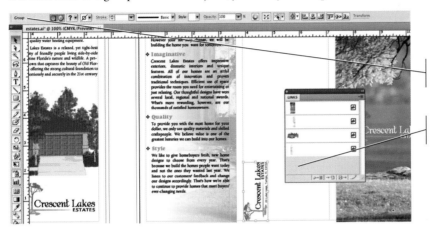

The selected object is now a group of native artwork objects.

After being embedded, the file is no longer listed in the Links panel.

7. **Save the file and then close it.**

When you work with linked files, the external files must be available and up to date when you output the file to print or PDF. The Links panel uses various icons to help you monitor these files and identify potential problems.

If a file has been **modified**, you can click the Update Link button to show the most current version of the linked file in your Illustrator layout.

If a file is **missing**, you can click the Relink button to open a navigation dialog box so you can identify the current location of the file (or the location of a different file if you want to replace the existing one).

When a file is linked but not embedded, clicking the Edit Original button opens the linked file in its native application

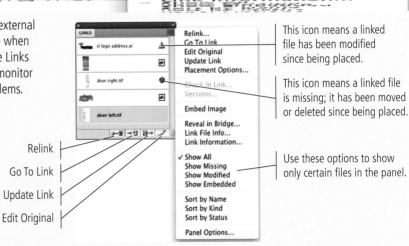

This icon means a linked file has been modified since being placed.

This icon means a linked file is missing; it has been moved or deleted since being placed.

Use these options to show only certain files in the panel.

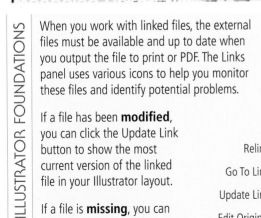

Relink
Go To Link
Update Link
Edit Original

(for example, Illustrator .ai files open in Illustrator, .tif and .psd files open in Adobe Photoshop, and so on). You can make whatever changes are necessary, save the file, and then return to Illustrator and update the link.

1. _____ is the size of a flat page, before folding, and after it has been cut from a press sheet.

2. _____ is the area where it is safe to place important content.

3. _____ is the amount you must extend objects beyond the actual Artboard edge for them to safely appear at the cut edge of the final job.

4. For a folding document, panels that fold in need to be at least _____ smaller than outside panels.

5. The _____ command can be used to convert any object into a nonprinting guide.

6. When guides are _____, you can use the Control panel or Transform panel to position them using precise measurements.

7. You can reposition the _____ by dragging from the intersection of the horizontal and vertical page rulers.

8. The _____ icon indicates that more text exists in the story, but does not fit into the current text area or chain.

9. You can use the _____ dialog box to change all instances of a selected font in the active file.

10. You can choose the _____ command to show visible, nonprinting indicators of spaces and paragraph return characters.

1. Briefly explain how the mechanics of printing affect the layout for folding documents.

2. Briefly explain two advantages created by using styles for text formatting.

3. Briefly explain the difference between linked and embedded files.

Use what you learned in this project to complete the following freeform exercise.
Carefully read the art director and client comments, then create your own design to meet the needs of the project.
Use the space below to sketch ideas; when finished, write a brief explanation of your reasoning behind your final design.

art director comments

The real estate developer was very pleased with your work, and has recommended your agency to a colleague at the local chamber of commerce. Your new client, Outdoor Adventures, specializes in "extreme tourism" — rock climbing, white water rafting, and similar activities.

To complete this project, you should:

❏ Create a letterfold brochure to present the client's information in an aesthetically pleasing layout.

❏ Reserve the middle panel of the brochure's outside for mailing information, including only the client's logo and return address.

❏ Use any or all of the client's supplied images to support the text. All files are in the RF_Builders>Adventures folder.

client comments

Our company caters to what we call the "extreme tourist." We put together tour packages for people who like to experience and challenge nature. Some of our most popular tours take people up Mount Whitney, go rafting down the Colorado River, and even hike through the Alaskan ice fields.

Our business is doing very well with people who live on the West Coast, but we would like to extend our reach to the entire United States. We've purchased mailing lists from magazines that have a similar audience as our clients, and we want to create a brochure that we can mail to approximately 10,000 potential new clients.

We've given you the text for the brochure — there isn't much of it, because the images tell a more dramatic story of what we do. We've given you a number of images from our previous tours, and you can use as many of them as you think are necessary. If you want to use any other images, just make sure they follow the general theme of "outdoor adventures."

project justification

To begin the letterfold layout, you built technically accurate folding guides for each side of the brochure, incorporating nonprinting fold guides and text frames into the slug area. To speed up the process for the next time you need to build one of these common letterfold jobs, you saved your initial work as a template.

Completing this project also required extensive work with imported text, specifically importing styles from a Microsoft Word file and controlling the flow of text from one frame to another. You also worked with several advanced text-formatting options, including paragraph and character styles and typographic fine-tuning controls.

Templates and styles are designed to let you do the majority of work once and then apply it as many times as necessary; many different projects can benefit from these tools, and you will use them extensively throughout your career as a graphic designer.

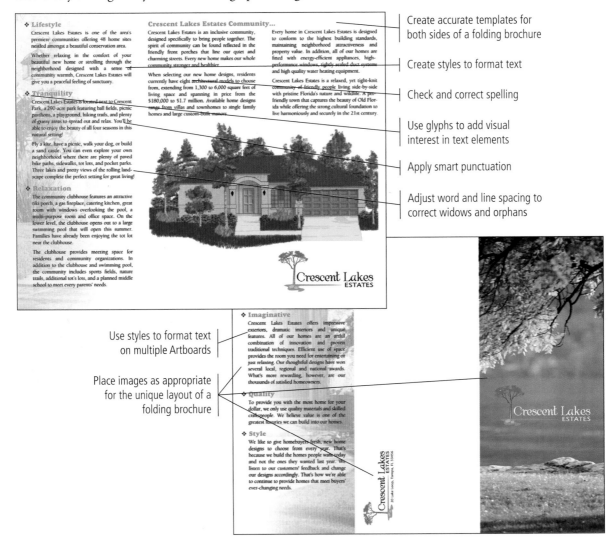

Create accurate templates for both sides of a folding brochure

Create styles to format text

Check and correct spelling

Use glyphs to add visual interest in text elements

Apply smart punctuation

Adjust word and line spacing to correct widows and orphans

Use styles to format text on multiple Artboards

Place images as appropriate for the unique layout of a folding brochure

Cereal Box

Your client, a food manufacturer, is redesigning the packaging for its primary product — a cereal targeted at the health-conscious consumer. The client hired you to build the new package. You will incorporate elements from the old design as you develop an attractive, modern packaging concept.

This project incorporates the following skills:

❏ Sampling colors to create custom swatches

❏ Placing a variety of external files in the appropriate locations to meet package design requirements

❏ Creating type on an irregular path

❏ Controlling object blending modes and opacity

❏ Using different methods to isolate parts of a group

❏ Using warp and 3D effects to add depth to artwork

❏ Understanding and defining raster effect settings

❏ Expanding appearance attributes

❏ Flattening transparent effects and attributes

Project Meeting

client comments

Our current package was designed about 20 years ago; it's little more than a white box with a bowl of cereal and our brightly colored logo on the front. We've conducted some focus group studies with our primary target market: women aged 25–50 with an expressed interest in eating well and living a healthy lifestyle. We've found this group prefers a less stark appearance — they find less empty white space and softer colors more appealing than a stark white background.

The new package should use the old logo, but we'd like it to be softer than it is in the basic file. It's vivid pink, which was popular in the 1980s when the old package was designed. We also want to add some color to the entire box to avoid the "sea of white space" syndrome.

We were recently endorsed by the Association for a Healthy America; the organization sent their endorsement logo, which should be included on the box. We also want to incorporate the "recycled" logo in some subtle way; using recycled materials wasn't a big deal in the '80s, but it is now.

art director comments

We have a template from the printer with the package structure already laid out, based on the existing die that's used to cut the flat box from the press sheet. There's no need to reinvent the wheel, so use this template to build the new cereal box artwork.

With the growing focus on breast cancer research and overall health awareness, pink has adopted a new symbolic meaning in American culture. Because the client is targeting the health-conscious female consumer, pink should play a prominent part in the design. Complement and contrast the pink with one or two other colors for various elements; the best bet is to simply pick some colors from the main image for the box cover.

The Food and Drug Administration requires food manufacturers to include product weight and nutrition information on every food package that will be sold in U.S. stores. Other elements are purely decorative, but all six sides of the box should work together to create a cohesive design.

project objectives

To complete this project, you will:

❑ Create the package file from a template

❑ Sample colors to create custom swatches

❑ Place a variety of external files in the appropriate locations to meet package design requirements

❑ Create type on an irregular path

❑ Create arrowheads with effects and filters

❑ Change object blending modes and opacity

❑ Apply raster effects to vector objects and placed images

❑ Apply effects to pieces of a group

❑ Create warp and 3D effects

❑ Define raster effect settings

❑ Expand appearance attributes

❑ Preview and control transparency flattening

❑ Flatten transparency in a PDF file

Stage 1 Building the File Structure

When you work on a package design, it's important to realize that many types of packages have a standard size and shape. If you look around your local grocery store, you'll see that similar products typically have similar packages. Although there is something to be said for standing out in a crowd, packaging design is often governed by the space allowed on store shelves — which means you probably won't have any choice regarding the size and shape of the package.

You also need to understand that packages, especially boxes, are typically designed and printed as a single flat layout using a template to indicate edges and folds; they are then die-cut, folded, and glued. The next time you finish a box of cereal, carefully tear it apart along the glue flaps to see how the package was designed. Because these types of packages are common job sizes, printers often have existing die-cut templates you can use.

 ## CREATE THE PACKAGE FILE FROM A TEMPLATE

The printer for this package has provided you with a template file that includes the die-cut layout and folding guides. You will use this file as the basis for the entire project.

1. On your desktop, drag the **Cereal** folder from the WIP folder on your Resource CD to the WIP folder where you are saving your work.

2. Create a new file by opening the template file named **cereal box.ait** from the RF_Illustrator>Cereal folder. If necessary, resize the view percentage so you can see the entire Artboard.

3. Using the Layers panel, individually show and hide the existing layers and review their contents.

   The file currently has three layers: one has guides that indicate the location of the folds, one has guides that define margin areas around the folds, and one has the die-cut lines for the box shape.

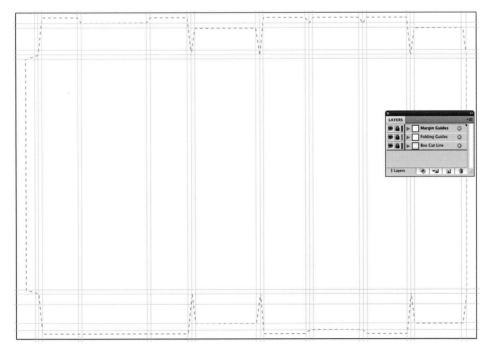

4. **Add four new layers, placing them in the following stacking order:**

   Back

   Jumpstart Side

   Front

   Nutrition Side

There are many ways to organize artwork. Placing each panel's elements on a separate layer makes this type of complex artwork easier to manage. The image below includes a different-colored overlay on the area of each panel, to help you avoid confusion later.

Note:

Even though the panel layers are above the guide layers, guides always appear in front of artwork.

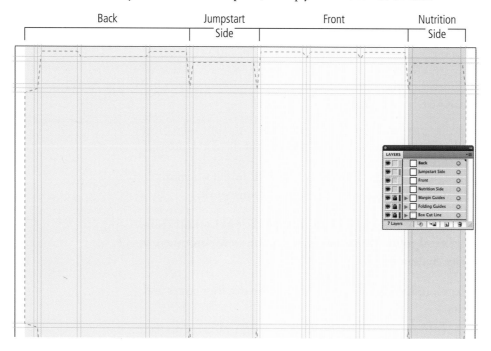

5. **Drag the Box Cut Line layer to the top of the layer stack.**

   Be careful how you drag the layer to reposition it. If you accidentally move the layer to the wrong place in the stack, or move it to be a sublayer of another layer, simply drag it again to the top of the layer stack.

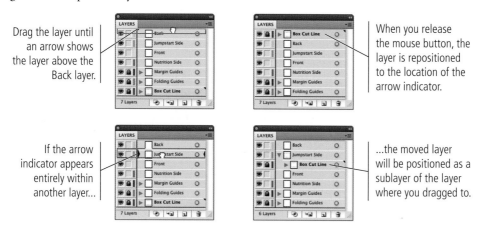

Drag the layer until an arrow shows the layer above the Back layer.

When you release the mouse button, the layer is repositioned to the location of the arrow indicator.

If the arrow indicator appears entirely within another layer...

...the moved layer will be positioned as a sublayer of the layer where you dragged to.

The Box Cut Line layer shows the location of the cut lines. Although it will not be printed, this layer needs to be visible while you create the basic package.

6. **Save the new file as a native Illustrator file named heartsmart.ai in your WIP>Cereal folder.**

7. **Continue to the next exercise.**

SAMPLE COLORS AND CREATE CUSTOM SWATCHES

Now that you have set up the basic box document and layers, the next step is to place the image that will fill the front cover. Then you can select colors directly from the image, enabling you to create a cohesive package design.

1. **With heartsmart.ai open, select the Front layer and lock the other layers. Hide the Margin Guides layer.**

   In the early stages of package design, the folding guides are important, but the margin guides are not yet necessary.

2. **Choose File>Place. Navigate to the file box front.tif in the RF_Illustrator>Cereal folder. Make sure the Link option is not checked, and then click Place.**

   Remember from Project 5: to embed an image when you place it, make sure the Link option is not checked in the Place dialog box.

3. **Position the placed image so its bottom-left corner aligns with the bottom-left corner of the front panel area (as shown in the following image).**

4. **Click the top-right bounding box handle of the image, press the Shift key, and drag down until the right edge of the image aligns with the right edge of the front panel.**

   By pressing Shift before scaling the picture, you maintain the original proportions or aspect ratio of the image.

Shift-drag this corner to resize the placed image proportionally until it fits in the width of the front panel.

5. **Display the Swatches and Color panels, and then choose the Eyedropper tool in the Tools panel.**

6. **Click the Eyedropper tool in the dark purple area at the left side of the image.**

   Clicking with the Eyedropper tool changes the color in the Color panel; this method is called sampling color.

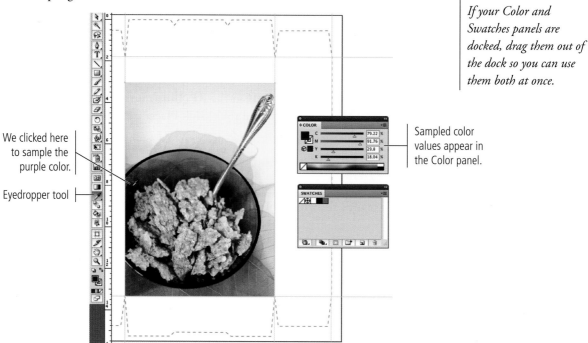

We clicked here to sample the purple color.

Eyedropper tool

Sampled color values appear in the Color panel.

Note:

If your Color and Swatches panels are docked, drag them out of the dock so you can use them both at once.

7. **Open the Color panel Options menu and choose Create New Swatch.**

   This option defines a new color swatch based on the current ink percentages.

Note:

You could also simply click the New Swatch button in the Swatches panel to create a custom color swatch.

8. **In the resulting New Swatch dialog box, activate the Global check box, and then click OK to accept the default swatch name and color values.**

   The sampled color is added as a saved swatch, so you can access the exact same color again later.

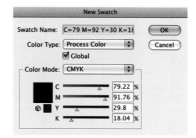

9. **Use the Eyedropper tool again to sample the light gold color in the image background, and then add the sampled color as a second global swatch.**

We sampled the light gold color in this area.

10. **Add a third swatch by sampling the light pink color in the leaf veins below the cereal bowl.**

    You might need to zoom in to sample the color in the thin line of the leaf vein.

We sampled this leaf vein.

11. **Add a fourth swatch by sampling the dark pink color in the leaves below the cereal bowl.**

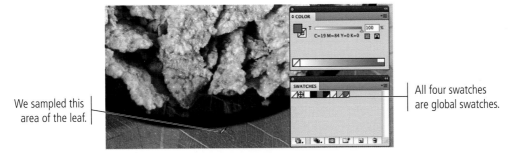

We sampled this area of the leaf.

All four swatches are global swatches.

12. **Save the file and continue to the next exercise.**

 ## CREATE THE BACKGROUND SHAPES

You are now ready to draw the basic background shapes for the design. Remember, the die-cut lines identify the outside edges of the box shape. The Folding Guides layer shows the location of the various folds; these guides also identify the edges of the four panels in the job. In this exercise, you use the folding guides and the die-cut template shape to create solid-colored background shapes for most of the box surface.

1. **With heartsmart.ai open, unlock and select the Back layer, and lock all other layers.**

2. **Choose the Rectangle tool from the Tools panel. Set the fill color to the light pink swatch, and set the stroke to None.**

3. **Draw a rectangle that fills the top-flap area, extending beyond the cut-line edges by at least 1/8″.**

Like any other job where ink is supposed to print all the way to the trim edge, packaging design also requires bleed allowance. Rather than trying to meticulously match the die-cut shape, a rectangle does the job far more easily.

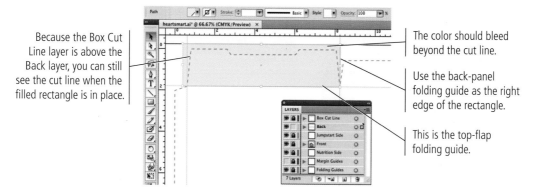

Because the Box Cut Line layer is above the Back layer, you can still see the cut line when the filled rectangle is in place.

The color should bleed beyond the cut line.

Use the back-panel folding guide as the right edge of the rectangle.

This is the top-flap folding guide.

4. **Deselect the pink rectangle.**

5. **With the Rectangle tool still active, change the fill color to the light gold custom swatch.**

6. **Draw a rectangle that fills the back panel area, including the bottom flap. Make sure the bottom edge bleeds past the bottom cut line.**

7. **Show the Margin Guides layer. Extend the left edge of the gold rectangle to the margin guide on the outside glue flap.**

The box will be glued together along this flap. The back panel color should extend past the folding guide so there will be no white space where the side meets the back panel.

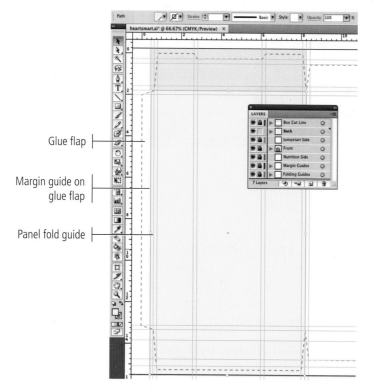

Glue flap

Margin guide on glue flap

Panel fold guide

8. **Lock the Back layer, and then unlock and select the Jumpstart Side layer.**

9. **Choose the light pink swatch as the fill color, and then use the Rectangle tool to draw the shape of the entire side panel. Bleed the rectangle past the top cut line and extend the rectangle to the margin guide on the bottom flap.**

   The white space remaining on the bottom flap will be used by the printer to add registration marks and color swatches for checking color on press.

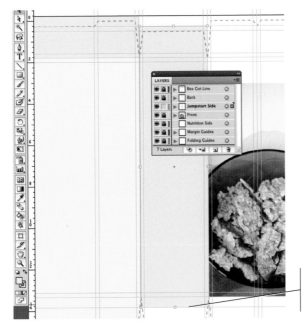

Extend the bottom of the shape to this margin guide.

10. **Hide the Margin Guides layer.**

11. **Lock the Jumpstart Side layer, and then unlock and select the Front layer.**

12. **Draw the top flap shape with a light pink fill, and extend its bottom edge into the front panel area. Leave a 1/8″ gap between the pink shape and the placed box-front image.**

13. **Draw the bottom flap shape with a light gold fill.**

Note:

When creating the background shapes, it's less confusing to show the margin guides only when necessary.

This is the shape from Step 12.

Note:

If you place an element on the wrong layer, simply select the element and drag the Selected Art icon in the Layers panel to the correct layer. Just make sure the layers involved are unlocked.

This is the shape from Step 13.

14. **Bring the placed image to the front of the stacking order (Object>Arrange>Bring to Front).**

15. **Lock the Front layer, show the Margin Guides layer, and then unlock and select the Nutrition Side layer.**

16. **Draw the second side panel shape with a light pink fill. Extend the shape to the same margin guide on the bottom flap as the Jumpstart Side shape. Extend the right edge of the shape at least 1/8″ past the right cut line.**

17. **Unlock all content layers. If necessary, adjust the objects so the only gap between background elements is the white line on the front panel.**

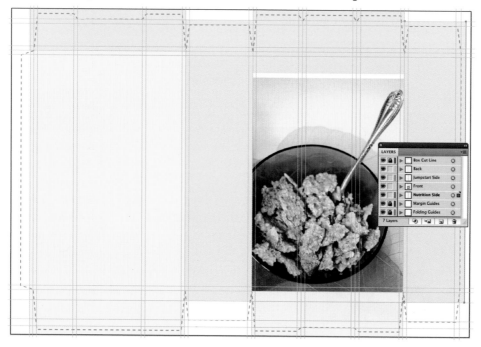

18. **Save the file and continue to the next stage of the project.**

Stage 2 Understanding Package Requirements

The nature of a specific package determines what standard elements you must include in the design. In this case, a cereal box generally requires nutritional information, the package weight (in both ounces and grams), the "best by" date, and a UPC bar code label. Since the box is resealable, you should also include some simple text explaining how to open and close the box. Additionally, HeartSmart cereal is being recommended by the Association for a Healthy America; this type of product endorsement should be displayed prominently on the package.

This package design has four basic panels, and each panel combines many elements. Most of these elements have already been created; you are going to use Illustrator to combine or composite the various elements into a single, unified layout. (You have already placed the primary image on the front panel, which was necessary to sample the colors you will use to build the rest of the layout.)

The most logical way to proceed is to place or create the rest of the basic design elements. You can then decide what, if anything, still needs to be done to create an attractive, finished package design.

PLACE THE NUTRITION PANEL CONTENT

When you design a complex project such as this package, it helps to decide on a logical approach to accomplish the task. Rather than jumping around in the layout, it makes more sense to work on one panel at a time.

You are going to start with the nutrition panel on the right side of the page, and then work your way across to the back panel. (You could just as easily work from left to right; but for this project, we decided to start with the simplest panel.)

1. **With heartsmart.ai open, make sure the Nutrition Side layer is active and all other layers are locked.**

2. **Choose File>Place. Place the file nutrition.ai from the RF_Illustrator> Cereal folder into your cereal box layout. Make sure the file is embedded (not linked), and base the placement on the Crop To Art option.**

   As you know, when you place a native Illustrator file into another Illustrator file, it is contained by a bounding box that marks the outermost edges of the selected Crop To area. All objects in the placed file are grouped together so you can treat the placed graphic as a single object.

Note:

All external files for this project are in the RF_Illustrator>Cereal folder. This is the last time we mention the full path.

3. **Center the placed nutrition information in the panel area (between the margin guides), and align its top edge with the top of the cereal bowl image.**

When you place another file into an Illustrator file, it is automatically centered in the workspace. Because the Nutrition Side layer is below a number of other layers, the placed file might not be visible until you move it into place. Although you can't see the actual file, you can still click within the visible bounding box of the placed file and drag to move it into place.

If you have difficulty working with placed files behind the locked layers, try zooming into the correct area before placing; the placed artwork will still be centered in the workspace, but by zooming you center the approximate area in the workspace so the placed file will be roughly centered in the correct position.

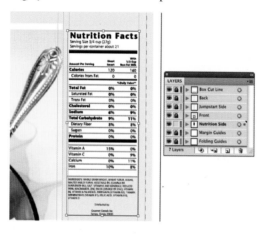

4. **Place (embed) the file afha.ai into the layout, using the Crop To Art option.**

5. **Position the placed endorsement graphic below the nutrition information. Center the graphic between the panel's vertical margin guides, and position the bottom edge at the bottom margin guide.**

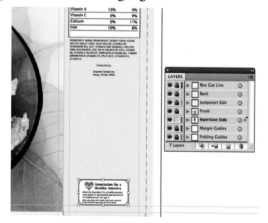

6. **Save the file and continue to the next exercise.**

PLACE THE FRONT PANEL CONTENT

1. With **heartsmart.ai** open, lock the Nutrition Side layer. Unlock and select the Front layer.

2. Place (embed) **bar code.eps** into the layout, positioning it on the right side of the bottom flap. Move the bar code so the bottom corner is 1/8″ from the front flap edge, and align the bottom edge with the bottom edge of the side flap.

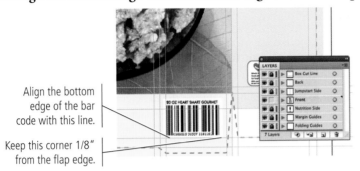

Align the bottom edge of the bar code with this line.

Keep this corner 1/8″ from the flap edge.

> **Note:**
>
> *UPC (Universal Product Code) barcodes are symbols containing look-up numbers that uniquely identify items in the distribution and retail chain. They are specially created files that contain information about the item's name, price, and so on. These files are created by specialist companies, based on specific requirements; you can't draw a series of lines and call it a bar code.*

3. Place (embed) **hs logo.ai** into the layout, based on the Crop To Art option, and positioned in the top center of the front panel area. Align the left edge of the file with the left margin guide of the front panel area.

   The crossbar of the "t" in "Heart" should overlap the line of empty white space, as shown below.

4. Using the Type tool, click to create a point-type object and then type:
   NET WT
   20 OZ (567 g)

5. Format the text as 12-pt ATC Maple Medium with centered paragraph alignment. Change the text color to the custom purple swatch you created earlier.

6. Place the type object in the bottom-right corner of the box front area (inside the margin guides).

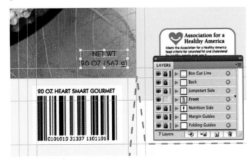

7. **In the top-left section of the top flap, create an area-type object and type BETTER IF USED BY. Format the text as black 11-pt ATC Maple Medium with centered paragraph alignment.**

8. **Resize the type area width to fit the top-left flap, as marked by the guides (and shown in the following image).**

9. **Directly below the text object, draw a rectangle filled with the dark pink custom swatch, positioned within the rectangle created by the guides.**

The sell-by date is typically stamped onto pre-printed boxes during the packaging process because every day's production has a different date. This area provides a defined space for stamping the date.

10. **In the center section of the top flap, click and drag with the Type tool to create a small area-type object. Type the following, formatted with 10-pt ATC Maple Medium, filled with black, with centered paragraph alignment:**

    To Open, Slide Finger Under
    Arrows to Left and Right

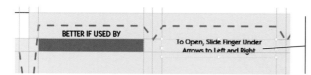

Draw the new area-type object here. If necessary, use the Selection tool to adjust the size and position of the area.

11. **Clone the type area and place the clone directly below the original. Format the text in the cloned area as 9-pt ATC Maple Medium with a horizontal scale of 80%, and change the text to:**

    TO KEEP YOUR CEREAL FRESH, REFOLD INNER BAG
    AFTER EACH USE AND CLOSE PACKAGE FLAPS

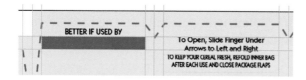

12. **Save the file and continue to the next exercise.**

1. With **heartsmart.ai** open, lock the Front layer. Unlock and select the Jumpstart Side layer.

2. Place (embed) the file **slogan.ai**, based on the Crop To Art option.

3. Position the placed logo at the top of the panel area. Center the logo between the left and right panel margin guides, and align the top edge of the logo to the top margin guide.

4. Using the Type tool, click and drag to create an area-type object that fills the Jumpstart Side panel below the placed graphic, snapping to the margin guides on the left, right, and bottom edges.

   Be sure the cursor is near the panel margin guide before you click and drag with the Type tool. If you click too close to the edge of the existing pink rectangle, clicking with the Type tool will convert the existing shape into an area-type object. Use the shape of the cursor as a guide for when you can click to create a new type area.

When you see this cursor, clicking will convert the existing shape to a type area.

If the cursor is far enough away from the edges of existing shapes, you can click and drag to create a new type object.

5. With the insertion point flashing in the new type area, place the file **side copy.doc** into the new type area. Accept the default Microsoft Word options, and click OK if you receive a Font Problems warning.

   You are going to reformat this text, so you don't need to worry about missing fonts.

6. Select all placed text and format it as 12-pt ATC Pine Normal with 21-pt leading. Change the Space After Paragraph setting to 5 pt.

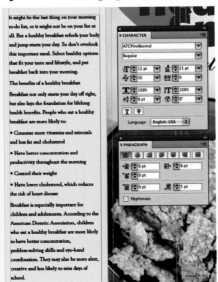

Note:

To work around this potential problem, you can also click and drag to create a small type area in the middle of the panel, and then use the Selection tool to resize the type area to fit in the panel's margin guides.

7. Select the entire second paragraph ("The benefits of a healthy breakfast"). Change the text to 14-pt ATC Elm Italic, apply the custom purple swatch, and change the Space After Paragraph value to 0.

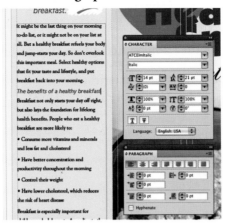

8. Select the four bulleted paragraphs and change the leading to 17 pt. Change the Left Indent setting to 15 pt, and change the First Line Left Indent value to −15 pt.

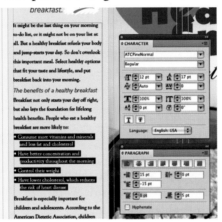

Note:

*This type of negative first-line indent is called a **hanging indent**.*

9. Select only the first bullet character and open the Glyphs panel (Type>Glyphs).

10. Search through the glyphs of various fonts to find a bullet that fits the overall product message (natural, healthy, heart-smart). When you find a glyph you like, double-click it to replace the selected character with that glyph.

Note:

In software terms, anything between two paragraph return characters is technically a paragraph, regardless of punctuation.

We used a leafy ornament from the Minion Pro font, but you can use whatever glyph from whatever font you prefer.

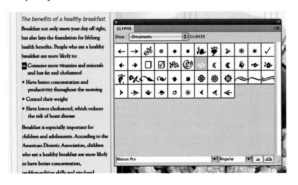

11. Change the color of the placed glyph to the custom purple swatch.

12. Copy the custom glyph, and then paste it to replace the remaining three bullets.

13. Save the file and continue to the next exercise.

PLACE THE BACK PANEL CONTENT

1. With heartsmart.ai open, lock the Jumpstart Side layer. Unlock and select the Back layer.

2. Place (embed) the file recycle.eps onto the bottom flap of the back panel. Rotate the logo 180°, and position it as shown in the following image.

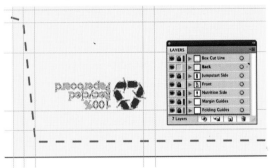

3. Create a type area below the middle of the top flap on the back panel. Type TO CLOSE, PUSH TAB UNDER HERE.

4. Format the text as 10-pt ATC Maple Medium with centered paragraph alignment.

5. Rotate the area 180°, and position it as shown in the following image.

6. **Choose File>Place. Navigate to the file flake heart.psd and click Place. In the resulting dialog box, check the Show Preview option.**

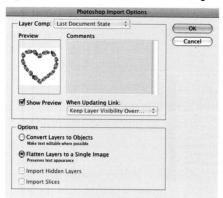

The resulting Photoshop Import Options dialog box allows you to control how Photoshop elements are translated into Illustrator:

- Use the **Layer Comp** menu to import a specific layer comp saved in the Photoshop file.

- If you link to the file instead of placing it (in the Place dialog box), you can use the **When Updating Link** menu to control what happens if you update the linked image.

- **Convert Layers to Objects** converts Photoshop layers to Illustrator objects. This option preserves type layers as editable text objects in Illustrator, as well as masks, blending modes, transparency, and slice information. (Adjustment layers and layer effects are flattened into the placed objects.)

- **Flatten Layers to a Single Image** combines all Photoshop layers into a single layer. The appearance of the image is preserved, but you can't edit the layers.

- **Import Hidden Layers** can be checked to include layers that are not visible in the Photoshop file.

- **Import Slices** is only available if the Photoshop file includes slices for Web layouts. If this option is checked, the slices will be maintained in the imported file.

Note:

For more information about the various Photoshop elements, we recommend the book **Adobe Photoshop CS4: The Professional Portfolio** *from Against The Clock.*

7. **Choose the Flatten Layers to a Single Image option and click OK.**

This image has only one layer, which you will not edit, so this option has the same result as converting Photoshop layers to Illustrator objects.

8. **Position the placed image in the center of the back panel area. Leave about two inches between the panel's top folding guide and the top of the placed image.**

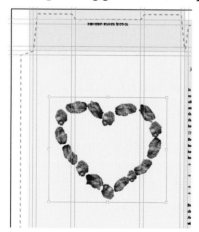

9. Using the Type tool, create an area-type object in the area below the placed heart image, using the sides of the heart to define the approximate width of the area. Place the top edge of the area about 1/2″ from the bottom of the heart graphic.

10. Place the file **back copy.doc** into the area, using the default Microsoft Word import options.

11. Select all placed text and format it as 18-pt ATC Pine Normal with 26-pt leading. Change the text color to the custom purple swatch. Apply justified paragraph alignment with the last line centered, and make sure the Hyphenate option is not checked.

12. Extend the bottom edge of the type area until all of the text is visible.

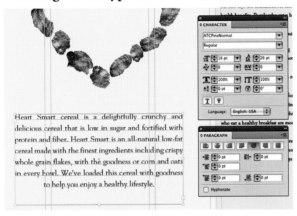

13. Unlock the Jumpstart Side layer.

14. Open the Smart Punctuation dialog box (Type>Smart Punctuation). Check all Replace options except ellipses, and choose the Entire Document option. Click OK, read the results dialog box, and click OK to continue to the next step.

Note:

It's a good idea to include this step whenever you work with client-supplied text files.

The Smart Punctuation utility does not work on locked layers.

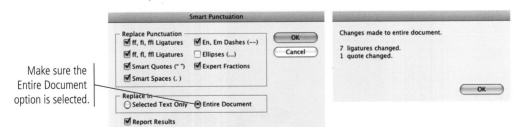

Make sure the Entire Document option is selected.

15. Place the insertion point in the last paragraph on the Jumpstart Side panel, and allow hyphenation in that paragraph.

This step fixes the widow at the end of the paragraph.

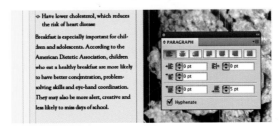

16. Save the file and continue to the next exercise.

CREATE TYPE ON A PATH

The final element that needs to be placed is the headline, which should appear above the heart graphic on the back panel of the box. Instead of simply flowing text into a type object, you can create unique typographic effects by flowing text onto a path. A text path can be any shape you can create in Illustrator, whether it's a simple shape created with one of the basic shape tools, a straight line drawn with the Line tool, or a complex graphic drawn with the Pen tool.

1. **With heartsmart.ai open, select the Back layer and lock all other layers.**

2. **Deselect everything in the layout.**

3. **Select the Pen tool. Change the fill to None and the stroke to 1-pt black.**

4. **Draw a curve above the top of the flake heart, as shown in the following image.**

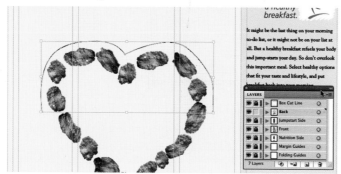

5. **Select the Type tool in the Tools panel, and then click near the left side of the path you just drew.**

   Clicking an existing path with the Type tool converts the path to a type path. You could select the Type on a Path tool (nested under the Type tool), but it's not necessary because when the Type tool cursor is near an existing path, it automatically switches to the Type on a Path tool cursor.

   When the Type tool cursor is near an existing path, it switches to the Type on a Path tool cursor.

   The 1-pt black stroke attribute is automatically removed when you convert the stroke to a type path.

   After converting the path to a type path, the insertion point flashes on the path.

   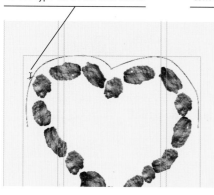

6. **With the insertion point flashing along the path, type A healthy start for your heart!**

7. **Select all the text on the path (Select>All) and format it as 36-pt ATC Laurel Book. Change the text color to the custom purple swatch, and apply centered paragraph alignment.**

Depending on where you clicked, some of the message might not be visible after you change the formatting. You will adjust the text position on the path in the next two steps.

The text is centered between the location where you clicked with the Type tool and the end point of the path.

8. **Click the type path with the Direct Selection tool.**

When you converted the path to a type path, the location where you clicked defined the starting point for text along the path. By selecting the path, you can modify the start and end points for type on the path. This is the same basic concept as changing the left and right indents for text in a regular type area.

This is the start bar for the text (basically, the left indent for the type path).

This is the center point of the type path, based on the current start and end points.

This is the end bar for the text (basically, the right indent for the type path).

9. **Click the start bar and drag to the left end of the path.**

If you change the start or end point, the center point also changes, based on the new available space. The text is now centered, based on the entire path.

Note:

Make sure you click the start bar and not the white square that represents the in point of the text path.

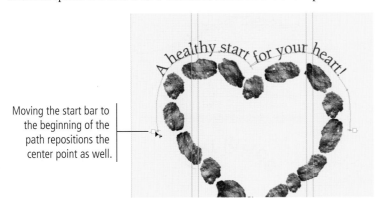

Moving the start bar to the beginning of the path repositions the center point as well.

10. **If necessary, place the insertion point and press the Spacebar enough times to separate the words "start" and "for."**

This might be necessary, depending on the shape of your type path; if the "t" in start and the "f" in for are too close together where the path dips, use extra spaces to move the letters away from the dip.

11. **Save the file and continue to the next stage of the project.**

You can control the appearance of type on a path by choosing Type>Type on a Path>Type on a Path Options. You can apply one of five effects, change the alignment of the text to the path, flip the text to the other side of the path, and adjust the character spacing around curves (higher Spacing values remove more space around sharp curves).

- The **Rainbow** (default) effect keeps each character's baseline parallel to the path.

- The **Skew** effect maintains the vertical edges of type while skewing the horizontal edges around the path.

- The **3D Ribbon** effect maintains horizontal edges of type while rotating vertical edges to be perpendicular to the path.

- The **Stair Step** effect aligns the left edge of each character's baseline to the path without rotating any characters.

- The **Gravity** effect aligns the center of each character's baseline to the path, keeping vertical edges in line with the path's center.

The **Align options** determine which part of the text (baseline, ascender, descender, or center) aligns to which part of the path (top, bottom, or center).

The **Flip** check box turns type onto the other side of the path; this option is useful for putting text inside shapes.

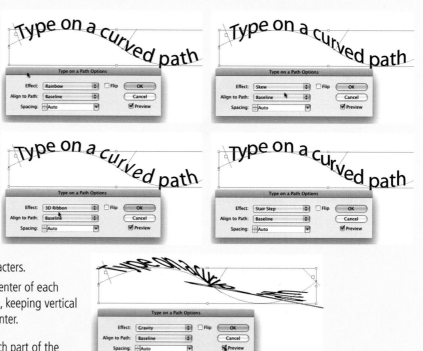

Stage 3 Working with Effects

Illustrator includes a number of non-destructive effects for enhancing objects in a layout. The Effect menu is separated into two primary sections: Illustrator functions and Photoshop functions.

Illustrator Effects are live and non-destructive, which means they can be edited or removed from an object without destroying the original object. The Photoshop Effects, on the other hand, can be applied to both raster- and vector-based objects.

When you work with effects, you should be aware that many of these options eventually result in rasterized elements, even when you apply them to vector objects. For example, a drop shadow (in the Stylize submenu) creates a soft-edge shadow object that blends from the shadow color to fully transparent. To achieve this effect on output, the shadow has to be rasterized into pixels that reproduce the visual effect.

The Drop Shadow, Inner Glow, Outer Glow, and Feather options in the Stylize submenu all utilize some form of graded transparency, and they all result in objects that reproduce as pixels (rasters) instead of vectors. In this stage of the project, you use effects and transparency controls to add visual interest to different elements of your artwork. In Stage 4 of this project, you learn how to control transparent objects that need to be rasterized before they can be successfully output.

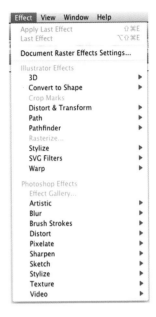

APPLY THE ADD ARROWHEAD EFFECT

In Stages 1 and 2, you placed all but one of the package design elements. The text on the top flap of the front panel mentions arrows, which you haven't yet created. You could draw these shapes manually, but Illustrator's built-in effects make it easy to add symmetrical arrowheads in one step, rather than meticulously measuring and drawing the shapes by hand.

1. **With heartsmart.ai open, unlock and select the Front layer. Lock all other layers.**

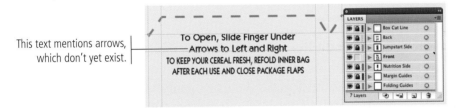

This text mentions arrows, which don't yet exist.

2. **Select the Pen tool. Set the Fill value to None and the Stroke value to 6-pt black.**

3. **In the Artboard area above the page, draw a horizontal line (from left to right) approximately 1/8″ long.**

   Because this line is so short, zooming in can be very helpful for this series of steps.

4. **Press Shift, and then click above and to the right to create a second straight segment at a 45° angle.**

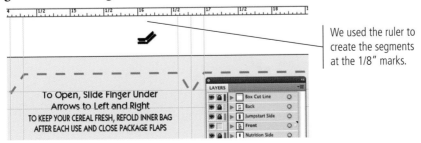

We used the ruler to create the segments at the 1/8″ marks.

5. **With the line selected, choose Effect>Stylize>Add Arrowheads, and then check the Preview option.**

The Add Arrowheads effect can create arrowheads at the start (where you first click) and the end (where you last click) of a line. The dialog box defaults to the last-used settings, so your settings might show different options than our screen shot.

Illustrator offers 27 arrowhead styles, which you can browse using the buttons below the previews. The scale defines the size of the arrowhead relative to the stroke weight.

Note:

The Add Arrowheads effect is in the Illustrator Effects Stylize menu, not the Photoshop Effects Stylize menu.

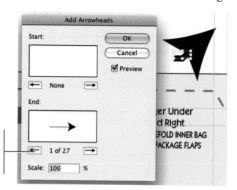

Use these buttons to navigate through the available arrowhead styles.

6. **Leave the Start arrow as None and choose 1 for the End arrow. Change the Scale field to 25.**

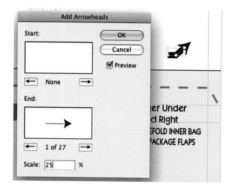

7. **Click OK to apply the arrowhead. With the line still selected, open the Appearance panel.**

Because Add Arrowheads is an effect, the arrowhead is applied in the same manner as a brush stroke. The arrowhead is considered an attribute of the line, which means it can be changed or removed at any time, unless you choose to expand the effect.

Note:

To remove the effect, simply drag it to the Appearance panel's Delete button.

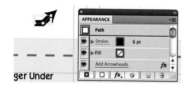

Note:

You can convert arrowhead effects into actual objects by choosing Object>Expand Appearance.

8. **Position the line on the top front flap, as shown in the following image.**

Because the arrowhead is an attribute of the line, it moves with the line.

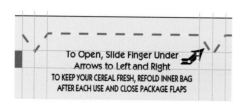

9. **Select the arrow and choose Object>Transform>Reflect. In the Reflect dialog box, choose the Vertical option, and then click Copy to create a reflected copy of the arrow.**

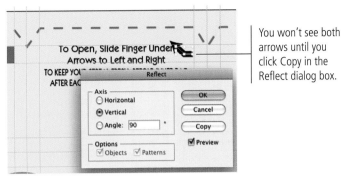

You won't see both arrows until you click Copy in the Reflect dialog box.

10. **Press Shift, and drag the reflected copy to the left side of the text.**

Note:

You can also open the Reflect dialog box by double-clicking the Reflect tool in the Tools panel.

11. **Save the file and continue to the next exercise.**

EXPAND THE APPEARANCE OF EFFECTS

As you have learned, effects such as Add Arrowheads are considered attributes of the object to which they are applied. As long as they remain appearance attributes, you can easily change or remove them. If necessary, you can convert these effects into actual objects, which can then be independently manipulated however you prefer.

1. **With heartsmart.ai open, unlock and select the Back layer. Lock all other layers.**

2. **In the Appearance panel Options menu, make sure the New Art Has Basic Appearance option is toggled on.**

   When this option is checked, new art has only the basic default fill and stroke attributes you define. When this option is not checked, new art maintains the same appearance attributes (arrowheads, etc.) of the previous object.

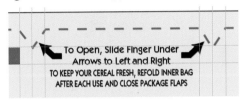

3. **Zoom into the Artboard around the "To Close…" text at the top of the back panel. Use the Pen or Line tool to draw a short vertical line, from bottom to top, with a 6-pt black stroke and no fill.**

4. **With the vertical line selected, choose Effect>Stylize>Add Arrowheads.**

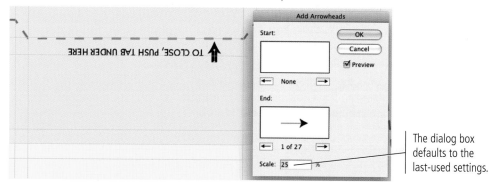

The dialog box defaults to the last-used settings.

5. **Click the button below the End option to find arrowhead 11. Make sure the Scale field is set to 25, and then click OK.**

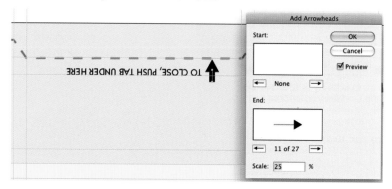

Note:

Illustrator remembers the last-used effect, and the specific settings you used to apply that effect. The top of the Effect menu includes the option to apply the last-used effect without opening the related dialog box, or to open the dialog box for the last-used effect.

6. **With the line selected, choose Object>Expand Appearance.**

This command creates a group of individual objects from effects.

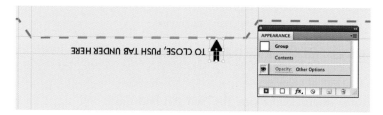

7. **Using the Direct Selection tool, select only the vertical line and delete it.**

8. **Select the remaining triangle. Change the fill to white and the stroke to 0.5-pt black. Drag the triangle into position as shown in the following image.**

9. **Clone the triangle and move the clone horizontally to the other side of the related text.**

10. **Save the file and continue to the next exercise.**

CHANGE OBJECT BLENDING MODES AND OPACITY

The effects and transparency controls in Illustrator allow you to add dimension and depth to virtually any design element. You can change the transparency of any object, apply different blending modes so objects blend smoothly into underlying objects, and apply creative effects (such as drop shadows) that incorporate transparency.

1. **With heartsmart.ai open, unlock the four content layers.**

2. **Select the recycle logo and open the Transparency panel.**

   All parts of this graphic have a white fill. You are going to change the blending mode so the logo blends into the background color (hence the term, "blending mode").

3. **Choose Color Burn in the Blending Mode menu.**

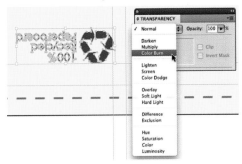

   After changing the blending mode, the logo is a blend of the original purple logo color and the gold color of the background object.

4. **Using the Direct Selection tool, select the heart shape in the cereal name on the front panel.**

5. **In the Transparency panel, change the Opacity value to 50%.**

The Opacity value determines how much of the underlying colors show through the affected object. If an object is 75% opaque, 25% of the underlying colors are visible.

Use the slider to experiment with different levels, or type a specific value in the field.

6. **Clone the logo. Scale the clone to 35%, and then position the resized version in the empty space of the nutrition panel (between the nutrition information and the AHA logo).**

Understanding Blending Modes

Blending modes control how colors in an object interact with colors in underlying objects. Objects are set to Normal by default, which simply overlays the top object's color onto underlying objects (i.e., the "base"). If the top object is entirely opaque — a solid color you can't see through — it is unaffected by underlying objects.

- **Darken** returns the darker of the blend or base color. Base pixels that are lighter than the blend color are replaced; base pixels that are darker than the blend color remain unchanged.

- **Multiply** multiplies (hence the name) the base color by the blend color, resulting in a darker color. Multiplying any color with black produces black; multiplying any color with white leaves the color unchanged.

- **Color Burn** darkens the base color by increasing the contrast. Blend colors darker than 50% significantly darken the base color by increasing saturation and reducing brightness; blending with white has no effect.

- **Lighten** returns whichever is the lighter color (base or blend). Base pixels that are darker than the blend color are replaced; base pixels that are lighter than the blend color remain unchanged.

- **Screen** is basically the inverse of Multiply, always returning a lighter color. Screening with black has no effect; screening with white produces white.

- **Color Dodge** brightens the base color. Blend colors lighter than 50% significantly increase brightness; blending with black has no effect.

- **Overlay** multiplies or screens the blend color to pre-serve the original lightness or darkness of the base color.

- **Soft Light** darkens or lightens base colors, depending on the blend color. Blend colors lighter than 50% lighten the base color (as if dodged); blend colors darker than 50% darken the base color (as if burned).

- **Hard Light** combines the Multiply and Screen modes. Blend colors darker than 50% are multiplied, and blend colors lighter than 50% are screened.

- **Difference** inverts base color values according to the brightness value in the blend layer. Lower brightness values in the blend layer have less effect on the result; blending with black has no effect.

- **Exclusion** is very similar to Difference, except that mid-tone values in the base color are completely desaturated.

- **Hue** results in a color with the luminance and saturation of the base color and the hue of the blend color.

- **Saturation** results in a color with the luminance and hue of the base color and saturation of the blend color.

- **Color** results in a color with the luminance of the base color and the hue and saturation of the blend color.

- **Luminosity** results in a color with the hue and saturation of the base color and the luminance of the blend color (basically the opposite of the Color mode).

Avoid applying Difference, Exclusion, Hue, Saturation, Color, and Luminosity blending modes to objects with spot colors.

7. **In the Layers panel, drag the Selected Art icon to the Nutrition Side layer.**

Drag the Selected Art icon from the Front layer to the Nutrition Side layer. This moves the scaled version of the logo onto the correct layer.

8. **Clone the resized logo. Place the new clone at the bottom of the Jumpstart Side panel and move the artwork to the appropriate layer.**

ILLUSTRATOR FOUNDATIONS

Three options at the bottom of the Transparency panel allow you to control transparency settings relative to grouped objects. If **Isolate Blending** is checked, blending changes only apply to other objects in the same group. The group effectively knocks out the underlying shapes.

The opacity of the purple letters has been reduced to 50%.

When Knockout Group is checked, the opacity only affects underlying objects that are not part of the grouped logo.

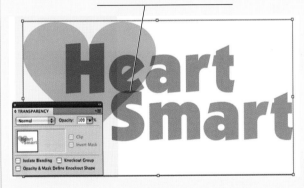

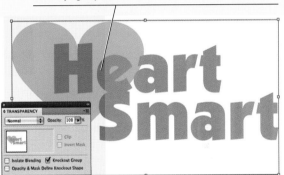

If **Knockout Group** is checked, transparency settings for elements within the group do not apply to other elements in the same group. The transparent effects are only applied to objects under the entire group. In this case, elements within the group knock out other objects in the same group.

The Hard Light blending mode is applied to the purple letters in the grouped logo.

When Isolate Blending is checked, the blending mode does not affect the underlying gold object.

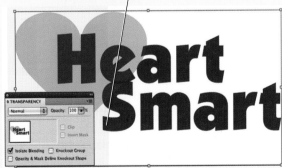

If **Opacity and Mask Define Knockout Shape** is checked (at the bottom of the panel), the mask object's opacity creates a knockout effect. Where the mask is 100% opaque, the knockout effect is strong; in areas of lower opacity, the knockout effect is weaker.

ILLUSTRATOR FOUNDATIONS

As you have seen, you can use the Transparency panel to change the blending mode and opacity of an object in Illustrator. If you only see the blending mode menu and opacity field/slider, you can choose Show Options in the panel Options menu to show several other options that allow you to control the behavior of transparency for more complex objects.

An opacity mask defines the transparency of selected artwork. In Illustrator, you can create an opacity mask by selecting two or more shapes and choosing Make Opacity Mask in the Transparency panel Options menu. The topmost selected object (or group) becomes the masking object; underlying objects in the selection are the masked artwork.

The best way to explain the concept of opacity masks is through example. The first image shows three separate objects: the top object (the word Autumn, converted to outlines), the gradient-filled rectangle, and the black-filled rectangle.

When you define an opacity mask, shades in the masking object (in this example, the word "Autumn") determine the degree of transparency in the masked artwork (the blue-gold gradient).

As you can see in the second image, the underlying gradient is entirely transparent — the black background shape shows through those areas of the gradient. Where the masking object is white, the masked artwork is 100% opaque.

Masked artwork
thumbnail

Mask thumbnail

If the **Clip** option is checked, the masking object also determines which parts of the masked artwork are visible.

If the **Invert Mask** option is checked, tones in the masking object are reversed (black becomes white and white becomes black). Transparency of the masked artwork is also effectively reversed.

By default, the masking object and masked artwork are linked, which means you can't move one without the other. If you click the Link icon between the masked artwork and the mask thumbnails, you can move the two elements independently.

Turn off the Link
option to move either
object independently
of the other.

9. **Clone the resized logo again. Rotate the new clone 180°, place it in the center of the top flap on the back panel, and move the artwork to the Back layer.**

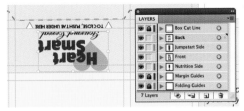

10. **Save the file and continue to the next exercise.**

 APPLY RASTER EFFECTS TO DESIGN ELEMENTS

Transparency and blending modes can help unify various elements of a design. Other effects — specifically glows, drop shadows, and similar styles — combine graded transparency and blending modes to add depth to otherwise flat artwork.

1. **With heartsmart.ai open, select the placed heart image on the back panel.**

2. **Choose Effect>Stylize>Outer Glow.**

   As with the Add Arrowheads effect, we are using the Illustrator Effects Stylize menu, not the Photoshop Effects Stylize menu.

   The Outer Glow effect adds a transparent effect behind the selected object. The Mode menu, color swatch, and Opacity menu determine the appearance of the glow effect. The Blur field defines the width of the apparent effect (how far the glow extends from the edges of the object).

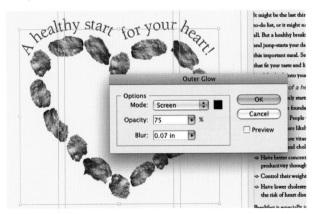

3. Check the Preview box, and then click the color swatch to the right of the Mode menu.

4. In the resulting Color Picker dialog box, click the Color Swatches button to show the swatches saved in the current file.

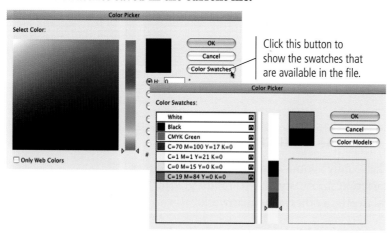

Click this button to show the swatches that are available in the file.

Note:

You can use any color for the glow, but using an existing swatch helps unify the design.

5. Choose the dark pink custom swatch and click OK.

6. In the Outer Glow dialog box, choose Multiply in the Mode menu and change the Blur field to 0.05 in.

The Multiply blending mode combines the base color (the light gold background) with the glow color (the dark pink at 75% opacity).

7. Click OK to apply the glow effect, and then look at the Appearance panel.

As with the Add Arrowheads effect, the outer glow is treated as an appearance attribute. You can edit the applied glow settings by double-clicking the effect in the Appearance panel. You can remove the effect by dragging it to the Appearance panel's Delete button.

8. Save the file and continue to the next exercise.

APPLY EFFECTS TO PART OF A GROUP

As you know, all elements of placed graphics are grouped together in the file where they are placed. Any groupings from the original file are also maintained, often resulting in a complex series of multiple nested groups — which can make it difficult to access specific elements to make changes or apply effects.

1. With **heartsmart.ai** open, use the Direct Selection tool to select one piece of the purple man in the slogan logo.

This icon identifies the layer where the selected object exists.

2. **In the Layers panel, click the arrow to the left of the Jumpstart Side layer.**

   Clicking this arrow shows the objects contained on the layer (called sublayers). You can further expand groups so you can show — and select — the individual elements in a group.

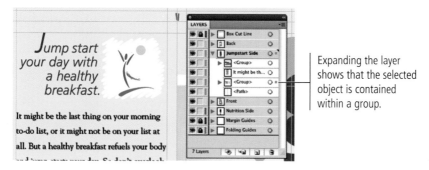

Expanding the layer shows that the selected object is contained within a group.

3. **Open the Layers panel Options menu and choose Panel Options. In the resulting dialog box, choose Large in the Row Size section, and then click OK.**

   Enlarging the panel rows makes it easier to see what is contained on each layer and sublayer.

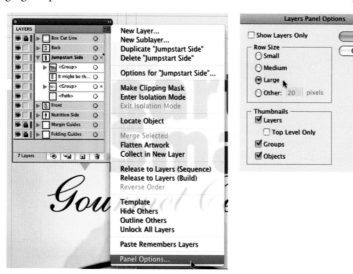

4. **Click the arrow to expand the group that contains the selected object.**

5. **Continue expanding groups until a group thumbnail shows the dancing man figure (with the grass and sun).**

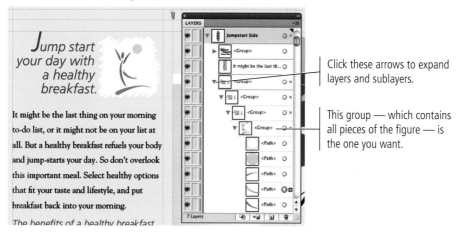

Click these arrows to expand layers and sublayers.

This group — which contains all pieces of the figure — is the one you want.

6. **Click the Target icon next to the small figure group to isolate it.**

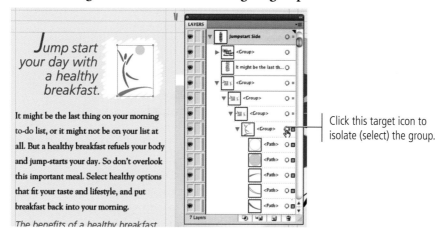

Click this target icon to isolate (select) the group.

7. **Choose Effect>Stylize>Drop Shadow and activate the Preview check box.**

The Drop Shadow dialog box has similar options to the Outer Glow effect. The primary difference is that you can change the horizontal (X) and vertical (Y) offset values of the applied shadow.

Note:

Effect dialog boxes default to the last-used settings, so your settings might be different than those in our screen shot.

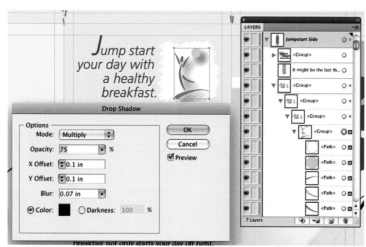

8. **Change the drop shadow settings to the following:**

Mode:	Multiply
Opacity:	75%
X Offset:	0.02 in
Y Offset:	0.02 in
Blur:	0.04 in
Color:	100% Black

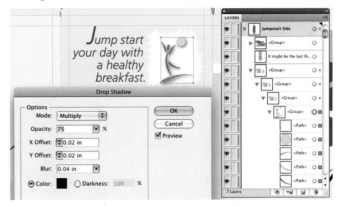

9. **Click OK to apply the drop shadow.**

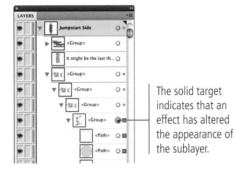

The solid target indicates that an effect has altered the appearance of the sublayer.

10. **Collapse the expanded layers in the Layers panel, save the file, and continue to the next exercise.**

 WARP DESIGN ELEMENTS

The final piece of the design is a banner across the bottom that announces a promotional premium (in this case, a recipe booklet). Rather than simply creating a flat banner, you're going to use effects to create a two-piece, three-dimensional banner that appears to wave across the box.

1. **With heartsmart.ai open, lock everything but the Front layer, hide the Margin Guides layer, and select the Front layer.**

2. **Create a rectangle near the bottom of the front panel area that is 5.5″ wide and 1″ high. Fill the rectangle with the dark pink custom swatch and set the stroke to None.**

3. **Using the Add Anchor Point tool, add an anchor point to the right edge of the rectangle, halfway between the corners. Use the Direct Selection tool to drag the point left, creating the basic banner shape.**

We added an anchor point to a basic rectangle to create the right side of the banner shape.

4. Using the Type tool, click to create a point-type object near the center of the banner shape.

5. Type Yummy! Cereal Recipes, and then format the text as 28-pt ATC Maple Ultra with 125% vertical scaling and a white fill.

6. Position the text relative to the banner shape (as shown in the following image).

7. Group the text and the banner. With the group selected, choose Effect>Warp>Arc.

8. In the resulting Warp Options dialog box, activate the Preview check box.

The icon for each warp style suggests the result that will be created.

The Bend value determines how much warping will be applied to the selected objects.

Distortion values change the horizontal and vertical perspectives of selected objects.

9. Choose Arch in the Style menu.

As the Arch icon suggests, the object's left and right edges are unaffected by an Arch warp.

Note:

You can choose from any of the 15 styles in the Style menu (these are the same as the options listed in the Effect>Warp submenu).

Note:

Similar warp options are available by choosing Object>Envelope Distort>Make with Warp.

10. **Change the Bend value to –25 and click OK to apply the warp.**

The warp effect is also treated as an appearance attribute. When selected, you can see the original object shape.

The bounding box and paths reflect the actual objects without the applied appearance attributes.

11. **Create another rectangle that's 2″ wide by 1″ high, positioned on the right side of the front panel area.**

12. **Using the same method from the first banner shape, add a point to the left side of the shape, and then drag it right to create the second banner shape.**

13. **Use the Type tool to add a point-type object with the words FREE INSIDE formatted as 20-pt ATC Maple Ultra with a white fill and a vertical scale of 125%. Group the second banner with its text.**

14. **Apply a warp effect using the Rise style and a 50% Bend value.**

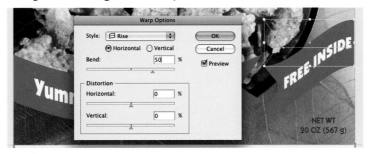

15. **Save the file and continue to the next exercise.**

CREATE A 3D EFFECT

3D effects allow you to create three-dimensional objects from two-dimensional artwork. You can create depth by changing an object's rotation along three different axes, or use extrusion settings to basically "pull" (extrude) an object in three directions. You can also control the appearance of 3D objects with lighting, shading, and other properties.

1. **With heartsmart.ai open, select the first banner group you created in the previous exercise.**

2. **Choose Effect>3D>Extrude & Bevel and activate the Preview option.**

   In the 3D Extrude & Bevel Options dialog box, the small preview shows the approximate position of the original object (the blue square) in relation to the object created by the settings in this dialog box.

Note:

The X Axis value rotates an object around an invisible horizontal line.

The Y Axis value rotates an object around an invisible vertical line.

The Z Axis value rotates an object around an invisible line that moves from the front of an object to the back.

3. **Click the preview icon and drag it around.**

   As you drag the preview icon, the values in the three fields change, based on how and where you drag. In the layout, the selected group also changes because the Preview option is active.

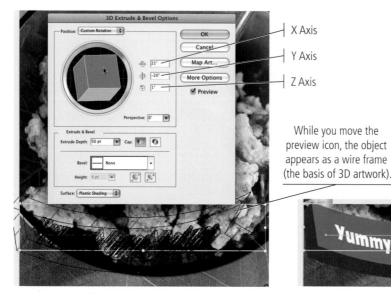

X Axis

Y Axis

Z Axis

While you move the preview icon, the object appears as a wire frame (the basis of 3D artwork).

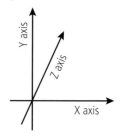

The surface of the object appears only after the wires are calculated internally.

4. When you're done experimenting with the preview, specify the following values:

   X Axis = 14°   Y Axis = 0°   Z Axis = 0°

5. Click OK to apply the effect.

6. Select the small banner group and choose Effect>Apply Extrude & Bevel.

   The top menu option shows the last-used effect. If you use this menu command, the effect will be applied with the last-used settings. You will not see the effect's dialog box.

7. Place the two banners across the bottom of the box, as shown in the following image.

   Since there is some variability in banner size and text placement, you might need to adjust the placement so your banners fit in the best possible way.

8. Save the file and continue to the next stage of the project.

Stage 4   Preparing Artwork for Output

For all intents and purposes, the box artwork is now finished. You've placed and formatted the client's text, composited a number of external graphics and images, created several design elements directly from within Illustrator, and enhanced many of the layout objects using built-in transparency controls and effects.

Whenever you design a file, however, it's important to consider the ultimate goal of the project — in other words, how the job will be output, and what needs to happen to ensure that what you see on your screen is what you receive from the printer.

For most Illustrator projects, you will probably use two or more formats for a completed job (depending on what you need to do with the file).

- If the file needs to be placed into Adobe InDesign or QuarkXPress 8, you can leave the file in its native Illustrator format. (Transparency in the file will be flattened when the page layout document is output.)

- If the file needs to be placed into a QuarkXPress 7 document, you need to save the file using the EPS or PDF format.

- If the file needs to be placed into a QuarkXPress 6 document, you need to save PDF files to be compatible with PDF 1.3 (which does not support transparency).

- If the file needs to be placed into an earlier version of QuarkXPress (version 5 or lower), you should save the file as EPS. (Some earlier versions of QuarkXPress do not support PDF files without an extra XTension; some do not support the PDF format at all.)

When an Illustrator file is output — whether exported to EPS or PDF, or printed directly — the elements in your design need to be converted to something that makes sense to an output device.

High-quality, professional output devices are driven by a **raster-image processor** (RIP) that processes the file data. Unfortunately, output devices don't understand instructions such as "put a red circle in the middle of the page." The PostScript language is used to translate visually designed elements into something the RIP can understand. The PostScript language mathematically describes each object on the page in terms of vectors and pixels.

PostScript does not have the ability to communicate information about transparency. So for transparent elements to output properly, they must be converted or **flattened** into information that can be described in the PostScript language. Flattening divides transparent artwork into the necessary vector and raster objects.

Define Raster Effect Settings

Flattening means dividing transparent elements into whatever elements are necessary to properly output the file. In some cases, flattening results in the creation of new rasterized objects (for example, where transparent text overlaps a raster image).

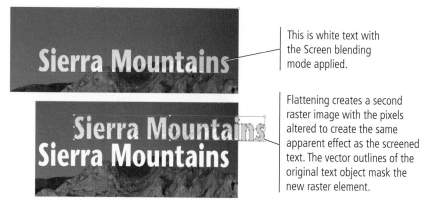

This is white text with the Screen blending mode applied.

Flattening creates a second raster image with the pixels altered to create the same apparent effect as the screened text. The vector outlines of the original text object mask the new raster element.

Some effects, such as drop shadows, create entirely new raster elements where none existed previously.

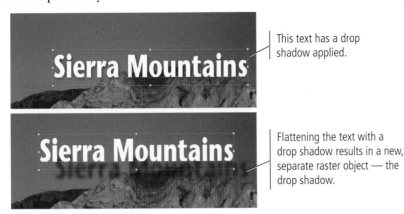

This text has a drop shadow applied.

Flattening the text with a drop shadow results in a new, separate raster object — the drop shadow.

If you are going to create raster objects — either manually or allowing Illustrator to manage the process — you need to be able to control the resolution of those elements. For high-quality print jobs, you should use at least 300 pixels per inch.

1. **With heartsmart.ai open, choose Effect>Document Raster Effects Settings.**

2. **Review the settings in the resulting dialog box.**

These settings are already optimized for high-quality output, applied in the printer's original document template. However, it's always a good idea to check the settings before you apply them.

The **Color Model** menu determines the mode that will be used for new rasterized objects (CMYK, Grayscale, or Bitmap for a document in CMYK mode; an RGB option replaces CMYK if the file uses the RGB color mode).

The **Resolution** options include three basic settings (72 ppi for low-resolution screen display, 150 ppi for medium-resolution desktop printers, or 300 ppi for high-resolution PostScript output). If necessary, you can also assign a custom resolution value in the Other field.

The **Background** options determine how unfilled areas of the file will be handled when placed into another file. If White is selected, underlying objects will not be visible through empty areas of the file.

In the **Options** area:

- **Anti-alias** helps to create smooth transitions, reducing stair-stepping around the edges of rasterized objects.
- **Create Clipping Mask** creates a vector mask that makes the background of the rasterized image appear transparent.
- **Add _ Around Object** creates a specific-sized border around a rasterized image. If you use the White Background option, this area will be filled with white.
- **Preserve Spot Colors** allows spot-color objects to be maintained as spot colors instead of being converted to CYMK.

3. **Click OK to close the dialog box.**

4. **Save the file and continue to the next exercise.**

Note:

Note the warning at the bottom of the dialog box that says, "Changing these settings may affect the appearance of currently applied raster effects."

EXPAND APPEARANCE ATTRIBUTES

When you output a file, the RIP processes the PostScript stream to create the print. Extremely complex designs can take a long time to output (depending on the processing capability of the output device) and can even "jam the RIP" — crash the device and cause an output error. To prevent output problems from overly complex designs, you might want to expand appearance attributes after the design has been finalized.

1. **With heartsmart.ai open, use the Selection tool to select the right banner shape. Display the Appearance panel.**

   At this point, you can still change or delete any attribute of any object. After expanding effects, the file will output faster, but you won't be able to change the effect settings.

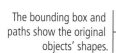

The bounding box and paths show the original objects' shapes.

Two effects have been applied to this object: Warp (Rise) and 3D Extrude & Bevel. Opacity values are those determined by the default settings for the effects you applied.

2. **Choose Object>Expand Appearance.**

The paths show the new objects created by expanding the effects.

The effects are no longer editable.

3. **Using the same process, expand the appearance of the left banner.**

   Fine-tuning and optimizing a complex file for output requires a tradeoff between editability and printability.

4. **Choose File>Save As. Save the file as** heartsmart expanded.ai **in your WIP>Cereal folder and continue to the next exercise.**

   We recommend saving the expanded version as a separate file so you can make changes to the original file if necessary.

Flattener Preview Panel Options

ILLUSTRATOR FOUNDATIONS

You can use the Flattener Preview Highlight menu to highlight different kinds of areas, enabling you to determine which flattener settings are best for the entire file or for a specific object.

- **None** (Color Preview) displays the normal layout.
- **Rasterized Complex Regions** highlights areas that will be rasterized based on the Raster/Vector Balance defined in the applied preset.
- **Transparent Objects** highlights objects with opacity of less than 100%, blending modes, transparency effects (such as drop shadows), and/or feathering applied.
- **All Affected Objects** highlights all objects affected by transparency, including the transparent objects and the objects overlapped by transparent objects. All these objects will be affected by flattening.

- **Affected Linked EPS Files** highlights all EPS files linked in the file but not embedded.
- **Expanded Patterns** highlights patterns that will be expanded by flattening. (Pattern effects must be expanded if they are affected by transparency; this takes place automatically when you output the file.)
- **Outlined Strokes** highlights all strokes that will be converted to filled objects when flattened. (For example, a 5-pt stroke with the Screen blending mode will be converted to a 5-pt-high rectangle filled with the underlying object when the file is flattened.)

PREVIEW TRANSPARENCY FLATTENING

If you are designing with transparency, it's a good idea to know exactly what elements will be affected when the file is flattened for output. Illustrator provides a Flattener Preview panel that you can use to review the file for potential problems.

1. **With heartsmart expanded.ai open, choose Window>Flattener Preview.**

2. **If nothing appears in the white space of the panel, click the Refresh button.**

Drag this corner to make the panel larger, and then click Refresh to enlarge the preview image.

3. **In the Highlight menu, choose All Affected Objects.**

   The red areas in the preview show all objects that are somehow affected by transparency in the file; all these objects will be somehow affected by flattening.

4. **In the Highlight menu, choose Transparent Objects.**

   The highlighted areas reduce to only the objects where transparency is applied.

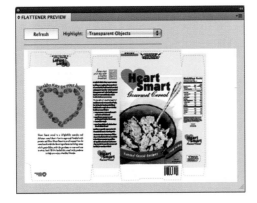

5. **Choose Show Options in the panel Options menu, and then click Refresh.**

The options show the specific settings that will be used to flatten the artwork, based by default on a flattener preset.

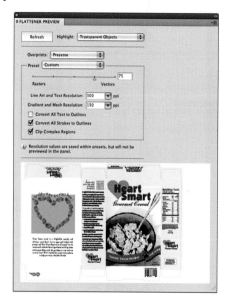

6. **Close the Flattener Preview panel, and then continue to the next exercise.**

Understanding Flattener Presets

Illustrator includes three default flattener presets, which are appropriate for most typical jobs:

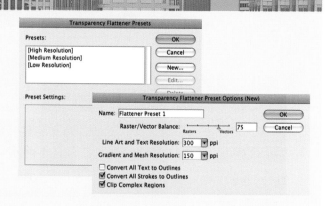

- **Low Resolution** works for desktop proofs that will be printed on low-end black-and-white printers, and for documents that will be published on the Web.

- **Medium Resolution** works for desktop proofs and print-on-demand documents that will be printed on PostScript-compatible color printers.

- **High Resolution** works for commercial output on a printing press and for high-quality color proofs.

You can also create your own flattener presets by choosing Edit>Transparency Flattener Presets and clicking New in the resulting dialog box. You can also use the Transparency Flattener Presets dialog box to load flattener presets created on another machine — such as one your service provider created for their specific output device and/or workflow.

- The preset **Name** will be listed in the related output menus. You should use names that suggest the preset's use, such as "PDF for XL Printing Company." (Using meaningful names is a good idea for any asset that can have a name — from color swatches to output presets.)

- **Raster/Vector Balance** determines how much vector information will be preserved when artwork is flattened, from 0 (all information will be flattened as rasters) to 100 (maintains all vector information).

- **Line Art and Text Resolution** defines the resulting resolution of vector elements that will be rasterized, up to 9600 ppi. For good results with commercial printing, this option should be at least 600–1200 ppi (ask your output provider what settings they prefer you to use).

- **Gradient and Mesh Resolution** defines the resolution for gradients that will be rasterized, up to 1200 ppi. This option is typically set to 300 ppi for most commercial printing applications.

- **Convert All Text to Outlines** converts all type to outline shapes; the text will not be editable in a PDF file.

- **Convert All Strokes to Outlines** converts all strokes to filled paths.

- **Clip Complex Regions** forces boundaries between vector objects and rasterized artwork to fall along object paths, reducing potential problems that can result when only part of an object is rasterized.

FLATTEN TRANSPARENCY FOR SELECTED OBJECTS

Although flattening is typically managed for you when you output a file, you can flatten selected objects manually at any point in the process. Like expanding an object's appearance, flattening is a permanent action — you can no longer edit any effect or setting that caused the transparency. This process should only be done at the very end of a project; again, we recommend maintaining your original file and saving a new version with the manually flattened artwork.

1. With **heartsmart expanded.ai** open, unlock the Back layer, and then select the heart image on the back panel.

2. Choose Object>Flatten Transparency and activate the Preview option.

3. Make sure the High Resolution option is selected in the Preset menu and the Preserve Alpha Transparency option is checked.

   To produce the outer glow effect applied to this object, the color blends outward to become fully transparent at the edges. In other words, the pixels toward the outer edge of the effect are more transparent than the pixels at the inner edge of the effect. This type of effect requires a mechanism to describe the degree of transparency for each pixel. Alpha transparency is a type of mask that defines the degree of transparency for each pixel in the resulting raster objects.

Note:

If Preserve Alpha Transparency is not checked, the flattened artwork will have a white background; the effect will not blend into the background color.

When the Preview option is checked, the file shows two bounding boxes — the result of flattening the applied outer glow effect.

4. Click OK to flatten transparency of the selected object, then deselect everything.

5. Using the Direct Selection tool, click one of the flakes in the image to select only the placed image file.

6. Choose Object>Hide>Selection.

   By flattening the object, a new raster object was created to reproduce the Outer Glow effect.

7. Choose Object>Show All to show the heart of flakes image.

8. Choose File>Save As. Save the file as **heartsmart flat.ai** in your WIP>Cereal folder and continue to the next exercise.

EXPORT A PDF FILE FOR PROOFING

Although packaging such as this box is commonly printed directly from the Illustrator file, you should still create a proof that your client can review either on screen or printed. The PDF format is ideal for this use because the client doesn't need Illustrator to open or print the proof file.

1. **With heartsmart flat.ai open, choose File>Save As.**

2. **Navigate to your WIP>Cereal folder as the destination and choose Adobe PDF in the Format/Save As Type menu.**

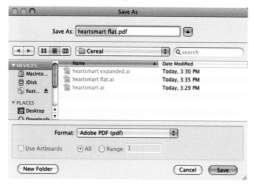

3. **Click Save.**

4. **Choose High Quality Print in the Adobe PDF Preset menu.**

   The Adobe PDF Preset menu includes six PDF presets that meet common industry output requirements.

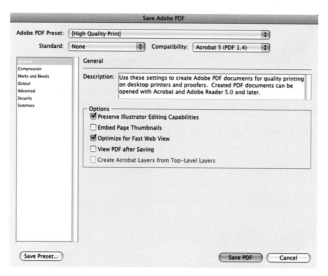

5. **Choose Acrobat 4 (PDF 1.3) in the Compatibility menu.**

   The Compatibility menu determines which version of the PDF format you will create. Not all clients will have the latest versions of technology, so you should consider saving all proof-quality PDFs to be compatible with the earliest version of PDF possible.

As soon as you choose a setting that is not part of the preset, the preset name shows "(Modified)."

Note:

You can manage PDF Presets by choosing File>Adobe PDF Preset>Define. The dialog box that appears lists the built-in presets, as well as any presets you have created. You can also import presets from other users, and you can export presets to send to other users.

Note:

Because there are so many ways to create a PDF — and not all of those ways are optimized for the needs of commercial printing — the potential benefits of the file format are often undermined. The PDF/X specification was created to help solve some of the problems associated with bad PDF files entering the prepress workflow. PDF/X is a subset of PDF specifically designed to ensure that files have the information necessary for and available to the digital prepress output process. Ask your output provider whether you should apply a PDF/X standard to your files, and if so, which version to use.

6. **Click Advanced in the list of options.**

PDF 1.3 does not support transparency, so the file will require flattening. If you save the file to be compatible with PDF 1.4 or later, the transparency information will be maintained in the PDF file; it will have to be flattened later in the process.

7. **Choose High Resolution in the Preset menu.**

Even though this PDF is for proofing purposes, high-resolution produces better results. If file size is not a concern, it's a good idea to use the high-resolution flattener even for proofs.

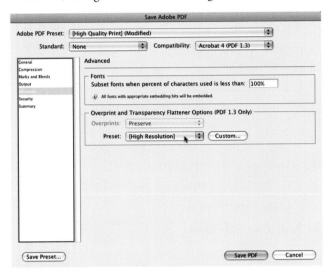

Note:

If you need a smaller file size for proofing purposes, try applying a higher amount of compression in the Compression options.

8. **Click Save PDF to output the file.**

9. **Close the file and continue to the final stage of the project.**

Stage 5   Preview the Box Design in 3D

In Stage 3, you used the 3D Extrude & Bevel feature to add depth to the banners on the front of the box. This effect can also be used to create a box shape and preview your flat box artwork in three dimensions, which is especially useful for showing a client how the art will look when the final piece is printed and folded.

CREATE SYMBOLS FOR BOX PANELS

For this process to work, you first have to do a bit of set-up work. The artwork for each panel has to be saved as a symbol before it can be applied to the 3D box shape. This means you have to do some cutting and clean up work so you have the exact shapes you need before you create the 3D box preview.

1. **Open heartsmart flat.ai from your WIP>Cereal folder.**

2. **Save the file immediately as box preview.ai in your WIP>Cereal folder.**

3. **Hide all layers but the Nutrition Side, Folding Guides, and Box Cut Line layers. Unlock and select the Nutrition Side layer.**

Note:

Depending on how you completed the exercises in this project, you might be able to open this file by choosing File>Open Recent Files. This menu stores the last ten files that were opened in Illustrator.

4. **Select the pink background shape, and use the Selection tool to drag the background shape edges to match the folding guides for the side panel.**

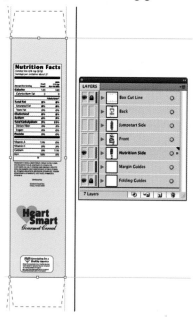

5. **Select and group all objects on the Nutrition Side layer.**

6. **Open the Symbols panel (Window>Symbols).**

7. **Drag the group into the Symbols panel. In the resulting dialog box, name the symbol Nutrition Panel and click OK.**

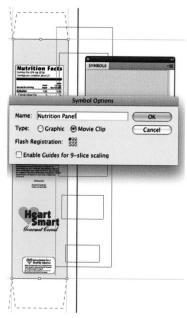

8. **Choose Large List View in the Symbols panel Options menu.**

The Large List views allow you to see both the thumbnail and name of the available symbols.

9. Repeat the process for the Front layer, Jumpstart Side layer, and Back layer, hiding and locking other layers as necessary. If an element only exists on a flap, delete it. Name the symbols Front Panel, Jumpstart Panel, and Back Panel, respectively.

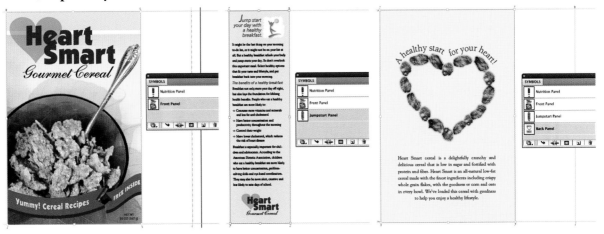

10. Save the file and continue to the next exercise.

APPLY THE ART TO A 3D BOX

Now that you have symbols for each side of the box, you have to create a shape that you can turn into a three-dimensional box. This shape needs to be the correct size for the existing artwork, so you will again use the panel folding guides to build the shape.

1. With box preview.ai open, create a new layer named Box Rendering and select it as the active layer. Hide the content layers, but leave the Folding Guides and Box Cut Line layers visible.

2. Using the Rectangle tool with the light gold fill and no stroke, draw a shape that fills the front panel area (excluding the flaps).

3. Using the Measure tool (nested under the Eyedropper tool), drag a horizontal line to measure the width of the Nutrition Side panel.

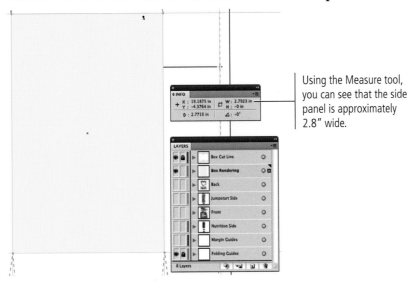

Using the Measure tool, you can see that the side panel is approximately 2.8" wide.

4. Hide the Box Cut Line and Folding Guides layers.

5. **Select the remaining large rectangle and choose Effect>3D>Extrude & Bevel. Make sure the Preview option is unchecked.**

   An active preview slows down the application because it re-renders the artwork after every change.

6. **Define the following parameters, and then check the Preview option to review the results:**

X axis	–3°	Perspective	50°
Y axis	32°	Extrude Depth	Width of the side panel
Z axis	–1°		(from Step 3)

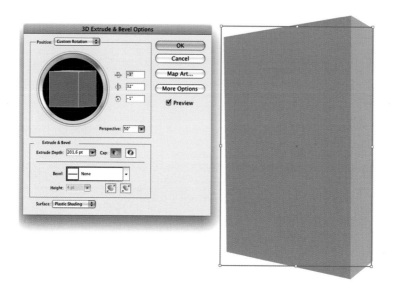

Note:

When you type the panel width in the Extrude Depth field, make sure you type the correct measurement increment ("in"). The dialog box automatically makes the correct conversion to points.

7. **Uncheck the Preview box, and then click the Map Art button.**

   When the Map Art dialog box is open, the object in the layout displays as a 3D wireframe preview even when the Preview option is unchecked. The red line around the preview shows which side (surface) of the shape is being mapped.

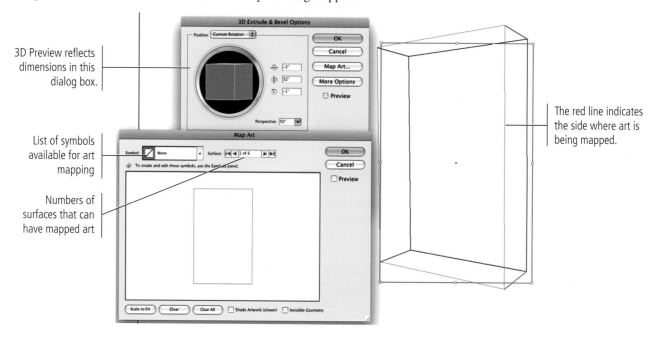

3D Preview reflects dimensions in this dialog box.

List of symbols available for art mapping

Numbers of surfaces that can have mapped art

The red line indicates the side where art is being mapped.

8. Choose Front Panel in the Symbol pop-up menu.

The picture of the front of the box is placed on the page, but you need to adjust it so it exactly fits the page outline; otherwise, there will be gray areas when you render the picture.

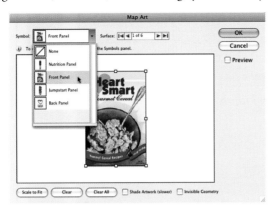

9. Check the Preview option in the Map Art dialog box.

Illustrator renders a preview of the symbol on the 3D box shape (this might take a few minutes to complete).

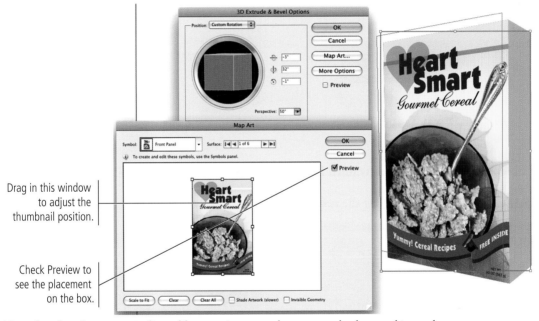

Drag in this window to adjust the thumbnail position.

Check Preview to see the placement on the box.

Note that the white stripe indicated by negative space shows a gray background instead of the white in the design. To solve this problem, you will edit the symbol (after you exit the 3D Extrude & Bevel Options dialog box) to create an actual white stripe in the symbol art.

10. Click the Preview check box to turn off the preview.

Rendering 3D artwork takes time, and must be redone every time you make a change in the dialog box. It's a better idea to turn off the preview while you're making changes, and then turn it on only when you want to review your progress.

11. Click the right Surface arrow until you are looking at Surface 3, and then choose Nutrition Panel in the Symbol menu.

The thumbnail is placed in the wrong orientation, so you need to rotate it. You can click an object in the Map Art preview and drag to move the symbol artwork, or you can use the bounding box handles to resize or rotate the symbol until it fits the gray surface shape.

12. **Click the symbol artwork in the preview and drag down so you can see the top bounding box handles.**

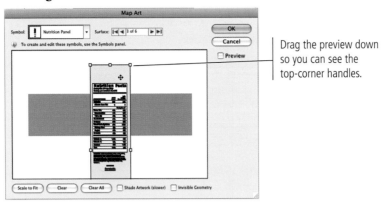

Drag the preview down so you can see the top-corner handles.

13. **Place the cursor near one of the top corner handles, press Shift, and drag around to rotate the artwork 90° counterclockwise.**

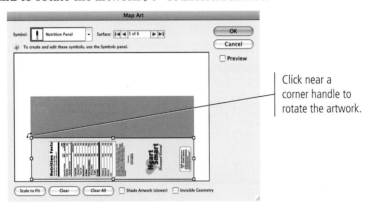

Click near a corner handle to rotate the artwork.

14. **Drag the rotated art in the preview until it aligns with the gray surface shape.**

15. **Check the Preview box and review the results.**

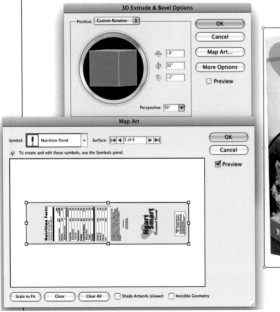

Surface 3 is selected in the Map Art dialog box.

16. Click OK to close the Map Art dialog box, and then click OK again to finalize the 3D box preview.

17. In the Symbol panel, double-click the Front Panel symbol to enter Symbol Editing Mode.

18. In the area of the empty white space, draw a white-filled rectangle the same width as the symbol artwork and send it to the back of the stacking order.

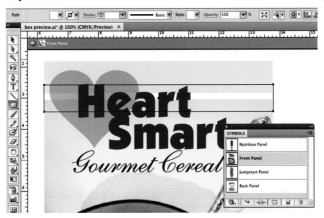

19. Click the arrow button in the top-left corner of the document window to exit Symbol Editing mode.

20. Save the file and close it.

Note:

Once art has been mapped, you can view the 3D virtual effect from different angles by changing the settings in the 3D Extrude & Bevel Options dialog box.

Project Review

fill in the blank

1. You can use the _____ tool to sample colors from placed images.

2. Unchecking the _____ option when placing images results in an embedded file.

3. The _____ can be used to review all the available characters in a font.

4. Checking the _____ option when you place a native Photoshop file results in a single object on a single layer in the Illustrator file.

5. The _____ determines the left-indent position of type on a path.

6. You can use the _____ panel to review and edit applied effects.

7. When the _____ option is not active, each object you create will adopt the last-applied attributes (including effects).

8. The _____ is the specific method used to blend the color of one object into the colors of underlying objects.

9. _____ refers to the degree to which light passes through an object.

10. A(n) _____ can be used to restrict opacity to selected objects; colors in the topmost object determine which areas of the underlying object are visible.

short answer

1. Briefly explain the concept of sublayers, including at least one example of their potential benefit.

2. Briefly explain the difference between Illustrator Effects and Photoshop Effects (in the Illustrator Effect menu).

3. Briefly explain how transparency settings relate to Illustrator files created for commercial printing.

Use what you learned in this project to complete the following freeform exercise.
Carefully read the art director and client comments, then create your own design to meet the needs of the project.
Use the space below to sketch ideas; when finished, write a brief explanation of your reasoning behind your final design.

art director comments

Your agency has been hired to develop packaging for a new video game called *Eye of Horus*, which is an adventure game set in Egypt when the pyramids were being built.

To complete this project, you should:

❏ Disassemble (flatten) an existing game box and measure the different elements. Create a die-cut template in Illustrator using those measurements.

❏ Design box artwork for the new video game, using images or creating illustrations that support the general theme of the product.

❏ Incorporate the product name on all sides of the box.

client comments

The new game is a typical action adventure game with a historical context. The goal is to the navigate a labyrinth inside one of the pyramids to find the Pharaoh's treasure without being captured by the various beasties that protect the hidden chamber.

One side panel needs to list system requirements for the game. We know it will work on both Mac and Windows, but we're still trying to work out the bugs on the latest system releases so we haven't finalized that information yet. For now, use place-holder bullets that say something like 'requirement listing'. That way we can see the formatting even though the actual text isn't ready yet. We'll also have to incorporate the Apple and Windows logos, so leave space for those logos on the same panel.

The back of the box will incorporate some screen captures, which we'll provide as soon as the development is finalized. For now, just leave placeholders to mark the space where those will be placed.

Finally, make sure you build a space on either the back or one side of the box for a bar code.

project justification

The large Artboard size and layer controls, coupled with the extensive set of creative tools, make Illustrator ideally suited to meet the complex needs of packaging design. You can design sophisticated artwork that can be wrapped or folded into virtually any shape to package virtually any product.

This project combined the technical requirements of packaging design — specifically using a custom die-cut supplied by the output provider — with the artistic capabilities necessary to create the final design for a standard-size cereal box. You composited a number of existing elements and created others, then used a number of features to modify artwork — adding interest and depth to unify the different pieces into a single, cohesive design.

Create artwork to fit a printer-supplied die-cut template

Place external elements as necessary for package design

Create type on a custom path

Use effects and filters to add design elements like arrowheads

Use transparency to unify artwork components

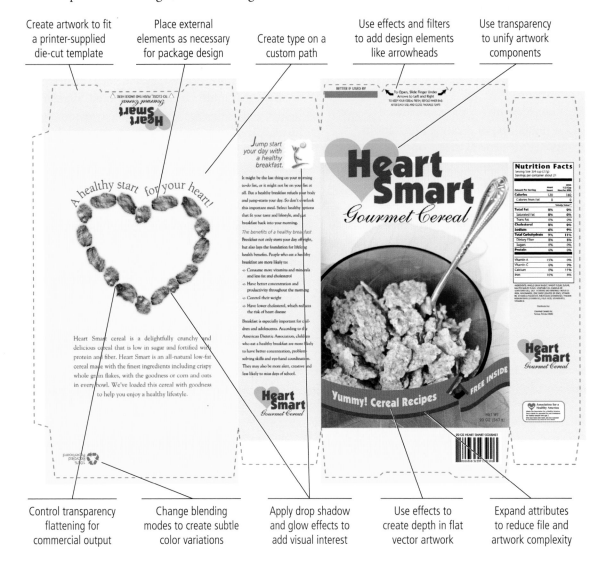

Control transparency flattening for commercial output

Change blending modes to create subtle color variations

Apply drop shadow and glow effects to add visual interest

Use effects to create depth in flat vector artwork

Expand attributes to reduce file and artwork complexity

Financial Infographics

As the illustrator for a magazine publisher, it's your job to create interesting graphics for articles in a variety of magazines. Next month's feature article is about trends in consumer spending and debt. You need to create a graphic that will accompany the article, presenting five different sets of data in a visually pleasing, easy-to-understand format.

This project incorporates the following skills:

- ❏ Creating graphs to present data in a visual format
- ❏ Editing graph data to change the appearance of a graph
- ❏ Importing data from an external file
- ❏ Managing fills, legends, and labels to create graphs
- ❏ Defining a perspective grid
- ❏ Creating objects on alternate horizontal planes
- ❏ Putting objects into the correct perspective

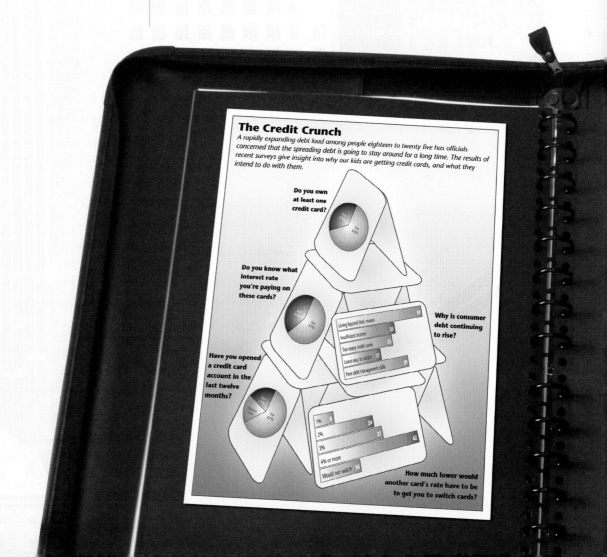

client comments

The feature article in next month's personal finance magazine is an investigation into the spending habits and debt load of the average 20-something American consumer. We conducted a survey through our Web site, and we have some interesting data that we want to include in support of the article text.

Since this is a general-interest consumer magazine, and not a cut-and-dry financial report, I'd like something more than just a set of plain graphs. I'd like you to put the graphs into some kind of context or overall illustration to make the presentation more interesting.

art director comments

Before you start creating the graphs, you should evaluate the kinds of data you have. That way, you can determine which type of graph will best suit the data. Illustrator's graphing tools support many graph types, but you probably won't need more than a few. Bars and pies are the most common types, but the others have important uses too.

You might want to look at some other consumer and personal financial magazines to see how different kinds of graphs and charts are typically used — and how they are incorporated into illustrations to make the data appear more attractive and interesting.

I sketched a "house of cards" idea that I think will be a good container for the five graphs (of course, we're talking about credit cards and not playing cards). I'll also send you the color library we typically use for this magazine — it has a series of "money" colored gradients that work well for financial infographics.

project objectives

To complete this project, you will:

❏ Create pie and bar graphs to present different types of data

❏ Edit live graph data to change the segment breakdown in a graph

❏ Import data from an external file to create a graph

❏ Edit fills, legends, and labels to create aesthetically pleasing, technically accurate graphs

❏ Create a perspective grid for complex, three-dimensional artwork

❏ Change the constrain angle to create objects on alternate horizontal planes

❏ Use the Free Transform tool to put objects into the correct perspective

❏ Ungroup graphs so they can be placed in perspective

Stage 1 Creating Charts and Graphs

The first stage of this project revolves around one of the most powerful but least-used functions in Illustrator — the ability to generate graphics based on variable data. Information graphics (referred to as "infographics") are illustrations that deliver information; bar graphs, pie charts, and area charts are all examples of information provided in a visual format that makes it easier to understand.

Successfully designing infographics requires knowing which kind of chart best shows which type of information. Once you know what kind of chart you need, Illustrator provides the tools and functionality to generate the chart.

Distinguishing Types of Graphs

You can create a wide variety of graphs in Illustrator.

Column graphs compare values using vertical columns.

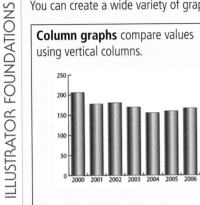

Bar graphs compare values using horizontal bars.

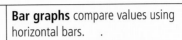
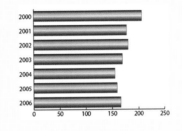

Line graphs plot a series of points across the graph, connecting those points with a line. These graphs show a progressive change in values, such as different prices over time.

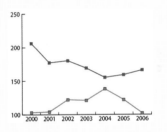

Stacked column graphs divide each column into segments to show the relationship between pieces of the total value.

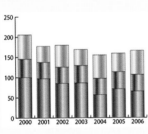

Stacked bar graphs are horizontal versions of stacked column graphs.

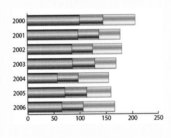

Area graphs are modified line graphs; the space below the line is filled to emphasize the plotted values.

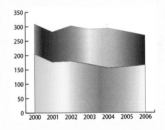

Scatter graphs plot multiple data points along the horizontal and vertical axes. These graphs are used to show trends or clusters in the data points.

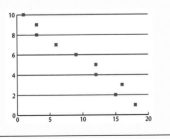

Pie graphs show values as a percentage of the whole.

Radar graphs compare sets of values in a circular format.

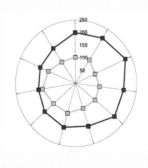

This project involves five different graphs, based on data from a survey of a specific number of people. The five survey questions were intended to determine:

- The number of people who have at least one credit card

- The number of people who know the interest rate of their credit card(s)

- The number of people who would switch to a 0% rate for one year, regardless of the eventual rate

- The point at which consumers say they would switch to a lower-rate credit card

- The perceived reasons for the overall increase in consumer debt

For the first three sets of data (and the resulting graphs), each person surveyed was allowed only a single answer. For the last two sets of data, respondents were allowed to check more than one option from a defined list.

Using this information, you can determine the best type of graph to represent each set of data. Because each person gave a single response to the first three questions, the combined percentages of responses will equal 100%. A pie graph is the best way to show values as a percentage of the whole, so you use pie graphs to visually represent the first three sets of data.

1. **On your desktop, drag the Cards folder from the WIP folder on your Resource CD to the WIP folder where you are saving your work.**

2. **Create a new file named credit, using a letter-size page with inches as the default unit of measurement and portrait orientation. Use the CMYK color model and the High (300 ppi) Raster Effects setting.**

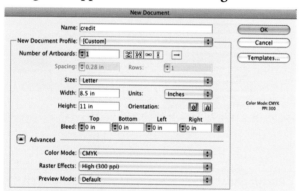

Note:

We've been lucky to work with one of the country's most respected information artists, Scott MacNeil, whose amusing presentations are among the best you'll see. The image you are creating in this project is based on one of MacNeil's illustrations.

3. **With the new file open, select the Type tool in the Tools panel. In the Control panel, change the font to ATC Oak Normal.**

By changing the font with nothing selected, you change the default font of any new type elements in the file — including the legends that will be attached to the graphs.

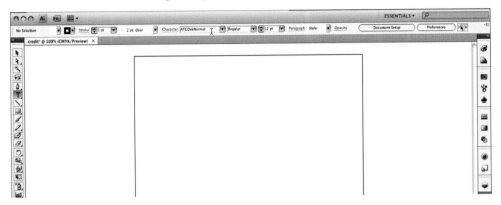

4. **In the Tools panel, choose the Pie Graph tool (it might be nested under one of the other graph tools).**

When you choose a specific graph tool, it becomes the default tool in the Tools panel. Depending on what was previously done in your version of the application, your default graph tool might be different than ours.

5. **Click once anywhere in the page.**

Like single-clicking with a basic shape tool, this method opens a dialog box where you can define the dimensions of the new object (in this case, the graph).

6. **In the Graph dialog box, change both the Height and Width values to 2 in and click OK.**

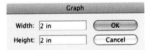

When you create a new graph, a window opens with what appears to be a spreadsheet. This is the Illustrator Data panel, where you enter (or import) the data that will make up your graph.

Note:

The size you define here represents the size of the graph shape only; it does not include the legend or axis labels. If you know the amount of space available for the entire graph (including labels and legend), you should define a smaller graph size so the labels and legend fit within the available space.

7. **Type Yes in the first cell.**

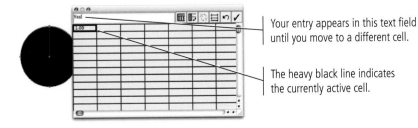

Your entry appears in this text field until you move to a different cell.

The heavy black line indicates the currently active cell.

8. **Press Tab to move to the next cell in the row, and then type No in the selected cell.**

   Pressing Tab moves to the next cell in the row. Pressing Return/Enter moves to the next cell down in the column. You can also use the Arrow keys to move through the cells.

   The first row of the chart can be used to add labels to each set of data. If you don't want to include data labels, you can simply type the data in the first row.

9. **Click the first cell in the second row to select it, and then type 63.**

10. **In the second cell of the second row, type 37.**

    On the Artboard, the graph is still a solid black circle.

Note:

You can create more than one pie graph by entering additional sets of values in subsequent rows.

Using Quotes in the Data Panel

Quotation marks have a specific use in the Data panel. By default, Illustrator's Data panel treats all numbers as parts of the data. In some cases, however, the first row or column of numbers might actually be labels for the data, such as years included in the data set. To prevent Illustrator from treating these numbers as data, you can enclose them within quotation marks in the Data panel.

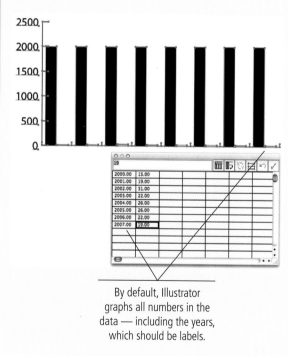

By default, Illustrator graphs all numbers in the data — including the years, which should be labels.

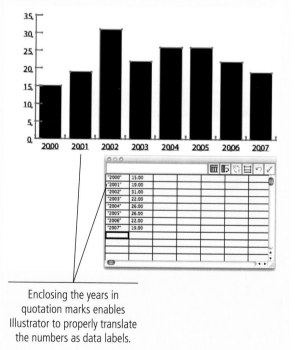

Enclosing the years in quotation marks enables Illustrator to properly translate the numbers as data labels.

11. **Click the Apply button at the top of the Data panel.**

The pie graph is now split into sections, based on the data you defined and applied. The total of the two data values is 100, so each wedge occupies a percentage of the graph that is the same as the related data.

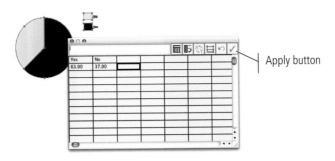

Apply button

12. **Click the Data panel Close button to close the panel.**

13. **Save the file as `credit.ai` in your WIP>Cards folder and continue to the next exercise.**

Edit Graph Data

When you create a graph in Illustrator, the graph, labels, and legend (if used) are grouped together as a single object. As long as the object remains grouped, you can edit the related data, which changes the graph as necessary.

1. **With `credit.ai` open, use the Selection tool to drag the existing graph to the top-left corner of the Artboard.**

2. **Press Option/Alt, begin dragging the graph down, then press Shift and continue dragging down to clone a second pie graph exactly below the first graph.**

3. Press Command/Control-D to repeat the last transformation (the cloning movement) and create a third version of the pie graph.

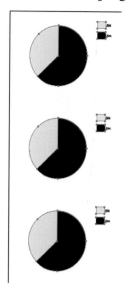

4. Deselect all objects on the Artboard, and then use the Selection tool to select the middle pie graph. Control/right-click the second graph and choose Data from the contextual menu.

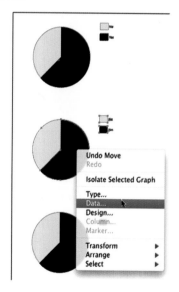

5. In the Data panel, change the Yes value to 57 and the No value to 43, and then click the Apply button.

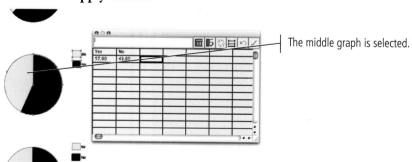

The middle graph is selected.

6. **Click the third graph to select it and show the related data in the Data panel.**

   You don't need to close and reopen the Data panel to see the data for a different graph.

7. **In the Data panel, drag to select the two fields in the second column.**

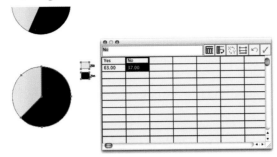

8. **Choose Edit>Cut (Command/Control-X) to cut the data to the Clipboard.**

9. **Click the first cell in the third column and choose Edit>Paste (Command/Control-V).**

   Unlike traditional spreadsheet applications, you can't drag data cells to a new location. You can, however, cut cells and paste them into a new position if you need to add new data in between existing data.

10. **Select the first cell in the second column and type** Maybe**.**

11. **Select the second cell in the second column and type** 18**.**

12. **Change the Yes value to** 61**, change the No value to** 21**, and then click the Apply button.**

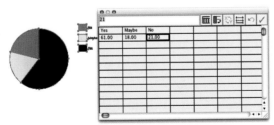

13. **Close the Data panel, save the file, and continue to the next exercise.**

CHANGE GRAPH LEGENDS

When the first row of your data defines labels for each set, the graph automatically includes a legend with a small block of the wedge color and the related label. You can change the type or position of the legend, or you can remove it completely by editing the graph type settings.

As we stated earlier, all elements of the graph object — including the legend — are grouped into a single object; as long as the group remains a group, you can edit the related data. If you try to select the legend elements and delete them from the Artboard, however, you'll see a warning that you can't delete the objects as long as the graph object remains grouped.

1. **With `credit.ai` open, use the Direct Selection tool to select the black wedge in each graph.**

   The Direct Selection tool allows you to change individual pieces of the graph without ungrouping the graph object.

   Don't worry about the Yes blocks in the legends; those blocks will be removed when you change the legend type later in this exercise.

2. **Change the fill of the selected shapes to 25% black.**

   This color change will allow you to see the black text when you change the legend type.

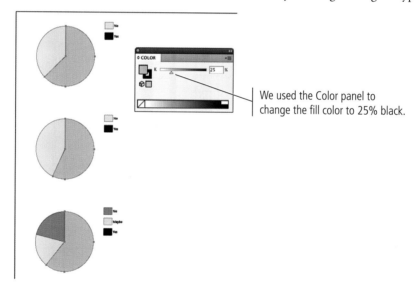

We used the Color panel to change the fill color to 25% black.

3. **Deselect all objects on the Artboard.**

4. **Using the Selection tool, select the top graph. Control/right-click the selected graph and choose Type from the contextual menu.**

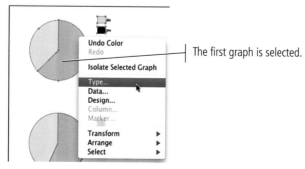

The first graph is selected.

5. **In the Options area of the Graph Type dialog box, choose Legends in Wedges in the Legend menu.**

This dialog box has different available options, depending on the type of graph you are creating. For a pie graph, you can use the Legend menu to remove the legend completely, create a standard stacked legend (the default), or place the legend labels inside the associated wedges.

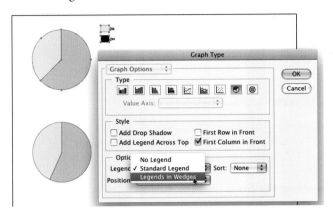

Note:

If you check Add Legend Across Top when the Standard Legend option is selected, the legend appears as a row above the graph.

6. **Click OK to close the Graph Type dialog box, and then zoom in to 200%.**

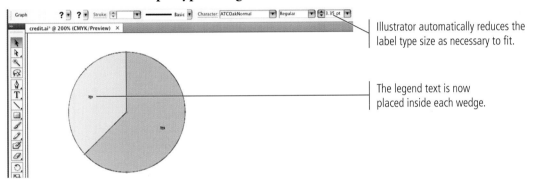

Illustrator automatically reduces the label type size as necessary to fit.

The legend text is now placed inside each wedge.

7. **With the graph still selected, use the Control panel to change the type size to 10 pt.**

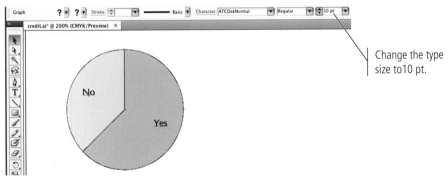

Change the type size to 10 pt.

8. **Control/right-click the graph and choose Data from the contextual menu.**

9. **In the , select the first label field.**

10. **In the field at the top of the Data panel, place the insertion point at the end of the existing label (Yes).**

11. Type |63%.

The pipe character (Shift-Backslash) is used to create a new line in the graph label.

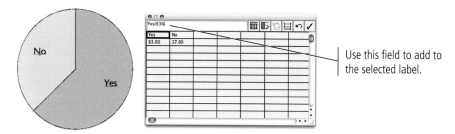

Use this field to add to the selected label.

12. Using the same method, type |37% after the No label.

The labels now reflect the actual data that was used to create the graph wedge. The point of infographics is to make data easy to view and understand; these enhanced labels are far more informative than the basic Yes/No labels.

13. Click the Apply button, and then close the Data panel.

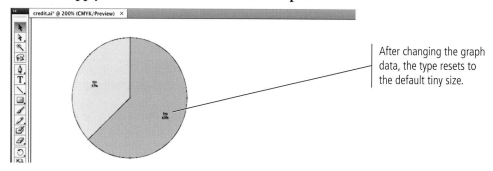

After changing the graph data, the type resets to the default tiny size.

14. With the graph selected, use the Control panel to change the type size to 10 pt.

Legend type is automatically scaled to some smaller size to fit the graph whenever you reapply the data.

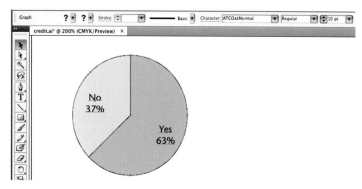

15. Repeat this process for the two remaining graphs: Move the legend text into the wedges, add the actual data value to the label text, and then change the label text to 10 pt.

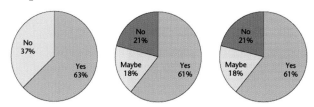

16. Save the file and continue to the next exercise.

COLOR GRAPH COMPONENTS

One of the advantages of building graphs in Illustrator is the ability to use the extensive artistic tool set to decorate the graphs. Rather than using the default shades-of-gray fills, you can fill the wedges with swatches — colors, gradients, patterns — to make the data more visually appealing.

1. **With credit.ai open, choose Window>Swatch Libraries>Other Library.**

2. **Navigate to the file money colors.ai (in the RF_Illustrator>Cards folder) and click Open.**

    This is a custom library of swatches that your magazine frequently uses to illustrate financial concepts. You're going to use these gradients to fill the various elements of the graphs.

3. **Using the panel Options menu, display the Money Colors library panel in List view (either small or large, whichever you prefer).**

4. **Deselect everything on the Artboard.**

5. **Using the Direct Selection tool, Shift-click the Yes wedge in each graph.**

6. **Make sure the Fill swatch is active in the Tools panel, and then click the Gold Radial swatch in the Money Colors library.**

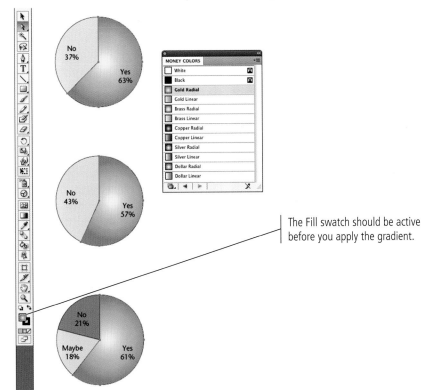

The Fill swatch should be active before you apply the gradient.

Note:

Radial gradients are automatically applied from the center of the object, as determined by the outermost edges of the selected shape. For a gradient to be centered in the entire graph area instead of just the wedge shape, you have to use the Gradient tool to reposition the gradient center.

7. **Deselect the three wedges, and then use the Direct Selection tool to select the Yes wedge in the first graph only.**

8. **Choose the Gradient tool in the Tools panel.**

As you learned in Project 2, selecting the Gradient tool activates the Gradient Annotator, which allows you to control the gradient's angle, position, and colors.

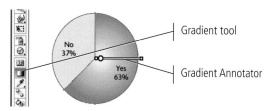

Gradient tool

Gradient Annotator

9. **Click the Gradient Annotator center point and drag it to the center point of the graph.**

The radial gradient now originates from the center of the chart, but the gradient does not extend to the edge.

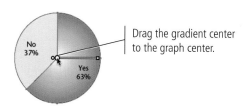

Drag the gradient center to the graph center.

10. **Drag the right end of the Gradient Annotator to touch the outer edge of the chart.**

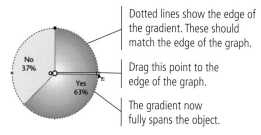

Dotted lines show the edge of the gradient. These should match the edge of the graph.

Drag this point to the edge of the graph.

The gradient now fully spans the object.

11. **Choose the Direct Selection tool and click away from the active wedge to deselect it.**

If you don't deselect the active gradient-filled object, you might have difficulty selecting and modifying the gradients in the other graph wedges.

Filling Wedges with Gradients

If a pie graph wedge is 75% or more of the graph area, a radial gradient will be correctly centered in the graph area because the outermost edges of the wedge are the same as the outermost edges of the graph. In the following images, dashed lines show the outer dimensions of the cyan wedge; you can see the white gradient center move as the wedge shape changes.

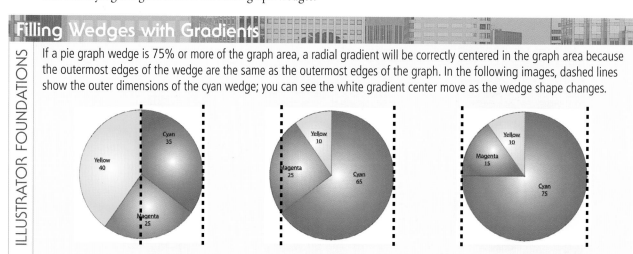

12. **Repeat Steps 7–11 to correct the center and endpoint of the gradient in the Yes wedge of each graph.**

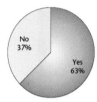 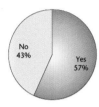 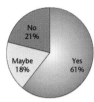

13. **Using the Direct Selection tool, select the No wedge of the top graph. Apply the Copper Radial gradient swatch, and then use the Gradient tool to correctly position the center and endpoint of the gradient.**

The center of the gradient should be at the graph center, and the endpoint of the gradient should be at the graph's outer edge.

Note:

You can toggle the Gradient Annotator on and off by choosing View>Show/Hide Gradient Annotator.

14. **Using the same process as in Step 13, apply the Copper Radial gradient to the No wedges in the other two graphs.**

15. **Apply the Dollar Radial gradient to the Maybe wedge in the third graph. Center and extend the gradient as necessary.**

16. **Using the Direct Selection tool, select all three No labels and change the text color to white.**

17. **Reposition each label element closer to the centers of the graphs.**

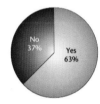 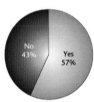 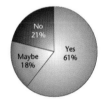

18. **Save the file and continue to the next exercise.**

 ## CREATE A BAR GRAPH WITH IMPORTED DATA

In this exercise, you create two additional graphs to show how many survey respondents selected specific answers to a posed question. Respondents were allowed to select more than one answer, so the data does not reflect percentages of a total — in other words, a pie graph is inappropriate for presenting this type of data. Bar and column graphs, on the other hand, are well suited for showing this type of data.

Orientation is the only real difference between a bar graph and a column graph. Bar graphs represent each data set as a horizontal bar, while column graphs use vertical columns. These two graphs need to be horizontally oriented (as you'll see when you get to Stage 2 of the project), so you will use bar graphs for the last two sets of data.

1. **With credit.ai open, choose the Bar Graph tool (nested under the Pie Graph tool) from the Tools panel.**

2. **Click in the right side of the Artboard to open the Graph dialog box. Define the new graph to be 4 inches wide by 2 inches high, and then click OK.**

3. **In the Data panel, click the Import Data button.**

4. **Navigate to the file rates.txt in the RF_Illustrator>Cards folder and click Open.**

   This data was originally a Microsoft Excel file, but it was exported as a tab-delimited text-only file.

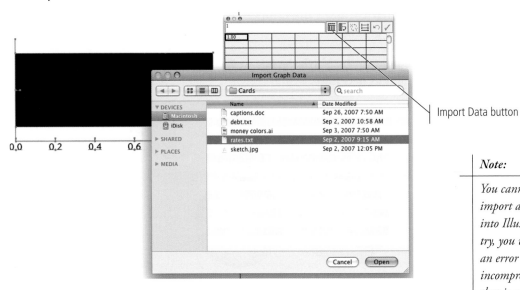

Import Data button

Note:

You cannot directly import an Excel file into Illustrator. If you try, you will see either an error message or incomprehensible data that is useless for making graphs in Illustrator.

5. **Click the Apply button, and then close the Data panel.**

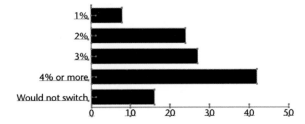

6. **With the graph selected, use the Control panel to change the type size to 10 pt.**

7. **Control/right-click the graph and choose Type from the contextual menu.**

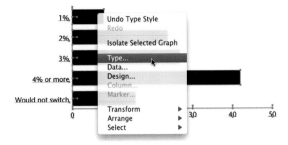

8. **In the Graph Type dialog box, choose Value Axis in the top menu.**

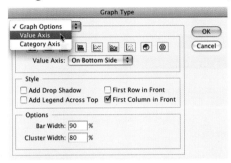

9. **Check the Override Calculated Values box. Type 42 in the Max field (the highest number in the data set) and type 1 in the Divisions field.**

   By default, Illustrator uses a range beginning with 0 and extending in increments as necessary to show the defined data. You can use the Min and Max fields to define a specific value axis, such as always extending to 100 instead of ending at 70 or some other lower value. The Divisions field determines how many tick marks and labels are added to the value axis (the horizontal axis for this bar graph).

   Because you changed the Max field to the largest number in the data set, the bar for that data field will extend the entire width of the graph.

10. **Choose None in the Tick Marks Length menu.**

    By default, tick marks are short lines on the inside of the graph area. You can also choose Full Width to extend the tick marks the full range of the graph, or you can choose None to turn off the value axis divisions.

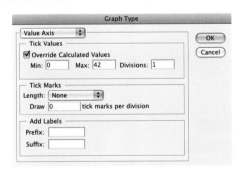

Note:

If you are including divisions in your graph, you can add subdivisions using the Draw _ Tick Marks Per Division option.

Note:

The Prefix and Suffix fields can be used to add specific characters in front of or at the end of defined value labels.

11. **Choose Category Axis in the top menu and change this Tick Marks Length menu to None.**

Similar to the value axis, categories are also separated by tick marks by default. In the case of a bar graph, tick marks are usually unnecessary.

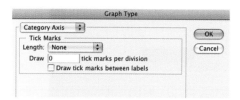

12. **Click OK to close the Graph Type dialog box and apply your changes.**

Note:

Unfortunately, the Graph Type dialog box does not include a Preview check box. You can't see the results of your choices until you click OK. As long as the graph object remains a graph object, you can always make changes.

13. **Save the file and continue to the next exercise.**

EDIT AND FORMAT GRAPH LABELS

When it comes to labeling graph elements for bar graphs, you can change the appearance and position of labels, and you can edit the label text by changing the fields in the Data panel. You cannot, however, add multiple labels to the same data.

In the pie graphs you created earlier, you modified the data labels to include the actual values of the wedges. You could use the same technique for bar graphs, but in some cases it's better to simply add new text elements as secondary labels.

1. **With credit.ai open, deselect everything on the Artboard.**

2. **Use the Direct Selection tool to select the first, third, and fifth bars in the graph. Make sure the Fill swatch is active in the Tools panel, and then apply the Gold Linear gradient.**

Remember, every part of the graph must remain grouped if you want to be able to edit the associated data. The Direct Selection tool allows you to access individual pieces of the graph group.

3. **Using the same process as in Step 2, apply the Dollar Linear gradient to the second and fourth bars.**

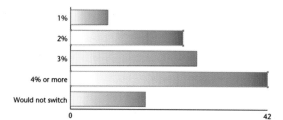

4. **Use the Direct Selection tool to select all five type objects on the left side of the graph.**

5. **Apply left paragraph alignment to the selected elements, and then Shift-drag the labels right so they are within the related bars in the graph.**

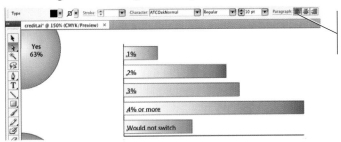

Click here to apply left paragraph alignment to the selected objects.

Note:

You can also use the Arrow keys to nudge the selected objects into place.

6. **With the same five elements selected, choose Edit>Copy.**

7. **Choose Edit>Paste to create copies of the selected objects.**

When you paste these objects, they are no longer considered part of the graph group. In this case, you cannot use the Option/Alt-drag cloning method or the Paste in Front/Paste in Back commands to make the secondary labels. Both of these methods result in duplicate labels that are still part of the graph, which will cause problems if you update the graph data or edit the graph type.

8. **Change the pasted type objects to ATC Oak Bold filled with white, and apply right paragraph alignment. Use the Direct Selection tool to position each secondary label at the right end of the associated bar.**

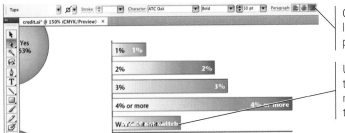

Change the secondary labels to right paragraph alignment.

Using right paragraph alignment, the right end of the type object will remain in place when you change the text in the object.

9. **Using the Selection tool, select the bar graph. Control/right-click the selected graph object and choose Data from the contextual menu. Write down the five values in the second column, and then close the Data panel.**

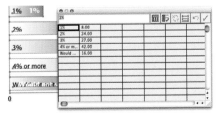

10. **Change each white label to show the actual value for the related bar.**

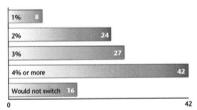

11. **Select the graph and the five extra type objects and group them.**

12. **Save the file and continue to the next exercise.**

EDIT GRAPH DATA

The final artwork for this project requires two bar graphs with different data but the same general appearance. Rather than repeating the entire process to create the second bar graph, you can clone the existing graph and edit the data to create the second graph.

1. **With credit.ai open, use the Selection tool to select the group that contains the existing bar graph.**

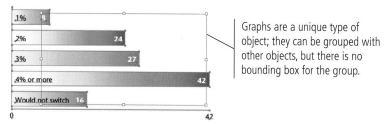

Graphs are a unique type of object; they can be grouped with other objects, but there is no bounding box for the group.

2. **Press Option/Alt-Shift and drag down to clone the group.**

3. **Double-click the duplicate group to enter Isolation mode.**

   In Isolation mode, you can access the graph group (and its Data panel) without ungrouping the graph from the secondary label-text objects.

4. **In Isolation mode, use the Selection tool to select the graph object. Control/right-click the selected graph and choose Data from the contextual menu.**

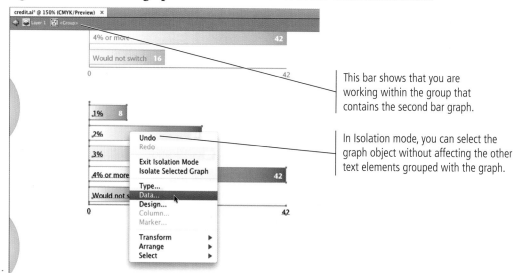

This bar shows that you are working within the group that contains the second bar graph.

In Isolation mode, you can select the graph object without affecting the other text elements grouped with the graph.

5. **In the Data panel, click the Import Data button. Navigate to the file debt.txt (in the RF_Illustrator>Cards folder) and click Open.**

6. **Write down the five values in the second column, and then click the Apply button.**

7. **Close the Data panel.**

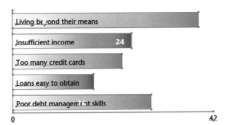

8. **Control/right-click the selected graph and choose Type from the contextual menu.**

9. **In the Value Axis options, change the Max field to match the largest number in the data set. Click OK to close the Graph Type dialog box.**

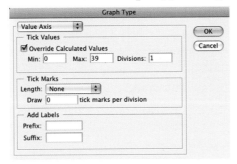

When you edit the graph type, the label formatting will return to the default settings — in this case, to right paragraph alignment.

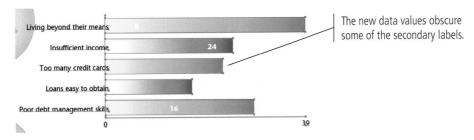

The new data values obscure some of the secondary labels.

10. **Using the Direct Selection tool, select the five changed label objects and reapply left paragraph alignment.**

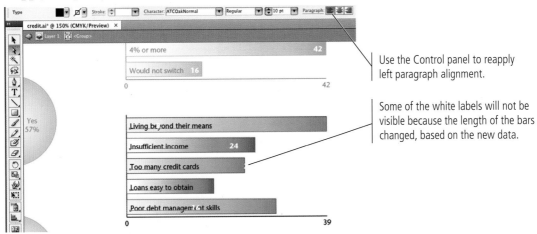

Use the Control panel to reapply left paragraph alignment.

Some of the white labels will not be visible because the length of the bars changed, based on the new data.

11. Choose View>Outline Mode so you can see all secondary labels.

Remember, outline mode shows only the edges of the objects — including the outline of type objects. This mode allows you to see and access the white-filled labels for the third and fourth bars, so you can change the text and position the type objects as necessary.

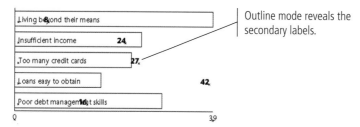

Outline mode reveals the secondary labels.

12. Change the text in the secondary labels to match the new data you wrote down in Step 6. Using the Direct Selection tool, move the secondary labels to the right ends of the bars.

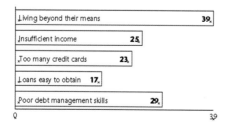

13. Choose View>Preview to return to the normal view.

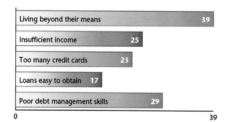

14. Click the arrow button (at the top of the document window) two times to exit Isolation mode.

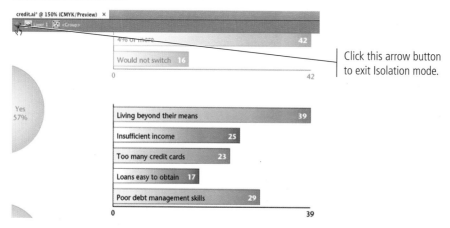

Click this arrow button to exit Isolation mode.

15. Save the file and continue to the next stage of the project.

Stage 2 Drawing in Perspective

The second half of the word "infographics" means adding visual elements that make the data seem more attractive and accessible to users. Although the graphs are already visual representations of data, true infographics typically refer to something more than just graphs — some type of visual context for containing the graphs.

The graphs you built for this project are all related to trends in consumer credit and debt. Following the theme of the data, you are going to create a stacked "house of credit cards" illustration, and then place the data on the visible faces of the stacked cards.

CREATE PERSPECTIVE GUIDES

In this series of exercises, you create the artwork for this project based on a pencil sketch. As you will see in the sketch, stacked cards create a three-dimensional object. To recreate this effect using two-dimensional drawing tools, you need to understand the basic artistic principle of perspective.

The concept of perspective means that all lines on the same surface (or plane) eventually meet at a single point, called the vanishing point. Lines move closer together as they get closer to the vanishing point, creating the illusion of depth.

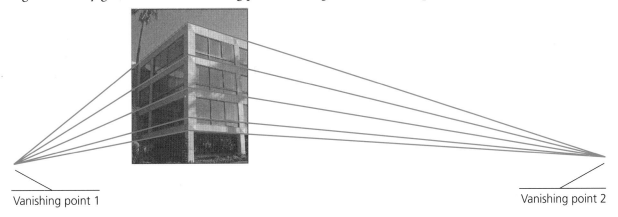

Vanishing point 1   Vanishing point 2

Artists using traditional media typically create perspective lines using tracing paper. You will use layers to build the digital equivalent of perspective guides.

1. **With credit.ai open (from your WIP>Cards folder), rename Layer 1 as Graphs, and then hide and lock the layer.**

2. **Create a new layer named Sketch. Place the sketch.jpg file (from the RF_Illustrator>Cards folder) into the Sketch layer, center the image horizontally and vertically to the Artboard, and then lock the layer.**

   The sketch shows that the artwork has four primary surfaces; each surface has two vanishing points (called two-point perspective). You need to define two-point perspective guides for each surface in the artwork so you can more easily draw and transform the card shapes.

3. **Create a new layer named Left Face Guides and select it as the active layer.**

4. **Using the Line tool with a 1-pt black stroke and no fill, draw a line along the left side of the cards on the left side of the stack. Extend the top edge of the line past the top edge of the Artboard.**

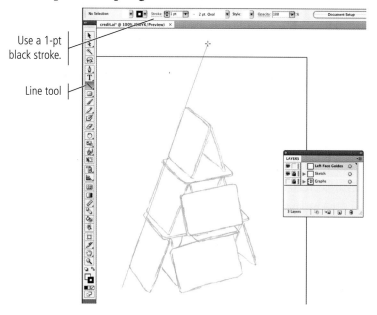

Use a 1-pt black stroke.

Line tool

5. **Draw a second line along the right edge of the same cards.**

6. **Using the Direct Selection tool, select the top anchor points of both lines.**

7. **Choose Object>Path>Average. Average the selected points based on both axes, and then click OK.**

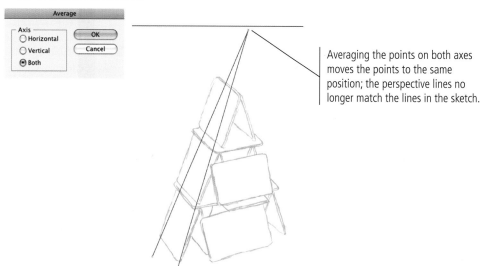

Averaging the points on both axes moves the points to the same position; the perspective lines no longer match the lines in the sketch.

8. **Choose Object>Path>Join. Join the selected points as a corner point and click OK.**

Note:

It's not mandatory that you join the two points, but it's easier to manage a single point than to control multiple points at the same location.

9. **Zoom out to 25% magnification. Using the Direct Selection tool, drag the joined point away from the sketch until the lines match the card edges in the sketch.**

Depending on your monitor size and resolution, you might have to zoom out farther than 25% to match the perspective lines to the sketch. However, 25% is a good starting point because you can still see the lines in the sketch.

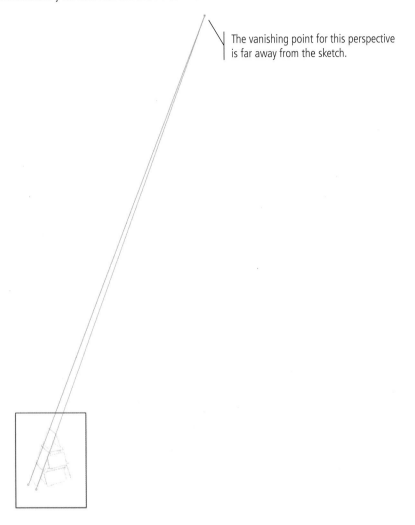

The vanishing point for this perspective is far away from the sketch.

10. **Zoom in and check the accuracy of the lines relative to the cards in the sketch.**

If the lines don't match the sketch, the vanishing point is either too close or too far away.

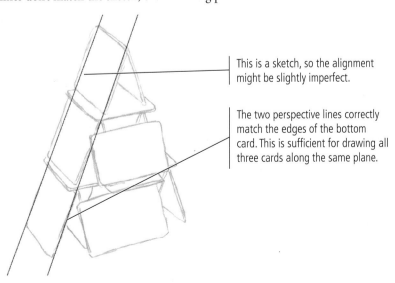

This is a sketch, so the alignment might be slightly imperfect.

The two perspective lines correctly match the edges of the bottom card. This is sufficient for drawing all three cards along the same plane.

11. **Adjust the location of the vanishing point (if necessary) until the perspective lines align correctly on the cards.**

12. **Using the same basic technique, create a vanishing point and perspective lines for the second perspective of the cards on the left side of the stack.**

    Use the following illustration as a guide.

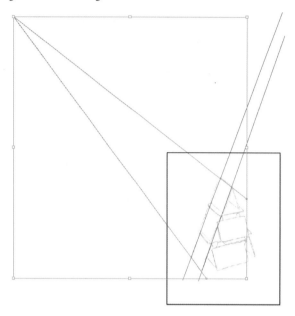

13. **Use the Selection tool to select both lines of the second perspective point.**

14. **Choose Edit>Copy, and then choose Edit>Paste in Front to paste a copy of the perspective lines in the exact same spot.**

15. **Deselect everything on the Artboard. Use the Direct Selection tool to drag the right endpoints of the copied lines so they mark the bottoms of the top and middle cards (as shown in the following image).**

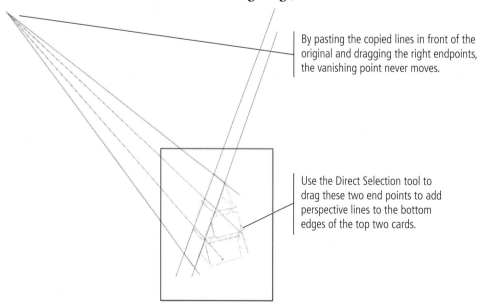

By pasting the copied lines in front of the original and dragging the right endpoints, the vanishing point never moves.

Use the Direct Selection tool to drag these two end points to add perspective lines to the bottom edges of the top two cards.

16. Select all six lines on the layer and choose View>Guides>Make Guides.

The Make Guides command can be used to convert any selected object — at any angle or in any shape — into a nonprinting guide. If necessary, you can convert custom guides to regular objects by selecting the guide object and choosing View>Guides>Release Guides.

Note:

To select and release object guides, guides need to be unlocked.

17. Save the file and continue to the next exercise.

IDENTIFY AND CREATE ADDITIONAL PLANES

The process for creating a vanishing point is fairly simple, as you saw in the previous exercise. The most complicated part of drawing in perspective is identifying the different planes you need to map with perspective lines.

As we said at the beginning of this series of exercises, this sketch contains four basic planes:

- The cards that face out on the left side of the stack
- The cards that face forward
- The cards that face out to the right side of the stack
- The cards that lay flat (the "support" cards for the upright cards)

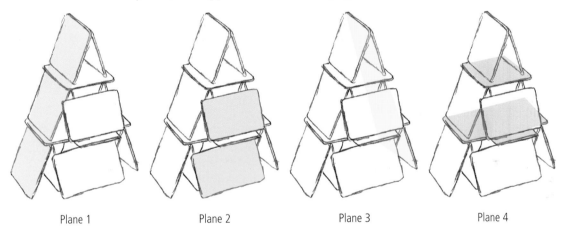

| Plane 1 | Plane 2 | Plane 3 | Plane 4 |

The cards on the inside of the stack also need to be created, but they will follow the same basic perspective as the outer cards. Because most of these cards are hidden, their perspective is not as critical as the primary planes.

1. With credit.ai open, hide and lock the Left Face Guides layer.

2. Create three new layers with the following names, arranged top to bottom as shown here:

Right Face Guides

Front Face Guides

Flat Guides

Because this is going to be a very complex file, you are placing the guides for each plane on a separate layer. Doing so allows you to show only the guides you need while you create specific cards.

3. **Starting with the Flat Guides layer, use the same techniques as in the previous exercise to create two-point perspective guides for each of the three planes.**

Make sure the perspective lines are on the appropriate layers, and convert each set of lines to guides. After you complete a particular set of guides, hide and lock each layer to make it easier to see and create the next set.

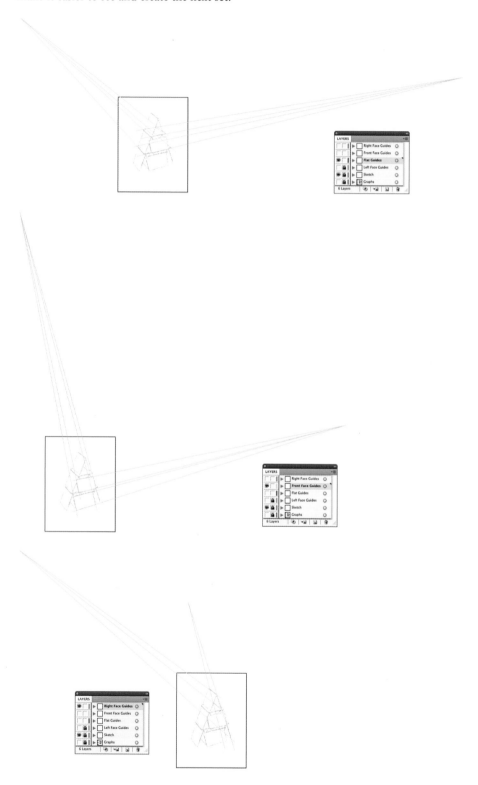

4. **Save the file and continue to the next exercise.**

CHANGE THE DEFAULT CONSTRAIN ANGLE

Now that you have four sets of perspective guides, it's time to start drawing the cards. There are many elements to draw, but they all require the same basic technique.

Because you are looking at the sketch from an angle, "horizontal" lines — where the card edges sit on a surface — are not really horizontal. Instead, they are at the angle necessary to create the depth effect of the related vanishing point.

If you know the angle of that implied horizon, you can use it as the basis of drawing the objects that will make up the artwork.

1. **With credit.ai open, make sure all layers are locked. Show only the Sketch and Front Face Guides layers.**

2. **Create a new layer named Front Card 1 at the top of the layer stack, and select that layer to make it active.**

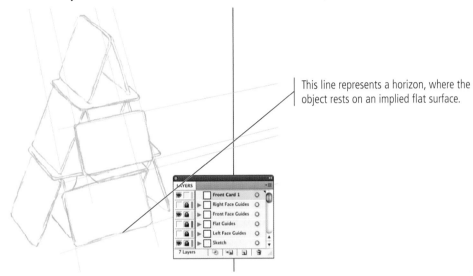

This line represents a horizon, where the object rests on an implied flat surface.

3. **Select the Measure tool (nested under the Eyedropper tool) in the Tools panel.**

4. **Click with the Measure tool near the left edge of the bottom-front perspective guide, and then drag along the line to end at the right side of the bottom card.**

   The angle is approximately 17°. If this were a technical illustration, "approximately" would be unacceptable. For the sake of this illustration, however, you can use "close enough" whole numbers.

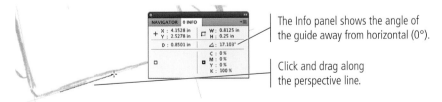

The Info panel shows the angle of the guide away from horizontal (0°).

Click and drag along the perspective line.

5. **Open the General panel of the Preferences dialog box.**

   Remember, Macintosh preferences are accessed in the Illustrator menu; Windows preferences are accessed in the Edit menu. You can also click the Preferences button in the Control panel when nothing is selected in the file.

6. **Change the Constrain angle to 17°.**

This option resets the X axis to the newly defined angle (instead of perfectly horizontal).

7. **Set the Corner Radius to 0.17 inch.**

This is the default corner radius for corner effects on basic shapes, such as the rounded rectangles you create next.

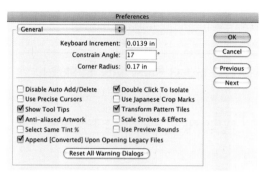

8. **Click OK to apply the change and return to the document.**

9. **Choose the Rounded Rectangle tool. Set the stroke to 2-pt magenta and the fill to None.**

Using a heavy colored stroke, the objects you create will stand out in contrast to the gray lines in the sketch image. We use magenta for this reason, but you can use whatever color you find easiest to work with. You'll change the magenta lines after you finish drawing the stack of cards.

10. **Click at the bottom corner of the lower front-facing card, and then drag to create a new rounded rectangle. Use the intersection of perspective lines to mark the start and end of the shape.**

As you draw the shape, notice that the bottom edge is angled, based on the new constrain angle — i.e., the new "horizon" or X axis.

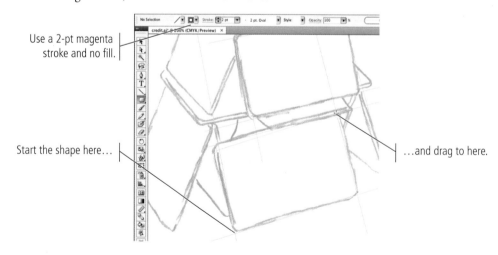

Use a 2-pt magenta stroke and no fill.

Start the shape here…

…and drag to here.

11. **With the new rectangle selected, choose the Free Transform tool in the Tools panel.**

12. **Click the top-left handle of the object's bounding box. Hold down the mouse button, press Command/Control, and drag the handle to the upper-left intersection of the two perspective lines.**

By pressing the Command/Control modifier key after you click the corner handle, you can reposition one corner of the object without affecting the other corners.

Note:

*You must click the object's handle **before** pressing the Command/Control key. If you press the modifier key before clicking the handle, this process won't work.*

Click-hold the corner handle, press Command/Control, and then drag to the intersection of the upper-left perspective guides.

Free Transform tool

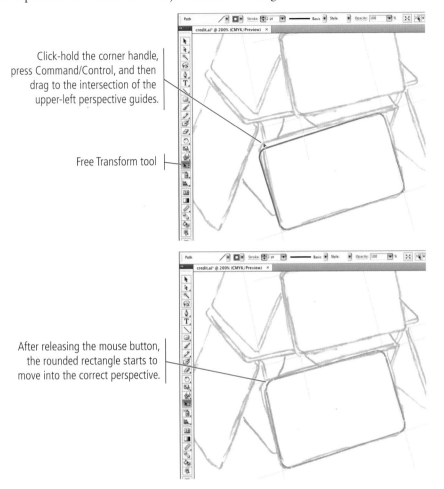

After releasing the mouse button, the rounded rectangle starts to move into the correct perspective.

13. **Repeat Step 12 as necessary for the other corners of the shape.**

14. **Deselect the object and review the results.**

The drawing does not match the sketch exactly, but it does match the perspective guides. When the sketch is removed from the artwork, the card will appear in the correct perspective.

15. **Save the file and continue to the next exercise.**

The Free Transform tool allows you to change the shape of selected objects by dragging the bounding box handles. Depending on where you click and whether you press a modifier key, you can use this tool to sketch, shrink, rotate, distort, or skew a selection.

Click a center handle to stretch or shrink the selection in one direction.

Click a corner handle to stretch or shrink the selection horizontally and vertically at the same time.

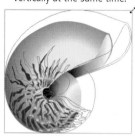

Click slightly outside a corner handle to rotate the selection.

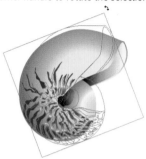

Click a center handle, then press Command/Control to skew the selection.

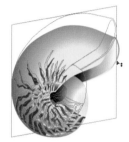

Click a corner handle, then press Command/Control to distort the selection.

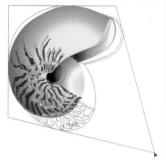

Click a corner handle, then press Command-Option-Shift/Control-Alt-Shift to alter the perspective of the selection.

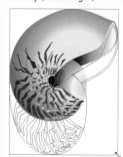

Press Option/Alt while making any free transformation to apply it equally on both sides of the selection center.

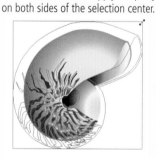

Press Shift and drag a handle to constrain the related transformation. For example, press Shift while dragging a corner handle to scale the selection at the same proportional height and width (below left) rather than scaling disproportionately (below right).

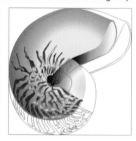

CREATE CARDS ON DIFFERENT PERSPECTIVE PLANES

The rest of this perspective drawing is more of the same — measure the apparent horizon, change the constrain angle, draw the rounded rectangle based on the perspective guides, and then use the Free Transform tool to drag the shape's corners into the correct perspective.

After all cards have been created, you will need to change the stacking order so the cards appear as they would in a real "house of cards." You can accomplish this task by creating each card on its own layer, or creating all cards on the same layer so you can rearrange the sublayers. This choice is mostly a matter of personal preference, but we find it easier to manage individual layers rather than organizing sublayers.

Some cards in the sketch are at least partially hidden by other cards. You will have to make an educated guess about the correct positions and shapes of these elements. The best way to create these implied elements is to clone existing shapes and make adjustments as necessary.

1. **With credit.ai open, create a new layer named Front Card 2 at the top of the layer stack and select it as the active layer.**

2. **Using the Rounded Rectangle tool, draw the second front-facing card.**

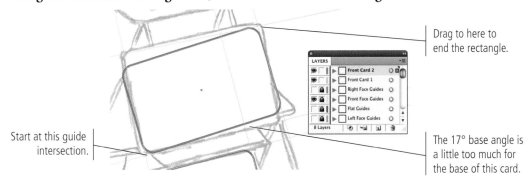

Drag to here to end the rectangle.

Start at this guide intersection.

The 17° base angle is a little too much for the base of this card.

3. **Using the Free Transform tool, adjust the corners of the card to fit the perspective guides.**

   Remember, you have to click-hold the handle first, then press Command/Control and drag to reshape the corner.

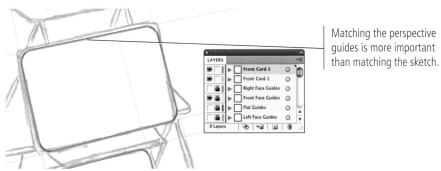

Matching the perspective guides is more important than matching the sketch.

4. **Hide the two Front Card layers and the Front Face Guides layer, and then show the Left Face Guides layer.**

5. **Open the General pane of the Preferences dialog box and reset the Constrain Angle to 0°. Click OK to close the Preferences dialog box.**

You need to find the base angle of the left-facing cards, but you need to find this angle from the actual horizontal X axis. If you don't change the constrain angle to 0°, the next measurement will be calculated from the altered horizon (17° instead of the original 0°).

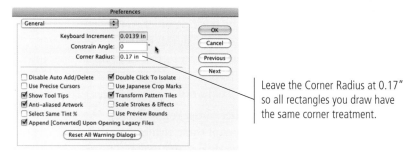

Leave the Corner Radius at 0.17″ so all rectangles you draw have the same corner treatment.

6. **Use the Measure tool to determine the angle of the bottom card edge on the left face.**

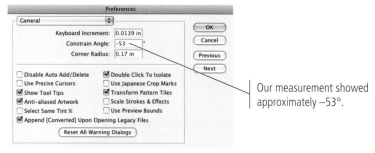

Drag from here…

…to here.

Note:

The Measure tool can measure objects on unlocked and locked layers.

7. **In the General pane of the Preferences dialog box, change the Constrain Angle value to match the angle value from the Info panel in Step 6.**

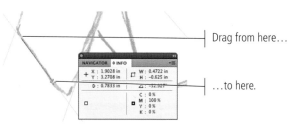

Our measurement showed approximately −53°.

8. **Select the Left Face Guides layer in the Layers panel, create a new layer named Left Card 1, and select that layer.**

9. **With the Left Card 1 layer selected, draw a rounded rectangle based on the bottom perspective line.**

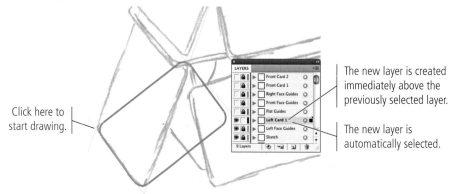

Click here to start drawing.

The new layer is created immediately above the previously selected layer.

The new layer is automatically selected.

10. Use the Free Transform tool to drag the rectangle's corners to match the perspective lines (as shown in the following image).

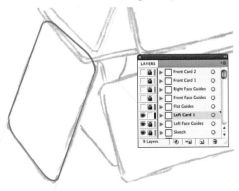

11. Create the remaining two left-facing cards, placing each card on its own layer.

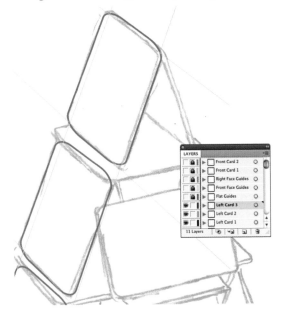

12. Hide the three left-facing card layers and the Left Face Guides layer.

13. Show the Flat Guides layer and select it. Create two new layers for the flat cards, named Flat Card 1 and Flat Card 2.

14. Draw the flat cards, each on its own layer.

On the Flat Card 1 layer, draw a single rounded rectangle for the lower flat card, and then transform the corners to match the perspective guides. Draw a second rounded rectangle on the same layer for the perpendicular card that sticks out from the lower flat card layer.

Note:

Reset the constrain angle, and then measure the base angle for the flat cards using the front edge of the bottom flat card. (We found the required angle to be approximately 13°.)

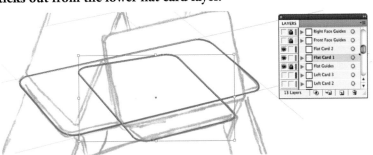

On the Flat Card 2 layer, draw a single rounded rectangle for the upper flat card, and transform the corners as necessary.

15. **Hide the two Flat Card layers and the Flat Guides layer. Show the Right Face Guides layer and select it. Create three new layers named** Right Card 1, Right Card 2, **and** Right Card 3.

16. **Reset the constrain angle in the Preferences dialog box. Select the Right Card 1 layer, and then draw the top right-facing card.**

You are creating the top card first because more of that card is visible than the other two.

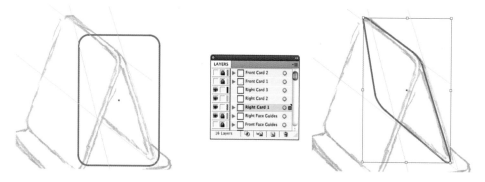

17. **Clone the card on the Right Card 1 layer, and move the clone onto the Right Card 2 layer. Move the card into place, and use the Free Transform tool as necessary to adjust the corners of the card (as shown in the following image).**

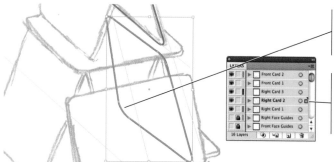

You will have to interpolate the areas where the cards are hidden by other cards.

A selected object shows this icon on its layer. To move an object to another layer, simply drag the icon to the new layer.

18. **Repeat Step 17 to create the bottom card on the Right Card 3 layer.**

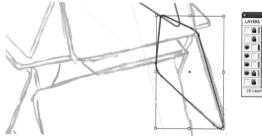

19. Create a final layer named `Hidden Cards` and select it to make it active.

20. Use whatever method you prefer to create shapes that represent the visible portions of the cards in the inner part of the stack (as shown in the following image).

    You can simply draw new rectangles and adjust their shapes; or you can clone existing shapes, move them to the hidden cards layer, and then make the necessary adjustments.

Note:

As you create these final shapes, hide and lock other layers as necessary to make your screen view less confusing.

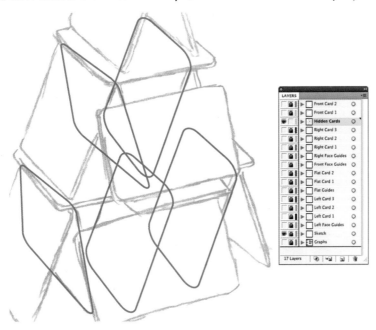

21. Save the file and continue to the next exercise.

 ARRANGE LAYERS LOGICALLY AND REALISTICALLY

You currently have a large number of layers, including one layer with five shapes in no apparent order. The final step in building this artwork is arranging the different shapes to appear as they would in real life.

1. With credit.ai open, drag all guide layers to the bottom of the stack. Drag the Hidden Cards layer directly above the Sketch layer.

2. Hide the Sketch layer, then show and unlock all card layers.

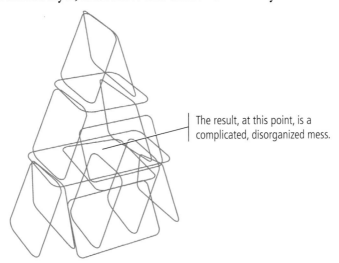

The result, at this point, is a complicated, disorganized mess.

Note:

You could delete the Sketch and guide layers at this point, but we prefer to leave that step for the very end of the process.

3. **Choose the Selection tool in the Tools panel. Select all card shapes, and then click the Default Fill and Stroke button in the Tools panel.**

When the card shapes are filled, you can begin to see why reordering is necessary — and why managing cards on individual layers is a better option than placing multiple cards on a single layer.

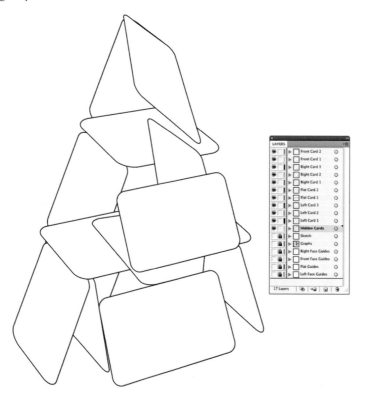

4. **Hide everything but the Hidden Cards layer.**

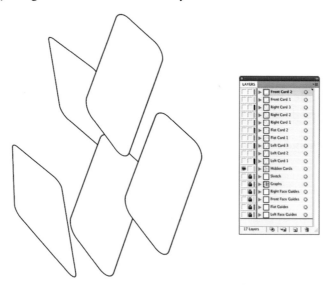

5. **Drag the Hidden Cards layer to the Create New Layer button.**

This creates a copy of the Hidden Cards layer.

6. **Hide the original Hidden Cards layer. With the Hidden Cards copy layer selected, delete the three shapes in the bottom row. Make sure the left shape is in front of the right shape.**

   Use the Object>Arrange menu to change the stacking order of objects on the same layer.

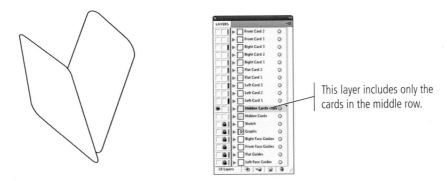

   This layer includes only the cards in the middle row.

7. **Hide the Hidden Cards copy layer and show the original Hidden Cards layer. With the Hidden Cards layer selected, delete the two shapes in the top row. Make sure the cards are arranged in the stacking order shown here.**

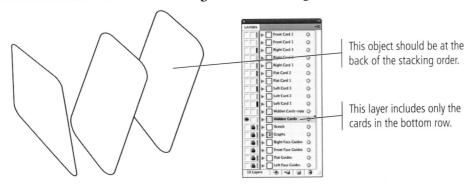

   This object should be at the back of the stacking order.

   This layer includes only the cards in the bottom row.

8. **Show all card layers except the two Front Card layers.**

9. **Rearrange the layers as necessary to reproduce a realistic-looking house of cards. Use the following points (and the image) as guides in rearranging your layers.**

   - **Cards in the bottom row should be below the Flat Card 1 layer.**

   - **Cards in the middle row should be above the Flat Card 1 layer and below the Flat Card 2 layer.**

   - **Left-facing cards should be above the right-facing and hidden cards in the layer stack.**

10. **Show the two Front Card layers, and then make any necessary adjustments to fine-tune the house of cards.**

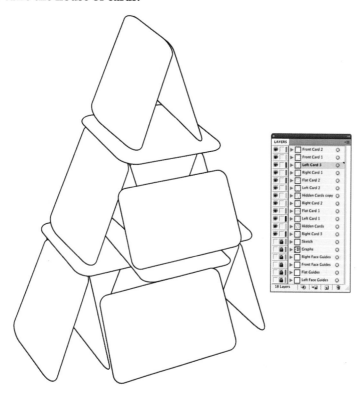

11. **Select all objects on the page and fill them with a radial gradient that blends from C=0 M=15 Y=50 K=0 to C=0 M=0 Y=25 K=0.**

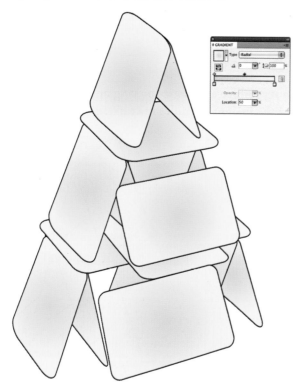

Note:

To change the color of gradient stops, double-click the stops in the panel to open the pop-up color panel for that stop.

12. **Save the file and continue to the next exercise.**

PLACE GRAPHS IN PERSPECTIVE

You have several choices for transforming the perspective of graphs to match the stacked cards. If you need to maintain the live link to the graph data, you can use the 3D Extrude & Bevel effect to apply a transformation effect to the graph object. This filter is complex, however, and can be particularly difficult to manage when you apply it to a text element.

If you don't need to maintain the live data link in the Illustrator graphs, you can apply the same transformation options you used to transform the card shapes. In this case, you have to ungroup the graph object before you can transform it.

Because the data will no longer be editable after you transform it, we recommend saving a working back-up copy of the illustration before you ungroup the graphs.

1. **With `credit.ai` open, choose File>Save As. Save the file as `credit transformed.ai` in your WIP>Cards folder.**

2. **Select all card layers in the Layers panel and choose Merge Selected from the Layers panel Options menu.**

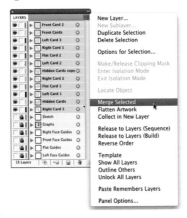

3. **Rename the merged layer `Cards` and then lock it.**

4. **Show and unlock the Graphs layer, and then drag it to the top of the layer stack.**

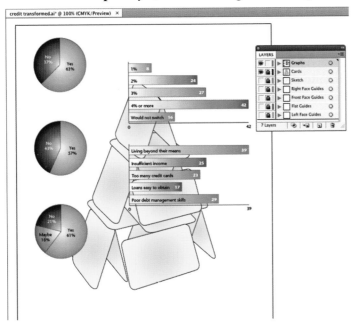

5. **Select all but the top pie graph and choose Object>Hide>Selection.**

   The card shapes are on the locked layer, so they remain visible. The Hide command only affects the selected objects on the unlocked layer.

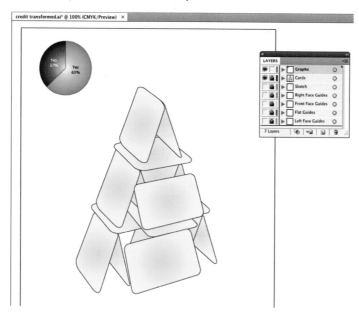

6. **Select the remaining graph and choose Object>Ungroup.**

7. **Read the resulting warning, and then click OK/Yes.**

   After you ungroup the graph, you won't be able to edit the graph type or data.

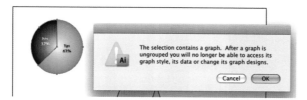

8. **With the resulting objects selected, choose Object>Group.**

   You have to ungroup the graph to convert it into regular vector objects. Regrouping the resulting vector objects allows you to maintain them as a single object, even when they are no longer technically a graph.

9. **Scale the group to 50%, drag it onto the top left-facing card, and rotate the group clockwise to match the approximate angle of the card.**

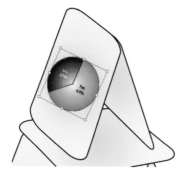

10. Use the Free Transform tool to adjust the corners of the group bounding box, placing the graph into the same approximate perspective as the card upon which it sits.

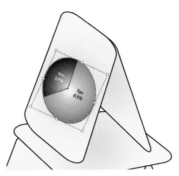

Note:

The type objects in the group will not be transformed. You would have to convert them to outlines if you wanted to free-transform them.

11. Lock the grouped object to the Artboard (Object>Lock>Selection).

12. Repeat this process to transform the remaining pie graphs onto the left-facing cards.

   • Show the remaining hidden graphs (Object>Show All).

   • Select all but one of the graphs and hide the others.

   • Ungroup the graph, group the resulting vector objects, and then transform the group to fit one of the left-facing cards.

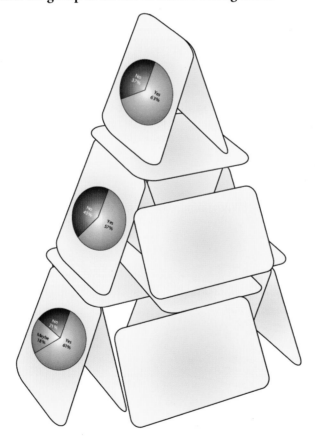

13. **Show the remaining hidden graphs (the bar graphs).**

- Hide the debt graph while you transform the rate graph.

- Double-click the debt graph to enter Isolation mode. Select the main graph object (without the secondary labels) and ungroup the graph.

- After the graph is ungrouped, delete the axis lines and axis labels.

- Using the Direct Selection tool, move each bar (and the related labels) to leave only a small gap between the bars.

- Select all objects and convert the type to outlines (Type>Create Outlines).

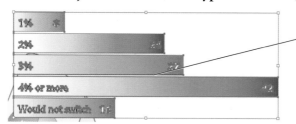

Use the Direct Selection tool to move the bars (and related labels), leaving only a small gap between each bar in the graph.

- Exit Isolation mode to return to the main Artboard. Scale, rotate, and transform the group to fit the bottom front-facing card.

14. **Repeat Step 13 for the final bar graph, placing it on the top front-facing card.**

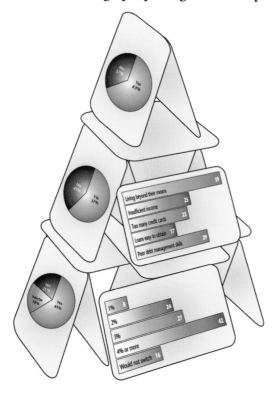

15. **Save the file and continue to the next exercise.**

FINISH THE DESIGN

Infographics aren't very informative without something to tell the viewer what the various graphs represent. Illustrator does not include a caption function, so you have to create those elements manually.

1. With `credit transformed.ai` open, create a new layer named `Background`.

2. Position the Background layer below the Cards layer, lock the Graphs layer, and make sure the Background layer is selected (active).

3. Open the General pane of the Preferences dialog box and make sure the Constrain Angle is reset to 0°. Click OK to close the Preferences dialog box.

4. Create a rectangle 6″ wide by 8″ high, centered horizontally to the Artboard and positioned with the top edge at Y:10.2″.

5. Fill the rectangle with the Brass Linear gradient (from the Money Colors library) with a −90° angle. Change the rectangle stroke to 1-pt black.

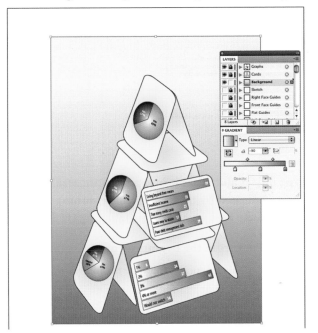

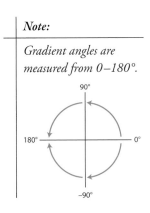

Note:

Gradient angles are measured from 0–180°.

6. Lock the Background layer, and then create a new layer named `Text` directly above the Background layer.

7. With the Text layer active, choose File>Place. Place the file `captions.doc` (from the RF_Illustrator>Cards folder) into the file, using the default options. Click OK in the Microsoft Word Options and Font Problems dialog boxes.

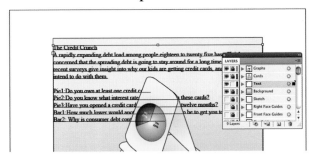

8. **Using the Selection tool, adjust the edges of the area-type object to leave 1/8″ from the edges of the gradient-filled rectangle to the edges of the type object.**

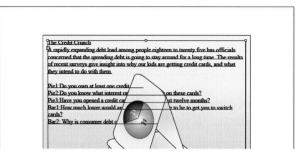

9. **Using the Type tool, select the first paragraph of imported text (the headline) and change it to 18-pt ATC Oak Bold Italic.**

10. **Change the second paragraph (the explanatory text) to 11-pt ATC Oak Italic.**

11. **Change all remaining text (the captions) to 10-pt ATC Oak Bold with 90% horizontal scaling.**

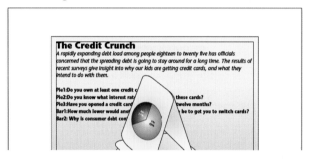

12. **Cut each caption from the main type object and paste it into a separate area type object. Position the caption objects as indicated by the text at the beginning of each line, and apply formatting to create the best possible result.**

13. **Delete the "Pie 1, 2, 3" and "Bar 1, 2" notes from the beginning of each caption.**

Make sure the captions match the cards where you placed each graph. Use the following image as a guide.

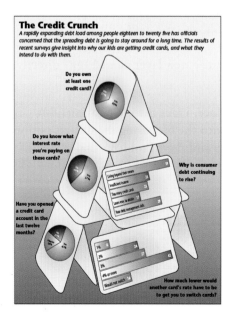

14. Lock the Text layer and hide the Graphs layer. Duplicate the Cards layer, and then hide the new Cards copy layer.

The duplicate layer — named Cards copy by default — automatically appears above the original Cards layer. The original is lower in the layer stack, so you need to combine the shapes on that lower layer.

15. Unlock the visible Cards layer and select all card shapes on the layer. In the Pathfinder panel, click the Unite button to create a single shape from all selected objects.

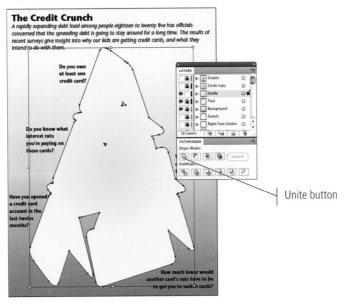

Unite button

16. With the combined object selected, apply the Outer Glow effect (Effect>Stylize>Outer Glow), using Screen as the blending mode, white as the color, 75% opacity, and a 0.35″ Blur value.

By combining the cards into a single object, you can apply the effect to the overall shape rather than to the individual cards.

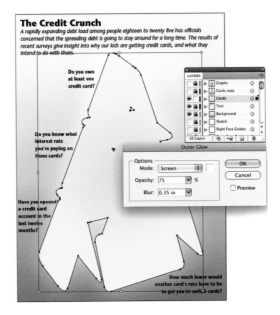

17. Show all but the Sketch and guide layers. In the Layers panel, move the Text layer to the top of the layer stack.

This prevents the cards' glow from affecting the text.

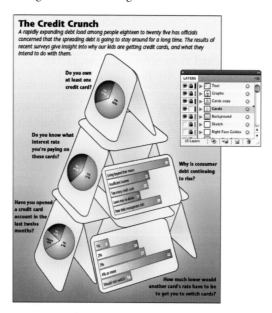

18. Save the file and close it.

Project Review

fill in the blank

1. A ______________ graph shows value as a percentage of the whole.

2. A ______________ graph plots values as a series of connected points, showing progressive change in value over time.

3. You must use ______________ to enter numbers as text in the Data panel.

4. You must use the ______________ to select one segment of a graph without ungrouping the entire graph.

5. You can click the ______________ button in the Data panel to increase the number of decimals that are included in each data cell.

6. A ______________ explains the colors used in different segments of a graph.

7. A pie graph segment must occupy at least ______________ of the graph for a radial gradient to automatically center on the overall graph center.

8. The ______________ of a bar graph appears across the bottom of the graph.

9. The ______________ is the spot where multiple lines on the same perspective converge.

10. Press ______________ while using the Free Transform tool to drag one corner of an object without affecting the other corners.

short answer

1. Briefly explain what is meant by the term "infographics."

2. Briefly explain the concept of "two-point perspective."

3. Briefly explain the function of the Constrain Angle setting.

Portfolio Builder Project

Use what you learned in this project to complete the following freeform exercise.
Carefully read the art director and client comments, then create your own design to meet the needs of the project.
Use the space below to sketch ideas; when finished, write a brief explanation of your reasoning behind your final design.

art director comments

The main theme for next month's magazine is "Living Green". The main articles all focus on some aspect of environmental conservation, such as renewable energy, recycling strategies, and landfill reduction. Your job is to create information graphics for data that will accompany the cover story.

To complete this project, you should:

❏ Use the supplied data (in the RF_Builders>Info folder) to create three information graphics that present the data in some visually interesting way.

❏ Create illustrations for each set of data that support the overall theme of the article.

client comments

The main focus of next month's cover story is the growing energy shortage in some areas of the country, and different methods that are being explored to supply affordable electricity to an ever-growing number of people in large metropolitan areas such as New York City and Los Angeles.

The author has compiled three different sets of data about renewable energy — wind power, water power, and so on — that will support the ideas and facts in the article. We need some type of illustrated graph for each of these data sets.

We want our readers to see the graphs even if they only flip through and skim the article. Create a compelling illustration for each one so they are more than just graphs. However, keep in mind that the data is the most important element — it needs to be clear and understandable.

Use a consistent color scheme in all three graphs; green should play a prominent role because people naturally associate that color with environmentalism and natural resources.

project justification

_____

_____

_____

_____

_____

_____

_____

_____

_____

_____

_____

_____

_____

Information graphics like the one you created in this project are frequently used in newspapers, magazines, and presentations to visually represent complex statistics or other numerical data. Information graphics range from simple pie charts and line graphs to elaborate full-color images.

When you create this type of illustration, keep in mind that "information" is the first word in information graphics. Also notice that this category of illustration work is not called "information decorating" — the information or data being presented is always the priority. Although aesthetic appeal is a primary concern of most graphic designers, the integrity of the information is the most important aspect of creating information graphics.

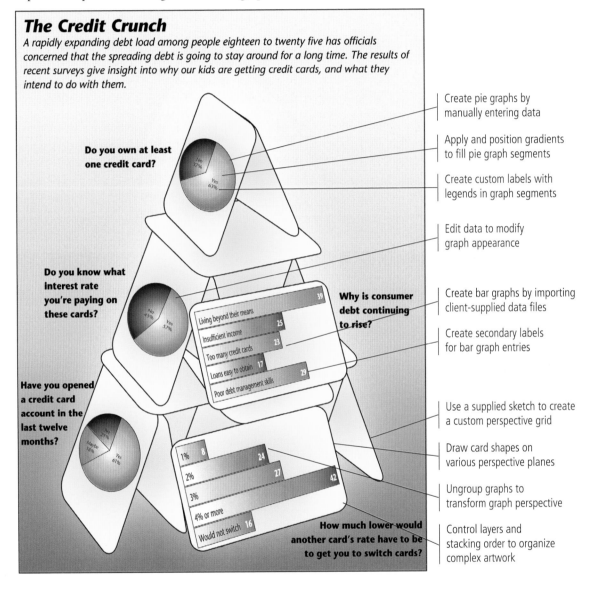

The Credit Crunch

A rapidly expanding debt load among people eighteen to twenty five has officials concerned that the spreading debt is going to stay around for a long time. The results of recent surveys give insight into why our kids are getting credit cards, and what they intend to do with them.

Do you own at least one credit card?

Do you know what interest rate you're paying on these cards?

Have you opened a credit card account in the last twelve months?

Why is consumer debt continuing to rise?

Living beyond their means — 39
Insufficient income — 25
Too many credit cards — 23
Loans easy to obtain — 17
Poor debt management skills — 29

How much lower would another card's rate have to be to get you to switch cards?

1% — 8
2% — 24
3% — 27
4% or more — 42
Would not switch — 16

- Create pie graphs by manually entering data
- Apply and position gradients to fill pie graph segments
- Create custom labels with legends in graph segments
- Edit data to modify graph appearance
- Create bar graphs by importing client-supplied data files
- Create secondary labels for bar graph entries
- Use a supplied sketch to create a custom perspective grid
- Draw card shapes on various perspective planes
- Ungroup graphs to transform graph perspective
- Control layers and stacking order to organize complex artwork

Web Site Interface

As an in-house designer for a multimedia services company, your job is to create the pieces that are required for the company's new Web site home page. The basic site structure has already been designed; you need to make changes that were requested by the marketing manager, and then slice the page into pieces that can be reassembled in a Web design application.

This project incorporates the following skills:

❏ Using Live Trace to create complex vector artwork from a photograph

❏ Using Live Color to make universal and individual changes to the colors in a group

❏ Slicing a page into pieces and defining settings for individual slices

❏ Saving images and pages in appropriate formats for display on the Web

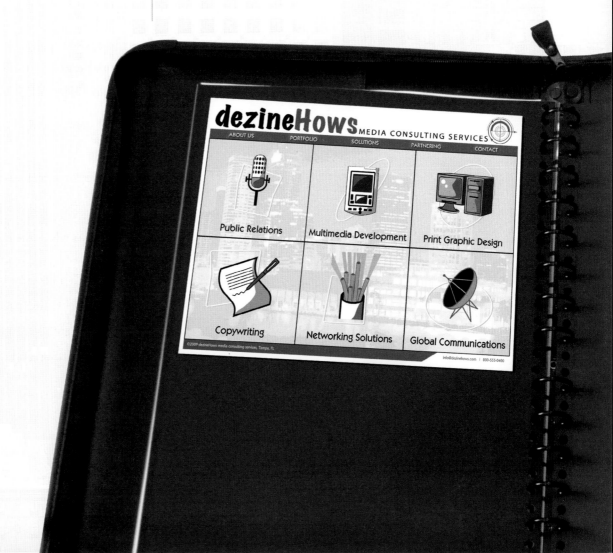

client comments

We're very happy with the overall look of the site, and the retro icons for the six service rollovers are great! Since the Tampa image is predominantly red, though, we want to change the blue to red in all the current design elements.

For the home page, we want the main area — where the Tampa photo is now — to include six rollovers that screen back the Tampa image and show one of the main branches of our service business.

We were also thinking that the skyline would look good as a "paint-by-numbers" kind of drawing rather than a basic photo. That will go better with the overall feel of the icons.

art director comments

Rather than taking days to manually create an illustration from the skyline photo, you can use Illustrator's Live Trace function to accomplish the same goal. Experiment with the different settings — specifically, the number of colors — until you get the look we need. You can create color groups to make it easier to adjust the colors in the site.

In addition to the rollovers in the main page area, the navigation buttons in the blue bar also need to be rollovers. Use some kind of subtle effect to create the second state (what the buttons look like on rollover).

Before you slice up the page, keep in mind that the six icons in the main area and the navigation buttons are rollovers. You're going to have to export the file twice to create all the necessary bits and pieces.

While you're making the necessary changes and cutting apart the pieces, I'll have the Dreamweaver developer start working on the Web site framework that will reassemble the slices you create.

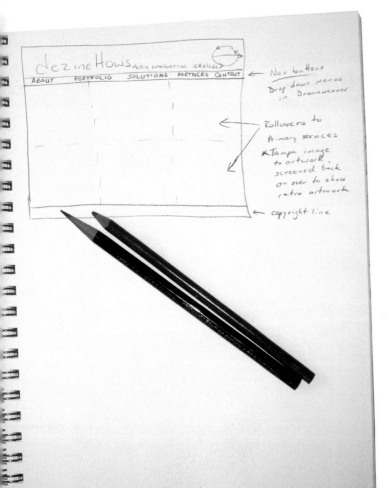

project objectives

To complete this project, you will:

❑ Use Live Trace to create a complex vector illustration

❑ Create color groups to manage the color swatches in the file

❑ Adjust global color attributes in all selected artwork

❑ Adjust individual colors in a group to change all objects where the color is applied

❑ Define a graphic style to easily apply multiple effects to objects

❑ Create slices from existing page guides

❑ Define individual slice settings

❑ Optimize image settings and export HTML

Stage 1 Using Live Trace and Live Color

As you learned in the previous projects of this book, you can use Illustrator to create virtually any type of illustration — from a basic vector drawing to a complex photo illustration to a folding-brochure layout. You can also use Illustrator to build and cut apart the pieces that make up a Web site (as you will do in this project), including specific styles for navigational buttons and multiple states of rollover areas. Those pieces can then be correctly reassembled in a professional Web design application such as Adobe Dreamweaver to create a fully functional Web site.

In the first stage of this project, you are going to use built-in tools to create a complex illustration, then you will use color groups and live color to adjust global and specific colors to unify the overall site design.

USE LIVE TRACE TO CREATE A COMPLEX IMAGE

If you have completed the other projects in this book, you should have a solid foundation for creating basic and complex vector graphics, whether based on a sketch, based on a photograph, or from scratch. Another option — Live Trace — makes it very easy to create vector graphics directly from an image, using a variety of options to determine how realistic the resulting illustration will be.

1. **Copy the Consulting folder from the WIP folder on your Resource CD to the WIP folder where you are saving your work.**

   This folder contains a number of HTML files with the necessary structure to properly display the images and rollovers you build in this project.

   Make sure you save files for this project using the exact names we define in the steps. If you use different file names — including misspellings or different capitalization — the HTML code will not be able to locate the necessary files.

2. **Open the file dh site.ai from the RF_Illustrator>Consulting folder.**

3. **Open the Layers panel and review the contents of the layers in the file.**

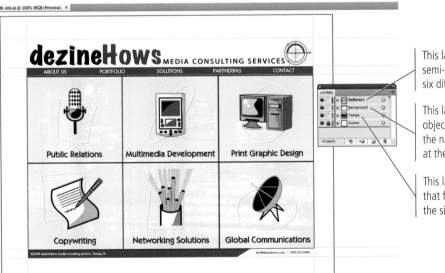

This layer contains the icons and semi-transparent overlay for the six different category rollovers.

This layer contains all persistent objects, such as the top banner, the navigation bar, and the bar at the bottom of the page.

This layer contains an image that fills the primary area on the site home page.

4. **Hide all but the Tampa layer, and then use the Selection tool to select the image on the visible layer.**

5. Choose Object>Live Trace>Tracing Options.

If you use the command Object>Live Trace>Make, Illustrator automatically traces the image using the last-applied settings. If you haven't used this function before now, the tracing defaults to black and white.

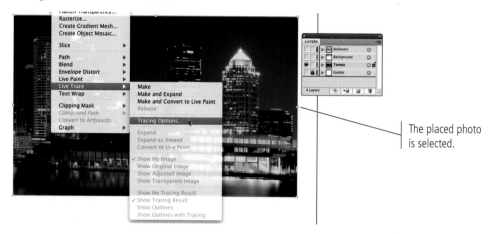

The placed photo is selected.

6. In the resulting Tracing Options dialog box, make sure the Preview check box is unchecked.

If you leave the preview turned on, every change in the dialog box requires Illustrator to reprocess the image to generate the correct curves. Because this is a rather large image, processing each change could take considerable processing power and time (depending on your computer). Rather than waiting to preview each change, it's a better idea to activate the preview after defining your initial choices; you can then toggle the preview on and off as necessary to reduce the time you spend sitting and waiting.

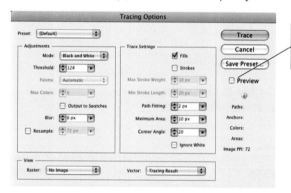

Turn off the preview to reduce processing time every time you make a change in the dialog box.

Note:

Illustrator includes a number of Live Trace presets that you can apply to any image. These can be accessed in the Trace Options dialog box or in the Control panel when a tracing object is selected.

7. Choose Color in the Mode menu and make sure the Max Colors field is set to 6.

The Live Trace function can produce black-and-white, grayscale, or full-color images.

By allowing only a small number of colors, you force Illustrator to create larger objects of solid colors — ultimately resulting in a "paint-by-numbers" effect.

8. Check the Output to Swatches option.

By checking the Output to Swatches option, each color used in the resulting illustration will be stored in the Swatches panel as a global swatch.

As you know, global swatches provide a distinct advantage if you want to later edit the artwork; by changing the definition of a global swatch, you change all artwork colored with that swatch.

Note:

Increase the number of possible colors to create a more realistic result (and a more complex illustration).

9. **Check the Preview option and review the results.**

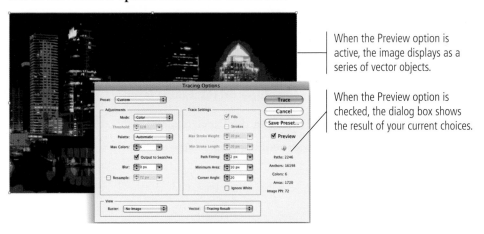

When the Preview option is active, the image displays as a series of vector objects.

When the Preview option is checked, the dialog box shows the result of your current choices.

10. **Click Trace to accept these settings and illustrate the photo.**

The original photo disappears, and the illustrated version appears in its place. However, the traced paths are neither visible nor editable. Unless you expand the tracing object (Object>Expand), you can't edit the anchors and paths that make up the resulting illustration.

Note:

To access the individual anchors and paths, you have to expand the tracing object (Object>Expand).

11. **Look at the Swatches panel.**

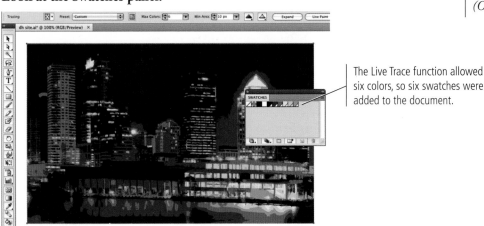

The Live Trace function allowed six colors, so six swatches were added to the document.

12. **Save the file as dh site working.ai in your WIP>Consulting folder, and then continue to the next exercise.**

EDIT LIVE TRACE SETTINGS

The result of Live Trace is a special type of object called a **tracing object** (which you can see in the Control panel). As long as you don't expand the tracing object, you can change the settings to produce different results from the same picture.

1. **With dh site working.ai open, select the tracing object on the Tampa layer.**

2. **In the Control panel, choose Outlines with Tracing in the Preview menu.**

   Without expanding the tracing object, these preview options allow you to view the paths that result from the Live Trace function.

Note:

By default, vector outlines that make up the tracing object are not visible in the document.

Choose a defined tracing preset.

Open the Tracing Options dialog box.

Use this menu to change the visibility of the original traced image.

Use this menu to change the preview of the resulting vector objects.

When Outlines with Tracing is selected, you can see the vector paths that will make up the resulting illustration.

3. **In the Control panel, change the Max Colors field to 8.**

   As long as you don't expand the tracing object, you can change the settings that generate the illustration.

   Note:

   If you expand the tracing object, you can no longer change the options that create the illustration.

4. **Open the Preview menu (in the Control panel) and choose Tracing Result.**

   This turns off the path outlines and restores the illustration to full opacity.

5. **Look again at the Swatches panel.**

   The image is reprocessed to allow eight colors in the tracing object. Those colors are added as new color swatches, in addition to the six swatches from the original tracing.

New swatches based on the revised tracing settings are added to the existing six.

6. **Make sure nothing is selected on the Artboard, and then choose Select All Unused in the Swatches panel Options menu.**

7. **With the original six swatches selected, click the panel Delete button. When you see the confirmation message, click Yes.**

After deleting the unused swatches, you have seven global swatches (generated by the last edit you made to the Live Trace options) in addition to the black and white swatches.

Note:

When you define the Max Colors setting in the Live Trace options, you determine the maximum number of colors that can be generated. The resulting number of swatches might be less than what you define as the maximum number of colors.

8. **Save the file and continue to the next exercise.**

Live Trace Options

With so many options and sliders, the Tracing Options dialog box might seem a bit intimidating at first. As with any tool, it's easier to get the desired results if you know the function of each option.

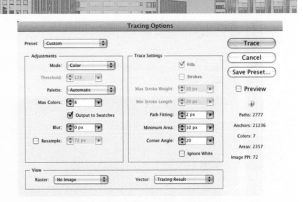

- **Mode** defines the color mode (color, grayscale, or black and white) of the resulting vector illustration.

- **Threshold**, which is only available when the Mode menu is set to Black-and-White, defines the maximum tonal value that will remain white before an area is filled with black.

- **Palette** defines the specific colors that can be used in a live trace; the default Automatic option allows Illustrator to use an unlimited palette to reproduce an image.

- **Max Colors** defines the maximum number of colors Illustrator can use to create an illustration. More colors create more depth, but also increase the complexity and number of points in the resulting illustration.

- **Output to Swatches** creates individual global swatches from the colors in the traced illustration.

- **Blur** adjusts the amount of blur applied to the original image before tracing. Higher values can help eliminate artifacts and noise (defects) in the illustration.

- **Resample** changes the resolution of a source image prior to tracing.

- **Fills**, when checked, results in solid-filled paths.

- **Strokes**, when checked, results in paths with an applied stroke color and weight.

- **Max Stroke Weight** defines the maximum stroke weight (when the Strokes option is checked) that can be applied before a stroke will be recreated as a fill object.

- **Min Stroke Length** defines the shortest allowable stroke (when the Strokes option is checked).

- **Path Fitting** adjusts how closely traced paths will follow the pixels of the original image.

- **Minimum Area** adjusts the smallest color area (in pixels) that can be drawn as a path.

- **Corner Angle** defines the minimum angle that can be traced as a sharp corner instead of a smooth curve. (By default, Live Trace attempts to create smooth curves.)

ILLUSTRATOR FOUNDATIONS

USE A COLOR GROUP TO CHANGE MULTIPLE SWATCHES

Color groups are useful for organizing color swatches into logical and manageable collections. You can also make changes that affect all colors within a group; this takes the concept of global color swatches one step further. In this exercise, you create a group from the tracing object swatches so you can make changes that will affect the entire illustration.

1. With **dh site working.ai** open, deselect everything on the Artboard.

2. Select all global swatches in the Swatches panel, and then click the New Color Group button at the bottom of the panel.

 — New Color Group button

3. Type **Tampa Colors** in the Name field, and then click OK to create the new color group.

  The selected swatches are now combined in a group (represented by the folder icon on the left).

4. Select the tracing object on the Artboard, and then click the Expand button in the Control panel.

   Before you can affect the object's colors by editing a color group, you must expand the tracing object to basic vector objects.

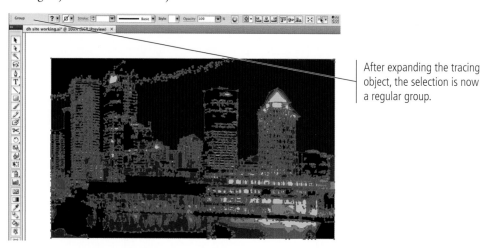 After expanding the tracing object, the selection is now a regular group.

5. With the resulting vector artwork selected, click the color group folder icon (in the Swatches panel) to select the color group.

6. **Click the Edit or Apply Color Group button at the bottom of the Swatches panel.**

Click the folder icon to select the color group.

Edit or Apply Color Group button

Note:

If you click a swatch instead of the group folder, you will change the fill/stroke attribute (whichever is active) of the selected objects.

7. **With the dialog box in Assign mode, review the list of colors in the left side of the dialog box.**

8. **Make sure the Recolor Art option is checked in the bottom-left corner.**

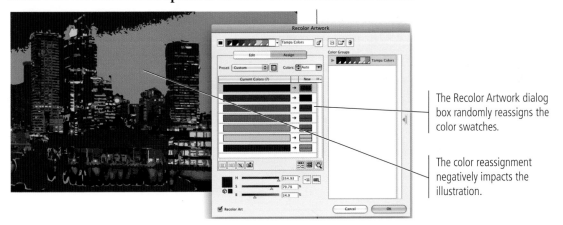

The Recolor Artwork dialog box randomly reassigns the color swatches.

The color reassignment negatively impacts the illustration.

9. **Click the first color bar and drag to the New swatch on the right to define the color assignment.**

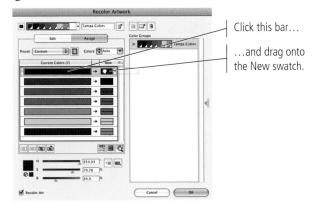

Click this bar…

…and drag onto the New swatch.

10. **Repeat Step 9 for each color in the list.**

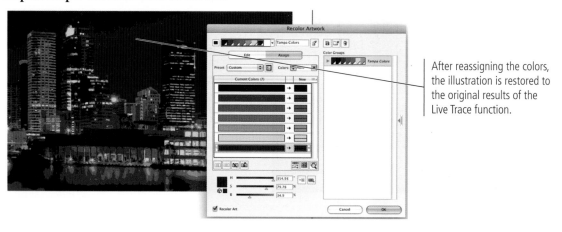

After reassigning the colors, the illustration is restored to the original results of the Live Trace function.

11. **Display the dialog box in Edit mode.**

12. **Make sure the Link Harmony Colors button is active. Drag the Brightness slider (below the color wheel) right to lighten all colors in the image.**

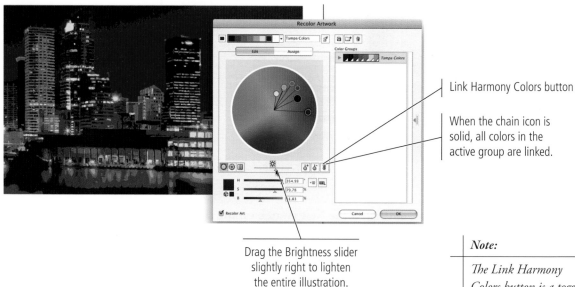

Link Harmony Colors button

When the chain icon is solid, all colors in the active group are linked.

Drag the Brightness slider slightly right to lighten the entire illustration.

Note:

The Link Harmony Colors button is a toggle. When it is already active, the tool tip for the button shows "Unlink Harmony Colors" (and vice versa).

13. **Click OK to apply the change. Click Yes when asked if you want to save the changes to the color group.**

14. **Save the file and continue to the next exercise.**

USE A COLOR GROUP TO MANAGE FILE COLORS

In addition to managing universal changes to all swatches in a group, color groups can also be useful for simplifying a design and managing the individual colors included in specific areas of a file. In this exercise, you use a color group to combine similar colors into tints of a single color swatch.

1. **With dh site working.ai open, lock the Tampa layer, and then show the Background and Rollovers layers.**

2. **Choose Select>All to select all artwork on the two unlocked layers.**

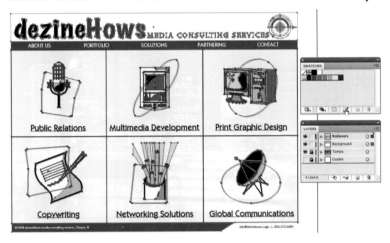

3. **With the artwork selected, click the New Color Group button at the bottom of the Swatches panel.**

4. **In the resulting dialog box, type Site Colors in the Name field. Choose the Create From Selected Artwork radio button, and make sure both check boxes are selected.**

5. **Click OK to create the new color group.**

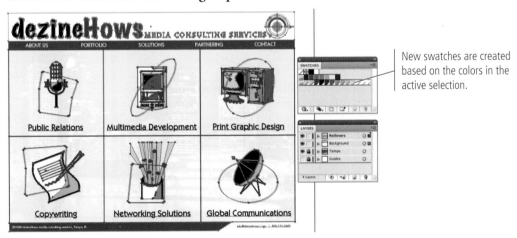

New swatches are created based on the colors in the active selection.

6. **With the artwork still selected, click the new color group folder icon to select the entire group, and then click the Edit or Apply Color Group button.**

This group currently contains 13 colors, but most of the colors are tints of black. It will be easier to manage the group if you combine the different gray swatches into tints of a single black swatch. You also have two very similar shades of gold, which might be combined to produce a more unified piece of artwork.

7. **In the list of colors, click each gold color and review the color contents at the bottom of the dialog box.**

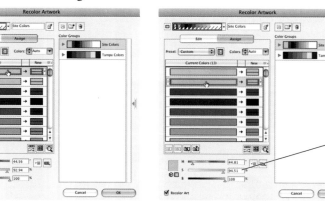

These values show that the two gold colors are virtually the same.

Note:

Unchecking the Include Swatches for Tints option does not solve this problem. You would still end up with a number of black and gray swatches that can be combined.

8. **Drag the second gold bar onto the first one to combine both colors into a single swatch.**

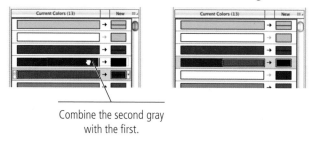

Click the second gold bar and drag it onto the first.

After releasing the mouse button, the Current Colors area shows that two original colors will result in a single new color.

9. **Click the fifth color in the list of current colors and drag it into the fourth row.**

Combine the second gray with the first.

10. **Repeat Step 9 to combine all gray shades (including the whites) into the first black color.**

When you get to the lower swatches in the Current Colors list, the one you're dragging to will have scrolled out of the window. You can click a Current Color swatch and drag to the top of the window to scroll up to the swatch you need to target.

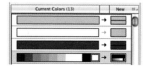

11. **Click OK to return to the document.**

12. Open the Swatches panel Options menu and choose **Select All Unused**. Delete the selected swatches from the file.

Consolidating the Site Group swatches has no visible effect on the selected artwork. Shades are created as tints of the single black swatch.

13. With the artwork still selected on the Artboard, reselect the Site Colors group and click the Edit or Apply Color Group button at the bottom of the Swatches panel.

14. Display the Recolor Artwork dialog box in Edit mode, and then show the Smooth Color Wheel. Below the color wheel, click the Link Harmony Colors button to disconnect the color spokes from one another.

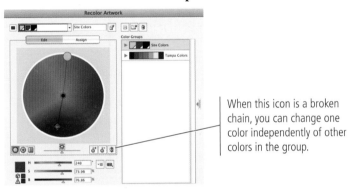

When this icon is a broken chain, you can change one color independently of other colors in the group.

15. Select the blue color spoke. In the bottom area of the dialog box, display the color sliders in RGB mode and then define the spoke to be R=196 G=35 B=22.

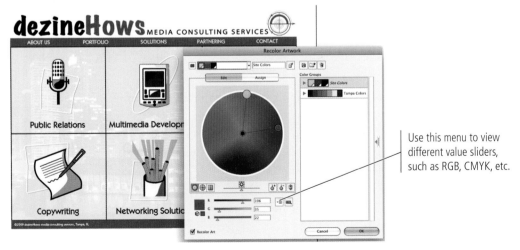

Use this menu to view different value sliders, such as RGB, CMYK, etc.

16. Click OK to change the color group, and click Yes when asked if you want to save changes to the current group.

17. Save the file and continue to the next exercise.

WORK WITH LIVE PAINT GROUPS

A Live Paint Group is a special type of Illustrator group. Using the Live Paint Bucket tool, you can navigate through various swatches in a color group and apply those colors to different areas of the selected group. The advantage to this type of group is that fills are not necessarily defined by object edges. Rather, Illustrator identifies overlapping areas and allows you to treat the separate areas as distinct objects, even though they are part of the same vector shape.

1. **With dh site working.ai open, deselect everything in the file and then click the microphone artwork with the Selection tool to select that group.**

2. **Choose the Live Paint Bucket tool in the Tools panel, and then click the Site Colors group icon in the Swatches panel to select that group.**

The Live Paint Bucket tool includes three sample swatches from the active color group. The center swatch is the active swatch.

Live Paint Bucket tool

Note:

If no color group is selected, the Live Paint Bucket tool shows the default ungrouped swatches.

3. **Press the Right Arrow key until the red swatch appears selected in the tool cursor.**

The Left and Right Arrow keys navigate between the swatches in the active group.

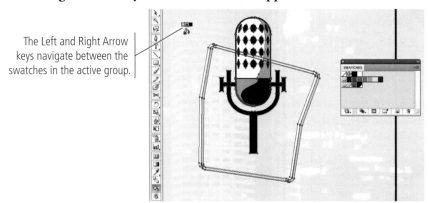

4. **Click the black area at the base of the microphone to change the fill color of that object.**

Before you click the group, cursor feedback provides helpful tips.

5. Using the Selection tool, click the Multimedia icon graphic to select that group.

6. Choose the Live Paint Bucket tool, and then activate the Site Colors color group. Press the Right Arrow key until the red swatch is active for the Live Paint Bucket tool.

7. Zoom in to the active selection so you can clearly see the black area in the top-left corner of the PDA screen.

8. Click the top-left section of the black area, as shown in the following image.

    The Live Paint Bucket tool identifies divisions in the selected artwork, even though they are not technically divisions.

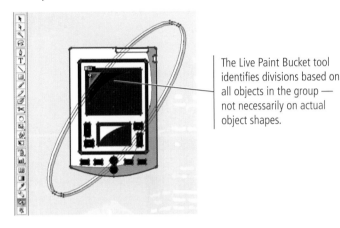

The Live Paint Bucket tool identifies divisions based on all objects in the group — not necessarily on actual object shapes.

9. Using the Direct Selection tool, click away from the active group to deselect it, and then click only the object you filled with the red swatch.

10. Click the selected object and drag right.

    Moving objects in a Live Paint group is different than moving individual objects in a regular group. Illustrator recognizes the original placement of the fill color, almost as if there is an underlay of the fill color, and the "filled" object is revealing that area of the color. Moving the individual object changes which part of the color "underlay" is visible.

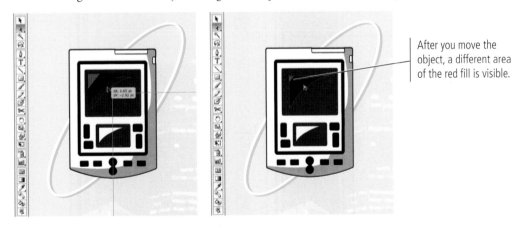

After you move the object, a different area of the red fill is visible.

11. Choose Edit>Undo to reposition the object you moved in Step 10.

12. **Select the entire group again. Use the Live Paint Bucket tool to fill the other three pieces of the reflection object with the red swatch.**

Note:

Use the Live Paint Selection tool to select pieces of a Live Paint group.

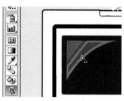

13. **Use the same techniques to change at least one element in each graphic to the red swatch.**

Note:

When working with the Live Paint Bucket tool, press Shift to paint the stroke of an object instead of the fill.

14. **Save the file and continue to the next stage of the project.**

Stage 2 Creating Web Site Graphics

It is common practice to create the look and feel of a Web site in Illustrator, and then hand off the pieces for a programmer to assemble in a Web design application such as Adobe Dreamweaver. In the second half of this project, you complete a number of tasks to create the necessary pieces for the final Web site, including the different states (versions) of areas that change appearance when the user's mouse rolls over those areas.

COMPOUND EFFECTS TO CREATE A GRAPHIC STYLE

The five type objects in the red bar will become navigation buttons; you will slice these elements and define targets for them in a later exercise. It is common practice to change the appearance of navigation buttons when the mouse rolls over them (called a **mouseover** or **rollover**).

Because of the way Illustrator manages page slicing, you need to be able to easily apply and remove the altered appearance from mouseover type objects — a process that is enabled by using graphic styles.

1. **With dh site working.ai open, use the Selection tool to select the About Us type object in the red bar.**

2. **Choose Effect>Stylize>Drop Shadow.**

3. **Apply a small drop shadow with a small Blur value, using the Multiply blending mode and black as the shadow color. Click OK to apply the drop shadow.**

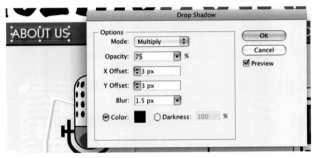

4. **Choose Effect>Stylize>Drop Shadow again.**

The drop shadow from Step 3 is already applied.

5. **When you see the warning message, click Apply New Effect.**

    You can apply multiple effects to a single object, including multiple instances of the same effect.

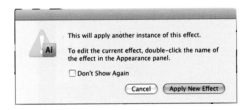

6. **Change the blending mode to Soft Light and the color to white. Change the X Offset and Y Offset fields to the inverse of the drop shadow from Step 3. Click OK to apply the second drop shadow to the text object.**

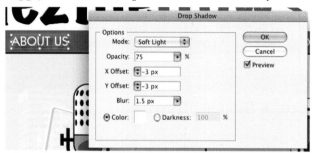

7. **Open the Graphic Styles panel (Window>Graphic Styles).**

   Graphic styles are managed in much the same way as the swatches and other libraries you used in Project 4.

8. **With the shadowed type object selected, click the New Graphic Style button at the bottom of the Graphic Styles panel.**

9. **With the new style selected in the panel, choose Graphic Style Options from the panel Options menu.**

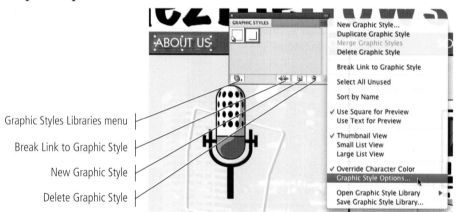

Graphic Styles Libraries menu

Break Link to Graphic Style

New Graphic Style

Delete Graphic Style

Note:

Illustrator includes several built-in style libraries, which you can access from the Window>Graphic Style Libraries menu, or by clicking the Graphic Styles Libraries Menu button at the bottom of the Graphic Styles panel.

10. **Name the new style Text Over State and click OK.**

   This graphic style contains all effects and attributes applied in the first text object (the one that was selected when you created the style). You can now use the Style button to apply multiple effects with a single click.

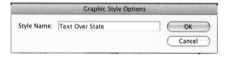

You can choose one of the List views (in the panel Options menu) to show the style names.

11. **With the About Us text element selected, open the Appearance panel submenu and choose Reduce to Basic Appearance.**

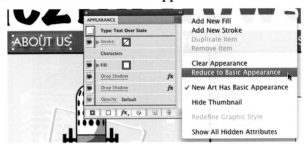

If you clicked the Clear Appearance button at the bottom of the panel, the type object would revert to the default appearance of black fill with no stroke. In this instance, you want to retain the same basic fill color but remove the drop shadows, so you need to use the Reduce to Basic Appearance option.

12. **Save the file and continue to the next exercise.**

 ## CREATE SLICES FROM SELECTIONS

The next step is to divide the file into **slices** (pieces) that can work properly on a Web page, and define hyperlink destinations for the main links. For most Web pages you design, each element that needs to link to a different location should become a slice, as should any element that requires unique output options (such as file format).

When you export the page, Illustrator can create an HTML file with the necessary information for assembling the slices into a functional Web page — which is useful for previewing your work. However, Illustrator is not a Web design application. You can create functional HTML for client review, but the final slices should be handed off to a programmer to reassemble in Dreamweaver, using the appropriate structure and code.

Illustrator includes three primary options for creating slices: based on guides, based on a selection, and based on a manually defined area.

1. **With dh site working.ai open, hide the Rollovers layer and make sure the Guides layer is visible. Unlock and select the Tampa layer.**

2. **Choose Object>Slice>Create from Guides.**

This heading banner will provide a link to the dezineHows home page.

Each button needs to link to a different HTML page.

This area will include the six rollovers, each of which navigates to a different page in the dezineHows site.

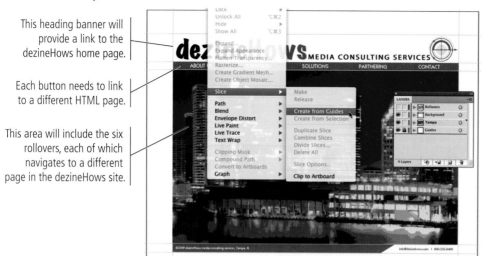

Because the original designer used guides to carefully align the different elements of this file, the guides are a perfect choice for beginning to slice the page.

Slices are identified by a small number and icon in the top-left corner.

Note:

If you need to work on actual content, the slice indicators can be distracting. You can easily toggle slice numbers and icons on and off by choosing View>Show Slices.

3. **Choose the Slice Select tool (nested under the Slice tool in the Tools panel). Click away from the artwork to deselect all slices, and then click the company logo to select only that slice.**

4. **With Slice 01 selected, choose Object>Slice>Slice Options.**

Note:

If you choose Create from Selection, whatever is selected on the Artboard will become a custom slice.

Selected slice

Slice Select tool

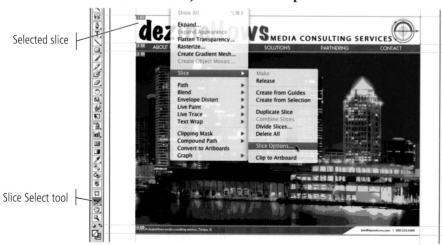

For every slice, you can define a number of settings:

- **Name** is the file name that will be used when you save the page or slice for the Web.

- **URL** is the page or file that opens if a user clicks the slice. (Slices don't have to be links; if you don't want a slice to link to something, simply leave the URL field blank.)

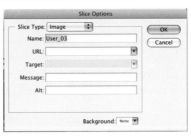

- **Target** is the location where the URL opens when you click the slice. Although there are other options available in full-scale HTML development applications such as Dreamweaver, you will primarily use "_self" to open the link in the same window or "_blank" to open the link in a new window. (This field is grayed out until you define a URL.)

Note:

You can also change the slice background type and color if the slice contains areas of transparency.

- **Message Text** appears in the browser's status bar. If you don't type a specific message, the URL link will display.

- **Alt Tag** appears in place of an image when image display is disabled in the browser, or when a Web page is being read by screen-reader software for a visually impaired user.

5. Define the following settings for the slice:

Name: dh_logo

URL: index.html

Target: _self

Alt text: dezineHows Media Consulting

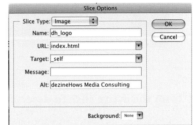

ILLUSTRATOR FOUNDATIONS

Although some slices can be created based on page guides or specific object boundaries, other slices will be easier to manage by simply drawing them manually. The Slice tool, nested under the Crop Area tool in the Tools panel, allows you to create custom slices for any area of the page.

When you define custom slices, automatic slices are added as necessary to support the ones you define. Those automatic slices will be named with sequential numbers based on the page name when you export the page. If you want to define a custom file name, link, or other option for a slice, you have to create a user slice instead of an automatic slice.

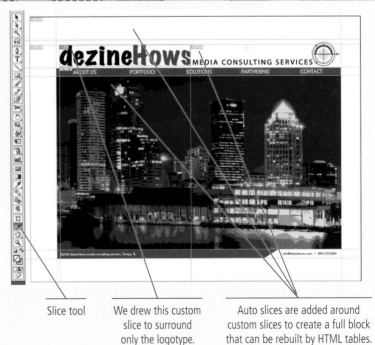

Slice tool

We drew this custom slice to surround only the logotype.

Auto slices are added around custom slices to create a full block that can be rebuilt by HTML tables.

6. **Click OK to close the Slice Options dialog box.**

When you return to the document window, the slices seem to jump and renumber themselves. This is a quirk in the software; Illustrator recognizes the edge of the Artboard as well as the page guides. When the file is output, you will see extra slices surrounding the actual page artwork, based on the size and position of the Artboard.

7. **Click away from the active slice to deselect it.**

The slices return to the correct positions and numbering.

8. **Save the file and continue to the next exercise.**

DIVIDE SLICES

Two areas of the page need to be divided into equal areas: the navigation bar and the main page area. Rather than trying to manually create these slices, you are going to divide the existing slice into equal pieces.

1. **With dh site working.ai open, use the Slice Select tool to click the navigation bar slice.**

2. **Choose Object>Slice>Divide Slices.**

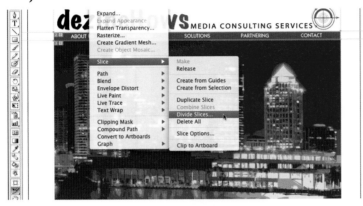

3. **Activate the Preview option in the Divide Slice dialog box and uncheck the Divide Horizontally option.**

   This bar includes five buttons that are distributed horizontally, which means you need to add vertical slices to separate the buttons.

Creating No Image Slices

In the Slice Options dialog box, you can change the slice type to No Image, which is useful if you want to create a slice to contain editable HTML text instead of a graphic representation of text. When No Image is selected in the Slice Type menu, you can define the HTML text that will appear in the slice after the page is exported. This text won't appear anywhere in Illustrator, except within the Slice Options dialog box.

The bottom options allow you to define the horizontal and vertical alignment of text within the exported slice (the word "cell" is used in this case because the exported text area is actually a table cell, not an image slice).

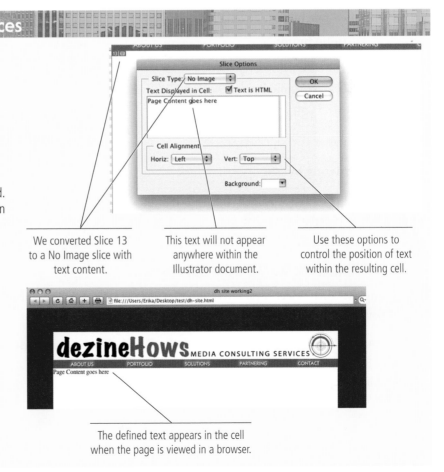

We converted Slice 13 to a No Image slice with text content.

This text will not appear anywhere within the Illustrator document.

Use these options to control the position of text within the resulting cell.

The defined text appears in the cell when the page is viewed in a browser.

4. In the Divide Vertically section, type 5 in the Slices Across field.

With the Preview option selected, you can see the five slices that will be created.

Note:

You can also create slices of a specific size using the Pixels Per Slice option.

5. Click OK to create the new slices.

6. Click away from the selected slices to deselect them.

You can change the options for only one slice at a time.

7. Using the Slice Select tool, click the first button slice, and then choose Object>Slice>Slice Options.

8. Define the following options for the slice.

Name: about_btn

URL: about.html

Target: _self

Alt: Link to About Us Page

9. Click OK to apply the slice options.

10. Using the same method, change the options for the remaining buttons.

Portfolio button		Solutions button	
Name:	portfolio_btn	Name:	solutions_btn
URL:	portfolio.html	URL:	solutions.html
Target:	_self	Target:	_self
Alt:	Link to Portfolio Page	Alt:	Link to Custom Solutions Page

Partnering button		Contact button	
Name:	partners_btn	Name:	contact_btn
URL:	partners.html	URL:	mailto:info@dezinehows.com
Target:	_self	Alt:	Email dezineHows
Alt:	Link to Partnering Page		

Note:

The mailto: protocol is the proper code format for creating an email link. Do not add a space between the colon and the email address.

11. Using the Slice Select tool, select the slice over the Tampa illustration and choose Object>Slice>Divide Slices.

12. With the Preview option active, check the Divide Horizontally option.

This area includes three icons across and two down, which means you need to divide this slice in both directions.

13. **Change the Divide Horizontally option to 2, change the Divide Vertically option to 3, and then click OK.**

14. **Show the Rollovers layer and use the following information to define slice options for the six new slices.**

Public Relations

Name: pr_btn

URL: pr.html

Target: _self

Alt: Link to PR Page

Multimedia Development

Name: multimedia_btn

URL: multimedia.html

Target: _self

Alt: Link to Multimedia Development Page

Print Graphic Design

Name: printdesign_btn

URL: print.html

Target: _self

Alt: Link to Print Design Page

Copywriting

Name: writing_btn

URL: copywriting.html

Target: _self

Alt: Link to Copywriting Page

Networking Solutions

Name: networks_btn

URL: networking.html

Target: _self

Alt: Link to Networking Solutions Page

Global Communications

Name: communications_btn

URL: communications.html

Target: _self

Alt: Link to Global Communications page

15. **Select the bottom slice and define the following options.**

Name: copyright_bar

Alt: Copyright 2009, dezineHows media consulting services

16. **Hide the Rollovers layer, save the file, and continue to the next exercise.**

OPTIMIZE IMAGE SETTINGS AND EXPORT HTML

After all content has been placed and the slices have been defined, you can safely export the page and create the necessary image files for the Web. When you use Illustrator's Save for Web function, only visible content will be included in the resulting slices. Because the Rollovers layer is currently hidden, and your navigation buttons are reduced to their basic appearance, the first export process will create all the basic images (the default states of the rollovers).

Note:

As you might have guessed, you need to export the page twice to produce all the necessary image files (the basic slices and the rollover slices).

1. **With dh site working.ai open, choose File>Save for Web & Devices.**

   The Save for Web dialog box defaults to show the optimized version of the image. You can use the tabs at the top of the preview to show the original image or split the window into two or four panes (each pane can have different settings for experimentation).

2. **Using the Slice Select tool, click the top-left illustration slice (Slice 10) in the main page area.**

   The large space around the page objects is the result of Illustrator's auto-slicing, based on the defined Artboard area. These slices will be removed in the Web design application when the final pages are assembled.

Note:

The tools in the Save for Web dialog box serve the same purpose as the related tools in the main interface.

   Illustrator defaults to export slices using the GIF format, which is appropriate for vector art with areas of flat color (such as this logo). If you review the optimization settings, you can see the optimized file will download in 7 seconds over a 28.8-K modem.

   Don't assume that all users have high-speed Internet access. Many people, especially in the general consumer and international markets, still use dial-up modems. If your target audience is one of these, you should optimize your files for slower download speeds.

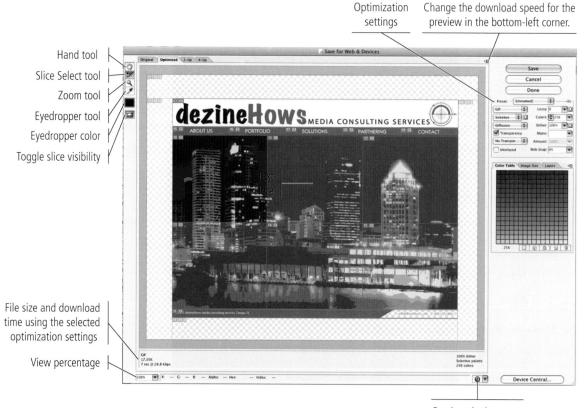

Optimization settings

Change the download speed for the preview in the bottom-left corner.

Hand tool
Slice Select tool
Zoom tool
Eyedropper tool
Eyedropper color
Toggle slice visibility

File size and download time using the selected optimization settings

View percentage

Preview the image or page in a browser

When optimizing files for the Web, the format you use affects the display of the colors in the exported file, as well as dictates compression and transparency capabilities. The Save for Web & Devices dialog box allows you to save images or slices in a number of formats (JPEG, GIF, PNG-8, PNG-24, WBMP, SVG, or SWF), and define options specific to the format you choose. WBMP (Windows Bitmap format) is not useful for anything that needs to be visible on a Macintosh computer; SVG (Scalable Vector Graphics) is rarely used because it is not widely supported by current browsers; and SWF is only relevant if you define JavaScript behaviors. Following is a brief explanation of the options for the commonly used formats.

JPEG

JPEG is the format of choice for continuous-tone images (such as photos) since it can store up to 24-bit color. The JPEG format compresses information using lossy compression, which means information is lost in the resulting file. It is not well suited for text or graphics, since its compression method introduces a blurring effect to the graphics.

You can choose a predefined compression level (Low, Medium, High, Very High, or Maximum) or define a specific quality percentage. These choices refer to the quality of the resulting image, not the amount of compression applied; the higher quality you want, the less compression you should apply.

- The **Optimized** check box creates an enhanced JPEG with a slightly smaller file size. Some older browsers don't support this feature.
- The **Progressive** option allows the image to appear in stages as more data downloads; this option is only available if the Optimized check box is selected.
- The **Blur** option applies a Gaussian blur to the exported image, which allows higher compression without destroying the image.
- The **ICC Profile** preserves the profile of the image in the exported file.
- The **Matte** option defines a color for any pixels that were transparent in the original image. The JPEG format does not support transparency.

PNG-8 and PNG-24

PNG is another format used for Web graphics and images. Two versions of the format — PNG-8 and PNG-24 — support 8-bit and 24-bit color respectively. For the PNG-8 format, the options are the same as for the GIF format, except that PNG-8 files cannot be compressed. PNG-24 can support continuous-tone color as well as transparency.

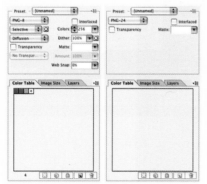

GIF

GIF is an 8-bit format typically used for graphics and artwork that don't have a large range of color. It is ideally suited for files with large areas of solid color, but it is ill suited for continuous-tone images that have subtle color variations.

When you save a file in the GIF format, all the colors are mapped to a color table (called **indexed color**). Indexed color is an 8-bit color model in which the specific 256 values are based on the colors in the image. You can remap the indexed colors using a number of options:

- **Perceptual** gives priority to colors to which the human eye is more sensitive.
- **Selective** is similar to Perceptual, but favors broad areas of color. This usually produces the best results.
- **Adaptive** samples colors appearing most commonly in the image.
- **Restrictive (Web)** uses a standard 216-color Web-safe color table. This option can result in drastic color shift.

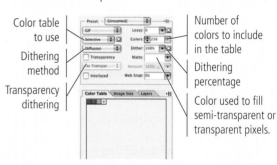

The **Lossy** option reduces file size by selectively discarding data; higher settings result in more data being discarded.

The **Dithering Method** option applies **dithering**, which blends two available colors to simulate additional colors. A higher dithering percentage creates the appearance of more colors and more detail, but can also increase the file size.

The **Transparency** and **Matte** options determine how transparent pixels are treated. If Transparency is checked, semi-transparent pixels blend into the defined Matte color.

The **Transparency Dithering** option allows you to dither transparency in a similar manner as dithering colors.

The **Interlace** option allows the image to display in stages as more data downloads (similar to progressive JPEG files).

The **Web Snap** option specifies a tolerance level for shifting colors to the closest Web palette equivalents.

3. **Choose JPEG in the Format menu, and choose High in the Compression Quality menu.**

Because this image is based on a photograph and does not require transparency, the JPEG format might be a better choice than the default GIF format.

Using the High compression option, the image will download in 7 seconds on a 28.8-K modem. This is an acceptable download time (especially since very few people still use 28.8K modems), and the image preview shows that the quality will be fine for an image such as this one.

Default optimization settings for a JPEG file

Optimized preview of the selected slice

File size and download time using a 28.8-K modem

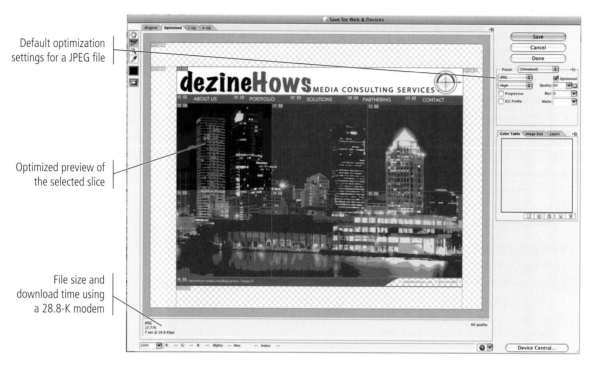

4. **Change all six of the Tampa slices to the JPEG format with High compression quality.**

5. **Double-click the bottom slice to open the Slice Options dialog box.**

6. **At the bottom of the dialog box, open the Background Color menu and choose White from the menu. Click OK to apply the change.**

You need to change the background color of this slice so the page background doesn't show through the area.

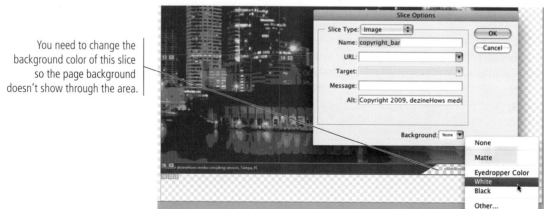

7. In the options for that slice, uncheck the Transparency option.

When Transparency is turned off for this slice, the background area is white (as you defined in Step 6).

8. Click the Save button. Navigate to your WIP>Consulting folder as the location for saving.

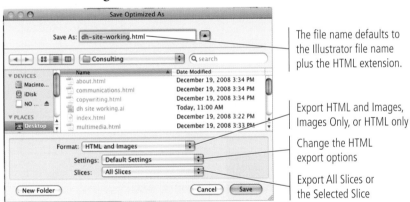

The file name defaults to the Illustrator file name plus the HTML extension.

Export HTML and Images, Images Only, or HTML only

Change the HTML export options

Export All Slices or the Selected Slice

Note:

Clicking Done closes the dialog box and saves your slice optimization settings. Clicking Cancel closes the dialog box without saving your choices.

9. Make sure HTML and Images is selected in the Format menu and All Slices is selected in the Slices menu.

Rather than changing these settings for each of the six pages you need to output, you are saving the settings so you can easily call them again later.

10. Click the Settings menu and choose Other.

Note:

Illustrator automatically replaces spaces in the file name with hyphens.

11. **In the resulting dialog box, display the Background options. Choose Other from the Color menu.**

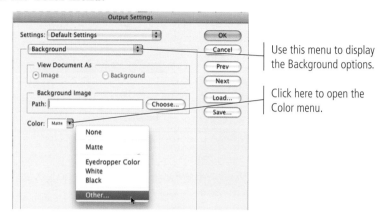

Use this menu to display the Background options.

Click here to open the Color menu.

12. **Use the resulting Color Picker to select a dark red color as the background color, and then click OK to return to the Output Settings dialog box.**

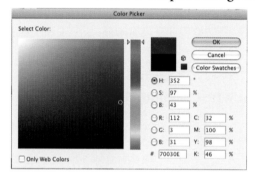

13. **Click OK to return to the Save Optimized As dialog box, and then click Save.**

14. **On your desktop, open your WIP>Consulting folder. Double-click dh-site-working.html to open the file in a browser window.**

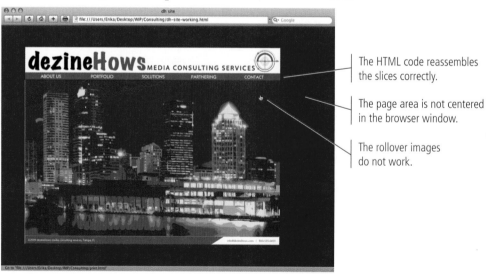

The HTML code reassembles the slices correctly.

The page area is not centered in the browser window.

The rollover images do not work.

15. **Close the browser and return to Illustrator.**

16. **Save the file and continue to the next exercise.**

    Using the Save for Web dialog box does not save your work in the native Illustrator file. You have to save the Illustrator file separately after the HTML and images have been exported.

ILLUSTRATOR FOUNDATIONS

When you use the Save for Web dialog box to output HTML, you can change the options for the resulting HTML by choosing Other in the Settings menu of the Save Optimized As dialog box. (Background Image, Default Settings, and XHTML are saved sets of options that you can call without opening the Output Settings dialog box.)

The Output Settings dialog box has four panes that you can access in the menu located below the Settings menu. Most of these options require a good understanding of HTML, CSS (cascading style sheets), and Web design structure; if you don't understand these concepts, you can safely use the default settings for most basic Web pages you design in Illustrator.

HTML Options

The **Output XHTML** option creates Web pages that meet the XHTML standard. Choosing this option disables options that might conflict with this standard; when this option is selected, the Tags Case and Attribute Case options are automatically selected.

The Formatting options determine how the resulting HTML code will be formatted:

- **Tags Case** defines the capitalization for tags.
- **Attribute Case** defines the capitalization for attributes.
- **Indent** defines a method for indenting lines of code.
- **Line Endings** defines the platform for line-ending compatibility.
- **Encoding** defines the default character encoding for the page.

The Coding options determine what will be included in the resulting code:

- **Include Comments** adds explanatory comments to the HTML code.
- **Always Add Alt Attribute** adds the Alt attribute to image elements to comply with Web accessibility standards.
- **Always Quote Attributes** places quotation marks around tag attributes, which is required for compatibility with some older browsers.
- **Close All Tags** adds closing tags for all HTML elements in the file (for XHTML compliance).
- **Include Zero Margins On Body Tag** removes default internal margins in a browser window and adds margin tags with zero values to the body tag.

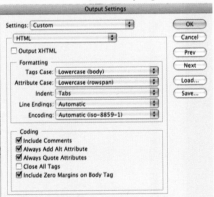

Slices Options

The **Generate Table** option creates an HTML table to reassemble the slices in the exported Web page:

- **Empty Cells** defines how empty slices are converted to table cells.
- **TD W&H** defines when to include width and height attributes for table data.
- **Spacer Cells** defines when to add empty spacer cells around the generated table.

The **Generate CSS** option creates a cascading style sheet to reassemble the slices in the exported page. The Referenced menu defines how slice positions are referenced in the HTML file (By ID, Inline, or By Class).

The **Default Slice Naming** options change the default file-naming conventions for the files created for auto slices and unnamed user slices.

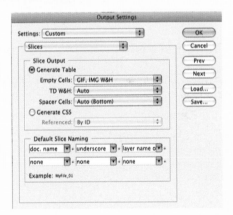

Background Options

The **View Document As** option allows you to define a specific image or color to use as the Web page background. If the Image option is selected, the page displays an image or color as the background behind the image or page you're exporting. If the Background option is selected, the page displays the optimized image as a tiled background.

In the **Background Image** field, you can determine which image to use as the page background, or you can click the Choose button to navigate to an image on your computer. The background image tiles behind the optimized image on the Web page.

The **Color** field and menu allow you to define a color to use as the background of the exported page.

Saving Files Options

The **File Naming** options change the default file-naming conventions for the files created when you export an image or page for the Web.

The **Filename Compatibility** options make the file name compatible with Windows, Mac OS, and UNIX. The default option (UNIX) is the most common server type; the two platform-specific options can cause problems for users or servers based on the other platform.

The **Put Images In Folder** option, active by default, defaults to "images," which is a standard convention for folder structure used in Web site design. If a folder named "images" does not exist where you save the optimized file, the images folder is created for you.

The **Copy Background Image When Saving** option preserves a defined background image as a single image.

The **Include XMP** option preserves any defined metadata that was added to the document. (**Metadata** is information about a file such as author name, resolution, color space, copyright, and keywords.)

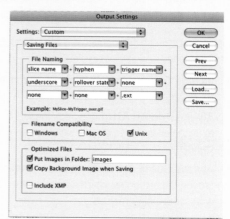

CREATE THE ROLLOVER IMAGES

The final step is to create the rollover images, which will be combined in the final HTML files by the Dreamweaver developer. The artwork is already complete, so you simply have to make the correct elements visible, change the slice names, and save the additional images into your WIP folder.

1. With **dh site working.ai** open, show the Rollovers layer.

2. Select all five type objects in the horizontal navigation bar and apply the Text Over State graphic style.

3. Choose File>Save for Web & Devices.

4. Using the Slice Select tool in the Save for Web & Devices dialog box, double-click the About Us slice to open the Slice Options dialog box for that slice.

5. In the Name field, change the letters "btn" to **over**. Click OK to make the change.

6. Repeat Step 5 for the remaining slices in the navigation bar and main page area.

7. Click Save. In the Save Optimized As dialog box, make sure HTML and Images is selected in the Format menu and All Slices is selected in the Slices menu.

If you continued directly from the previous exercise, these options are already selected.

8. **Click Save. When you see the Replace Files dialog box, click Replace.**

This dialog box shows that some slices already exist in the location where you are saving the files; these are the slices you created when you exported the first time. Because these slices haven't changed, you can safely overwrite the original slices with the new versions.

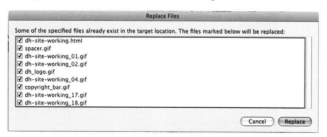

9. **On your desktop, double-click dh-site-working.html (in your WIP>Consulting folder) to open it in your browser.**

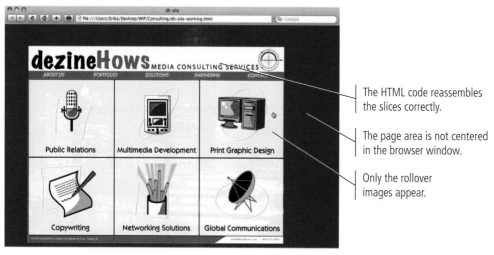

The HTML code reassembles the slices correctly.

The page area is not centered in the browser window.

Only the rollover images appear.

10. **Close the browser window and return to Illustrator.**

11. **Save the native Illustrator file and close it.**

12. **On your desktop, open the file index.html (from your WIP>Consulting folder) in a browser window.**

This file was built in Dreamweaver to read the images you generated with the Save for Web function.

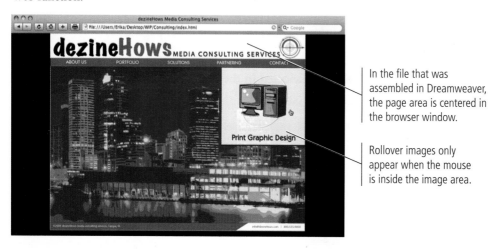

In the file that was assembled in Dreamweaver, the page area is centered in the browser window.

Rollover images only appear when the mouse is inside the image area.

13. **Close the browser window.**

fill in the blank

1. Choosing the _____ option in the Control panel Preview menu reveals the vector objects that result from the Live Trace function.

2. You can check the _____ option in the Recolor Artwork dialog box to reflect color changes in selected objects.

3. If the _____ option in the Recolor Artwork dialog box is active, you can make universal changes (such as brightness) to all colors in a group.

4. The _____ tool can be used to apply color swatches from selected groups based on overlapping areas rather than entire vector objects.

5. Choosing the _____ option in the Appearance panel removes applied effects and resets an object to only its fill and stroke.

6. Use _____ at the beginning of a link target to create a link that opens a pre-addressed email message.

7. When defining slice settings, the _____ option defines the file that should open when a user clicks that slice.

8. The _____ tool is used to manually cut apart a page into smaller pieces for Web delivery.

9. When setting image optimization settings in the Save For Web & Devices dialog box, the _____ format allows lossy compression and does not support transparency; it is best used for photos.

10. The _____ format supports transparency but not a large number of colors; it is best used for artwork or graphics with large areas of solid color.

short answer

1. Briefly explain the differences between the JPEG, GIF, and PNG formats for exporting Web images.

2. Briefly explain two advantages of designing a Web site interface in Illustrator.

3. Briefly explain two disadvantages of designing a Web site interface in Illustrator.

Portfolio Builder Project

Use what you learned in this project to complete the following freeform exercise.
Carefully read the art director and client comments, then create your own design to meet the needs of the project.
Use the space below to sketch ideas; when finished, write a brief explanation of your reasoning behind your final design.

art director comments

Every professional designer needs a portfolio of their work. If you've completed the projects in this book, you should now have a number of different examples to show off your skills using Illustrator CS4.

The eight projects in this book were specifically designed to include a broad range of *types* of projects; your portfolio should use the same principle.

client comments

For this project, you are your own client. Using the following suggestions, gather your best work and create printed and digital versions of your portfolio:

❏ Include as many different types of work as possible.

❏ Print clean copies of each finished piece that you want to include.

❏ For each example in your portfolio, write a brief (one or two paragraph) synopsis of the project. Explain the purpose of the piece, as well as your role in the creative and production process.

❏ Design a personal promotion brochure — create a layout that highlights your technical skills and reflects your personal style.

❏ Create a PDF version of your portfolio so you can send your portfolio via email, post it on job sites, and keep with you on a CD at all times — you never know when you might meet a potential employer.

project justification

The Live Trace and Live Color options extend Illustrator's basic drawing tools, allowing you to create complex vector graphics with a degree of detail that would be extremely difficult to create otherwise. The paint-by-numbers effect that you created from the Tampa photo would require significant time and skill to create from scratch. Consolidating color swatches into groups provides an easy way to make color changes to existing artwork, whether created by Live Trace or using conventional drawing tools.

Although many developers use dedicated Web design software like Adobe Dreamweaver to build sophisticated Web sites, the images for those sites have to come from somewhere. It is very common for a designer to build the "look and feel" of a site in Illustrator, then slice and export the pieces so the developer can reassemble them in the Web design application.

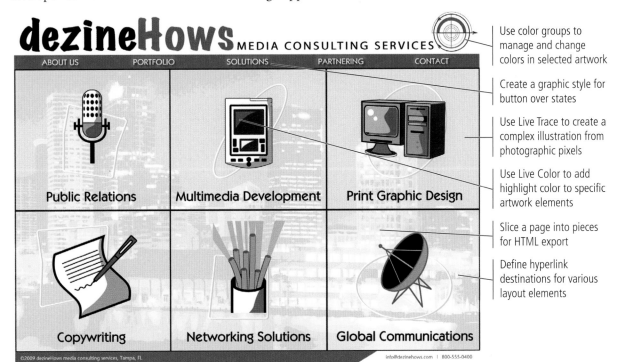

Use color groups to manage and change colors in selected artwork

Create a graphic style for button over states

Use Live Trace to create a complex illustration from photographic pixels

Use Live Color to add highlight color to specific artwork elements

Slice a page into pieces for HTML export

Define hyperlink destinations for various layout elements

Index

PROJECT PORTFOLIO
Design Awards

The **Against The Clock Project Portfolio Design Awards** are your chance to gain recognition for your creative and technical design skills. Prizes range from your work being displayed in the Against The Clock Web Gallery, to cash prizes, to having your design published in an upcoming ATC book.

The **Project Portfolio Design Awards** are designed to test both your creative talents and technical skills. Submit your Portfolio Builder project from any of the Professional Portfolio Series books for your chance to win. Entries will be judged on design quality, originality, understanding of client needs, and technical skills.

Go to **www.againsttheclock.com/contest.html** for complete contest details and rules, and to download the official contest entry form.

AGAINST THE CLOCK
mastering graphic technology

Use our portfolio to build yours.

The Against The Clock Professional Portfolio Series walks you step-by-step through the tools and techniques of graphic design professionals.

Order online at www.againsttheclock.com
Use code **PFS409** for a 10% discount

Go to **www.againsttheclock.com** to enter our monthly drawing for a free book of your choice.